Second-Generation
Client/Server Computing

T5-CVQ-452

Other McGraw-Hill Books of Interest

BATES • *Client/Server Internetworking,* 0-07-005442-8

BERSON • *Client/Server Architecture,* Second Edition, 0-07-005664-1

BERSON/ANDERSON • *Sybase and Client/Server Computing, Featuring System 11,* Second Edition, 0-07-006080-0

DEWIRE • *Client/Server Computing,* 0-07-016732-X

DEWIRE • *Application Development for Distributed Environments,* 0-07-016733-8

SACKETT/SILVERMAN • *Internetwork Routing: Design, Performance Management, and Tuning,* 0-07-057688-2

VAUGHN • *Client/Server System Design and Implementation,* 0-07-067375-6

WEADOCK/MARTIN • *Bulletproofing Client/Server Systems,* 0-07-067622-4

WISE • *Client/Server Performance Tuning: Designing for Speed,* 0-07-071173-9

Second-Generation Client/Server Computing

D. Travis Dewire

McGraw-Hill

New York   San Francisco   Washington, D.C.   Auckland   Bogotá
Caracas   Lisbon   London   Madrid   Mexico City   Milan
Montreal   New Delhi   San Juan   Singapore
Sydney   Tokyo   Toronto

Library of Congress Cataloging-in-Publication Data

Dewire, Dawna Travis.
    Second generation client/server computing / D. Travis Dewire.
        p.   cm.—(The McGraw-Hill series on client/server computing)
    Includes index.
    ISBN 0-07-016736-2 (pbk.)
    1. Client/server computing. I. Title. II. Series.
QA76.9.C55D5 1997
004'.36—dc20   96-35817
                                                CIP

McGraw-Hill

A Division of The McGraw-Hill Companies

1 2 3 4 5 6 7 8 9 0 DOC/DOC 9 0 1 0 9 8 7

ISBN 0-07-016736-2

The sponsoring editor for this book was Jennifer Holt DiGiovanna, the editing supervisor was Fred Bernardi, and the production supervisor was Pamela Pelton. It was set by Decision Tree Associates.

Printed and bound by R. R. Donnelley & Sons Company.

McGraw-Hill books are available at special quantity discounts to use as premiums and sales promotions, or for use in corporate training programs. For more information, please write to the Director of Special Sales, McGraw-Hill, 11 West 19th Street, New York, NY 10011. Or contact your local bookstore.

 This book is printed on recycled, acid-free paper containing a minimum of 50% recycled, de-inked fiber.

To Andy, Travis, and Gregory

Contents

List of Figures

Preface

Client/server technology was hyped as the wave of the 1990s. And it has lived up to its advance billing. New applications are being deployed on client/server platforms. Organizations are reengineering their IT architectures to take advantage of the cooperation inherent in client/server architecture. These new applications pull data and services from legacy systems as just another link in the network.

My original book, *Client/Server Computing*, focused on a newly emerging technology. It covered the assumptions that were made and the realities that early adopters of the technology faced. At the time, it was predicted that all new developments would be client/server-based by 1995. This seems to have come true. In the four years since the first book was published, technology has enhanced the capabilities of the hardware and software, and users have clamored for more and more features and functionality. The result is second-generation client/server computing.

Second-generation client/server computing takes the original view of client/server computing—all work is done on the client, the server accepts requests for data from client and returns the data—to higher expectations. Clients and servers now share the load—especially servers, since there is often more than one server in the architecture, hence, a multitier architecture. The way these components interoperate is the strength of this improved technology.

That strength is supplied by the network, which has evolved into an infrastructure for the organization. It links every node together to form "the system." Data is also distributed within this infrastructure. It may be fragmented or it may be copied (replicated). The ability to easily access data wherever it resides and whatever data source it is in becomes the life-blood of the organization.

Client/server technology is significant to both business users and IT organizations. Information management is improved with centralized validation and access rules. Easy access to data improves users' productivity. Organizations can rightsize applications to the platform that provides the most benefits.

But on the flip side is the multivendor environment. Because client/server applications rely on communication networks for process results as well as data retrieval, managing the network becomes critical. Maintaining and updating client software requires new methodologies and controls. Second-generation client/server computing changes the organization's virtual structure and can be disruptive.

This book is intended to educate. Insights into second-generation client/server computing are based on research and hands-on experience. The intent is to provide the reader with a sense of the history of this technology, where the technology is today, and where it is headed. Some questions will be answered, hopefully others are raised. Little attention is paid to actual product reviews. The technology is changing so fast that anything said about a product today could be enhanced next month. And new technologies are introduced at every trade show as well.

This book is divided into five parts. The first part deals with the history of client/server computing and its premises. It also deals with why client/server technology is still important and why it hasn't been supplanted (yet!).

The second part deals with how all the components—clients, servers, networks, operating software, data, and middleware—fit together in today's client/server environments. The chapters in this section also focus on what these components look like today—what technology they are using, how robust their software is, what alternative implementations there are, and how data is handled in this enhanced environment.

The third part of this book focuses on how to apply the client/server approach and, once it is deployed, how to manage and operate in the client/server environment. An entire chapter is devoted to multitier environments, a major component in this enhanced technology. Managing the data and managing the client/server environment are dealt with in separate chapters, which speaks to their complexity as well as their importance.

The fourth section covers application development within this environment. Rather than review a lot of products, the chapters in this section discuss what features organizations should look for in development tools and why each of them is important. The products reviewed were included as a represented sample of existing development products.

The fifth and final section is a glimpse into the future (although the year 2000 doesn't sound that far away anymore): what is happening with hardware and software and what improvements have already been announced or speculated; what are some new uses of this technology; and finally, the Internet and intranets. A year ago, the Internet was still used primarily for E-mail and as a way to send files. Tools like Netscape and Explorer and the multimedia presentations on World Wide Web sites have opened up a whole new set of possibilities to organizations.

If you haven't started to explore the possibilities of client/server computing, don't wait too much longer. Your competitors are using it. Prices are coming down, which makes it more affordable. If you love your mainframe and its applications, great. Just build a link to the mainframe or wrap the applications so that they are accessible by client/server applications. Most application software being developed today is for client/server platforms.

If you wait too long, you'll be forced into it for survival. So find an application, plan your client/server strategy, and go for it.

Have fun!

Acknowledgments

I wouldn't be finishing up this, my fourth book, with ideas for the next one without the early encouragement and ongoing support from Pieter Mimno. I look forward to his continued support.

There really are so many who have encouraged me along the way. To all of you, my thanks.

And, of course, this wouldn't be possible without the support of my family. My thanks to Travis and Greg, who got so they knew when I was working on this book and held off asking me to play with them (so I'm off to make up for lost time!). And to Andy, who took over the reins when I was holed up in my office. Without him, none of this is possible.

D. Travis Dewire

Trademarks

The following trademarks are listed in order of company, not in the order in which they appear in the book. Other company and product names may be trademarks of the respective company with which they are associated. Casual use of company names and products in this book does not imply that those trademarks are in the public domain.

Company name	Product name
American Telephone and Telegraph	AT&T, Xt+
Apple Computer and International Business Machines Corp.	Common Hardware Reference Platform, PowerPC, PowerPC Platform
Apple Computer, Inc.	Apple, AppleTalk, Cyberdog, Mac OS, MacDraw, Macintosh, Open Transport, Power Mac, Power Macintosh, System 7, System 8
Attachmate Corp.	Remote LAN Node
Banyan Systems, Inc.	Banyan, Banyan VINES, StreetTalk
BMC Software Inc.	Patrol
Borland International, Inc.	Object Component
Business Objects, Inc.	BusinessObjects
Centura Software Corp.	Application Server, Centura, Gupta, Gupta Technologies, Ranger, SQLWindows, Team Developer, Web Data Publisher
Client/Server Technology, Inc.	GUISys/400
Computer Associates International, Inc.	CA-Ingres/Replicator, CA-Unicenter
Compuware Corp.	EcoTools, EcoNet, Playback for Client/Server
Corporate Computing International	RADPath
Creative Sales & Marketing	English Wizard
DASCOM, Inc.	DASCOM, IntraVerse
Digital Equipment Corp.	DECwindows, Digital, Ultrix
Dynasty Technologies, Inc.	Dynasty, Dynasty Development Environment
Forte Software	Forte, Forte Application Environment
Gradient Technologies, Inc.	Gradient, Web Crusader
Hewlett-Packard Corp.	Alpha, HP, HP-UX, Odapter, OpenView, PerfView
Information Builders, Inc.	API/SQL, EDA, EDA/Extender, EDA/Link, EDA/WebLink, EDA/SQL, EDA/Start
Informix, Inc.	Informix, Informix Online, NewEra, Online Dynamic Server
Insignia Solutions, Inc.	Softwindows

Company name	Product name
Intel Corp.	430HX, 430VX, 440FX, Intel, LANDesk Manager, Merced, Pentium, Pentium Pro, Triton
International Business Machines Corp.	AIX, APPC, APPN, AS/400, CICS, Common User Access, Customer Information Control System, CommonPoint, DB2, DB2 PE, Distributed Console Access Facility, Distributed Data Management Architecture, Distributed Relational Database Architecture, External Presentation Interface, IBM, LAN Distance Remote, LAN Server, LU6.2, MQSeries, NetView, Networking Solutions, OS/2, OS/2 Data Base Manager, OS/2 Warp, OS/2 Warp Connect, OS/2 Warp Fullback, OS/400 Database, SAA, SP2 System, SQL/DS, SystemView, Web Explorer, Workplace Shell
JavaSoft	Java
Landmark Systems Corp.	PerformanceWorks
Lotus Development Corp.	Lotus Notes
Lucent Technologies, Inc.	Lucent, MMCX, Multimedia Communications Exchange
Massachusetts Institute of Technology	Kerberos, X Windows
Mercury Interactive Corp.	LoadRunner Client/Server
Micro Decisionware Inc.	Database Gateway
Microsoft Corp.	ActiveX, BackOffice, Component Object Model, Distributed Component Object Model, Dynamic Data Exchange, FrontPage, Index Server, Internet Information Server, JET Database Engine, LAN Manager, Microsoft, Microsoft Exchange, Microsoft Internet Explorer, Object and Embedding, Open Data Services Interface, Open Database Connectivity, PowerPoint, SQL Enterprise Manager, SQL Server 95, Visual Basic, Windows, Windows 95, Windows Applications Binary Interface, Windows for Workgroups, Windows Internet Name Service, Windows New Technology, Windows NT, Windows NT Server, Windows NT Workstation, Windows Open Services Architecture, Winnet, WinSock, XENIX
Momentum Software Corp.	InterFlow, X*IPC
Natural Language, Inc.	Natural Language
NCR Corp.	NCR, TOP END
Netscape Communications Corp.	Netscape, Netscape Navigator, Netscape Navigator Gold
Network General Corp.	Sniffer
Neuron Data Inc.	Data Access Element, Open Interface Elements
NeXT, Inc.	NeXTStep
NobleNet Inc.	EX-RPC
Novell, Inc.	ManageWise, NetWare, NetWare Directory Services, NetWare Management System, NetWare Web Server, Novell, Tuxedo
Object Management Group	Common Object Request Broker Architecture
Open Environment Corp.	Entera

Company name	Product name
Open Group, The	DCE, DCE Web, Distributed Management Environment, Distributed Computer Environment, DME
Open Software Associates Inc.	OpenUI, OpenUI Development Environment
Open Software Foundation	Motif, OSF, OSF/1
Open Vision Technologies, Inc.	OpenV*Event Manager
Optimal Networks Corp.	Optimal Networks Tool Kit
Oracle Corp.	Designer/2000, Developer/2000, Oracle, Oracle 7, Oracle 8, Parallel Query Option, Parallel Server Option, PowerBrowser, SQL*Net
PeerLogic Inc.	Pipes Platform
Performix, Inc.	Empower
Platinum Technology Inc.	InfoPump, Platinum Open Enterprise Management System
Powersoft Corp.	PowerBuilder, Powersoft, PowerScript, PowerBuilder Desktop, PowerBuilder TEAM/ODBC, PowerBuilder Enterprise, InfoMaker, Optima++, S-Designer
Prolifics	JAM 7/Transaction Processing Interface
Remote Data Access	International Standards Organization
Santa Cruz Operation Inc., The	SCO, SCO OpenServer, UNIX, UnixWare
SAS Institute, Inc.	SAS/English Software
Seagull Software Systems Inc.	GUI/400
SQL Access Group	OpenSQL
Star Division Corp.	StarView
Sterling Software Inc.	STAR:Flashpoint
Sun Microsystems, Inc.	NeWs Development Environment, NFS, Sun, XView
SunSoft	Open Network Computing, OpenWindows, Solaris, Transport-Independent Remote Procedure Call
Sybase, Inc.	Enterprise SQL Server Manager, Navigation Server, OpenClient/Open Server, SQL Server System, SQLWindows, Sybase, Sybase IQ, Sybase MPP, Sybase Replication Server, Sybase SQL Anywhere
Sybase, Inc. and Microsoft Corp.	SQL Server
Template Software Inc.	SNAP
Tivoli Systems, Inc.	Tivoli, Tivoli Management Environment
Transarc Corp.	Encina, Encina++, EncinaBuilder, Encina Monitor, Encina Peer-to-Peer, Encina Recoverable Queuing Service, Encina Structured File Server
ViewSoft Inc.	Utah
X/Open Corp.	X/Open, X/Open Transport Interface
Xerox Corp.	Xerox Network System
XVT Software Inc.	XVT, XVT-Design, XVT Portability Tool, XVT-Power++
Zinc Software Inc.	Zinc Application Framework

Acronyms

3GL	Third-generation language
4GL	Fourth-generation language
AMS	Application Management Specifications
ANSI	American National Institute of Standards
API	Application programming interface
APPC	Advanced Program-to-Program Communication (IBM)
APPC/LU6.2	APPC/Logical Unit 6.2 (IBM)
APPN	Advance Peer-to-Peer Network (IBM)
ATM	Asynchronous transfer mode
BISDN	Broadband ISDN
BLOB	Binary large object
BOOTP	Bootstrap Protocol
BPR	Business process reengineering
CASE	Computer-aided application system engineering
CCITT	Consultative Committee on International Telephone and Telegraph
ccNUMA	Cache-coherent nonuniform memory access architectures
CDE	Common Desktop Environment (OSF)
CGI	Common gateway interface
CHRP	Common Hardware Platform
CICS	Customer Information Control System (IBM)
CIDR	Classless Interdomain Routing
CISC	Complex instruction set computing
CLI	Call level interface
COM	Component Object Model (Microsoft)
CORBA	Common Object Request Broker Architecture (OMG)
CPI-C	Common Programming Interface for Communications (IBM)
CSMA/CD	Carrier Sense Multiple Access with Collision Detection
CUA	Common User Access (IBM)

DAO	Data Access Objects (Microsoft)
DBMS	Database management system
DCE	Distributed Computing Environment (The Open Group)
DCOM	Distributed COM (Microsoft)
DDE	Dynamic Data Exchange (Microsoft)
DFS	Distributed File System (DCE)
DHC	Dynamic Host Configuration group of IETF
DHCP	Dynamic Host Configuration Protocol
DII	Dynamic Invocation Interface (Microsoft)
DIMM	Dual in-line memory module
DIVE	Direct Interactive Video Extension (Microsoft)
DLC	Data Link Control (IBM)
DLL	Dynamic link library (Microsoft)
DME	Distributed Management Environment (The Open Group)
DMI	Desktop Management Interface
DMTF	Desktop Management Task Force
DNS	Domain Name Service
DRAM	Dynamic RAM
DRDA	Distributed Relational Database Architecture (IBM)
DSA	Dynamic Scalable Architecture
DSOM	Distributed SOM (IBM)
DSS	Decision support systems
DSSS	Direct-sequencing spread-spectrum
DTP	Distributed transaction processing
ECC	Error-correction code
EDA	Enterprise Data Access (Information Builders)
EDI	Electronic data interchange
EDO RAM	Extended data out RAM
EIS	Executive Information Systems
EPI	External Presentation Interface (IBM)
EPS	Enterprise Parallel Servers (Hewlett-Packard)
ESSM	Enterprise SQL Server Manager (Sybase)
FAP	Formats and protocols
FDDI	Fiber Distributed Data Interface
FHSS	Frequency-hopping spread-spectrum
FNPNW	File and Print Services for NetWare (Novell)
FRAD	Frame relay access device
GOSIP	Government Open Systems Interconnection Profile
GUI	Graphical user interface
HTML	Hypertext markup language

HTTP	Hypertext Transport Protocol
IBI	Information Builders Inc.
IBM	International Business Machines
IDL	Interface definition language
IEEE	Institute of Electrical and Electronic Engineers
IETF	Internet Engineering Task Force
IIS	Internet Information Server (Microsoft)
IP	Internetwork protocol
IPC	Interprocess communications
IPCP	IP over PPP
IPng	IP—Next generation
IPv4	IP version 4
IPv6	IP version 6
IPX	Internetwork Packet Exchange (Novell)
IPX/SPX	IPX/Sequenced Packet Exchange (Novell)
IPXCP	IPX over PPP
ISDN	Integrated Services Digital Network
ISO	International Standards Organization
IT	Information technology
ITU-T	International Telecommunications Union
JAD	Joint application development
JDBC	Java Database Connectivity (JavaSoft)
JOE	Java ORB Environment (JavaSoft)
LAN	Local area network
LDAP	Lightweight Directory Access Protocol
LSAPI	License Service API (Microsoft)
MAN	Metropolitan area network
MAPI	Mail API (Microsoft)
MAU	Multistation access unit
MIB	Management information base
MMCX	Multimedia Communications Exchange (Lucent Technologies)
MMX	Multimedia instruction set extensions (Apple and HP)
MOM	Message-oriented middleware
MPP	Massively parallel processors
MUD	Multistation access unit
NDS	NetWare Directory Services (Novell)
NetBEUI	NetBIOS Extended User Interface (Hewlett-Packard)
NetBIOS	Network Basic Input/Output Operating System
NNM	Network Node Manager (Hewlett-Packard)
NNTP	Network News Transport Protocol

NUMA	Nonuniform memory access
OCX	OLE custom controls (Microsoft)
ODBC	Open Database Connectivity (Microsoft)
ODSI	Open Data Services Interface (Microsoft)
OLAP	On-line analytical processing
OLE	Object Linking and Embedding (Microsoft)
OLE DB	OLE Database (Microsoft)
OLTP	On-line transaction processing
OMA	Object Management Architecture (OMG)
OMG	Object Management Group
ONC	Object Network Computing (Sun Microsystems)
OODBMS	Object-oriented database management systems
ORB	Object request broker
OSF	Open Software Foundation, now The Open Group
OSI	Open Systems Interconnection
OSQL	Object SQL
PCI	Peripheral Component Interconnect
POEMS	Platinum Open Enterprise Management System
POSIX	Portable Operating System Interface
PPCP	PowerPC Platform
PPP	Point-to-Point Protocol
PQO	Parallel Query Option (Oracle)
PSO	Parallel Server Option (Oracle)
RAD	Rapid application development
RAID	Redundant arrays of inexpensive disks
RARP	Reserve Address Resolution Protocol
RAS	Remote Access Service (Windows NT)
RDA	Remote Data Access (ISO)
RDRAM	Ramus Dynamic RAM
RIP	Router Information Protocol
RISC	Reduced instruction set computing
RLN	Remote LAN Node (Attachmate)
RMON	Remote network monitoring
RODM	Resource Object Data Manager (NetView)
RPC	Remote procedure call
RTAS	Run-time abstraction services
S-HTTP	Secure Hypertext Transfer Protocol
SAA	System Application Architecture (IBM)
SAG CLI	SQL Access Group Call level interface

SCO	The Santa Cruz Operation
SDLC	System development life cycle
SDRAM	Synchronous dynamic RAM
SLA	Service level agreement
SLC	System life cycle
SMDS	Switched Multimegabit Data Services
SMI	Structure of management information
SMP	Symmetric multiprocessors
SMS	System Management Server (Microsoft)
SNA	Systems Network Architecture (IBM)
SNAP	Subnet Access Protocol (Template Software)
SNMP	Simple Network Management Protocol
SOM	System Object Model (IBM)
SP2	Scalable Parallel Processor (IBM)
SQL	Standard Query Language
SSL	Secure socket layer (Netscape Communications)
SVR4.2	UNIX System V Release 4 (SCO)
TAPI	Telephony API (Microsoft)
TCP	Transmission Control Protocol
TCP/IP	Transmission Control Protocol/Internetwork Protocol
TME	Tivoli Management Environment
TP	Transaction processing
TX	X/Open Transaction interface
UDP	User Datagram Protocol
UNI	User-network interface
URL	Uniform resource locator
USB	Universal Serial Bus
VBS	Visual Basic Script (Microsoft)
VBX	Visual Basic Control (Microsoft)
VLAN	Virtual LAN
VPN	Virtual private network
VRML	Virtual Reality Modeling Language
WABI	Windows Application Binary Interface (Microsoft)
WAN	Wide area network
WINS	Windows Internet Name Service (Microsoft)
WOSA	Windows Open Services Architecture (Microsoft)
WWW	World Wide Web
XA	X/Open Resource Manager
XMP	X/Open Management APIs

XNS	Xerox Network Services
XOM	X/Open Object Manager
XPG4	X/Open Portability Guide Issue 4

Client/Server Revisited

Client / server computing was heralded as the technology that would revolutionize the 1990s, allowing businesses to work smarter. Organizations were promised smaller application development backlogs as well as lower development costs. There was the promise of lower operating costs, and even of the demise of the mainframe.

Some organizations have realized these promises, most have not. But yet, organizations are still looking to client / server technology to pave the way toward a better business environment. They need the flexibility that client / server technology can provide.

The second generation of client / server computing has evolved from a very simple premise: The client requests data and the server serves data. Organizations stretched that premise by distributing the processing, adding dedicated servers, and upscaling applications ported to client / server environments (enterprise-wide rather than departmental). Today's client / server–based applications still have clients making requests. But their requests are now viewed as requests for services: processing or data. And the end node for a request might not be the server connected to the client, in which case the server becomes a client requesting services from another server.

Local area networks create "islands of information." Enterprise networks connect these islands so that they can share information. In the process, the organization can also gain some efficiencies, reengineer the business

1

processes, and build an architecture that can grow or shrink in reaction to outside as well as inside business forces.

The goals of client/server computing are to allow every network node to be accessible, as needed by an application, and to allow all software components to work together. When these two conditions are met, the environment can be successful and the benefits of client/server computing, such as cost savings, increased productivity, flexibility, and resource utilization, can be realized.

These goals can be achieved in part by adhering to industry standards and creating open systems. However, some of the components of client/server computing have multiple standards to choose from, whereas others have none.

Knowing where to start or how to start is difficult. The decision on which standards to use is also not always obvious. But start you must. Make a plan. Do some research. Build a pilot. Scale up the pilot. Scale down the pilot. The separation of duties between clients and servers is not going away.

1

Today's Client/Server Technology

Client/server architecture is based on the premise that the key components of an application should not be tightly intertwined. Organizations should be able to add, remove, or replace components as necessary without affecting the applications themselves.

Client/server computing is based on distributed computing with data closer to the end user, thus lessening the impact of server failure and improving response time. The client/server computing model implies cooperation between a client—the requester—and at least one server—the responder which accepts the requests, fulfills them, and sends the results back to the client. In this form of distributed computing, the resources required to complete a task are spread among components, and the required data also may (or may not) be spread among components.

Users want more local processing power, and they want immediate access to the data they need on their portable or desktop computers. The Information Technology (IT) group within organizations is providing that access to data by distributing common applications and the appropriate data to "nodes" in the network. Data now exists in a central database and also in databases on various nodes. In some cases, the data on these nodes is a copy of data in the central database (remember when IT's primary purpose was to make sure that there was one and only one copy of a data element?).

1.1 Today's Definition

Client/server technology has always been an implementation of a distributed environment. Distributed environments are made up of secure subsystems with data flowing freely over a variety of networks. This interoperability is critical and is usually achieved through adherence to standards.

This structure makes optimal use of network protocols and bandwidths, operating systems, hardware, and databases. A distributed environment provides users with transparent access to computing resources within the network. Users are aware only of the computer on their desk.

Distributed environments can provide real benefits to organizations. These benefits include:

- Ability to develop enterprise-wide solutions
- Increased responsiveness to customer requests using a decentralized operation
- Transparent access to data located at multiple sites
- More efficient use of computer-related resources
- Reduced operating costs

In distributed environments, client applications request services and server applications provide services. Messages are the sole means of communication between these applications.

When the components of an application—the processes—are distributed, they:

- Communicate via messages
- Request and receive services
- Are distributed among applications
- Reside across multiple, geographically distinct processes
- Cooperate to complete a business transaction

In the past (and, unfortunately for many, still), the steps needed to complete a job might be similar to those detailed in the left column of Fig. 1.1. To a user in a distributed environment, the process would be more like the steps listed in the right column of Fig. 1.1.

A distributed environment allows a user to access the data on the mainframe (or on any connected machine, for that matter), do the analysis, upload it into a spreadsheet package, route the graphs to the graphics computer, access the CD-ROM "jukebox" (multidisk CD-ROM reader), and upload saved text into a word processing package. While there may not be fewer steps, each step is more straightforward and logical from a user's point of view, and the transitions between steps are painless and often transparent.

1.2   The Evolution toward Distributed Environments

The idea behind distributing the computing load is not a new one. Front-end communication controllers have off-loaded network-related processing from mainframes for years. But to the applications themselves, there was only one box which contained everything except what was displayed on the

Nondistributed Environment	Distributed Environment
– Use a mainframe to access and extract data. – Switch software to download the data to a micro. – Start up a spreadsheet package and load the data into the spreadsheet. – Perform some analysis, save some graphs, and save the spreadsheet. – Switch software to access a CD-ROM "jukebox" and extract text. – Start up word processing software and load the text files. – Edit the text files into a document format. – Import the spreadsheet into the document. – Print the document. – Switch to a graphics computer. – Print the saved graphics.	– Click on the spreadsheet icon. – Pick the menu choice for nonlocal data. – Specify the data object and extract criteria. – After the data has populated the spreadsheet, perform the analysis. – When a graph format is finalized, click on the graphic computer icon to have it print. – Save the spreadsheet and exit the package. – Click on the word processing icon. – Click on the CD-ROM "jukebox" icon. – Specify the text to be retrieved and do a search. – Click on the return icon. – Perform any editing necessary. – Use DDE or OLE to implement transparent data sharing with the spreadsheet. – Click on the print icon.

Figure 1.1 Steps required to complete a task

screen, and even that was sent line by line by the host to the receiving terminal.

1.2.1   Host-based

As organizations began to computerize their operations, they developed applications that resided on a central mainframe computer. In such applications, the processing is performed by this one machine and users are connected via "dumb" terminals. Data for these applications was stored on the same machine. An application running on a stand-alone micro is just as much a host-based application as those that are running on an mainframe or mini. In one case the terminal is "dumb," and in the other it is "intelligent" and seen as an integral part of the same machine.

As the price/performance ratios of micros and micro/servers improved, centralized application processing was no longer the only cost-effective alternative as an environment for applications. Today, businesses are

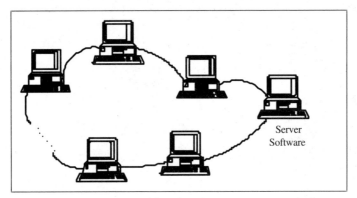

Server
Software

Figure 1.2 First generation of distributed computing

looking to distributed environments to meet the corporate goal of reducing costs while improving customer service.

1.2.2   File servers and LANs

The first generation of distributed computing connected workers in a department or group, as illustrated in Fig. 1.2. The impetus for this move was to share files and peripherals, usually laser printers. The micro that runs the software that facilitates the sharing is called the *server*. This micro might more appropriately be called the *coordinating workstation*.

As local area networks (LANs) began to appear within departments, the individual departments were connected, as illustrated in Fig. 1.3. E-mail facilities were often the justifying capability for this move. Most of the software ran on the coordinating workstation, and the connected networks were homogeneous. Security and reliability were not major features of these architectures.

1.2.3   First-generation client/server

The first generation of client/server computing was a natural extension of the idea behind file servers: specialization. The clients did all the application processing, and the server accepted requests for data and returned the results of the requests, rather than the file itself.

These micro-centric applications were usually simple decision-support applications for single users or workgroups, with data accessed from a single LAN-based database server (although it was simply called a server in those days!). Because of the visual development tools which could easily generate graphical user interface (GUI) screens for these applications, these early applications were easier to develop and deploy than their host-based counterparts.

In the early file-server LAN implementations, even if a client application needed only one record from a database, the entire database file was sent

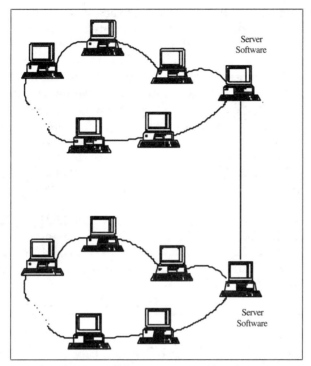

Figure 1.3 Extension of first generation of distributed computing

over the network to the client machine, at which point the client application did its own search. In the first generation of client/server computing, the client platform does most of the work, as illustrated in Fig. 1.4. The client application asks for a record and gets only that record.

As organizations adopted this first phase of client/server computing, they saw productivity gains as the primary benefit of this new environment. Once the infrastructure was in place, working reliably and readily accepted, organizations moved on to the second phase: distributing the application processing. Some of the application processing was off-loaded to the server.

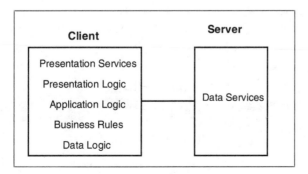

Figure 1.4 First-generation client/server computing

For example, instead of sending hundreds of records that would be used for a calculation within an application, the calculation is done on the server, and only the results are returned to the client application. Benefits from this move are more strategic, such as improved customer service, flexibility to react to changes in the market, and faster product introductions.

As shown in Fig. 1.5, many organizations connected heterogeneous resources used by various departments to create a enterprise system.

Most client/server applications are two-tier installations, departmental in scope, designed to support 15 to 20 users, and run non-business-critical applications. As a two-tier architecture, they were designed to run the user interface and application logic on the client. The client issued SQL calls across a LAN to a relational database on the server to retrieve data for processing.

These smaller, homogeneous, less complex applications had a high success rate, which prompted organizations to expand the scope and complexity of the applications. Developers were asked to increase the number of users, data sources, and functions of these early success stories. However, two-tier architectures do not scale well. The result was lower

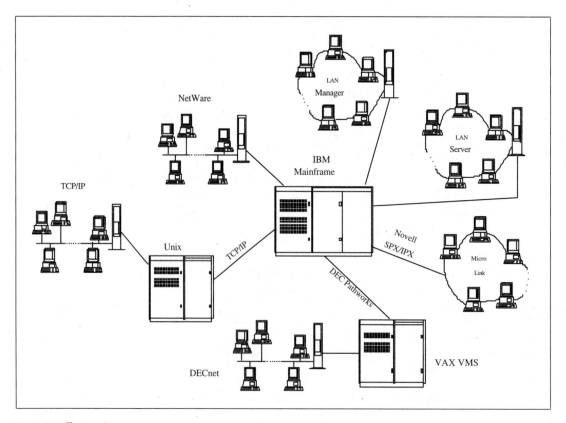

Figure 1.5 Enterprise system

performance, slower response times, and reduced reliability and availability. A successful pilot was doomed to failure.

1.2.4   Second-generation client/server

As the technology began to mature and client/server networks were interconnected, an application could make a request to its server for data that resided on another server. The idea of distributed access became commonplace. The machines at the users' desks provide almost all of the presentation services and logic, as illustrated in Fig. 1.6. Business-specific application processing can be done by the client machine, a multipurpose server, or an application server. Data is managed by a server. The data can be distributed among nodes in the network or be resident on only one machine, which may or may not be the server the client was directly connected to.

Organizations began to build multitiered client/server architectures and began to view the structure as support for the enterprise rather than just for individual departments. Servers evolved from multipurpose servers to specialized machines optimized for only one task and perform only that task.

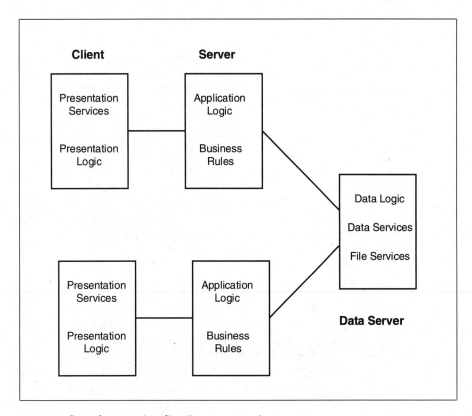

Figure 1.6 Second-generation client/server computing

These multitier architectures extend two-tier architectures by adding additional platforms (sometimes referred to as intermediate servers) to support application logic, database access, and distributed services. The simplest way to think of this new structure is as three tiers: user interfaces, servers, and data sources. The presentation services and logic are addressed by the user interface tier, the application logic by the server tier, and the data access by the data sources tier. These enterprise networks make use of application servers, database servers, compute servers, and communication servers.

These additional specialized platforms are critical in today's environments for providing location transparency and flexibility and scalability for the environment. (Two-tier and multitier architectures are discussed in detail in Chap. 10.) The multitier architecture also recognizes that in larger systems, the application logic is more common (shared by multiple applications and, for a single application, used by more users) and more complex.

As the hardware technology matured, so did the support for distributed processing: A node could perform a task for any other node, all transparent to the application and the user. The distinction between a server and a desktop client machine became blurred. Either computer could be a client or a server, depending on whether it was making a request or responding to a request.

When a mobile user connects to a desktop micro from the road, the desktop micro is a server. When the mobile user returns to the office and uses the desktop micro "as is," it is a client. The entire enterprise network—the users' machines, the servers, the network, and the network connection devices—becomes the computer system.

Applications can now share reusable modules. Data can reside at the nearest node. Components are easily scalable. Middleware technology provides many options for accessing heterogeneous data sources and for executing code.

As this technology evolves, the idea of objects and distributed objects is beginning to take hold. Most of the newer, high-end development tools use distributed objects as their development paradigm.

1.3   Categories of Applications

Client/server applications are traditional applications recast for the new environment. In most cases, organizations are not developing applications that are radically functionally different. What is different is how these applications make use of the architecture of this new environment.

It is important to understand how applications can be categorized to help understand how they can best be implemented in the client/server environment.

1.3.1   Transactional versus informational

Transaction processing applications are the lifeblood of an organization. These applications are the link between the organization and its customers and suppliers. There are very specific rules as to what data needs to be captured and what is to happen to the data once it is captured. If these applications are slow or unavailable, the operations of the organization suffers. If an order entry application is not working, no orders can be taken. In today's environments, most transaction processing applications have real-time capabilities (such as calling an 800 number to place an order) and therefore need real-time access to internal information (such as whether the item being ordered is in stock).

Informational applications are based on transaction applications. There is little processing in these applications other than aggregation. These applications provide information to management concerning what has happened in the transaction processing applications. Typically this information is supplied in a report, either hard copy or soft copy (on a screen). The contents and format of the report are prespecified.

With the easy-to-use query tools on the market today, many organizations are aggregating transactional data and depositing it in a data warehouse for access by users. In some cases, the reports are now derived from the warehouse data. This easy access allows a user to obtain more information than is currently supplied in report form.

Executive information systems (EISs) are a hybrid informational application. The screen-based reports are hot-linked to reports with lower levels of detail, allowing the user to click on a number in an upper-level report and see the details that make up that number (called drill-down).

1.3.2   Operational versus DSS

Operational applications access data in a procedural manner, and the data to be accessed can be identified in advance. The process might be to first access data element A, then data element B, and so on. The applications outlined above fall in this category.

Users of decision-support applications (DSS) access data in a nonprocedural manner. A user might review data element A, then access some portion of data element C, then access a different view of data element A, and so on. In some cases, the user may not be able to determine in advance what data elements will be needed for a particular session, task, or time. Given the business climate of the moment, data element A might be more important than data element B. As the business climate changes, data element C might become more important than either data element A or B.

Since most of the data accessed by DSS applications is generated by functional areas of the organization, the required data will most likely not be on the connection nodes of the DSS users. DSS data is massaged and aggregated before it is put in a DSS data source. In some cases, this is a proprietary format used by the DSS tool used in the organization. DSS data is usually stored as a multidimensional array—or on-line analytic processing (OLAP) structures. In other cases, database gateways or overlays to relational database structures are used to access the data.

DSS applications are not applications as we understand applications. They have no specified inputs, outputs, or processes. They do, of course, have data stores. DSS applications give users the functional tools (modeling, statistical analysis, user-defined aggregations, rotation of views, graphics, etc.) needed to access the data and make better decisions.

DSS applications are also known as "business intelligence" applications.

1.3.3   Workflow applications

Workflow through an organization is documented by forms. This process is one of the last information areas to benefit from computer technology. Forms are completed, sometimes manually, sometimes on-line (such as an order taken over the telephone). Multiple copies of manually prepared forms are made (or printed) and routed—and usually stored—by different departments.

In contrast, electronic forms—the image can include the form's graphics and fonts—can be routed electronically like E-mail messages. But automating an ineffective process will yield a faster ineffective process. Workflow software can streamline processes, but the greatest benefits from automating work processes are realized when the processes themselves are effective. Organizations first need to study the processes to determine where improvements can be made and take appropriate actions. For some organizations, a minor fix is all that is required; for other organizations, a major overhaul is needed.

Electronic forms can go beyond maillike messages—they allow users to electronically sign the form. Such a signature might indicate approval or that the form has been read. To support workflow, routes could be automatic. For example, when an employee "signs" an electronic timecard, the software locks in the hours and the timecard is automatically forwarded to the employee's supervisor. The supervisor reviews it and "signs" it, signifying approval, and the timecard is then automatically sent to the payroll application for processing.

Electronic data interchange (EDI) has revolutionized and formalized the way workflow among businesses can be, and is, processed. EDI is the transmission of data for standard business transactions, such as orders, order change requests, invoices, and requests for quotations, from one firm's computer to another firm's computer—sent and received by the software running on the computers. The transmission is almost instantaneous.

In the case of purchase orders, the receiving application can check for availability and respond quickly with a confirmation and an invoice. There is no manual intervention between the transactions that are exchanged among the various applications. There is no form, there is no paperwork—just a computer-generated transaction and a computer-generated audit trail.

Standards are beginning to be accepted for EDI formats and protocols within industries. Currently, the United States and Canada use the ANSI X.12 protocol, and Europe uses a standard called EDIFACT. Until these standards converge, multinational organizations will have to support both protocols.

EDI was originally adopted for competitive advantage but is quickly becoming a competitive necessity. For large companies, the benefits of speed, reliability (the data is keyed only once), reduced past-due payments, and reduced cost per purchase order far outweigh the implementation and operation costs. Smaller companies that need EDI to stay competitive are using commercial value-added networks that provide EDI services.

1.4   The New Terminology

Most of the new terminology arrives in the form of an acronym: SMP, MPP, ATM, MOM, WOSA, OLAP, ODBC, RMON, DMI, XMP, XOM, DHCP (listed in order of introduction in this book). Some of the other terms used today are still in code-name status: Cairo, Merlin, Copland, Kagera, Nile, Comet, Eiger, Gershwin, Nashville, Gemini, and Sting.

Network-centric is the term given to the new enterprise-wide environment: Each of the components is network aware, and connections are made as users need them. The Internet has spawned its own set of new terms: Java, applets, intranets, and WWW (World Wide Web) to mention just a few.

It should quickly become obvious that this once seemingly simple notion of separating presentation logic, application logic, and data access so that each could run on a platform best suited for the task has become much more complex. Installing and maintaining a client/server environment has never been for the faint at heart. That continues to be the case.

1.5   Why Client/Server Is Still Important

Despite the cost overruns and the missed deadlines, organizations are still willing to pay the costs and assume the risks. Why? Client/server technology has the potential to streamline operations and improve productivity without compromising performance and stability. It can deliver higher-quality and more flexible applications in shorter amounts of time, provide faster access to data when it is needed, reduce network logjams, and allow users to work smarter and faster (be more productive).

As organizations try to reduce their time to market, provide information to those needing to make decisions, and improve customer service, the flexibility of client/server technology is no longer a luxury, it is a necessity.

1.5.1   Geographical dispersion

If it is true that information is the business, then it is also true that the network is the organization.

Distributed environments allow an organization to build subnetworks at sites within the organization—on the same floor, in the same building, city, state, or country, or somewhere else in the world—and connect them into one network, thus sharing applications and data transparently to the user.

Mobile users add another dimension to this geographical dispersion. Mobile users aren't hard-wired into any subnetwork, they attach to the subnetwork as needed from wherever they happen to be: in a car, their home, a hotel, a shared office. This flexibility provides organizations with a new delivery vehicle for applications that require that the internal user be closer to the customer.

1.5.2   Changing levels of information systems

Improved response time is the goal of most IT organizations today. To support that goal, applications have to be able to access data very quickly—most response time is a function of data access speed rather than cycle times for computations.

With client/server technology, data can live anywhere in the network and still be accessed by any node needing it. By putting data closest to the point where it is used most often, organizations can improve response time. In some cases the data is a replica of the "real" dataset and the environment takes care of updating it on a scheduled basis.

We are also living in an information-driven business environment. The current focus of most of our applications is on providing information rather than automating tasks—most of those applications were written a long time ago and still run as legacy systems. Since our business environment is ever-changing, so are our information needs. Organizations must be able to respond quickly to those changing needs.

1.5.3   Distributed applications

Client/server technology allows an organization to review the structure of its applications. Applications can now be broken into pieces that are common to more than one application and therefore stored, maintained, and executed in a central location (a server), with the results sent back to the requesting client.

In addition, computation-intensive tasks can be routed to a server that is optimized for computation. In many ways, we are coming full circle again: The decentralized notion of the first-generation client/server computing architecture is evolving into a much more centralized notion (if all servers are considered as one group).

1.5.4   Scalability

Scalability is related to the architecture. Scalability means being able to unplug one server and plug in a new one (of either greater or lesser capacity) or put in additional disk capacity without changing the system.

Scalability allows an organization to design an application and "size" it to individual sites. An increased number of users or applications could mean adding another server to the network to share the processing load. An alternative would be to to add a dedicated server for a particular functional area of the organization to the network. Scalability also means fine-tuning a server for a particular function such as data access or computations.

1.5.5   Business forces

In the 1990s more than ever, organizations exist in an ever-changing environment. They are faced with reduced times to market, reduced profits, a quickly changing market, and increased competitive pressure.

They are rightsizing and reengineering business process to react to these forces. Organizations are looking to client/server technology to provide them with weapons to stay even in the market and tools that will allow them to create a competitive advantage.

1.5.6   Business process reengineering

Reengineering means to use information technology to improve the performance of a business and cut costs by redesigning work and business processes from the ground up ("out of the box") rather than simply automating existing tasks and functions. Reengineering is customer-oriented and, as such, has as its goal reducing service time, whether it's to respond to a service call, process an order, process an application, or respond to a question. Reengineering is about time to market. It is about radical improvement, not incremental change. Reengineering was popularized by the book *Reengineering the Corporation* by Michael Hammer and James Champy, published by Harvard Press in 1993.

When tasks were first automated and on-line processing started to become the norm, departments were fairly autonomous—remember, databases had just forced organizations to think very differently about what data was, how it was used, and how it might be used. So a new order-entry system didn't affect very many departments—probably two at the most. To those departments, the new system was mostly viewed as a radical improvement, although with the benefit of hindsight it seems more like an incremental change.

However, in today's environments, there is an enterprise view of the organization's data and cross-functionality between departments. Any new use of technology or new method for handling the data of the organization affects many, and for that very reason will take on a radical air.

The benefits of business process reengineering (BPR) include:

- **Streamlined operations**: more reliable and minimal cycle times
- **Flexibility**: faster responses to changes in the market
- **Metrics**: built-in controls and monitoring

Planning is, of course, key to a successful BPR project. Careful attention must be paid to why the process is being altered in the first place. Managers need to identify specific targets and outcomes, and most of the goals should be quantifiable—for example, not "to process loan applications faster" but "to process loan applications within 48 hours." The organization must recognize the mistakes that have been made so as to not repeat them in the new design.

An organization needs to think of its business processes from two points of view. The external point of view is how the customers, suppliers, distributors, etc.—the outsiders—interface with the organization. The internal point of view is what happens internally when an outsider interfaces with the organization. For example, what happens when a customer places an order or an order is sent to a supplier. Organizations can become more efficient and effective from both points of view through new uses of technology and redesigning the interface with the organization (such as the ATM machines) or the internal processes (how long it takes to process a loan application). EDI is an example of business process reengineering. Using the Touch-Tone phone to allow customers to key in data is process reengineering. Using handheld computers to capture onsite data is process reengineering.

Since customer service is the major focus for most of today's businesses, looking at business processes from both sides maintains the focus on the outsiders without losing sight of the internal activities required to support the outsiders.

Automating business processes is not as easy a task as one might imagine. Identifying all the processes, analyzing them, understanding how they interrelate, and then redesigning them takes time and a special skill set. The identification process does not need to be performed by outside consultants. An employee who understands the business but is not part of the business area being reviewed is often as good a choice as a consultant.

There are some rules of thumb to follow. Once a customer-oriented model of the area being reviewed has been determined, pick a critical *core* process to reengineer. Identify the value-added processes related to this critical core process and the value-added processes that are part of the critical core process. Which of those is the customer willing to pay for? Be sure to benchmark performance, simulated if possible, to see if the ends justify the means. If it's a go, then restructure the organization, apply technology, redefine job descriptions, and communicate the plan. Do a pilot program, if possible.

Recommendations usually include workflow automation or new uses of technology.

Workflow automation involves multiple stages and distribution between the internal members of the organization and the outsiders. There are automated process analysis tools available that provide graphical tools for capturing a process and a methodology for reviewing processes to ensure that all the information has been captured and all the relationships identified.

Some of the newer object-oriented tools get the end users more involved in the process of process reengineering. End users create descriptions of the business tasks they need to accomplish, and the software converts these descriptions into more formal object models and checks the results for inconsistencies and omissions.

There are also products called workflow builders, which are mapping tools that allow an organization to lay out workflow processes and integrate them with existing applications. The output is an automated workflow application. The analysis tools help the organization do the analysis, and the workflow builders translate it into an implementation model, complete with activity labels, process logic (flow and conditions), roles, and description information.

Workflow automation software uses imaging to move a document through a process. The focus is on who gets what piece of the document, in what order they get it, and under what conditions. These are known as routes, roles, and rules. The software then keeps track of who got what document and checks such things as how long that person has had it; if too long, the software reassigns the document to another worker's electronic in-box. If a worker has completed work on the document, he or she releases it to the software, which routes it to the next station depending on the built-in rules. Ideally, no document gets stuck in someone's electronic in-box or out-box.

Workflow within an organization isn't always so formal that it needs rules and roles. Lotus Notes is a prime example of software being used to coordinate processes. The roles and the rules are decided by the worker, not hard-coded into software.

The major hurdles of BPR are resistance to change, getting and maintaining cross-functional cooperation, and sustaining top management support. Add to these, the inability to manage expectations about the new technology that is going to make the BPR project successful. Adding structure to a worker's tasks is usually seen as restrictive rather than something that will make the job easier. In fact, once workers get past their initial reaction to the changes, they should see them as an opportunity to do better, more fulfilling work.

1.5.7   Rightsizing

Rightsizing means making sure that the IT architecture fits the business environment and its applications. In the past, applications ran on a host machine, and that machine had to be powerful enough to support the applications and their data requirements for the entire organization, and still have a decent response time. If the host machine was running out of steam, usually the only solution was to buy a more powerful machine—a large expenditure!

With the flexibility of client/server technology and the diversity of hardware and software options, organizations can build the architecture for today's requirements, knowing that if they need additional power, they can unplug the existing box and plug in a new box or plug in additional boxes. These boxes are usually micro/servers and don't have anywhere near the same impact on the corporate budget as host machines do.

1.5.8   Shift in computing paradigm

Computers were originally considered the workhorses of an organization. They were used to automate manual tasks and then used to streamline these tasks with on-line processing. As organizations come to the point where most of their operational systems are automated, they are looking to the computer to provide better ways to do business since the price/performance ratio of today's technology is so favorable.

Users today are much more computer-literate. They expect to use computing power to do their daily jobs. They more often ask, "Why can't I do this?" rather than yesterday's, "Can I do this?" These new users expect to be able to communicate with the world via the machine on their desk.

1.5.9   Emerging use of multimedia

Multimedia, the current rage, is presenting information in more than one form, which can include text, audio, images and graphics, animated graphics, and full-motion video. The original multimedia programs were typically games, encyclopedias, and training courses on CD-ROM.

Organizations are now looking at using multimedia to market their existing products. Many organizations now offer on-line and CD-ROM–based catalogs. Another example is information available on an organization's Web pages accessible via the Internet

Much of today's multimedia focus is aimed at the Internet and the World Wide Web (WWW). Since the Internet connects nodes from homes and businesses into one giant network, it's a new market channel for organizations. WWW interfaces are multimedia-based so an organization can provide images as well as text to deliver its message to those Internet users that stop at the organization's WWW home page.

The Internet and WWW are the focus of Chapter 17.

It is still too early to tell how the Internet and WWW will ultimately affect users and organizations. The Internet is not secure, so conducting on-line transactions is not routinely done and firewalls have to be built so that the outside Internet connections cannot access internal data or applications. Many organizations and groups are working on the security issue. A solution can't be too far off. But for now, most of the WWW applications are providing information (or sound or voice or video!) to the connected user. And if an organization's competitors have a WWW home page, then the organization had best get one up as well.

1.6   Advantages and Risks

Most of the risks surrounding the implementation of client/server computing can be minimized by careful planning and realistic expectations. An organization should not begin a client/server pilot just for the sake of technology—there has to be a real need for the flexibility that client/server computing brings. But be sure that the pilot can be delivered within a three- to six-month window, and the results of the pilot are tangible and measurable. Also manage the expectations of management—prototypes don't scale well! Converting a prototype involving a few users to a working application that can handle large volumes and a large number of users is not an overnight task.

Even when a need has been identified, an organization must be sure that it is ready for the changes client/server computing brings to the culture of the organization.

Some other risks that can be avoided with proper planning include:

- Improper application selection
- Inadequate server procedures
- Inadequate client processing methods
- Inadequate interface procedures
- Lack of consistency in processing
- Improper data usage
- Lack of integration
- Inadequate security
- Inadequate client/server administration

1.6.1   Technological advantages and risks

GUIs allow users to be more comfortable with applications. Users tend to feel that they are more in control. The flexibility of the technology allows an organization to fit the architecture to the application rather than the application to the architecture. With standards, open systems allow the support of heterogeneous environments, and organizations can use the best environment for the particular application knowing that it can still be part of the network.

However, distributed applications and heterogeneous environments are more complex to manage and to develop. Robust tools are beginning to appear on the market to help.

The early adopters of client/server technology would point to lack of quality as a major reason for any failures that occurred along the way. Poorly designed client/server applications were the result of the lack of knowledge of the "new" environment, ill-defined requirements, and failure to adequately test, especially simulating the expected operational environment.

Data can be closest to the source that uses it, resulting in improved response time, which can mean improved customer support. However, users come to expect that same response time for applications and requests that are off their location subnetwork.

As organizations move from two-tier architectures to multitier architectures, they often try to use the same development tools. Many of the first-generation client/server development tools are just not robust enough to build enterprise-wide solutions.

1.6.2   Operational advantages and risks

Client/server technology uses components that are supplied by multiple vendors. In some cases, the vendor's products may be written to communicate with other products via standard interfaces. In other cases, they may not be. In either situation, the organization has to make sure the products work together—and deal with the vendor finger-pointing that will occur when they don't.

To get the greatest benefit from client/server technology, an organization needs to do some form of reengineering and reorganization. This will result in changes to the corporate culture that need to be anticipated and be part of the planning process. Those subnetworks were as much fiefdoms as they were disparate systems. Tying them together requires a unified effort on the part of all the managers—and a loss of political power.

1.6.3   Economic advantages and risks

Client/server computing allows an organization to leverage its technology expenditures. The price/performance ratio for the smaller machines is much more favorable than that for larger machines. Scalability is easily accomplished.

The days of insisting that client/server technology will save lots of money because applications can be run on inexpensive client workstations and servers are over. The success stories rarely, if ever, talk about coming in on budget or the accuracy of the savings projections. The stories do talk about supporting the ever-changing business structure, being able to quickly respond to user requests, and easily scaling applications up or down.

Most of the focus of client/server costs is on the hardware, but hardware is a small piece of the pie. The client/server budget is actually labor intensive. An organization needs to acquire new personnel or train current personnel (and COBOL programmers don't quickly—if ever—take to event-driven programming), and provide ongoing support for thoese newly trained employees. For an example outside of client/server computing, consider moving users and their applications to Windows 95. Buying the software and any necessary hardware is a small percentage of the overall costs. Most of the upgrade costs are for labor.

Many organizations assume that because they have LANs, they are ready for client/server computing. But lessons learned in the local area network environment do not scale up at all.

The individual local area networks have to be upgraded to overcome some of their limitations. System management and security tools for LAN environments are not robust enough for enterprise use. In fact, system management and security tools for distributed environments are just now becoming available.

System management is also labor-intensive. Staff have to back up and recover system data, keep track of licenses for all the software running on all the client machines, distribute software upgrades, etc. Automated tools that will handle all or some of these functions are beginning to appear, but they aren't inexpensive. In addition, if the corporate data center is accessible through the LAN, the LAN-based system management software should integrate with its system management software.

LANs are expensive to troubleshoot. Reasonable downtime for E-mail and file transfers is usually not acceptable for environments running business-critical applications. Additional network expertise is required as LANs scale up. Installing a network is one thing. Maintaining it and troubleshooting it are not so easy.

The configuration that worked for the original LAN may not work for a scaled-up environment. Adding a server raises the complexity exponentially. It is not a simple fix to a resource problem. In addition, the two-phase commit protocol used to ensure data integrity when transactions span multiple data sources and/or platforms creates network traffic and may necessitate a network upgrade.

Internetworking heterogeneous LANs, DBMSs, operating systems, and applications can lead to surprises. Layer after layer of middleware need to be implemented to make the connections appear seamless. This translates to unexpected dollars and worker-hours.

In host-based environments, data administration is centralized. The data is located in one place, and there is only one copy of it. In client/server environments, copies of the same data could exist in many different places. Data is spread among many servers. Data is used by many applications, and in some cases are accessible to the users through query tools. In addition, the data is probably contained in different DBMSs and file structures.

The development tools with their wonderful GUI interfaces do improve programmer productivity (once programmers have been trained and have progressed along the learning curve, that is), but these event-driven applications require a lot of testing. The user is in control, and how the application behaves when the user does something unexpected (like miniaturizing the application and starting up something else) needs to be anticipated when the application is written and tested for during testing.

Increased testing and additional design requirements more than offset improved programmer productivity.

The other misconception about the development tools for client/server applications concerns their strengths. They are really great at creating the GUIs for an application. They are really great at simple applications that retrieve existing data and display it. They start falling apart when it comes to handling transactions that have complex business logic—then the developer is back to coding in the development tool's script language.

The costs of training the technical staff and allocating time for them to progress along the learning curve are also often underestimated. The staff members need to understand the new computing paradigm and its concepts. They need to understand the processes that are now used to construct an application. They need to learn the new platform. And while all this training and learning is going on, they are not productive at work.

These costs can be limited. One method is to not incur the costs all at once. They can be spread over two or three years. During development, only the hardware and software needed by the developers has to be purchased. Hardware and software for client workstations can be added as rollout approaches. Development can be done on a low-end server and moved to a production platform for final testing and rollout. If users are to be added over time, hardware and software can be purchased on an as-needed basis.

Not every developer needs a developer's license for every product. For some, a less expensive run-time license should be adequate.

Approaching a client/server project from this standpoint requires a different budgetary approach as well. Client/server implementations do not fit well with a year-to-year budget process. Instead, it is better to budget for shorter periods such as three months or six months. This allows the organization to have a better grasp of what will actually be needed based on its experience to date.

Don't let one project take the hit for all costs that are associated with putting an infrastructure in place. For example, developing GUI standards takes a great deal of time The investment should be spread over multiple projects. Loading these costs into a single application when the standards will be used in several projects is guaranteed to create a cost overrun.

Inventories are minimized. Costs for client/server hardware and software are declining every day. What is purchased today at even a hefty discount will be selling on the street for substantially less in six months.

Organizations must also remember that most client/server applications are not replacing those currently on the mainframe. Usually they are augmenting existing applications or are entirely new. This means that the mainframe doesn't suddenly disappear, and in fact may not disappear at all. So why think that IT costs are going to go down drastically if what has actually happened is that the IT structure has expanded? As the client/server environment matures and expands, its related costs will begin to diminish because the staff is trained and has progressed along the learning curve, the network support is in place, and the cost of the components needed as the structure expands will be lower.

1.7   Then Why Bother?

So why do organizations bother if the costs are so high and the risks so many? It's a quick rollout to users. Pieces of the environment can be rolled out without having the entire functionality ready. However, this process can backfire if adequate planning isn't done to ensure that the next piece fits with the first piece. Pieces should not totally replace the existing pieces if it requires users to learn the application over again.

GUIs are more user-friendly and tend to encourage users to try things on their own to understand the functionality of the applications. On-line help replaces documentation and has a chance of being accessed and read. Users are more involved in the actual development and are up to speed quickly with the new application.

Client/server environments allow organizations to implement business process reengineering endeavors. By redesigning workflow and jobs, an organization can achieve operational improvements, which should generate dollar savings.

Some organizations have little choice. They need the flexibility, and they will endure the growing pains that accompany the new technology. They recognize that it is the first step on the learning curve and that the next implementation will be better as a result of these hard-learned lessons.

2

Client/Server Concepts

As was discussed earlier, in client/server technology, the components of an application are separated and can be implemented on different resources within the network.

2.1 Client/Server Components

Each client/server application has three components. The architecture is broken into two or more tiers to support the execution of the application components. Each tier has its own hardware and software, as illustrated in Fig. 2.1.

2.1.1 Application components

Client/server applications can be broken into three components:

- Presentation, which refers to the user interface
- Application logic
- Data handling

The presentation component is the part of the application that controls what the user sees and captures what the user does.

The application logic component consists of the tasks and rules that are in place so that the application can complete its task and also includes any services required to implement these tasks and rules. Business rules, rules that are generic to the business rather than specific to the application, are handled as part of the application logic component.

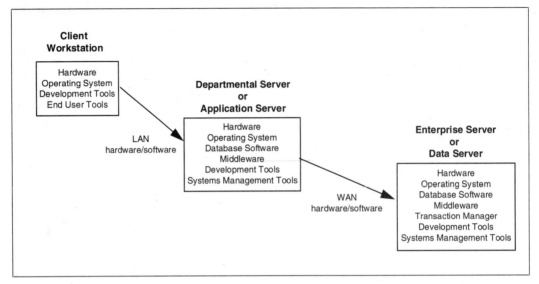

**Client
Workstation**

Hardware
Operating System
Development Tools
End User Tools

**Departmental Server
or
Application Server**

Hardware
Operating System
Database Software
Middleware
Development Tools
Systems Management Tools

LAN
hardware/software

**Enterprise Server
or
Data Server**

Hardware
Operating System
Database Software
Middleware
Transaction Manager
Development Tools
Systems Management Tools

WAN
hardware/software

Figure 2.1   Client/server hardware and software components

The data handling component includes the data required for the application as well as the services needed to access, manage, and retrieve the data.

2.1.2   Hardware

Each of the components in a client/server application has their own hardware needs. While there may be some overlap in their requirements, the hardware should be optimized for that particular component.

Client

A client workstation is usually a uniprocessor machine running Microsoft Windows, Apple Mac OS, IBM OS/2, or UNIX. As end users increasingly need to run multiple client applications in real-time, there will be a trend toward upgrading client machines to multiprocessor machines with true multitasking support.

Client hardware is discussed in more detail in Sec. 3.1.1.

Servers

Key requirements for servers are performance and scalability.

Servers are usually broken down by the number of users they can support. Today's high-end uniprocessor machines will support workgroup (2 to 20 users) and departmental (20 to 100 users) client/server systems. Enterprise-wide systems with over 100 users usually require multiprocessor machines, either tightly coupled symmetric multiprocessors (SMPs) consisting of up to 30 processors or loosely coupled massively parallel processors (MPPs) with hundreds or thousands of processors.

As is typically the case in computer technology, software development lags hardware advances. If an organization is considering a multiprocessor configuration, it must take care to ensure that the operating system under consideration can exploit the SMP/MPP hardware and that the DBMS can exploit the server operating system. The server operating system must be able to schedule and coordinate multiple concurrent tasks. The DBMS and the operating system must be able to work together to maintain consistency of updates across processors on an MPP with replicated versions of the DBMS.

At the other end of the spectrum are single-user desktop servers used by disconnected laptop, notebook, or mobile computers. The server aspect of this machine may coexist on the same box as a client application in the network.

Server hardware is discussed in more detail in Chap. 4, "Servers."

2.1.3 Operating system software

The operating systems for each component also have different requirements.

Client operating systems

Most client machines use Windows 3.1, Windows for Workgroups 3.11, Windows NT Workstation 3.5, or Apple Mac OS. Less common on clients are IBM OS/2 and UNIX.

Windows 3.1 is by far the most common operating system on client machines (perhaps because it is the oldest). Windows 3.1 can easily connect to most major server environments. It does provide virtual memory and task switching but cannot run as a true multitasking operating system. Windows for Workgroups 3.11 adds peer-to-peer networking to the basic Windows product.

Windows 95, released in August 1995, supports true multitasking and provides a remote procedure call. However, it needs 12 Mbytes of RAM to run efficiently in a client/server setting. In addition, if history repeats itself, it will take a full year for the product to stabilize and another year for organizations to justify the cost of upgrading all the hardware as well as buying either individual licenses or a site-license for Windows 95.

Windows NT Workstation is a portable version of Windows NT that runs on Intel and RISC microprocessors, and provides many of the required features of servers. However, it is restricted to 10 inbound network connections.

Client operating systems are discussed in Sec. 3.9.

Server operating systems

Most uniprocessor servers use IBM OS/2, Microsoft Windows NT, Novell

NetWare, or UNIX as their operating system. Server operating systems are discussed in Sec. 6.3, "Hybrid Operating Systems."

OS/2 runs on Intel and Intel-compatible platforms. A PowerPC version was released in late 1995. OS/2 Warp Connect provides a LAN Server Requestor, a NetWare Requestor, and a remote dial-up feature, LAN Distance Remote. The final release is expected to include TCP/IP support and peer-to-peer networking.

Windows NT Server 2.5 supports two- and four-way SMPs.

Novell NetWare is primarily a network operating system. Its strengths are in file and printing sharing; its weakness is as a database platform. The primary client/server database vendors (Sybase and Oracle) run their databases as NetWare Loadable Modules (NLMs). Other deficiencies include memory protection and preemptive scheduling.

UNIX comes in a variety of sizes and flavors. The common standard long promised by the UNIX vendors continues to be just that—a promise. UNIX basically comes in two sizes: workgroup and departmental server support or enterprise server support. The lighter versions of UNIX operate on Intel and RISC uniprocessors. The industrial-strength versions of UNIX are for enterprise systems running on SMP and MPP machines.

2.1.4   Database software

DBMSs typically rely on few operating system or underlying hardware features. This independence allows them to be more portable. In addition, since most operating systems weren't written with database processing and performance in mind, a DBMS can achieve better performance by providing its own equivalent functions.

As the operating systems become more robust and the hardware more complex with symmetric multiprocessor (SMP) and massively parallel processor (MPP) machines, it is more difficult for a DBMS to support and exploit the full range of hardware and operating systems.

SMP and MPP machines enable operating systems and database products to support parallel query processing, parallel transaction processing, or both. A parallel transaction processing system increases the transaction throughput of high-volume on-line transaction processing (OLTP) client/server systems by supporting multiple transaction processing applications. The efficient scheduling of transactions in parallel can be aided by using a transaction manager. (See Sec. 11.4.2 for more on transaction managers.)

Most of the leading database products support the leading transaction managers and parallel transaction processing on SMP machines. Using MPPs for parallel transaction processing usually involves running a copy of the DBMS on each processor and employing a distributed lock manager to maintain consistency across the memory caches of each processor.

If applications on multiple processors try to access the same data, distributed lock managers can create a performance bottleneck.

Consequently, to exploit parallel transaction processing on MPP machines requires special application design approaches. (See Sec. 4.6 for more information on SMP and MPP machines.)

2.1.5   Network hardware and software

Networks communicate through the use of protocols which specify the rules and the formats for the transmission. The major protocols in client/server architectures today are TCP/IP, OSI, and IPX/SPX.

Local area networks (LANs) allow a group of users to communicate and share data and resources. LANs are interconnected using network hardware such as routers, bridges, and hubs. The actual routing or switching of the message packets is performed using Frame Relay, ISDN, FDDI, ATM, and Fast Ethernet.

2.1.6   Middleware

Middleware holds all the pieces together. Middleware is a software layer that sits between the client and the server and supports all the facilities needed for a client request to be serviced. It is the link between the application program and the resources in the environment.

2.1.7   Development requirements

This architecture requires robust development tools that can support the developer with the user interfaces as well as partitioning the application for a distributed environment. The tools themselves are visual-oriented. The degree to which a tool can accommodate complex application logic varies among the tools. In addition, first-generation client/server development tools in most cases are not robust enough for second-generation implementations of client/server technology.

2.2   Architecture

Client/server applications can be divided into seven components as illustrated in Fig. 2.2:

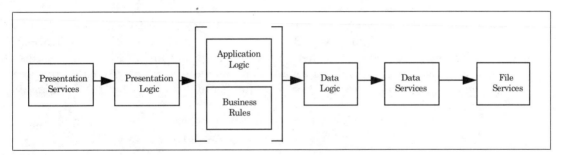

Figure 2.2 Components of a client/server application

- **Presentation services** accept the input from the user and display output from the presentation logic.
- **Presentation logic** controls the interaction between the user and the application. It specifies the actions that take place when a button is pushed or a menu choice is taken.
- **Application logic** is the collection of actions, calculations, and decisions that the application must carry out. It could be a payroll calculation, the evaluation of a loan application, or taking an order.
- **Business rules** are those rules that are global to the organization. They might be coded as triggers or stored procedures within the database itself or as subroutines (or objects) that are referenced by individual applications.
- **Data logic** is the actual formation of the data request for the application following the requirements of the application logic and business rules. For a relational database, this would require formulating an SQL statement.
- **Data services** accept the data logic output and handle all the front-end and back-end work of the request, such as compiling the request, handling data manipulation, and performing transaction commit and rollback functions.
- **File services** actually go to the disk and retrieve the data from the DBMS in question.

The lines between most of these levels are very gray. For example, the federal requirement that any banking transaction of over $10,000 in cash be reported could be a trigger on an amount field in a transaction record of a banking database. (See Sec. 9.2.2 for more about triggers.) Any transaction that meets this criterion would result in a message being sent to a vice president of the bank or a line written to a report. This business rule is tied to the data services function (as a trigger), and the action (the report or message) is part of the application logic.

Interest calculation could be a stored procedure on an interest field in a banking database. (See Sec. 9.2.1 for more about stored procedures.) Whenever a banking application needed to calculate interest, the application would automatically use the stored procedure for the field. This application logic is tied to the data services function.

Both of these examples are global to a bank and therefore could be considered business rules, and in a two-tier architecture they would be expected to be on the server. But they may in fact be considered application logic and executed by the client. Or they could be considered business rules and be coded as part of the application logic and therefore executed by the server. Or their execution site could be determined by the available resources at run time.

As illustrated in Fig. 2.3, two-tier client/server applications implement the application logic and business rules in one of three ways:

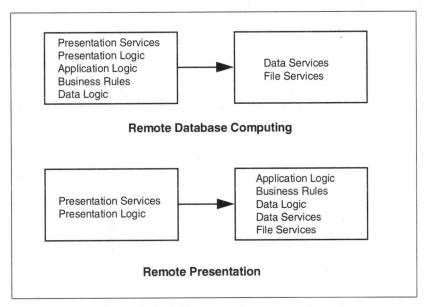

Remote Database Computing

Remote Presentation

Figure 2.3 How application logic and business rules can be implemented

- **Remote database computing.** In this approach, also known as the "fat client," the presentation services and logic for the business, application, and data all reside on the client, and the data and file services are on the server. This simple definition is the one used most often to explain client/server architectures. While many organizations begin with this architecture, they usually quickly convert it to a split logic model for resource efficiencies.
- **Remote presentation.** In this approach, only the presentation logic and services are on the client. All other application requirements are on the server. This is used primarily with screen-scraping applications that in effect put a GUI front end on a legacy application.
- **Split logic model.** In this popular approach, some of the business rules, application logic, and data logic reside on the server and some on the client.

This two-tier approach to client/server architectures works best in homogeneous environments with business logic that is not very complex.

As an organization's client/server architecture evolves into a multitier architecture, the implementations become split logic. More of the application logic comes to reside on servers. Data access logic continues to reside on servers. The client is still responsible for the presentation services and a smaller and smaller portion of the application logic.

The differences between two-tier architectures and multitier architectures are discussed in Sec. 4.8, "Two-Tier, Three-Tier, and Multitier Architectures," and Chap. 10, "Two-Tier and Multitier Environments."

2.3   Open Systems

Today's organizations use many different platforms and architectures to run their business. In addition, organizations are expanding their own enterprise networks to include links to their customers, distributors, and suppliers. They need to minimize the risk of incompatibility among the components in the enterprise network by adopting open systems.

Open (nonproprietary) systems allow organizations to mix and match hardware and software from a variety of vendors. The resulting enterprise network is not dependent on any one vendor for features or support.

Open systems applications are portable across all platforms and are not locked into one vendor. This can happen only if the applications are built according to industry-accepted standards. The network can then talk to and port applications to and from other standard-compliant systems.

In addition, application specifications for open systems can be developed independent of the target environment. Developers focus on the application, not the technology.

Open systems start with standard operating platforms and conform to a broad set of formal and de facto standards for distributed computing, networking, and application development. Open systems must support platforms from a variety of vendors.

Open systems, a methodology for integrating divergent technologies, create a flexible environment for solving business problems using open (or nonproprietary) software and open hardware. Open systems can provide maximum availability across standard and scalable system platforms, interoperability between different vendors' systems, a greater choice in system procurement, and optimized management of resources. All elements of the system can talk to one another. The focus is on solving problems for the entire organization, not for one group (not even IT).

Open systems demand the strategic adoption of standards throughout the organization. To succeed, the open system standards must be acceptable to both the user community and system manufacturers and be adopted by all levels of the organization.

The current movement toward open systems makes client/server computing easier to accomplish. Openness allows many different machines, software, and applications to be plugged together like the components of a stereo system. New components can be plugged into existing systems at any time. Application program interfaces (APIs) can be used to link the different products.

Open systems can increase the productivity of IS professionals. With only one development environment, skills are immediately portable. Applications do not have to be reengineered to be ported to another platform. The IS infrastructure is flexible and can quickly and easily adapt to changes in the business environment.

International Data Corporation (Framingham, Massachusetts) outlines three interdependent components that must be in place to create a true open systems environment. The components, summarized in Fig. 2.4, are:

Standards-based products and technology	Open systems technology provides portability and interoperability. Closed technologies will dead-end progress. While some proprietary technology is beneficial, the trick is to provide proprietary functionality within a structure of common APIs.
Open development infrastructure	Standards must ensure that current implementations of technology build on the prior implementations and are able to support future implementations.
Management directives	These directives, established by consensus by those with a vested interest in the IS infrastructure, ensure that technology does not benefit one group at the expense of the organization.

Source: International Data Corp.

Figure 2.4 Components of an open systems environment

- Standards-based products and technology
- Open development infrastructure
- Management directives

2.4   Standards

Adherence to standards offers the key to   some of the client/server computing promises. By adhering to standards, organizations can achieve portability, scalability, and communication among heterogeneous systems. The major standards organizations that play a role in the client/server computing arena are discussed in Sec. 2.4.3.

2.4.1 Standards areas

Standards address four areas of client/server computing:

- **Platforms**. These standards are developed by hardware and software vendors, usually in response to de facto standards, such as Intel chips, UNIX, and DOS with Windows.
- **Networks**. Industry-standard networking protocols such as the OSI model and TCP/IP are being used instead of vendor-specific networking protocols.
- **Middleware**. This new term, used to classify the software that sits between the application and the operating system, includes GUIs, databases, E-mail systems, software development tools (such as CASE), and IS management tools (such as encryption and recovery routines).
- **Applications**. Organizations decide on standard applications to facilitate workgroup interaction and work-product compatibility.

Standards specifications should be developed by consensus and be publicly available. For a standard to be effective, its specification must be widely accepted (used). It is difficult to predict which specification will gain wide acceptance and be considered a standard. Consider those organizations that standardized on OS/2 and Presentation Manager early in the GUI revolution—only to watch Windows and Window-based products take off.

Interoperability and portability are provided through adherence to standards. Portability means that software will run on other platforms without requiring modifications to application code, although system-oriented code may have to be modified. Interoperability means that the software can work with software (both itself and other vendors' software) on other platforms.

However, even though standards exist at this hardware, software, operating system, and network levels, they do not provide a complete solution. In some cases, there are multiple standards; in other cases, there are none at all.

2.4.2   Existing standards

Currently, there are recognized standards for the server operating system environment and for network protocols. Some standards have been set forth by a standard-setting body. Others are de facto standards.

UNIX

UNIX, originally from UNIX System Laboratories (USL), then a division of AT&T, and now a product (and trademark) of The Santa Cruz Operation (SCO), was developed as an operating system for scientific, engineering, and technical applications. It is written in C, and its source code is inexpensively licensed. It takes advantage of the power of the RISC (reduced instruction set computing) technology and offers multitasking and multiuser support. It can deliver excellent price/performance characteristics. Vendors such as IBM, Digital, and Microsoft offer their own versions of UNIX—AIX, Ultrix, and XENIX, respectively.

The latest version of the base product, UNIX System V Release 4 (SVR4), provides a desktop-metaphor GUI on top of the traditional UNIX system. Because it has reduced memory and hard disk requirements, it can be used on client machines.

UNIX is discussed in detail in Sec. 6.3.6.

POSIX

Portable Operating System Interface (POSIX) from IEEE (Institute of Electrical and Electronic Engineers) is a UNIX-based specification that is viewed as a standard for server operating systems. POSIX defines a uniform means for an application written in C (a high-level programming language for developing commerical software) to request services from an operating system, regardless of the underlying hardware architecture or operating environment. Programmers choose from a list of standard library functions and system header files that will work on any POSIX-compliant operating system.

TCP/IP

Transmission Control Protocol/Internet Protocol (TCP/IP) is a de facto standard for interconnecting otherwise incompatible computers. TCP/IP is used to connect LAN-based micros to corporate data on a (typically) UNIX host.

TCP/IP is a set of network and transport protocols that enable higher-level applications to communicate; however, it lacks much of the functionality of a regular network operating system. TCP, which runs on top of IP, controls the packet's delivery. IP takes care of the interplatform and internetwork communications.

TCP/IP is discussed in detail in Sec. 5.3.2.

OSI model

The Open Systems Interconnection (OSI) model was developed by the International Standards Organization (ISO) to provide a common basis for communication system standards. It adopted the best features of existing architectures and added features to support heterogeneous communications. The OSI model is discussed in Sec. 5.3.1.

The OSI model provides a hierarchical layer structure, in which each layer performs a specific network function, services the next higher layer, and accepts requests from the next lower layer. Nodes in the network communicate peer-to-peer with corresponding layers in other nodes.

The Government Open Systems Interconnection Profile (GOSIP) specification states that all government networking purchases must comply with or show long-term migration to OSI.

RDA and DRDA

Distributed data management, when the data and the DBMS are distributed among multiple systems, allows organizations to spread enterprise data over a network of computer systems. Distributed data management raises a variety of issues that are being addressed by ISO's Remote Data Access (RDA) architecture and IBM's Distributed Relational Database Architecture (DRDA). Both of these are discussed in detail in Sec. 7.7.

2.4.3 Standard-setting organizations

Consortia of vendors and developers are working on developing standards for information technology. Practically all hardware and software vendors belong to the Open Software Foundation. End users of the technology are beginning to join these consortia to help develop the standards, work with early versions of the developed technology, and receive compliant products ahead of commercial availability.

Open Software Foundation

The aim of the Open Software Foundation (OSF), a nonprofit consortium of computer vendors, software developers, and chip suppliers based in Cambridge, Massachusetts, is to develop standards-based software that will become widely accepted technologies, as its Motif GUI has. Under the umbrella of its Application Environment Specification, OSF focused on developing a standard UNIX-based operating system, which, using microkernel technology, can be ported to many different hardware platforms.

OSF has also announced specifications for related application environments, such as the Distributed Computer Environment, and user interface standards, such as Motif. Some of the standards announced by OSF include:

- **GUI standards**, as implemented in OSF's Motif.
- **OSF/1**. This UNIX-based operating system for client/server platforms is a standards specification as well as a product. HP, IBM, and Digital have announced that they would have compliant software, but they have opted for their own variants of UNIX until a production-quality OSF/1 is available. Currently, Digital is the only announced vendor that is actively using OSF/1, with its DEC/OSF/1. OSF/1.1 was commercially released in June 1992.
- **Distributed Computer Environment** (DCE). Announced in September 1991 and available as of September 1992, this set of products (and the standards they represent) provides the necessary services for distributing applications in heterogeneous hardware and software environments—all transparently to the user. Extensions to DCE, such as Transarc Corp.'s Encina products, support additional open functionality, including transaction management, two-phase commits, recovery, and rollback.
- **Distributed Management Environment** (DME). These standards were finalized by mid-1993, and products were expected in 1994. DME standards focus on the tools that are necessary to manage heterogeneous environments. DME was being designed for both UNIX and proprietary systems. It is based on DCE but does not require DCE for execution. As the industry began to focus on object orientation, support for DME began to dry up and OSF halted the project in 1994.

DCE is discussed in more detail in Sec. 9.9.1 and Motif in Sec. 3.5.1.

X/Open

The Transaction Processing Working Group of X/Open Ltd. Co., a London-based international open systems standards consortium, is working on the

Distributed Transaction Processing (DTP) model, which provides vendors with industry-standard APIs and architectures.

X/Open's XA protocol specifies the interface between a transaction manager and multiple, heterogeneous distributed DBMSs in an OLTP environment. XA supports two-phase commits, conversational transactions, and other advanced OLTP functions among multiple distributed XA-compliant heterogeneous databases. Its XA+ protocol allows communications managers and transaction managers to interface.

The X/Open Transport Interface, a POSIX-compliant transport application programming interface (API), provides reliable message transportation, regardless of the underlying network protocol.

The X/Open APIs, XMP and XOM, are used to isolate applications from the structure of system management protocols. These are discussed in Sec. 12.5.6.

The X/Open Portability Guide Issue 3 (XPG3) outlines X/Open's specifications for a Common Application Environment, which supports system interoperability and portability.

Open Group

In March 1996, Open Software Foundation and X/Open merged to form the Open Group. In August 1996 the Open Group began shipping its DCE Web technology which is available in Gradient Technologies, Inc.'s Web Crusader and DASCOM's IntraVerse product suits. Other vendors, including IBM, Digital, and HP, plan implementations as well.

The Open Group operates by identifying user requirements, conducting research into them, adopting specifications, and creating brands. The group is currently addressing five tactical areas: security, interoperability, distributed systems management, architecture, and the Internet.

The Group released two new standards in mid-1996. Baseline Security 96 is aimed at securing the operating platform. Baseline Security 98 is already in the works, which will incorporate single sign on and firewall into a base operating system.

The other standard, Secure Communciation Server, is aimed at securing communications services. Secure Communication Server is an extension of its Generic Security Service–API specification. The Open Group is also working towards securing trade over the Internet through the development of a public key infrastructure. Proposed standards for certificates would be used to verify the holders of keys, protocols for shipping keys, and a federated directory of keys. Their efforts have the support of many security developers.

One of their first acts was to offer a Web-based procrement aid dubbed the Open Software Registry (at http:/www.opensoftware.com) that lists products that conform to standards and describes their portability and inter-product dependencies. The Registry includes a browser and is free to users.

In the spring of 1997, the Open Group expects to begin shipping its Jade (Java and DCE Enhancements) technology, which will allow Java applications to talk to the DCE infrastructure. Jade is a set of technologies that will bring DCE security, naming, and integrity services to the World Wide Web.

The Group also plans to release a fast Java compiler, Turbo-Java, in 1997. It is expected to be a real-time, Java-compatible runtime compiler.

Object Management Group

The Object Management Group (OMG) of Framingham, Massachusetts, is an industry consortium of computer-related vendors, along with many organizations whose primary business is not computer software or systems and some government organizations. In addition, other industry consortia are nonvendor members. The OMG, an international organization of system vendors, software developers, and users, advocates the deployment of object management technology in the development of software. By applying a common framework to all object-oriented applications, organizations will be able to operate heterogeneous environments.

The OMG provides vendor-neutral interface specifications for a wide range of components required in the distributed object computing (DOC) environment. The OMG does not sell or provide products; vendors sell products based on OMG specifications. The specifications are designed to promote object computing products that are plug-compatible from different vendors and interoperable. The OMG members adopt (by vote and after public discussion) interface standards in the area of distributed object computing. These interface standards are based on the OMG interface definition language (IDL) and existing implemented and working technology. The OMG IDL is a neutral way of defining the interfaces needed in a DOC environment. Products written by different companies in different programming languages can be connected across any OMG-compliant object request broker.

OMG and a number of vendors, including Digital, NCR, Hewlett-Packard, and Sun Microsystems, have defined the Common Object Request Broker Architecture (CORBA), a mechanism that allows objects (applications) to call each other over a mixed network. CORBA compliance provides a high degree of portability.

Within CORBA, objects are identifiable entities which provide one or more services to clients. CORBA manages the identity and location of the objects, transports the request to the target object, and confirms that the request is carried out. CORBA is based on the service technology found in Digital's Application Control Architecture.

Microsoft, although a member of OMG, has rejected the OMG standards and is using its own object technology. Microsoft envisions OLE being at the low end of the enterprise and the OMG standards ruling at the high end of the enterprise.

SQL Access Group

SQL Access Group is an industry consortium working on the definition and implementation of specifications for heterogeneous SQL data access using accepted international standards. (Currently, each vendor has its own, slightly different implementation of SQL.) SQL Access Group is supported by most DBMS developers except IBM. The focus of the group is to provide an environment in which any client front end can work with any compliant server database. SQL Access Group supports TCP/IP as well as OSI protocols.

The OpenSQL standards from SQL Access Group are based on ANSI SQL. Current specifications include SQL Access and a call-level interface. Compliance with these specifications allows relational DBMS products from different vendors to access distributed databases without using special gateways. SQL Access Group is also working on a Persistent SQL Function, which uses a high-performance compiler to compile and store an SQL statement, and a data type strategy for two-phase commits.

Microsoft's Open Database Connectivity (ODBC) is an extension of SQL Access Group's call-level interface (CLI) specification. The SQL Access available in Windows 3.x is CLI-compliant, as is Borland's Object Component architecture. X/Open has announced its intention to use the SQL Access Group standards in its Portability Guide.

IBM does not back OpenSQL. Instead, IBM developed the Distributed Relational Database Architecture (DRDA), which third-party vendors can use to link to SAA (System Application Architecture) relational DBMSs (DB2, SQL/DS, OS/2 Data Base Manager, and OS/400 Database). DRDA is discussed in more detail in Sec. 7.7.1.

The SQL Access Group formally merged with X/Open in 1995 (which has since merged with OSF creating the Open Group). The charters of SAG and X/Open's Data Management Working Group were essentially the same, and X/Open had always edited and published the work of the SQL Access Group. The merger made it possible to eliminate duplicate efforts, reduce costs, and unify development efforts. The X/Open Data Management Technical Committee disbanded, and the X/Open SQL Access Group, now functioning within the X/Open Technical Program, has assumed all of its responsibilities.

2.5   Distributed Computing Environment

In a distributed computing environment, the processing or the data (or both) are distributed among the nodes in the network.

2.5.1   Distributed data

Data can be distributed throughout the enterprise network. Locating data on or close to the node that uses it most often (usually the update source) but still allowing the data to be accessed from any node eliminates islands of data. In addition, copies of data can be located at multiple nodes and synchronized by a distributed database management system. (A node is any processor on the enterprise network, such as a client machine or a server.)

2.5.2 Distributed processing

The days of strictly centralized processing or strictly decentralized processing are disappearing fast. Today's environments use a hybrid. Processing can occur anywhere in the enterprise network. Where a process executes could be under the control of any of the following:

- **The operating system**, which looks for underutilized resources and assigns tasks to them
- **The central processing unit** on the machine, which assigns certain tasks to specific processors
- **The application**, which codes assignments into the application

Distributed processing implies that the application logic and business rules can run on more than one node in the network. Some of the execution might be on the client machine, and some of the application code might be split among multiple servers.

If the logic and business rules are placed entirely on the client, there is little network traffic and the processing is close to the data source. However, multiple copies of the logic and rules may need to be maintained, eliminating the benefits of modular, sharable, reusable code.

If the logic and business rules are placed entirely on servers, there is more network traffic and the server may be overutilized. On the plus side, there is only one copy of the logic and rules to maintain.

If the logic and business rules are split among nodes, resources can be optimized for specific functions and execution code can be placed where it makes the most sense from an operational point of view.

2.6 Event-Driven Computing

Applications running in mainframe and midrange environments are process-driven. They are easily described by their input, output, and processes. Applications running in client/server and distributed environments are event-driven. Event-driven applications are described by their interfaces, data, and events, as illustrated in Fig. 2.5.

Events are initiated when a user selects an area on a GUI screen, such as a button. Each area is associated with a response (e.g., open a file) or the execution of a processing task (e.g., update). The application development process consists of defining the screen format and the event areas. The responses for each event area are then specified, using a high-level scripting language supplied by the development product or a source-level procedural language, such as C.

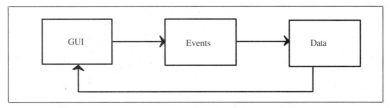

Figure 2.5 Event-driven applications

2.7   Network Role

The network provides the link between all the hardware and software in the client/server architecture. The network must know where all the nodes are and how to reach them. It must be able to handle peak traffic times. It must be able to react to nodes that are not functioning and reroute traffic automatically.

The network is the most important part of the client/server architecture. No matter how well client requests are generated or how well distributed the processing and data is, if the message can't get through, there is no processing.

2.8   Multivendor Environments

One way to build multitier applications today is to assemble a solution from components from various vendors. Such a customized solution will deliver the required benefits, but at the expense of greater programming effort and more complex integration of tools from multiple vendors.

Client-to-server connectivity can be developed in-house as the application itself is being built, using the capabilities of middleware software. (See Chap. 8 for more information on middleware.) Most of the RPC and messaging vendors support Windows-based client applications built with tools such as Powersoft's PowerBuilder, Centura Software Corp.'s SQLWindows, and Microsoft's Visual Basic. The technology for doing this is available from such vendors as NobleNet Inc. (EZ-RPC), Open Environment Corp. (Entera, formerly Encompass), PeerLogic Inc. (Pipes Platform), Transarc (Encina and DCE tools), and Momentum Software Corp. (InterFlow).

Connecting the application server to the database server is straightforward, especially in homogeneous server environments. Transactions can rely on the DBMS's TP-lite capabilities (the transaction management is handled by the DBMS itself) to ensure integrity. For large-scale applications, organizations should look to TP monitors for communications infrastructure and scalability. For distributed transaction integrity, especially across heterogeneous environments, organizations should use a transaction manager such as Novell's Tuxedo or Transarc's Encina. As middleware becomes the battleground of the late 1990s, DBMS vendors will be adding more TP monitor- and ORB-like features to their own interoperability products.

2.9   Who Does What

Before committing to a vendor for a complete multitier solution, consider how the organization is tied to the vendor on the different tiers of your architecture. Evaluate the vendor's proprietary language, object model, or RPC mechanism. Consider the robustness and openness of the languages and environments, and their flexibility for designing your application software.

Because these tools are complex and are intended for complex enterprise solutions, verify the performance and reliability of any tool in a real-life environment. Conduct in-house tests and carefully audit the results of other users' experiences in applications with characteristics similar to your own. Pay special attention to scalability and heterogeneous platform issues.

2

Client/Server Components

Client/server architectures have three elements: clients, servers, and networks. Each of these has a hardware component and several software components.

The major functions of the client in a client/server environment are to perform the presentation functions and the user's interactions with the interface, and execute any client-resident business logic.

Although servers are the workhorses in a client/server environment, the client needs enough power to process its end of the application and handle the presentation requirements. The client operating systems are providing more functionality and the GUI tools are more robust in this latest generation of client/server computing.

A server is a machine that offers multiuser access to its services and data. There are different types of servers: database, data warehouse, application, computation, communications, and general all-purpose servers. If they are specialized servers, they are optimized to perform that service.

Servers are more powerful with faster chips and newer instruction sets. The machines themselves are multiprocessor rather than uniprocessor. Server operating systems have integrated network operating system requirements into their offerings. Organizations no longer need one operating system for the server and one operating system for the network.

The second generation of client/server management tools are providing the features taken for granted in the mainframe world, such features as security, backup and recovery, monitoring software, and reliability.

Client/server applications rarely confine themselves to their own networks. In addition clients in the same network can use different software. Servers in the network can use different operating systems and server database software. When client/server applications need to go outside their own physically connected network, the environment must be able to communicate with the accessed environment, accept data, and then transport it back to its own environment.

All the connectivity should be transparent to the user. The network should provide self-healing capabilities that can reroute network traffic around broken cables and failed components. It would also be flexible enough to allow users to move around within the organization without requiring rewiring.

Today's networks can transmit at faster speeds, can have built-in intelligence, and can reach out into the world via the Internet.

Second-generation client/server environments offer more choices for where data resides. It can be split among nodes or it can copied among nodes. On-line analytic processing (OLAP) can use a special data structure called multidimensional. Data warehouses are being used to store data that has been reorganized to support business intelligence in one place.

The glue for all this connectivity is middleware. Data or processing can be distributed. Connections are made via remote procedure calls or messaging. Transaction managers monitor transaction processing to ensure integrity.

In an initial implementation of client/server computing, an organization has many choices—the hardware for the client, server, and network; the software for the client, server, and network; middleware; development tools; and management tools. None should be chosen in isolation.

3

Clients

To some, a client machine is a micro, to others it is a UNIX-based workstation. In this book, the term *client machine* refers to the desktop machine the worker uses, whether it is a Macintosh, a DOS- or OS/2-based micro, or a UNIX-based workstation. This is the worker's view of the application and the network.

3.1   Client Components

The components of the client side of the equation are fairly easy to understand. They are:

- Hardware
- Software
- Interface

3.1.1   Client hardware

The front-end client machine runs software that is responsible for the presentation and manipulation of data. The client software generates a data request and sends it to the server. The client machine must be powerful enough to run the required presentation software. A server can also act as an agent, requesting data from another server.

All clients in client/server computing require similar hardware. The memory and storage required for an efficient client machine depend on the class of application and the complexity of those applications.

The hardware must have enough memory to load and execute application logic. Higher processing speeds, a more powerful chip, and memory caching will improve response times. Storage requirements are based on the amount of data that is to be stored locally.

Most of the literature seems to assumes that client hardware is Intel-based. Today that is probably true. But that may change with the introduction of the PowerPC from IBM and Apple and the combination of Apple's new Power Macs and Softwindows software from Insignia Solutions, Inc.

PowerPC systems built to the PowerPC Platform, formerly referred to as the Common Hardware Platform (CHRP) and discussed in Sec. 4.5.1, will be able to run the Mac OS as well as Windows NT, OS/2, and variants of UNIX for the PowerPC.

Power Macs have a peripheral component interconnect (PCI) bus and use the PowerPC 604 chip. Softwindows software can emulate a 486, enabling Power Macs to run Windows 3.1 386-enhanced applications at 486 speeds.

3.1.2   Client software

All client/server applications use client software. How robust that software needs to be depends on the application itself.

A client machine could be running as many as four software packages, as illustrated in Fig. 3.1. At a minimum, a client machine runs an operating system and an interface environment, such as Windows 3.x, Windows 95, OS/2 Workplace Shell, Motif, or OpenLook. It also runs a portion of the network software.

Any application logic processed on the client machine requires a compiler or a run-time version of the application development tool used to generate the application. The machine used to develop the application is used to compile the application code, which is usually written in C, the de facto standard language for client/server computing. The compiled code is distributed to the client machines, where it is executed by a run-time version of the development tool.

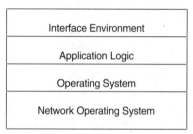

Figure 3.1 Possible software on a client machine

3.1.3   Interface environments

The interface component of a client/server application does not know where the data is located. The interface is concerned with accepting data requests from the user, sending those requests to the server, receiving the results data from the server, and manipulating and formatting those results according to stated requirements.

Graphical user interfaces

Most client/server applications use a graphical user interface (GUI). Information is presented in areas called windows. Tasks are presented as small pictures, which are called icons. Tasks are chosen by clicking a mouse button when the mouse cursor is positioned over the icon for that task.

The major GUI environments are Windows from Microsoft, OS/2 Workplace Shell from IBM, Motif from Open Software Foundation (OSF), and OpenLook from SunSoft, Inc. Each GUI environment has its own style guide—the rules for how the screen should look and react. To achieve the major benefit of GUIs—improved productivity from applications looking and acting the same—these rules must be followed.

Earlier GUI development software followed guidelines for IBM's Common User Access (CUA) methodology. IBM has developed a new set of guidelines, CUA '91, that specifically address GUI standards. These standards include:

- **Drag and drop**. This is best explained with an example: To change the color of an object, the color is chosen from a palette and *dragged* to the object, where it is *dropped*.
- **Control features**, such as container, notebook, spin button, slider, and value set.
- **Standard dialogues** for such operations as Open, Save As, and font changes.

GUIs are discussed in more detail later in this chapter.

Other interfaces

A client/server environment does not have to confine itself to GUIs. GUIs provide a static approach to accessing data. They do not reflect a user's vocabulary or allow the user to follow his or her own train of thought. Natural languages are more appropriate than GUIs for some applications and user communities. They combine an understanding of English with knowledge about the database to understand the user's terminology and queries.

Natural languages allow users to develop a query essentially free of syntax without having their thought processes proceduralized through menus and pop-up windows. The language processor parses the words in the query statement, asks for more information for unrecognizable words, generates the necessary SQL code, and sends the request to the server. The language processor then accepts the results of the query and formats it into the requested output form, graph, or report.

For example, to a college's alumni office, the phrase *students* refers to those students that have graduated. To the registrar's office, the phrase refers to those currently enrolled. If all past and present student records were in one database, each office would have to remember to include a WHERE clause when doing queries with SQL. A natural language can be programmed to include the appropriate WHERE clause based on the user ID.

Natural Language from Natural Language, Inc., one of the first natural languages, supports a variety of relational databases. SAA LanguageAccess from IBM supports DB2 and SQL/DS. SAS/English Software from SAS Institute, Inc., can access any database accessible by the SAS System. English Wizard from Creative Sales & Marketing is compatible with most ODBC-compliant databases.

3.2   What Is a GUI?

A graphical user interface (GUI) presents its users with information in windows, rectangular areas on a screen. Tasks displayed on a window are chosen by pressing (clicking) a mouse button when the cursor is on an icon, a small picture that is an illustration of the task. For example, some de facto standard icons are a file cabinet for storage and a trash can for discard.

A GUI entity is any area on the screen that is "clickable." Clicking in that area will result in an action.

3.2.1   Screen characteristics

The user can change the color, size, and position of a window and can open a new window (task) almost at will. Windows can overlap or be placed side by side. A window can be miniaturized to become an icon. The user can restore the iconized window by clicking on it with the mouse pointer.

Each window has a label bar along the top that indicates what task it contains. The corners of the label bar are used to size or close the window. Other features, such as sliders (sometimes called elevators) for scrolling and buttons for choices, reduce the need for keyboard use and allow users to control the interface and interact with the application.

3.2.2   Native API

Every GUI environment has its own application programming interface (API). An API consists of a set of programming routines that are used to provide services and link different types of software. For example, a GUI

API would consist of function calls such as CreateWindow and CloseWindow. APIs can also be used to access database servers and network services.

Coding an interface using a native API is similar to coding CICS screens with macros. GUI screens can be developed using APIs to the windowed environment of choice or by using one of the many available tools, such as those discussed in Chap. 16. These tools make the process easier, just as screen painters make CICS screen development easier.

3.2.3   Event-driven

To the IT professional, the real difference in GUI use is that the user is in control. For example, a user can start another application at any time.

Whereas conventional interfaces are data-driven, GUIs are event-driven. Common events for GUI interactions include the following:

- **Mouse events**. The mouse is moved in or out of an entity, or a mouse button is clicked.
- **Keyboard events**. The user has pressed and released a key on the keyboard.
- **Window update events**. An overlaid window must be redrawn to its original version.
- **Resizing events**. The user changes the size of the window.
- **Active/deactive events**. The user picks a new current (active) window.
- **Menu events**. The user chooses from a menu.
- **Start/stop events**. An application executes setup or cleanup logic when a GUI entity is created or destroyed.

The processing for user-driven events is distributed among the GUI itself, the API for that GUI, and the application logic, if any exists. There are several models for distributing this processing:

- **Event loop**. Shown in Fig. 3.2, the event loop, which consists of an event-handling routine and a dispatcher, calls a specific library routine

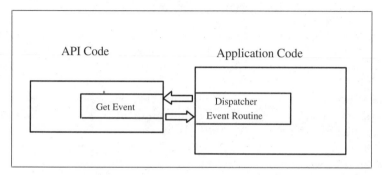

Figure 3.2   Event loop

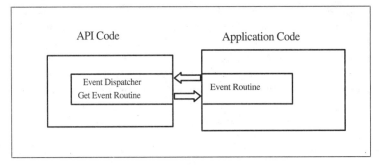

Figure 3.3   Event callback

that checks for pending events. If there are any, the application dispatches an event-handling routine before control is returned to the event loop.

- **Event callback**. An application registers an event-handling function for each GUI entity that it creates. When an event is detected, the GUI calls the appropriate event routine for that entity, as shown in Fig. 3.3. The event routine is called once for each event.

- **Hybrid**. This model combines an event loop model and an event callback model. For example, the Microsoft Windows model requires an application to contain an event loop for calling library routines but also registers functions for created entities.

3.3   Features of a Standard GUI

Currently there is no standard GUI, although some might argue that because it is the mostly widely used, Windows 3.x or Windows 95 is a de facto standard (with Windows 95 gaining ground fast). However, open systems implies portability, and Windows just isn't that portable.

A standard GUI for open systems would have the following features:

- **Adherence to standards**. This goes without saying, of course. The only GUI standard in existence today for open systems is the X Window System from MIT (see Sec. 3.4.1)

- **Portability**. A standard GUI would have the same "look and feel" on all platforms and would have a standard API for each platform. This would eliminate retraining when an application was ported to a new platform and allow for an easy port to the new platform.

- **Independence**. Open systems implies independence. A standard GUI for open systems would be independent of operating systems, hardware platforms, and network protocols.

- **Flexible**. To accommodate changes in technology and user requests, a standard GUI must be flexible.

- **Development tools**. In order for a standard GUI to be readily accepted by organizations (a standard without wide-scale acceptance and installations is worthless), development tools that support quick application development for a wide variety of platforms have to exist. However, most software developers wait to see how well accepted the standard is before they invest in developing the software—a Catch-22.

3.4 X Window vs. Windowing

Currently there are two GUI camps. One, called X Window, runs on UNIX-based systems. The two major X Window environments are Motif from Open Software Foundation (OSF) and OpenLook from SunSoft Inc. The other is called, in this book, windowing. It includes Windows 3.x, Windows 95, and Windows NT Desktop from Microsoft; OS/2 Workplace Shell from IBM; Macintosh from Apple Computer; and NeXTStep from NeXT, Inc.

Vendors are also trying to implement the Windows environment on non-Windows (typically UNIX) platforms. One camp is developing Windows APIs (Windows Applications Binary Interface or WABI) to run Windows applications natively under UNIX. The other camp is emulating Windows APIs under UNIX by running an emulator program such as SoftWindows from Insignia Solutions Inc., which allows users on Digital, Hewlett-Packard, IBM, SGI, Sun, and Motorola workstations to share data, as well as to cut, copy, and paste data from Windows applications into UNIX applications.

3.4.1 X Window interface

The X Window System was developed jointly by Massachusetts Institute of Technology, IBM, and Digital. The X Window System architecture is based on the client/server model and provides:

- A network-transparent protocol between an application and its presentation logic and services that reside on a remote display workstation
- High-performance device-independent graphics
- A hierarchy of resizable, overlapping windows

The X Window System allows applications to access displays on networked client stations transparently. In effect, the client acts as a presentation server, and the server runs as a client for that presentation server. This process is illustrated in Fig. 3.4.

An X Server program controls the display and provides an interface between itself and X Clients, which are usually application programs. The X Clients and X Server may be running on the same or different network nodes and communicate by exchanging messages using the X11 protocol. To communicate with an X Server, an X Client builds X11 protocol requests

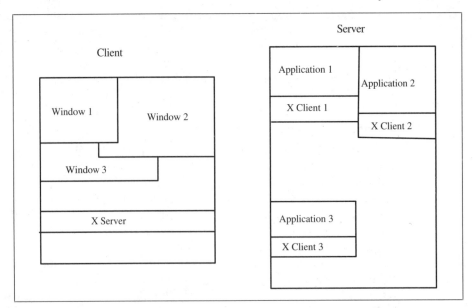

Figure 3.4 X Window System

using a library of C routines (called Xlib). To augment these routines, toolkits provide high-level graphics functionality, including menus and special window objects called *widgets*, which are data objects such as scroll bars and buttons.

An X Client is constructed using widgets from the Widget Library, also called a toolkit. The user can change the size or contents of the widget, but its appearance is determined by the native GUI functions supported by the toolkit. The Widget Library uses an Intrinsics Library for managing widgets (creating, deleting, etc.) and event message handling.

A window manager is used to move, resize, and iconize windows. An X Window Manager acts as an X Client. It interacts with the client applications through the X Server, controls the positioning and size of the client's windows, and determines the way input is directed to client applications. The window manager determines the look and feel of the GUI. The popular X Window GUIs, Motif and OpenLook, behave and look differently because they use different window managers.

The client and server terminology in X Window is the reverse of that usually used for client/server computing. In X Window, the X Server allows the windows to be displayed (even though the presentation logic resides on the client, it is controlled by the X Server) and the window manager determines the look and feel of the GUI. X Clients are the application programs and actually reside on the "server." But clients still initiate requests with servers and servers support more than one client—so it is still a client/server architecture.

The X Consortium is revising the X Windows protocol to make it possible to access X Window applications over the Internet. Broadway, a revision of the Low-Bandwidth X specification, will enable a Web browser to access X Window applications over TCP/IP. They are also developing the X.fast specification which will provide increased bandwidth, improved management, and better security. The Broadway code is expected to be released before the X Consortium turns the stewardship of X Windows systems over to the Open Group at the end of 1996.

3.4.2   Windowing interface

In the windowing environment, each interface has its own look and feel and there are some commonly available functions in each environment. Both Windows and OS/2 Workplace Shell adhere to IBM's Common User Access (CUA) standards. Motif's style is closer to CUA guidelines than OpenLook's.

In contrast to the X Window System environment, windowing GUIs can provide the application's processing logic as well as the application's presentation logic. The server is a data repository and data manager for the application. Any processing it might do is data-related, such as integrity checks and validation, or is application logic that has been assigned to the server for processing. In an X Window System, the server is in control; in windowing systems, the client is in control.

Motif is the GUI of choice for UNIX-based systems. Some variety of Microsoft Windows is the GUI of choice for most non-UNIX-based systems. Windows 95 is more than just a GUI, it is its own operating system and provides an open architecture that allows Windows workstations to connect across heterogeneous platforms. Windows 95 is discussed in more detail in Secs. 3.6.2 and 3.9.1.

Windows Open Services Architecture (WOSA) provides an open architecture and consistent standardized set of APIs to provide this interoperability. Microsoft expects that WOSA will help establish Windows as a universal client. WOSA is discussed in detail in Sec. 8.10.1.

3.5   X Window GUIs

X Window GUIs are UNIX-based graphical user interfaces.

3.5.1   Motif

OSF's Motif GUI is implemented using a single API for all supported platforms. Based on the DECwindows technology, Motif was enhanced to support OS/2 Presentation Manager–style behavior and therefore has some CUA compliance. Presentation Manager was the former OS/2 GUI. Motif is based on OSF standards and is compliant with OSF's Common Desktop

Environment (CDE) specifications. Motif is considered an enabling technology—it is open. The resource definition is stored separately from the application code, which simplifies enhancements. Motif contains few, if any, operating system and network protocol dependencies.

Motif's development environment includes the following tools:

- **User Interface X Toolkit**. This toolkit contains the graphical objects (widgets and gadgets) used by Motif.
- **User interface language**. This language is used to describe the visual aspects of the Motif GUI for an application, such as menus, forms, labels, and pushbuttons. Developers create a text file that contains a description of each object and its associated functions. The text file is compiled by the user interface language into a resource file, which is loaded at run time. ·
- **Window Manager**. Motif Window Manager allows windows to be moved, resized, and reduced to icons. It supplies Motif's three-dimensional appearance.
- **An API**.

Motif supports X/Open's XPG4 and POSIX (see Sec. 2.4.2) standards for native language support and is supported by most hardware and software vendors that provide a version of UNIX. Motif supports drag-and-drop and utilizes standard X11 mechanisms while maintaining network transparency. Drag-and-drop works between Motif clients running on different host machines in a network.

3.5.2   OpenLook

OpenLook was developed by Sun Microsystems and AT&T and is offered by SunSoft, Inc., a subsidiary of Sun Microsystems, Inc. OpenLook is very popular on AT&T and Sun systems. OpenLook Window Manager is required for interclient communication. The look and feel of OpenLook differs significantly from that of CUA-based interfaces, such as Windows 3.x, Presentation Manager, and Motif. It also contains few (if any) operating system and network protocol dependencies.

One of the following three APIs can be used to develop OpenLook-compliant applications:

- Sun's **NeWS Development Environment** API for Sun's platforms is an emulated PostScript interpreter modified to support a windowing system. It consists of client and server portions interacting to produce the OpenLook GUI.
- AT&T's **Xt+** API for AT&T platforms contains the graphical objects used by OpenLook.
- Sun's **XView** API for Sun SPARC and Digital VAX systems, Intel 80386, and Motorola 680x0 architectures implements the OpenLook API on top of the Xlib level of the X Window System. (In comparison, Motif

implements its API in the X toolkit built on the X Window System X11 Intrinsics level, which is a higher level than Xlib.)

SunSoft also offers OpenWindows, a GUI development environment for creating OpenLook point-and-click GUIs. It includes icons, windows, menus, X11/NeWS window system, and the Xview tool kit for designing OpenLook applications. It also includes OpenFonts for creating high-resolution fonts and DeskSet, a set of tools which includes a file manager, mail tool, icon editor, wastebasket, and clock.

3.6   Windowing GUIs

Windowing GUIs are the ones most users are familiar with. The most popular ones are offered by Microsoft. Windows 3.x is strictly a GUI (the operating system is DOS). Windows 95 and Windows NT are operating systems with a GUI interface.

3.6.1   Windows 3.x as a GUI

Microsoft Windows 3.x relies on Microsoft's MS DOS as its base operating system and therefore inherits some of DOS's limitations such as 64-byte segments and 640-kbyte memory ceiling. Its strengths are its ability to perform multitasking, its powerful memory management, and its Dynamic Data Exchange (DDE) protocol. DDE provides automatic information exchange between applications.

Windows Object Linking and Embedding (OLE) technology allows users to build compound documents and focus on their data (words, numbers, and graphics) rather than their application.

The Winnet driver is a set of APIs that links the Windows front end with a network operating system. By using Winnet, a developer can write network-aware applications that are not specific to a particular network operating system.

Windows 3.1 has optimized performance for DOS-based applications running within Windows. Graphical operating systems tools include Program Manager, File Manager, Print Manager, and Control Panel. Windows 3.1 also includes desktop applications such as a communications program, calendar, calculator, clock, card file, and notepad.

3.6.2   Windows 95 as a GUI

Released in 1995, Windows 95 does not rely on or require MS DOS. It is an operating system in its own right. It provides 32-bit support for Pentium-based machines, preemptive multitasking and multithreading, improved support for video and sound, and allows long filenames (DOS, and therefore Windows 3.x, is restricted to eight-character filenames). The interface is redesigned to provide easier navigation. Windows 95 also offers an enhanced file management tool called Windows Explorer.

Windows 95's plug-and-play technology automatically discovers and configures all desktop devices. Windows 95 also has built-in access to Microsoft Network, a fee-based access to E-mail, the Internet, and electronic bulletin boards; and to Microsoft Exchange, a facility for sending and receiving E-mail and faxes.

Windows 95 requires a minimum of 8 Mbytes of RAM (with 12 or 16 Mbytes recommended) and requires 60 Mbytes of hard drive space.

3.6.3   Windows NT Workstation as a GUI

The interface to Windows NT Workstation 3.x is similar to that of Windows 3.x. Windows NT 4.0 has an interface similar to Windows 95 but does not include plug-and-play capabilities. The next version of NT (version 5.0 and code-named Cairo), expected to be released in 1997, will include plug-and-play capabilities.

3.6.4   OS/2 Warp Connect as a GUI

OS/2 Warp's interface is object-oriented and supports links to files, folders, or directories located elsewhere on the hard drive. It is similar to Windows 95's ShortCuts.

Users can run DOS, Windows, and OS/2 applications, and access them directly from the Workplace Shell interface, a customizable launch pad that allows the user to put commonly used commands and tools in convenient locations. Multiple Windows sessions can run concurrently. The operating system features crash protection. The Easy Install feature automatically identifies the user's hardware, then prompts the user to insert diskettes at the proper time. OS/2 Warp provides enhanced graphics, multimedia support, 32-bit multitasking, drag-and-drop, plug-and-play, Internet access, and long-filename support.

3.7   Other Environments

DECwindows is a GUI for Digital's UNIX-based Ultrix and VMS systems. It is the foundation for OSF's Motif and is built on top of the X Window System. It adds features such as text fields and scrolling.

Another environment is the Macintosh. A primary benefit of Apple's machines, ease of use, has finally been ported to non-Apple machines. The Windows 95 interface is the closest interface to the Mac interface that Microsoft has released.

The Macintosh interface has been the basis for new GUI styles, such as NeXTStep from NeXT Computer, Inc. The NeXTStep object-oriented techniques allow a developer to work with visual representations of tasks and their corresponding code and add consistency to the appearance of application screens. Based on the UNIX operating system and the Mach kernel, NeXTStep provides a distributed object messaging architecture that allows objects residing on one computer to transparently send messages to objects residing on another computer. In addition, users have transparent client access to enterprise data residing on servers and mainframes.

3.8   Interface Independence

Portable applications is one of the most discussed benefits of client/server computing. Typically, applications written for one GUI are not portable to other GUI environments. To introduce a new GUI interface to users causes confusion, requires retraining of users and developers, and requires rewriting of applications to support both the new GUI and the platform it runs on.

But, if the GUI is not portable, the application is not portable. For a GUI to be truly portable, the GUI interfaces should be able to be moved, for example from Motif to Windows 3.x, with no application changes and no impact on the fundamental look and feel of the interface. This reduces application development time and allows an application to be written for multiple target GUI platforms. However, to be truly portable, most tools cannot take advantage of the native GUI toolkit. When the native GUI toolkits are used, the development tool supports portability for only those functions that are common to the supported GUI environments.

Tools that allow development on one platform and deployment on another platform promote this portability. For example, an application developed for Windows could be moved to Motif without changing the application itself. Developers and users should be able to learn and use one GUI environment and, if they begin to use a new application, specify the GUI environment of their choice.

However, each of today's GUIs has its own library of APIs, as illustrated in Fig. 3.5. Run-time portability is not possible unless third-party tools (these tools have been referred to as compatibility tools and are referred to

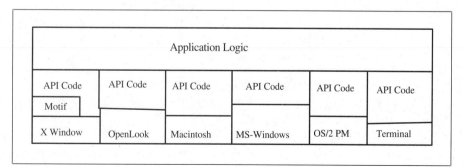

Figure 3.5 GUI libraries of APIs

as portable GUI frameworks) are used, such as Open Interface Elements from Neuron Data Inc., XVT-Design and XVT Portability Tool from XVT Software Inc., OpenUI from Open Software Associates Inc., and Utah from ViewSoft Inc.

Cross–development user interface tools cut development time for applications that must work similarly on Macs, and on micros with Windows and other GUIs, despite the look-and-feel differences among these environments. C++ products of this type include Zinc Application Framework from Zinc Software Inc., XVT-Power++ from XVT Software Inc., and StarView from Star Division Corp. These framework products supply C++ classes for building GUI components such as windows, menus, dialog boxes, buttons, and scroll bars. Developers visually design applications by laying out the elements and compiling the application using the supplied classes. Platform-specific routines can then be added if necessary. These products allow developers to interactively create GUIs without coding interface dependencies into their program objects and without writing interface code.

The benefits from these portable GUI frameworks include:

- Faster development for multiple platforms as than with native code development
- Simplified maintenance since there is only one source-code copy
- Consistent look and feel for applications across all platforms
- Reduced reliance on developers having platform-specific expertise

Neuron Data offers a product family called Elements Environment. Products in the Elements Environment from Neuron Data work together as components of a cross-platform development system. **Open Interface Elements** is a toolkit for building GUIs that are instantly portable and support the active look and feel of the six major windowing environments: Windows, Windows NT, OS/2, Motif, OpenLook, and the Macintosh. Open Interface Elements can incorporate C and C++ code. It provides an object-oriented, extensible development toolkit with a superset of all the widgets and functionality of the native toolkits. Open Interface also includes event management, font support, and X Window Manager compliance.

The widget library includes business graphics, tree browsers, color icons and images, text-edit validation, hypertext help, and a palette widget. Using the visual editor and script language, developers can create custom widgets as subclasses of standard widgets, so that the custom widgets can inherit features and functions of all Open Interface widgets. The Open Interface script is a high-level language that allows developers to select from a menu of verbs to evoke an action within their application. The script is extensible and can access third-party libraries.

Open Interface can be used to link flat-file, object-oriented, relational DBMS, and other data environments. Neuron Data also offers Data Access

Element, software that can be used to link these environments from within Open Interface, as an alternative to writing C code.

XVT Development Solution combines **XVT-Design** and **XVT Portability Tool** to form a GUI portable development solution. XVT-Design, a visual programming tool, is used to design, lay out, and prototype GUIs. It generates portable ANSI C or C++ code, application resources, and make-files. The generated code is compatible with the XVT Portability Toolkit, which is a development library that works with XVT-Design to build, maintain, and port applications to seven GUIs on more than 30 hardware platforms. GUI features such as windows, menus, controls, and dialog boxes and custom GUI objects are supported.

XVT Portability Toolkit then implements the portable XVT interface over native GUI functionality. The XVT toolkit is implemented as a layer on top of the native GUI API to provide access to native functionality and ensure native look and feel on all platforms. GUIs supported include Windows, Windows NT, Macintosh, OS/2, OSF/Motif, OpenLook, and character screens for DOS, UNIX, and VMS.

XVT-Power++ (3.0) is an object-oriented application framework that works with XVT Portability Toolkit. Compared to XVT-Design, discussed above, XVT-Power++ has improved support for portable bit-map images, access to fonts which gives developers access to font selection through the native system resources, and a hypertext help system for applications built with the tool. The hypertext feature compiles and builds the hypertext links for the target environment of the application.

XVT-Power++ also includes Rogue Wave Software Inc.'s Tools.h++, which is a multiple-platform library of C++ classes for handling a variety of data types. Tools.h++ replaces XVT's own data structures.

OpenUI Development Environment (3.5) from Open Software Associates, Inc., uses a high-level API to derive cross-platform compatibility to create a user interface. Applications are developed in a supported third- or fourth-generation language. The resulting applications will work on Windows 3.1, Windows NT, Macintosh, OS/2, and UNIX platforms. The application runs with native appearance and behavior for the installed GUIs.

Utah (2.0) from ViewSoft, Inc., is a cross-platform C/C++ GUI development tool with a user interface builder that provides virtual views, reusable views, view inheritance, and a resolution-independent screen designer. The product frees users from routine interface event management. Utah is available on Windows 3.1 and NT, X/Motif, Macintosh, and OS/2.

Zinc Application Framework (5.0) from Zinc Software allows developers to develop GUI applications on DOS, Windows, OS/2, Macintosh, and Unix platforms and has excellent internationalization support. It will work with database-access mechanisms provided by or compatible with any supported C++ compiler and tool set. Developers can deploy Zinc-based applications using many different languages, without duplicating code. Zinc centralizes the translation of prompts and other on-screen text and stores only the differences between multiple versions.

These tools provide a uniform cross-platform C++ wrapper for accessing each platform's own high-level GUI functions, such as menu and window routines. Some cross-platform development products handle GUIs by creating similar functionality. These products include Galaxy from Visix Software Inc. and C/S Elements from Neuron Data.

3.9   Client Operating Systems

Many of the characteristics of the next-generation client/server operating systems are clear. They are 32-bit designs that support 32-bit applications with far more advanced features than the 16-bit DOS and Windows software we're used to. However, these new operating systems can still run most existing 16-bit applications. All provide more protection for these new applications, so that one errant program won't be as likely to crash the whole system. All offer true multitasking (the ability to run multiple programs at the same time) as well as multithreading (the ability to have a single program do multiple things at the same time). All provide (or, in the case of Windows NT, will soon provide) a new user-friendly interface with object-oriented characteristics. And all offer broad network connectivity out of the box.

Today's 32-bit operating systems take advantage of the native 32-bit architectures of advanced microprocessors such as the 486, Pentium, and Pentium Pro. Under a 32-bit operating system, programs can manipulate 32-bit chunks of data and address large memory areas in a logical, streamlined manner. Application code can be smaller and, depending on the type of operation it is performing, noticeably faster. Using a 32-bit architecture means that programmers don't have to deal with the complexity of 16-bit segments and offsets.

Windows 3.1's simple cooperative multitasking scheme is often anything but cooperative. The 32-bit operating systems offer preemptive multitasking, a far more robust way to divvy up system resources. The unit that is multitasked is a program thread, a fully functional subset of a program. Applications can have multiple threads performing separate tasks at the same time. The net result is far smoother multitasking, better program response, and less waiting for the hourglass to go away. Apple's System 7.5, Windows 95, and OS/2 (and soon Windows NT) bring an object-oriented metaphor to the user interface. The screen becomes a true desktop. The screen hosts objects that represent programs, files, drives, devices, and directories. An object-oriented shell also has the intelligence to tell you about the objects it contains. Right-clicking on any object brings up a context menu with details on all the object's properties and all the things you can do to it. Windows NT 4.0 has a Windows 95-style.

Networking has finally become a standard operating system component. Using one of these advanced operating systems provides automatic connectivity. Out-of-the-box support for Novell and other common micro LANs is commonplace, and TCP/IP is fast becoming a standard offering in the operating-system bundle. Connectivity features may also include priceless aids for mobile users such as remote dial-up and high-speed cable connections. OS/2 Warp provides a World Wide Web browser to get you on the Internet. Windows 95 offers a browser in Microsoft Plus. Windows NT includes dynamic addressing for TCP/IP and support for dial-up connections.

Some closing thoughts on the interface race. Microsoft recently began releasing Service Packs for Windows 95. These will be released periodically and will contain device drivers, functions, and components, as well as bug fixes. In addition, the next major commercial release, code-named Nashville, is due out by the end of 1996.

A new version of the OS/2 user interface (code-named Merlin) is due out in early 1997. This OpenDoc-based, customizable user interface is network aware—connections are automatically made as the user needs them. Merlin is discussed in more detail in Sec. 6.3.5, "Merlin, the next OS/2 Warp."

So expect upgrade releases to be often—which means that if one of these operating systems doesn't have a feature that its competitor does, it will within six months—if not sooner!

3.9.1   Windows 95

Windows 95 is an extremely easy to use environment for users and developers alike. It is a natural upgrade path for Windows 3.x users and requires fewer resources than its competitors. To maintain backward compatibility with Windows 3.x, designers had to forgo some of the security features that would have been nice to keep.

Windows 95 provides hundreds of network drivers and supports plug-and-play networking. Windows NT and OS/2 Warp support plug-and-play only with PC Card network interface cards (as of right now!).

Microsoft Corp.'s forthcoming Windows update, code-named Nashville and due out by the end of 1996, promises to make Web browsing much easier. Nashville will include a new version of the Internet Explorer that will enable users to browse LANs, PCs, or the Internet using the same menu commands and screens. Such flexibility threatens to make separate Web browsers obsolete. Nashville promises to provide a single environment for browsing through various types of information, resulting in more opportunities for software developers but higher on-line bills. Nashville also is expected to include Web page development and Internet Information Server (IIS) Web server duties capabilities. IIS will offer ActiveX technology to improve the interoperability of Microsoft's pending server products.

Nashville will also include the next version of the Microsoft-Intel Advanced Power Management APIs, which let applications manage battery use on laptops, as well as features such as drivers for infrared transmission ports, ISDN support, the Direct X 2.0 multimedia technologies, and an image viewer, code-named ImageVue, that is being developed by Wang Laboratories Inc.

3.9.2   Windows NT Workstation

Windows NT Workstation 3.51 (a 32-bit operating system) uses the same engine that drives the server version of NT. It features preemptive multitasking and can access up to 2 Gbytes of virtual memory per application. It provides protected subsystems, memory protection, hardware isolation, and built-in backup and security features that meet U.S. government standards.

The Windows NT high-performance file system is used to manage files and directories and permits long filenames. It also can port to Alpha, MIPS, and PowerPC workstations.

The interface to Windows NT Workstation 3.x is similar to that of Windows 3.x. Windows NT Workstation 4.0 has an upgraded interface which is a Windows 95 look-alike. Windows NT Workstation 4.0 does not require additional memory to run because the layer of software that translates 32-bit function calls to 16-bit function calls is be eliminated. This version also includes plug-and-play capabilities, access to Microsoft Network, the universal Inbox Exchange client, and PCMCIA support comparable to that in Windows 95. This version of Windows NT Workstation is a more robust and more secure alternative to Windows 95. Windows NT 4.0 is discussed in more detail in Sec. 6.3.2.

Windows NT Workstation isolates applications in its own virtual machine, which uses more system resources but is more reliable. Windows NT Workstation also provides true multitasking and multithreading and support long filenames.

Windows NT has built-in networking features but no automatic link to Microsoft Network. Windows NT Workstation also provides crash protection for 16-bit applications, support for full 16- and 32-bit OLE, and symmetric multiprocessing.

NT Workstation can also compress individual files and entire subdirectory trees on NTFS files.

The price for this power is high-end hardware: at least a 66-MHz 486 and 16 Mbytes of RAM.

Although the long list of new features in NT 4.0 sounds compelling, the real reason most organizations will consider upgrading is because it will sport the Windows 95 user interface. The interface is simple to use and should help reduce support costs.

3.9.3   OS/2 Warp Connect

OS/2 Warp Connect, Version 3, provides object-based desktop flexibility for power users. It supports the System Object Model (SOM) and Distributed SOM (DSOM), so it is distributed object–ready. OS/2 Warp Connect is based on OS/2 Warp, IBM's 32-bit, multithreaded, preemptive, multitasking operating system.

OS/2 Warp Connect's networking options include connectivity with other Warp Connect or Windows machines, as well as connections to TCP/IP, NetWare, Microsoft NT, and IBM LAN Server networks. Support for IBM's LAN Distance for remote connections and Lotus Notes Express (a slimmed down version of Notes that includes E-mail and discussion applications) is also included. The Internet Access Kit provides IBM's Web Explorer, Gopher, a news reader, an FTP client, and a Telnet terminal. In addition, OS/2 Warp Connect has built-in support for a heterogeneous peer network that allows machines running OS/2 Warp Connect, Windows 3.11, Windows 95, and Windows NT networks to share resources.

Recommended hardware for running OS/2 Warp Connect is at least 8 Mbytes of RAM (16 Mbytes is even better and it can actually run in 4 Mbytes) and at least a 486DX2/66 processor.

OS/2 Warp Connect gives the user a choice for running Windows 3.x applications in its 32-bit environment. Each application can run in its own isolated area (called a virtual machine), which protects it from other applications but requires lots of RAM. The alternative is to run all DOS applications in one virtual machine, which conserves RAM but increases the risk of one bad application taking down the rest. Users can choose which configuration to use. Windows NT Workstation runs each application in its own virtual machine, trading reliability for resources.

OS/2 Warp Connect also offers OS/2 Warp Fullback, which runs Windows applications without requiring Windows.

OS/2 for PowerPCs was released in early 1996. This version allows IBM to call OS/2 a truly portable operating system. IBM has no announced plans for the next release of OS/2 for PowerPCs.

3.9.4   Copland

Copland is the code name for Apple Computer Inc.'s 32-bit, microkernel-based Mac OS version System 8, which is due to be released in stages during 1997. Copland is a complete rewrite of the Mac OS engine and is designed to improve performance. Copland is integrating a new hardware abstraction layer to help peripheral vendors get smooth plug-and-play upgrades for Mac users.

It will incorporate OpenDoc, which is similar to OLE, to support multiapplication data sharing. Copland will have the drag-and-drop capability of OpenDoc to link to a site on the Internet. Open Transport,

Apple's network operating system and communication system, will extend the MacOS network transparency: users will be able to connect to local or global networks as if they were on the desktop. Open Transport upgrades the feature set and performance of TCP/IP in the Mac OS. Open Transport 1.1, the successor to AppleTalk, released in early 1996, supports speeds of up to 100 Mbps.

Copland is designed to improve operating speed. It supports preemptive multitasking as well as cooperative multitasking. Many processes, such as copying and deleting files, will execute in background. Another important improvement is Copland's memory-on-demand system, which moves small pieces of code into RAM as needed, allowing the machine to accomplish more with existing memory.

Copland has a "layered" customizable interface. The low-end users can work in a simplified version that provides only the OS services they need. With a couple of clicks, power users can customize their interface to their own liking.

The new operating system is designed for the Power Mac and will run almost entirely in PowerPC native mode. Copland will support 256 terabytes of storage. Copland is also designed to recognize and support new types of motherboards and add-ons—clone users just need to add the right software hooks or drivers, thus giving clone vendors the ability to design their own systems and clone users more choices when choosing one.

Read-only memory (ROM) units will also be available for users whose PowerPC systems came with no ROM in the required socket. One of the design goals for Copland is to eliminate the need for Mac ROMs. When that goal is reached, either in Copland or in a subsequent update, system makers and users can stop worrying about Apple ROMs and just load the Mac OS from disk, as they do with other operating systems.

Apple has long promised that the Mac will be an active assistant, helping users wade through their data and make sense of it, not just serving as a repository for data. Some of the expected new capabilities include:

- **View by content**. This new technology, tentatively called a view window, lets users organize information based on criteria. Copland will be able to find and organize documents based on their content. This feature also lets a user to select a document and have the Mac OS find documents with similar content without entering search text. The view window can be saved and then automatically updated with any new or changed documents the next time it is opened, thanks to Copland's multithreaded design that allows powerful background processing.
- **Interface refinements**. Copland will have refinements to the user interface throughout. Copland's Finder shows part of the beginning of the filename and part of the end, so that a user would have enough context to readily tell files apart. The list view is also customizable.

- **Restructured system folder**. Apple also plans to restructure the System Folder so that users can tell which extensions the system needs and how recent they are. It is possible that this restructuring may not make it into the first version of Copland. For Apple to meet its end-of-1996 release date, the company may have to pull some features and deliver them in 1997 as an upgrade.
- **Custom configurations**. Multiple users can be set up on one system, each with different preferences and access capabilities. For example, a notebook user might have one group of settings on the road, when server access is unnecessary, and a different group when plugged into the office network.
- **Internet access**. Apple's Cyberdog Internet interface will be integrated into Copland. Copland users will be able to browse the Internet from any OpenDoc application, including the MacOS file manager and Finder, and drag and drop Internet links directly into applications.

Some promised but now not expected features include PowerTalk electronic mail system and its PowerShare directory services. Apple's revised messaging plans call for Copland to support and deliver E-mail and collaborative services via OpenDoc and industry-standard Internet protocols such as Simple Mail Transfer Protocol, Post Office Protocol, and Multipurpose Internet Mail Extensions. The plan is intended to foster collaboration and communication.

OpenDoc isn't an industry-standard protocol for communication via the Internet, but it will be built into Copland, and there is a Windows version of it. Jointly developed by IBM, Novell, and Apple, OpenDoc provides developers with a set of application programming interfaces that offer a consistent method for exchanging data among applications and across platforms.

The PowerTalk E-mail system, which offers a single in-box as a repository for all types of mail, will remain part of System 7.5, the current version of the Mac OS. It will be added to future updates of that version of the operating system.

4

Servers

To be a successful server, the platform chosen has to provide the following:

- **Scalability**. Adding computing resources to increase capacity, performance, throughput, or the number of supported users should not require changing any application. This includes updates to the server itself or adding a server into the environment to share the load.

- **Availability**. Today's servers are expected to be operational 24 hours a day, 7 days a week. RAID disk subsystems, hardware and software fault tolerance, disk duplexing, and mirroring increase a system's chances of a transparent and speedy recovery from failures. On-line monitoring and backup and recovery procedures will allow an organization to maintain its environment without bringing the environment down to do it.

- **Network support.** The hardware itself and the software running on the hardware must be designed to support networking. This is not an area to be treated lightly.

4.1 Platform Independence

Platform independence (hardware and software) is a major benefit of client/server computing. Upgrading hardware should be almost as simple as backing up the data and restoring it on a more powerful machine (micro, midrange, or mainframe) running the same server database software. The same should be true for downward migration.

To maintain vendor independence and provide a flexible migration path for future decisions regarding data sources, it is better to provide such functionality at a higher level than database management software and, ideally, independent of the database vendor.

Software should be compatible between platforms. Data, programs, and front-end software should need only system-related modifications.

4.2   Connectivity

Server software must support access to a variety of data sources and not be restricted to vendor-supplied sources. Database gateways (see Sec. 8.7.2 for more details) provide such links. This connectivity is in part due to vendors' opening up access to their data structures via APIs.

Database gateways provide access to external databases. Most database gateways use SQL as the access language. With a simple pass-through database gateway, the vendor provides software only on the requester side. The SQL request has to be acceptable to the target database. Intelligent database gateways have software on both the sending and receiving nodes. This allows the software to optimize the query and supports portability but does not allow the use of any special features that might be in the SQL of the target database.

Microsoft's Open Database Connectivity (ODBC) API permits applications to communicate with relational and nonrelational data sources. ODBC is based on the call-level interface (CLI) developed by the SQL Access Group. ODBC drivers allow developers to write Windows-based applications that transparently access the data sources supported by the drivers. Announced ODBC drivers include links to SQL Server, Oracle, and EDA/SQL from Information Builders, Inc. ODBC is discussed in Sec. 9.9.5.

4.3   Eight Layers of Software

There could be as many as eight categories of software working on a server, as illustrated in Fig. 4.1:

- Network management environment
- Network computing environment and extensions
- Network operating system
- Server operating system
- Loadable modules
- Database manager
- Database gateways
- Application

The application develops requests for data that are sent via the network operating system to database gateways, database managers, or a loadable module. They translate the request into machine code and pass it on to the server operating system. The server operating system is guided by the network computing environment software, which handles the services required to support distributed applications in heterogeneous environments.

Application		
Loadable Modules	Database Manager	Database Gateways
Server Operating System		
Network Operating System		
Network Computing Environment		
Network Management Environment		

Figure 4.1 Eight categories of software on a server

The entire networked enterprise is guided by the network management environment software.

4.3.1   User connections

One little-discussed aspect of server software is how it handles user connections. A connection is a single interprocess communication channel between a client program and the server database. Server software differs in memory requirements for each connection and in the number of connections it can support. The server database treats each connection as a separate user even though a front-end program can open several connections to a client (to display multiple tables on a screen or to improve performance).

Each connection requires a set amount of server random-access memory (RAM). When adding connections, server databases using multithreaded connections require less RAM than those that require additional sets of connection logic and, therefore, can handle more simultaneous connections. When the amount of RAM used for connections is limited, the RAM cache increases, thereby increasing performance.

4.4   Data Manager Features

Pioneers in server technology maintain that server database software is the critical piece of software in the client/server environment. It handles all the data management (storage, retrieval, updating, and deletion) and should support on-line transaction processing, referential integrity, and recovery procedures. It should handle distributed data, whether the data is fragmented or replicated. Server data managers are discussed in detail in Sec. 7.11, "Server DBMSs."

Server databases, a new class of software, reside on dedicated networked servers. Ideally, server databases should provide the integrity, security, functionality, and robustness of mainframe database technology. Most provide some subset of mainframe database technology, and more features are added regularly.

4.5   RISC vs. CISC

Complex instruction set computing (CISC) has been traditionally used by computer architectures. These instructions are decoded by the microcode which is placed in the microprocessor hardware. A newer implementation is reduced instruction set computing (RISC), which is decoded directly by the hardware, thus increasing speed. The system hardware is actually optimized to decode instructions.

The first implementations of RISC included only the simplest of the CISC architecture, which meant that there were very few instructions at all. The second generation of RISC designs includes more complex instruction sets and increases the number of instructions to rival those offered by CISC.

The important feature of RISC is that each instruction is simple enough to be executed in one CPU cycle. To support tasks that actually need several single-cycle instructions, a superscalar design is used to split the processor into separate units, with each unit executing separate instructions. This design allows the processor to execute two or more instructions per clock cycle. Examples of superscalar RISC implementations are IBM's RS/6000 and PowerPC, and Digital's Alpha.

RISC architectures also use pipelining, a technique that allows more than one instruction to be processed at a time. A pipelined CPU uses several execution steps to execute one cycle-long instruction. This results in high performance and increased throughput.

To date, most UNIX-based operating systems and Windows NT are capable of supporting RISC architectures.

4.5.1   PowerPC Platform

In late 1995 the Common Hardware Reference Platform (CHRP) standard was released by IBM and Apple. Now formally called the PowerPC Microprocessor Common Hardware Reference Platform (PowerPC Platform or PPCP for short), this is a single standard hardware design that uses the PowerPC microprocessor which uses RISC technology and is capable of supporting a variety of operating systems. The PowerPC Platform specifies the kinds of input/output interfaces, bus standards, and other system-level elements needed to produce a single micro capable of running multiple operating systems natively. Any developer could build hardware, using components readily available from mainstream sources, that would provide maximum compatibility with peripherals and programs designed for use with older Macs and micros and could run any PowerPC-supported operating system. The currently PowerPC-supported operating systems are Windows NT, OS/2 Warp, Solaris (Sun Microsystems, Inc.'s UNIX), AIX (IBM's UNIX), NetWare, and the Mac OS.

Apple expects to release a PowerPC-based PowerMac in early 1997. With PowerPC chip sets—the supporting circuitry necessary to implement the architecture—available from well-known suppliers, new players should be able to easily design their own systems. The user decides which operating system to run on the machine. Each machine, of course, will only be running one operating system at a time, but the machine can now be used at some point in time by another user that needs to use a different operating system, minimizing "obsolete" machines. The PowerPC chip is discussed in Sec. 16.2, "More Powerful Chips."

Some of the new technologies that PowerPC Platform is using include:

- **Open Firmware**. This standard is used to manage the startup process independently of the operating system to be launched. When a PPCP machine is powered up, code in Open Firmware tests and initializes the system, scanning it to detect available devices and load configuration information into memory. It then locates and loads the selected operating system, which then takes control of the startup process.

- **Run-time abstraction services** (RTAS). This layer of low-level software provides standard interfaces to underlying functions, simplifying the operating system and device driver development.

- **New memory map**. Each operating system supported by PPCP assigns different addresses to the system's various components. To prevent conflicts, the designers designed a new map that all the operating systems will use on PPCP systems.

- **New interrupt model**. Interrupts are the messages the various components of the systems send to the CPU to signal that they require attention or have completed a task. To standardize this, PPCP designers adopted the Open PIC standard.

- **Integrated I/O controllers**. For the PPCP platform, IBM, Apple, and Motorola designed a new high-performance bridge chip linking the CPU and PCI buses.

4.6   Multiprocessing Systems

As CPU costs decline, organizations are finding it more cost-effective to add processors to their existing equipment rather than augment their equipment with new machines.

Multiprocessing systems use one of three architectures.

- **Shared memory**. All processors have access to shared memory. Symmetric multiprocessor platforms are shared memory.

- **Shared disk**. Processors have their own private memory but are able to access all data on disks. This architecture is used in system clusters.

- **Shared nothing**. Each processor has its own memory and its own access to disks. Massively parallel processing systems are shared nothing.

4.6.1   Symmetric Multiprocessors

A symmetric multiprocessor (SMP) incorporates a number of processors

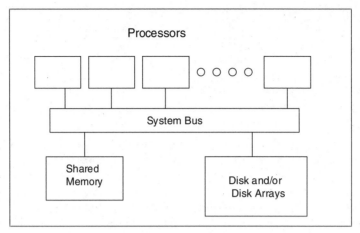

Figure 4.2 Symmetric multiprocessors

(somewhere between 4 and 12 typically, although some vendors have pushed SMP to 64 and 96 processors and still retained benefits) that share common memory as well as I/O and other system resources, including the operating system, as illustrated in Fig. 4.2. To reduce shared memory traffic, each processor has its own memory cache. The SMP machine coordinates the interprocess communication (IPC) through a global memory that all the processing units share.

Using SMP, organizations can quickly and cheaply boost performance—within limits. Adding more processors increases performance only until the number of processors contending for memory access and bus space reaches the point where they create bottlenecks. Vendors are pushing SMP scalability through special optimization algorithms and increasing bus speed so that more data can travel faster between memory and the processors. Organizations can also boost performance by swapping the processors for more powerful versions. Increased bus speeds also allow organizations to incorporate more processors into SMP systems.

Processors select tasks to be executed from a common task pool and are interconnected via a high-speed common system bus. Any processor that completes one task is immediately assigned another task. SMP machines have typically been the offerings of such big hardware names as IBM, Digital, Sequent Computer Systems, and Unisys but the micro players such as Intel and Dell are adding SMP machines to their offerings as well.

Not all operating systems can support SMP. An operating system that can support SMP must be able to assign work to available processors based on some algorithm.

SMP operating systems support threads, a single sequential flow of control within a process, as discussed in Sec. 6.1.3, "Multithreading." Multithreaded operating systems automatically allocate process threads to optimize the use of the processors. As long as the applications and databases are multithreaded, the system optimizes use of all the processors automatically.

SMP operating systems must provide memory protection, multithreading support, and load balancing but most provide these capabilities in different ways. Most server vendors have an implementation of SMP. The number of processors these implementations support varies greatly.

4.6.2   Clusters

Shared-memory clusters take over when straight SMP runs out of scalability. Shared-memory clusters link multiple logical SMP machines into a single system using an interconnect. For example, a shared-memory cluster might connect sets of four-processor SMP servers (usually referred to as nodes) into one logical machine. Intel's Pentium Pro four-processor SMP-on-a-board has fueled interest in shared-memory clusters.

Shared-memory clusters offer considerable flexibility, allowing an organization to link or unlink clusters of nodes as needed. Clusters also provide fault tolerance with their ability to quickly shift workload to another SMP should one SMP fail.

The ability of clusters to share processing across SMP nodes does not come without problems. Unlike SMP, standard operating systems do not automatically spread the processing beyond a single SMP node to all the other processors in the cluster. Operating systems need to get smarter to take advantage of clustering. Networks will also need to evolve to support the message-oriented communications that clusters require.

Another problem is memory management. In a shared-memory cluster, each SMP node has its own local memory as well as peer-to-peer access to memory on other nodes. A node cannot simply look at the results generated by the processors on another node. Nodes have to communicate by explicitly sending messages and data across the interconnect. This requires special software and complex locking to perform messaging and maintain cache coherency and memory integrity. System vendors are looking to specialized interconnect communication chip sets from companies such as Vitesse Semiconductor Corp. to solve some of these problems.

Historically, clustering works best when a single vendor develops the hardware, operating system, communications, and applications. Vendors such as Digital and Tandem fine-tune all elements of the system for optimal use of clustered architecture. Such optimization would be difficult, if not impossible, with hardware and software from multiple vendors.

Hallway clusters use a shared-nothing approach. A hallway cluster is a series of stand-alone systems connected by the network so that they can share processing cycles. The software distributes processing to every system that has spare processing cycles; this automatically increases performance because cycles are not sitting idle. However, with their technical and cultural problems, hallway clusters work best for compute-intensive problems with very light I/O demands.

4.6.3   Massively Parallel Processors

As vendors are trying to resolve the challenges of shared-memory clusters, organizations are turning to shared-nothing technology. Shared-nothing systems avoid the bottleneck of shared memory and shared I/O by giving each processor its own memory and I/O. Each independent processor node communicates with all other nodes via proprietary messages controlled by the operating system. The interconnect is more sophisticated than the one used in clusters. Its bandwidth is designed to increase as more nodes are added. Consequently, massively parallel processor (MPP) platforms can handle hundreds of nodes, but coordinating that many nodes using the message-passing communication mechanism can be a challenge.

The down side of this technology is that the data must be divided among the various processors in ways that minimize the amount of messaging between processor nodes.

MPP machines, in contrast to SMP machines, do not share memory. MPP machines are actually dozens of computers configured into a single computing system. MPP operating systems are optimized to execute programs that can be easily partitioned for parallel execution.

An MPP system could consist of hundreds of processors, all executing in parallel, with each having its own assignment memory, as illustrated in Fig. 4.3. Multiple processors can be simultaneously executing different instructions on different data. The results of the multiple executions must then be "combined" to provide a single result, if appropriate.

MPP machines have not taken the market by storm yet. Software that can take advantage of the parallel architecture is limited. However, MPP machines should be considered for applications that can partition either the

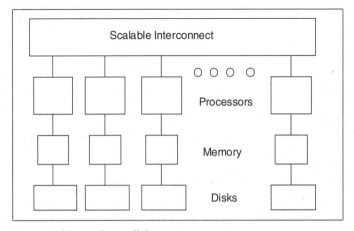

Figure 4.3 Massively parallel processors

processes or the data. For example, a text search application might run on an MPP machine, with each processor handling a specific subset of the text base being searched.

The MPP machines on the market today are from major hardware vendors such as IBM, AT&T, Pyramid Technology Corp., and Siemens Nixdorf Information Systems Inc. (a subsidiary of Siemens AG).

An interesting side note: Sequent Computer Systems is beginning to use SMP units to create a parallel design. The original offerings link four SMP units into one parallel configuration. The SMPs are arranged in a design that can treat the cache memory of each CPU as shared across the system. Sequent is moving data between the processors over a backplane at the rate of a gigabyte per second. Even though the nodes are arranged in parallel, applications and the operating systems address them as if they were running with a shared-memory pool, just like a regular SMP. The parallel SMP machines don't equal a massively parallel system with a thousand processors, but the design is easier to scale up than today's SMP systems.

In contrast, Hewlett-Packard recently announced its Enterprise Parallel Servers (EPS) strategy, which utilizes high-performance SMP systems and, Hewlett-Packard claims, has the following advantages over MPP systems:

- EPS nodes can be existing high-performance SMP systems; MPP can use only uniprocessor systems within a node.
- The very high speed Fiber Channel switch can move data among nodes at an advanced rate of speed.
- EPS models will be able to use 64-bit PA-8000 processors by the end of 1996. Most of the MPP suppliers have indicated 64-bit processors rolling out in 1997.

Leading independent software suppliers such as Oracle, Informix, Sybase, and Red Brick have all announced their support for EPS.

4.6.4   Comparisons

Bear in mind that the distinctions between SMP, cluster, and MPP are getting grayer all the time. Currently the categories refer to architectural design choices made by the hardware vendor regarding how multiple processors will be incorporated into a single computer. Each platform has its limitations. Shared-memory systems tend to develop bottlenecks in interprocess communication, making scalability limited. Shared-disk systems can have lock contention problems, making their scalability also limited. Shared-nothing systems are often difficult to administer because each processor has its own disk and its own memory. These systems require robust system management tools, but they can linearly scale up to hundreds of processors.

SMP usually means more than one CPU in a single box. When additional processors are added, the size of the footprint and the power and air conditioning requirements remain unchanged. However, that also means there is a single point of failure, such as memory or power supply. The number of processors that can be in the box is a function of the box itself. If the server holds only six processors and another processor is needed for performance, a new box has to be purchased.

Clustering adds a level of fault tolerance because if one box goes down, the others keep running. Adding processors for performance means simply adding a new box without affecting the existing components.

Which approach is the best depends on the type of application processing and the size of the application. OLTP works best on shared-memory systems when application growth is slow and the data is in the range of 10 to 100 Gbytes. Decision support works well with shared-nothing, MPP systems. Small databases (under 100 Gbytes) with less than a few hundred users would do well on commodity SMP servers. Databases up to 1,000 Gbytes with up to 1,000 users should perform well on big bus SMP systems or shared-memory clusters. For anything larger, organizations should look to shared-nothing platforms.

4.7   Multipurpose Servers

The basic premise behind client/server computing is that one machine asks for something and the other machine gets it and sends it back to the asking machine. A client application asks a server for services. This was the original implementation of client/server computing. All the application work—the presentation services, presentation logic, application logic, business rules, and data logic—was performed on the client. The server was basically a data storage device that retrieved data and returned it to the asking client. This very straightforward ask-and-you-shall-receive approach works very well for homogeneous database applications and for business problems that are not very complex.

As organizations began to implement client/server architectures, some organizations began to split more of the work between the client and the server. Business rules began to be part of the database itself in the form of triggers and stored procedures. This provided consistency (whenever an application accessed the data, the rules were evoked) and less maintenance (the business rules were in one place instead of being coded into application software residing on countless clients).

As applications became more complex, some of the application logic was off-loaded to the server. This was critical for applications that required large volumes of data to be handled at one time such as statistical sampling. Instead of returning hundreds of records that the client would have to access to perform statistical analysis, the analysis is done on the server and only the results are passed to the client. This improves response time and greatly reduces network traffic. The notion that a machine just served data to requesting applications had run out of steam.

The idea of a server as a high-powered computer is also changing as the workforce becomes more mobile. The remote worker's desktop machine may be a server to the laptops, personal digital assistants, or other portable equipment used by the untethered worker. When the worker is in the office, the desktop machine acts as a client.

4.8   Two-Tier, Three-Tier, and Multitier Architectures

Before we get into a discussion of architectures of more than two tiers, please consider one overriding fact: Two-tier architectures will still solve many of today's problems. The discussion of multitier architectures gives organizations some insight into how their own architectures can evolve, but organizations should not draw the conclusion that more than two tiers are required for client/server architectures.

As applications continued to evolve, they required data from other servers, usually heterogeneous sources rather than homogeneous sources, and other platforms in the organization. Data had to be used by multiple applications. Architectures that worked fine with a few hundred users and two servers didn't scale up well to several thousand users and ten servers. Partitioning a database across multiple servers required major application changes. Putting more processing on the server slowed down the server, as it had to handle application processing and database services. Putting more application processing on the client reduced network performance because of the increased communication between the client and the server and created maintenance headaches. It is easier to change a copy of an application on one or two servers than on hundreds of client machines.

The two-tier architecture started to became unacceptable. Organizations started to add additonal tiers to their client/server architecture, as illustrated in Fig. 4.4. Data in this server could be shared by all applications in the network.

The impetus behind this evolution is the same thing that drove the original concept of client/server computing into the mainstream: Put the specialized processing for each task on the appropriate platform and thereby create flexible and fast applications on the user's desk. A three-tier architecture divides the applications into pieces that will run on separate machines: clients, application servers, and data sources. The client handles the presentation processing and productivity tools such as spreadsheet and word processing packages, the application servers handle the business processing, and the data sources range from relational databases to host-based legacy data.

As enterprise networks connected more heterogeneous platforms and organizations began embracing open systems, the view of applications changed from a hierarchical view of clients and servers to one of cooperative peers. Since many of these applications need to interact with one another,

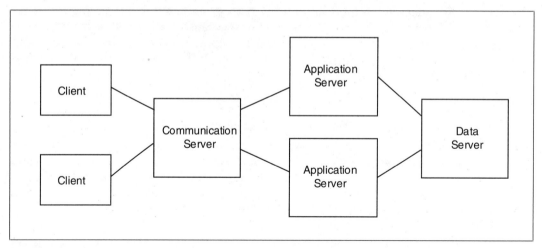

Figure 4.4 Multitier client/server architecture

the need for transactional integrity was answered with transaction managers.

Transaction processing (TP) monitors are finding a place in larger three-tier applications to improve the reliability of the clients that access an application on a local server which in turn requests information from database servers distributed throughout the organization. Some of the features of TP monitors that organizations have found useful in multitier architectures are the ability to roll back transactions in the event of a crash, to move applications from one machine to another, to replace an application without taking the server off-line, to set access controls and security, and to establish processing priorities.

While the original extension of the client/server architecture expanded two tiers to three tiers, most organizations today are looking at multitier architectures. In some cases, the additional tiers are dedicated servers, as discussed below. In other cases, organizations are extending their architecture to accommodate remote and mobile workers.

Organizations are developing stripped-down versions of LAN applications for laptops, personal digital assistants, and other mobile devices. Apple Computer calls these architectures client-client-server. Mobile users relay communications through a desktop computer or server before connecting to other computers on an office LAN. The portable machine is used for display and data entry; all other processing is partitioned to the desktop client or server tier.

To support this type of architecture, organizations must also synchronize large corporate databases with smaller subsets of the data that will reside on the mobile devices.

Many in the industry feel that this evolution is an natural extension of the concept of distributed objects. Discrete software components or objects will include their own intelligence for finding their peers on the network, regardless of their hardware platform, operating system, and network protocols. Constructing new software applications will be a simple as mixing and matching these discrete components. Each component resides on whatever node makes the best sense: close to the data, close to the work that handles the data, or close to the client that displays the data.

Chapter 10, "Two-Tier and Multitier Environments," is devoted entirely to this subject.

4.9   Dedicated Servers

The idea of a dedicated server is feasible because of the ever-decreasing cost of server hardware, its ever-increasing power, and the newly emerging enterprise-wide focus of client/server architectures in larger organizations. A dedicated server performs only one service to all those that ask for its resources. The client in this case would be a LAN server, another dedicated server, or a desktop client machine.

This allows a server to be optimized for computation cycles or data access. By configuring a server to do one or the other (compute or retrieve data) well, an organization is able to improve the performance of the environment.

By building multitiers into an architecture, an organization can also support mixed processing environments. An EDI server can handle the peaks and valleys of EDI transmissions without tying up other applications. A batch client can be used to offload report generation and other batch-type processing, freeing up other clients for query and transaction applications.

Organizations gain some obvious benefits with an n-tiered environment. It offers client/server systems the opportunity to be more scalable and portable. The separation of functions within the overall architecture allows IT staffers to specialize and fine-tune their skills. Developers can specialize in GUI development or application logic development instead of having to be jacks-of-all-trades.

The most common types of dedicated servers are

- Database servers
- Communication servers
- Compute servers
- Application servers

4.9.1   Database servers

The reality in every organization is that data is shared, business rules are corporate-wide, and most applications do not function in a vacuum. With database servers optimized database servers for data access and retrieval, data can be accessed by any application that requires it. Database servers also provide a single point for storing and updating files. The separation of dedicated database servers leaves application logic, business rules, presentation logic, and services to be handled by dedicated machines.

A data server is used in conjunction with a compute or application server and may be used by more than one such server. A data server does not perform any application logic processing. The processing done on a data server is rule-based procedures, such as data validation, required as part of the data management function.

Data servers perform multiple searches through large amounts of data and frequently update massive tables. These tasks require fast processors, large amounts of memory, and substantial hard disk capacity. However, for the most part, these computers send relatively small amounts of data across the network.

4.9.2   Communication servers

Some organizations put a communication server between the client machines and the actual processors in the network. This intermediate tier decides which processing server is the best one to handle the request. The application load is balanced among the available processors in the network, and the network traffic flows more smoothly. In addition, if a processing computer goes down, another can take up the slack.

Also, a central routing point provides security, a consistent environment for system monitoring, and a focus for performance load balancing.

4.9.3   Compute servers

For organizations that do a lot of number crunching, like weather stations or insurance companies, having a server optimized for computation makes sense. There is very little storage on such a machine. It expects to be given the data, perform computations, and return results. It therefore must be able to handle large data files both on the network link and in memory.

4.9.4   Application servers

One view of multitiered client/server architectures is that there is a middle tier of one or more application servers that handle most of the business and data logic. The client handles all the presentation logic and services, and a database server handles data services and file services. The actual placement of a particular application-related function would depend on ease of administration, scalability, and performance factors for both processing and network load.

Having the bulk of the application logic on a central server reduces the maintenance headaches significantly. The code needs to be modified in only one place rather than on hundreds of clients.

An application server can also manage transactions and ensure distributed database integrity by implementing a heterogeneous two-phase commit process based on the XA transaction protocol which is supported by most major DBMSs. It can also handle asynchronous queues to ensure that transactions are completed while the client proceeds to other tasks.

4.10   When Is a Server Not a Server

In multitier environments, servers become clients by requesting services from other servers. The request might be for data from a database server or for a computation from a compute server. The infrastructure needs to be able to handle this kind of interchange.

5

The Network

A network provides the link between the clients and the many servers. To facilitate that communication, a network must have the following features:

- **Name and address services**. The network must be able to translate user-supplied names with network addresses. This is usually done through the use of directories. The messages are then routed to the appropriate network address based on the destination address in the directory.
- **Segmentation**. Large messages or files must be split into multiple segments and reassembled before delivery. This maximizes network traffic for all users and allows parallel transmissions.
- **Blocking**. Short messages from different users can be combined into a single block for transmission to minimize network protocol overhead.
- **Synchronization.** The sender should not be transmitting faster than the receiver can receive.
- **Prioritizing**. Priorities should be assignable to messages, both statically such as all alarms or alerts, or dynamically according to message content, sender, or receiver.
- **Peak-traffic management**. The network needs to be able to manage those times when traffic actually exceeds network throughput to prevent deadlock and optimize network performance in these situations.
- **Error handling**. The network must be able to detect errors, including redundant data, correct errors through either retransmission, possibly over a different route, or error-correction codes, and recover from errors.

5.1   Definitions

Some definitions are necessary before we begin.

5.1.1   LAN, MAN, WAN

A local area network (LAN) supports communication between nodes that are a relatively short distance away from each other—usually under six miles, and usually limited to a single building or a group of buildings that are close together.

A metropolitan area network (MAN) operates within a city or a facility that resembles those normally found within a city, supporting distances of 1 to 50 miles.

A wide area network (WAN) connects users that are widely dispersed geographically; these distances are measured in hundreds and thousands of miles. WANs usually use public switched communication facilities such as satellites, microwave dishes, and spread-spectrum radio transmissions, to name just a few.

5.1.2   Bandwidth

Bandwidth is the capacity of a communications channel. It is measured in cycles per second: bits per second (bps) for a digital channel and hertz for an analog channel. The actual bandwidth is the difference between the lowest and highest frequencies transmitted.

The amount of bandwidth a channel can carry dictates what kinds of communications can be carried on it. A wideband circuit, for example, can carry one video channel or 1,200 voice telephone channels.

Bandwidth compression is a technique used to reduce the bandwidth needed for a particular transmission; it is usually used in image transmissions such as fax, imaging, or videoconferencing. Bandwidth compression can be used for voice and video as well as data. Any compression done at the sending node must be decompressed at the receiving node, and the routines must be compatible.

Bandwidth allows a network to ask for (and ideally get) additional circuits for a short period of time. Bandwidth on demand is provided only with digital circuits because they are easier to combine; it is usually carved out of an existing T1 circuit.

Fixed-bandwidth services provide point-to-point links at constant rates. T1 consists of twenty-four 64-kbps (kilobits—one thousand bits—per second) channels and can transmit at rates up to 1.544 kbps. E1 consists of 32 channels and can transmit at rates up to 2.048 Mbps (million bits per second). Although the bandwidth is fixed, T1 and E1 channels are often subdivided to suit the needs of a particular business. T1 and E1 channels are leased from a telecommunication service provider or installed through privately owned cable, microwave, or satellite links.

5.1.3   T1 and T3

T1 is a channel that can handle 24 voice or data channels at 64 kbps, giving it a capability of 1.544 Mbps speed. The standard T1 frame is 193 bits long, which includes one synchronization bit. Eight thousand frames are transmitted per second. E1 is the European counterpart to T1 and transmits at 2.048 Mbps.

T3 combines 28 T1 lines giving it a capability of 44 Mbps. T3 requires fiber optic cabling and is sometimes called FT3. It can carry 672 voice or data channels at 64 kbps.

5.1.4   10Base-T, 100Base-T, 100VG-Anylan

10Base-T is today's common standard for local area network transmission (10 megabit-per-second rates). It is an Ethernet local area network which works on twisted pair wiring that looks and feels remarkably like telephone cabling because 10Base-T was invented to run on telephone cable. 10Base-T cards for micros typically cost the same as those for Ethernet running on coaxial cable.

With 10Base-T, if a machine crashes, it doesn't bring down the whole network, unlike the case with coax Ethernet LANs, which are typically one long line, looping from one machine to another. In addition, a 10Base-T Ethernet network is easier to manage because the 10Base-T hubs often come with sophisticated management software.

100Base-T is a proposed standard for a 100-megabit-per-second local area network. 100Base-T would be completely compatible with today's 10Base-T networks, but would be ten times faster. 100Base-T is becoming the de facto Fast Ethernet standard.

100VG-Anylan, a proposal from AT&T and Hewlett-Packard, is a competing standard for 100-megabit-per-second networks. It uses all four pairs in a twisted pair wiring scheme to transmit or receive instead of just the two used in today's systems.

These networking standards are discussed in Sec. 5.10.6, "Fast Ethernet."

5.1.5   Connection-oriented and connectionless

The services provided for the exchange of data between two nodes in a network can be connectionless or connection-oriented, depending on whether a logic link is established or not.

Connection-oriented

Connection-oriented protocols provide a reliable two-way connection service during a session. These protocols are also called session-based protocols, virtual circuits, and sequenced packet exchanges.

Each packet that is exchanged during a session is given a unique sequence number. This number is used to track the packet and allows it to be uniquely acknowledged. Duplicate packets are detected and discarded by the session services.

A logical link is established prior to any exchange of user data. The services provided include sequence of delivery and error detection and correction.

Connection-oriented services provide reliable end-to-end service that is capable of supporting high traffic rates with minimal impact on the processing capacities of the individual devices being served. This type of protocol is used by the TCP portion of TCP/IP and X.25.

Connectionless

In a connectionless service, frames are transmitted with source and destination addresses, but the establishment of a logical link is not required. This service, also called datagram service, does not acknowledge frames or provide error recovery procedures. Since no link is made, and therefore no session actually exists, there are no guarantees that the frames that are sent will be received by the destination. For this reason, connectionless services send acknowledgments to senders to indicate that the data arrived.

The higher layers of the stack must provide recovery and frame sequencing. Consequently, this capability must reside on the nodes.

The Internet protocol (IP) of TCP/IP is an example of a connectionless protocol.

5.1.6   Types of switching

There are four types of switching.

- **Circuit switching** sets up a temporary connection of two or more communication channels. Users have full use of the circuit until the connection is terminated. Circuit switching is used by telephone companies for voice networks to guarantee steady, consistent service for people engaged in telephone conversation.
- **Packet switching** breaks the message into smaller packets for transmission. All packets contain address information. Individual packets are sent along the path that is most expedient at that moment, which means that the packets of a single message do not necessarily travel over the same path, or arrive at the same time, or arrive in order. The packets are reassembled in proper sequence (using the address information), ideally at the last switching node, before they actually arrive at their destination.
- **Message switching** sends a message to a holding area, where it is picked up by the receiving station. The message is received by the storage area in one block, stored as one block, and picked up as one block. This is usually referred to as store-forward.
- **Cell switching**, used by ATM, combines the efficiency of packet switching with the guaranteed bandwidth of circuit switching.

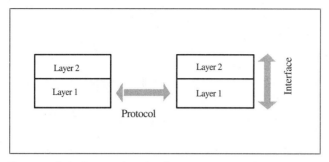

Figure 5.1 Interfaces and protocols

Packet switching is the form of data transmission most commonly used in LANs, WANs, and MANs. Packets are dynamically routed over the network as circuits become available. A message can be broadcast to many recipients. Packet switching also handles messages of different lengths and priorities.

The international standard for packet-switching networks is X.25, which was defined when all circuits were analog. Newer technologies such as Frame Relay and ATM use today's almost-error-free digital lines. Public packet-switching networks may provide value-added services, such as protocol conversion and electronic mail.

5.2   Layers, Interfaces, and Protocols

A network architecture defines the protocols, message formats, and standards used within that architecture. Products created within this network architecture (or that support it) are compatible.

The more robust network architectures use a layered structure, also referred to as a stack. Each *layer* consists of entities that are hardware components and/or software processes. The rules and formats for communications between adjacent layers are collectively called the *interface*.

Protocols are the rules and formats for communications within the same layer across different devices. Protocols include formats, the order of the data exchange, and any actions to be taken on the transmission and receipt of data. Figure 5.1 shows the differences between protocols and interfaces.

If two stations transmit at exactly the same time, they destroy each other's transmissions. Protocols are used to prevent this by providing rules for transmissions.

By using a layered structure, protocol changes can be made without affecting the other protocols (functions) in the stack (the protocols for all the layers). Each layer needs to be aware only of the services provided by the layer directly below it. Hardware and software from the same or different vendors can communicate as long as the same protocols and data formats are used.

5.2.1   Types of protocols

There are two types of protocols.

- A **transport protocol** prepares the message for transport and forwards it to another network node.
- A **service protocol** defines the format and meaning of messages before they are readied for transport.

Each network operating system has its preferred transport protocols. NetWare uses IPX, LAN Manager uses NetBEU, and UNIX usually uses the IP protocol of TCP/IP. A DOS system usually manages stacks of transport protocols as terminate-and-stay resident modules.

Network operating systems also have their preferred service protocols. UNIX uses the Network File System. NetWare uses NetWare Core Protocol. LAN Manager (and OS/2 Warp) uses the Service Message Block protocol.

5.3   Major Client/Server Protocols

The transport stacking protocols, such as TCP/IP, NetBIOS, IPX/SPX, AppleTalk, OSI, and SNA/APPN, provide reliable end-to-end communication across WANs and LANs, using routers, bridges, and hardware gateways to move the messages across the networks.

Communication software breaks down these complex protocols into layers. Each layer builds on the services provided by the layers below it. Because these layers are stacked, the name given to this type of protocol is transport stacking.

At each layer, both nodes cooperate to provide a service, even though only one node does all the actual work. The protocol is the set of rules the two nodes use to provide the service: how the work is divided, how messages are exchanged, and what the handshake sequences are.

An interface, also called a service interface, specifies how a layer obtains services from the layer directly beneath it. The services become more abstract in the higher layers as they become more application-oriented and less hardware-oriented.

In theory, each layer in the stack would have its own set of APIs and protocols so that organizations could mix-and-match vendor offerings. We aren't there yet.

The lowest layer belongs to the device drivers that interface to communications hardware adapters. The highest layer sits below the network operating system.

Stacking protocols are usually compared to the OSI model, which is covered in the next section. Not all stacking protocols cover all the OSI layers. SNA and IPX/SPX do. NetBIOS does not provide a network layer. TCP/IP does not support a link layer and depends on sockets for its sessions. Named Pipes has developed into a peer-to-peer protocol that sits on top of other protocols such as NetBEUI and IPX/SPX as an interface layer.

5.3.1   OSI model

The Reference Model of Open Systems Interconnection (OSI) is one of the most popular models for networks. It is not an actual product; it represents the published standards for a common network model. Developed by the International Standards Organization (ISO), this seven-layer model, illustrated in Fig. 5.2, covers all aspects of networking, from the physical wiring to sophisticated application support. The Layer 1 functions in one machine interact with Layer 1 functions in the connecting machine, the Layer 2 functions interacts with Layer 2 functions, and so on.

The lowest level is the **Physical layer**, which specifies the hardware and software necessary to place the data bits in the communication channel and transport them to their destination. This link is concerned with the physical transmission of signals. It does not provide data recognition services.

The second layer, the **Data Link layer**, is concerned with error-free transmissions and shields the upper layers from details concerning the physical transmission. This layer performs the following services:

- Data link activation and deactivation
- Transportation of data between data links
- Data link sharing
- Data link error detection, notification, and recovery
- Transparent data flow

The Data Link address, known as the local address, is used for send and

Layer		Function
7	Application	Support for application programs
6	Presentation	Code and format translations
5	Session	Dialogue management between users
4	Transport	Quality control of packet transmissions
3	Network	Internetwork routing
2	Data Link	Creation of frames
1	Physical	Transmission of signals

Figure 5.2 Open Systems Interconnection (OSI) model

receive identification. This address is used by network bridges to pass frames (blocks of data) between segments in a LAN.

The functions of these first two layers are performed by the hardware components of the network. The software on the adapter card in the micro takes the data and turns it into network-compliant packets. The transceiver located on the adapter card listens to the LAN and copies any packets addressed to it.

The Physical and Data Link layers are also addressed by the standards outlined in the Institute for Electrical and Electronic Engineers (IEEE) Project 802. IEEE also proposes a Physical layer but divides the Data Link layer into two sublayers. The Media Access Control sublayer interfaces with the Physical layer protocols. The Logical Link Control sublayer creates a logical data link between the sender and the receiver.

The functions of the layers above the Data Link layer are handled by software. The **Network layer** (Layer 3) establishes, maintains, and terminates the network connection between two users and transfers messages and data over that connection. Its services are included in X.25, the international standard for packet-switching data networks from CCITT (Consultative Committee on International Telephone and Telegraph). These services include:

- Network addressing
- Blocking and segmenting message units
- Sequencing data units
- Switching and routing
- Controlling local flow
- Controlling congestion
- Error detection, notification, and recovery

The fourth layer, the **Transport layer**, corrects all failures that occur at the Network layer and provides control functions between the user nodes. It takes packets of data from the Network layer and assembles them into messages.

The **Session layer** (Layer 5) creates, manages, and terminates the dialogues between the users. IBM's Advanced Program-to-Program Communication using Logical Unit type 6.2 (APPC/LU6.2) was used to develop the standards for this layer. Its services include:

- Session initiation and activation
- Session termination and release
- Dialogue control
- Synchronization and resynchronization of the session connections
- Normal and expedited data transfer

The **Presentation layer**, Layer 6, handles network security, character-code translations, and format translations. This sixth layer also creates pipes, which are areas of memory used for transferring data from one place to another.

The **Application layer** contains utilities that support application programs. This top layer does not include applications. It provides services that are not provided elsewhere in the model. The layer consists of three parts:

- **Common application services**. These services, which can be used by all communicating parties, provide control protocols for commitment, concurrence, and recovery and conversion protocols for specifying the type and structure of conversions between user nodes.
- **Specific application services**. These are the protocols for user information exchanges, such as private standards or internationally recognized communication standards.
- **User element**. If the user element (the user presentation) is defined, a user interface above this layer is not needed.

It is important to know which layer(s) network software handles. As illustrated in Fig. 5.3, Ethernet and Token Ring, for example, handle the Physical and Data Link layers. NetBIOS and APPC/LU6.2 are IBM protocols for the Network, Transport, and Session layers.

Application	Network services such as print services and data-base services
Presentation	
Session	LAN Support Programs such as NetBIOS and APPC/LU6.2
Transport	
Network	
Data Link	Logical Link Control
	Media Access Control
Physical	Ethernet, Token Ring

Figure 5.3 Comparison of network software

5.3.2   TCP/IP

Transmission Control Protocol/Internet Protocol (TCP/IP) was designed to allow military research laboratories to communicate if a land war broke out. Independent of any one vendor's hardware, TCP/IP lays out the rules for the transmission of datagrams (transmission units) across a network. It supports end-to-end acknowledgment between the source and destination of the message, even if they reside on separate networks. TCP/IP is used by the Internet, a large internetwork that connects major research organizations; universities; and government agencies.

As illustrated in Fig. 5.4, TCP/IP is a four-layer architecture that is built on a physical network interface, and that specifies conventions for communications and network interconnection and traffic routing. It allows networks to communicate by assigning unique addresses to each network. Nodes in different networks can have common names. Think of each network as a state and each node as a city. Two cities can have the same name as long as they are in different states. But to find the right city, you need to know which state it's in.

The internet protocol (IP) layer deals with delivery of data packets. It provides packet processing rules, identifies conditions for discarding packets, and controls error detection and error message generation.

Data delivery, concurrency, and sequencing are handled by the transmission control protocol (TCP) layer. TCP also handles connection to applications on other systems, error checking, and retransmission. TCP uses connections between two points, not individual end points, as its fundamental concept.

TCP/IP uses a three-way handshake to ensure synchronization between two end points. The requestor sends a synchronized signal and an initial sequence number to the destination end point. The receiver receives the synchronized signal and sends back acknowledgment, sequence number, and synchronization signals. On receiving these signals, the requester sends the acknowledgment back to the receiver. This handshake is necessary to ensure that messages are not lost, duplicated, or delayed.

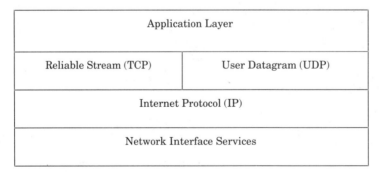

Figure 5.4 TCP/IP's architecture

IPng (IP next generation)

As the Internet explodes in popularity, the IP portion of TCP/IP, which deals with addressing, is approaching its limits. The 32-bit address size of the current version of IP, Version 4.0, also called IPv4, simply cannot provide enough name spaces to handle probable demand past, say, the year 2015. In addition, the routing tables are becoming too bulky to be of quick use. IPv4 will soon evolve to IPng (which stands for IP next generation), which needs to be deployed some time between 1999 and 2003 to prevent addressing and routing breakdowns.

To ready themselves for this demand, in late 1991 the Internet Society's Internet Architecture Board began crafting the next generation of the Internet Protocol. IPng had as its goal the connection of 1 quadrillion computers (10 to the 15th power) networks. Ultimately, three proposals hit the Internet Engineering Task Force's table in 1994 which blended them all together into Ipng and then renamed it IPv6. (I don't know what happened to Version 5!)

IPv6 will include a variety of enhancements, including simplified header format, quality-of-service capabilities, and expanded addressing routing. Security measures will be mandated in IPv6. Both authentication and privacy will be implemented as extensions to the main IP header.

Another important feature of IPv6 is its support for an expanded number of network addresses. Address space is expanded to 128 bits. IPv6 will also allow providers to offer different grades of services as well as support for real-time delivery of video and audio traffic.

To minimize the impact of the Internet explosion while work was being done on IPng, the IETF developed a new technology to reduce the size of routing tables, called Classless Interdomain Routing (CIDR, pronounced "cider"). It reduces routing table growth by having routers advertise groups of routes to networks rather than every individual route. This aggregation can be carried to higher and higher levels: Once routers advertise the collections of routes they "know," the next level up in the routing hierarchy also can advertise aggregations of routes. Internet service providers could aggregate their subscriber networks behind a single routing table entry, shrinking the routing table even farther.

It will be some time before IPv6 is ready for general use. Protocols that are to become Internet standards go through a series of maturity levels: proposed standard, draft standard, and standard. Each level calls for increased scrutiny and testing.

In mid-1996, all of the main components of the new protocol had been agreed upon, and router vendors had begun to develop software to accommodate the new standard. For the system manager who uses TCP/IP as a part of the enterprise network, several changes are in store as a result of the transition. The transition to the new standards will be aided by tools that help network managers renumber their networks, automatically configure the IP addresses of hosts throughout a network, tunnel IPv4 traffic through IPng links, and support dual-layer TCP/IP networks.

The ability of IPv4 (the current version) hosts to communicate with IPng hosts will be critical to the success of Ipng. There is also growing concern that Ipv6 will not be the answer to the addressing problem. IETF is already working on IPv8 and there is even talk of an IPv10.

TCP/IP Addresses

An internet protocol address is 32 bits long, divided into a network number and node number, and looks something like 140.170.42.65. In contrast, Domain Name Service (DNS) addresses are user-friendly, for example, DLTDewire@aol.com.

The number of bits assigned to the network node components is determined by the address class, and by the upper three bits of the IP address. For example, a class C address with high bits of 110 uses 24 bits for its network number and 8 bits for each node number. IP network addresses are assigned by a central authority (Network Information Center); administration of node numbers is done locally.

TCP/IP also requires configuration of the host computer. A TCP/IP host machine needs to know its own host name, the name of its network domain, the subnet mask for its network, the IP addresses of any gateways (necessary for communicating with other networks), and the IP addresses to DNS servers to resolve names to IP addressees.

Configuring TCP/IP means going to each local machine and entering this information into local files on each system. This is not too burdensome if the network consists of only a few dozen nodes, but it is overwhelming if the network consists of thousands of nodes.

To help manage and assign IP addresses, two protocols were developed in the mid-1980s: Reverse Address Resolution Protocol (RARP) and the Bootstrap Protocol (BOOTP). IETF established the Dynamic Host Configuration (DHC) working group in 1989 to develop techniques for configuring hosts dynamically. Their proposal Dynamic Host Configuration Protocol (DHCP) builds on the existing BOOTP protocol and supports all BOOTP vendor extensions. These three assignment methodologies are discussed in Sec. 13.1, "Assigning Network Addresses."

5.3.3   SNA model

Systems Network Architecture (SNA) from IBM uses a seven-layer architecture similar to the OSI model, although there is not a one-to-one correspondence between the layers, as illustrated in Fig. 5.5. SNA, a mature product, was built as an open-ended architecture to accommodate newer technologies This has allowed SNA to support such technologies as fiber optics, digitized voice, and distributed systems. SNA allows users in one

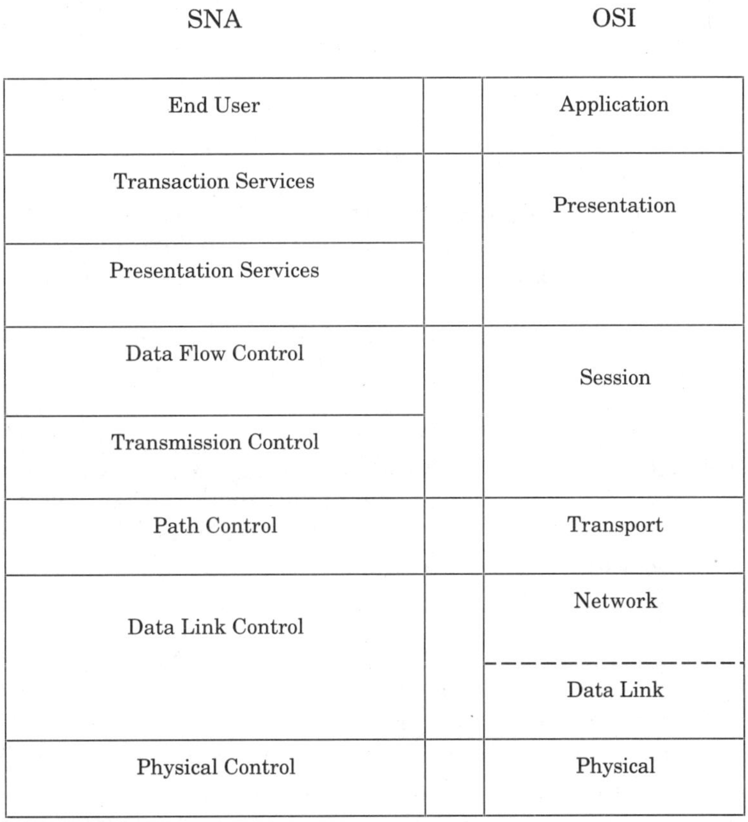

SNA   OSI

SNA		OSI
End User		Application
Transaction Services		Presentation
Presentation Services		
Data Flow Control		Session
Transmission Control		
Path Control		Transport
Data Link Control		Network
		Data Link
Physical Control		Physical

Figure 5.5 Systems Network Architecture (SNA)

SNA network to transparently access data and programs in other SNA networks by using SNA gateways. SNA provides resource sharing and includes reliability features such as alternative routing and backup host. Security is provided through logon routines and encryption facilities.

SNA is designed to provide networking facilities for IBM systems only. The OSI model can support homogeneous or heterogeneous networks. Recognizing the importance of OSI compliance, IBM has been reevaluating the possibility of developing gateways from SNA to OSI-compliant architectures.

5.3.4 APPC and APPN

Advanced Program-to-Program Communication (APPC) is part of IBM's SNA and permits peer communications between distributed processing programs running on different machines. APPC is based on SNA LU6.2 and is a set of protocols used by applications on different processors to communicate with each other as peers in executing a distributed transaction.

In order to communicate via APPC, a program must identify itself to the local SNA network management facility as a transaction program (TP). The SNA network management facility assigns the program a unique TP ID. Each TP accesses the SNA network via a SNA software socket, referred to as a logical unit. A TP issues APPC calls to its local logical unit in order to communicate with a partner logical unit. This communication requires the allocation of a conversation between the two logical units over an SNA session. Multiple conversations, usually short in duration, can serially share the same session.

APPC conversations use a half-duplex flip-flop protocol based on send and receive states. At any given time in the conversation, one partner should be in send state and the other in receive state. Invalid-state problems are avoided by using a simple send request/receive request protocol.

APPC itself supports OS/2 Named Pipes, and workstations use the APPC connectivity in the OS/2 communications server, keeping memory requirements on the DOS workstations to a minimum. Because APPC is used to communicate with most IBM platforms, micros can access data and facilities throughout an organization without the users' knowing or caring what platforms are being accessed.

APPN (Advanced Peer-to-Peer Network) from IBM focuses on integrating IBM's larger systems into an enterprise network. First introduced in 1986 for IBM's AS/400 midrange line, APPN has been adapted to other IBM platforms such as OS/2 and, to some, is a possible successor to TCP/IP.

APPN spans the Network and Transport layers of the OSI stack. It sets up client and server sessions and dynamically routes data through the network. Network nodes maintain tables of all resources and keep maps of the network topology.

When an end node needs to locate a network resource, it contacts the nearest network node, which checks its resource database for a location. If the requested resource is not in its resource database, the network node broadcasts a location request. Once a location has been found or provided, the originating network node checks the topology, chooses a route, and transmits the message.

5.3.5   IPX/SPX

IPX/SPX is NetWare's native stack. It is an implementation of the Xerox Network Services (XNS) transport and network protocol. Banyan VINES is also an adaptation of XNS but uses a TCP/IP-like addressing scheme.

The network layer is provided by the Internet Packet Exchange (IPX) protocol. This is a connectionless protocol which has no delivery guarantees. As such, it is used by network applications as the foundation protocol for sending and receiving low-overhead datagrams over the network.

The transport layer is provided by the Sequenced Packet Exchange (SPX) protocol, which provides a reliable connection-oriented service over the connectionless IPX. SPX builds a reliable protocol service on top of IPX.

5.3.6   Named Pipes

Named Pipes is OS/2's local interprocess communication mechanism. Named Pipes runs on NetBIOS, IPX/SPX, and TCP/IP stacks.

Using Named Pipes, processes can exchange data as if they were writing to or reading from a sequential file. A server application can set up a pipeline whose receiving end can exchange data with several client processes. Named Pipes handles the scheduling and synchronization issues.

Named Pipes uses a conversational communication technique. The communication requires a dedicated logical connection between partners as well as the identification of each partner by the other. Pipes may support one or several concurrent transport mechanisms. The details of the transport mechanism are hidden from a user and the pipes impose minimal protocol and format restrictions on users. Pipes also provide facilities for marking the boundaries of discrete messages, determining the identity of the sender, and performing verification of the receipt of a message.

5.3.7   NetBIOS

Network Basic Input/Output Operating System (NetBIOS) was developed in 1984 as an interface between the LAN hardware, in those days the network interface card implementing Ethernet or Token Ring, and DOS. Until the release of DOS 3.1, NetBIOS was the only option.

NetBIOS provides the following functions:

- Supports communication at the session layer for users on the LAN
- Sends and receives broadcast information to and from network nodes
- Supports the establishment of multiple user names within one node which is a Session layer function
- Interfaces with the network interface card and performs basic control and management functions

NetBEUI is the transport layer driver used by Microsoft LAN products (LAN Manager, Windows for Workgroups, and Windows NT). NetBEUI (NetBIOS Extended User Interface), an enhanced version of the original NetBIOS protocol, provides datagram and connection-oriented services and also offers a dynamic naming service. NetBEUI's weaknesses are a lack of security and lack of a network layer.

5.3.8   AppleTalk and Open Transport

Macintoshes have always been extremely friendly as AppleTalk network clients. And they have been extremely unfriendly when running other protocols. Apple's Open Transport ushers in the next generation of Macintosh networking architecture, boasting not only easier configuration and administration (there is even support for dynanmic HCP addressing) but native PowerPC performance, more flexible protocol configurations, and standardized APIs.

In addition, Apple made great efforts to allow backward compatibility. APIs for the older network functions are still there, but only to aid migration to the new Open Transport architecture. For instance, current TCP/IP applications still work, even without Open Transport support, because the MacTCP APIs are still available. You can also still use MacIPX.

For the first release, Open Transport is bundled with Power Macintosh 9500 models. This helps Apple release these new Macintoshes, which sport the Peripheral Component Interconnect (PCI) bus. Open Transport is the only networking architecture for PCI-equipped Macs.

The new Open Transport networking service will replace AppleTalk-centric networking services by including a wider variety of network protocols, including AppleTalk, Novell IPX, and TCP/IP. Open Transport will also handle interactions between programs and the network protocol, so that developers won't have to support every protocol and users won't have to worry about installing the right one.

This architecture also embraces many other industry standards, such as STREAMS and the XTI interface. STREAMS is a method used by UNIX to get data from the application to the network. XTI is an open, standardized API to access network services. Developers can expect to write network-based applications, using any protocol, with the same ease with which they can write any TCP/IP-based UNIX program.

Configuring the Open Transport protocol is straightforward and offers help. There are three levels of configuration, beginner, advanced and administrator. Beginner level asks for some simple information, such as IP address, router, and DNS server, and assumes default for other fields. Advanced level allows the user to configure all fields, including subnet mask and others. Administrator mode lets the user set a password and lock portions of the configurations.

Static addresses can be used which can help administrators locate problem machines easily, using AppleTalk node addresses instead of MAC addresses. Locating problem machines using MAC addresses can be difficult across routers. Dynamic addresses will still be the norm, but the static option is there.

And if there isn't a feature your organization needs, just wait a bit. Apple is already working on what promises to be a total revamping of the Mac OS, dubbed Gershwin. An interm release of System 7 (the current version) code name Harmony is expected to be released by first quarter 1997. The interm release will include some of the functionality planned for System 8, code name Copland. Copland is expected to be released by the middle of 1997.

Gershwin, Copland's successor, will add Windows 95-like preemptive multitasking for applications themselves. Gershwin is due in 1997.

5.4   Local Area Networks

Currently LANs can support data transmission rates of 1 to 100 Mbps as a result of advances in physical transmission and fiber-optic technologies. Each workstation on the LAN must be able to handle the communications. The links in the LAN (workstations and servers) are connected with twisted pair, coaxial cable, and/or fiber optics. Many LANs use twisted pair cabling from the desktop to the wall "plug" and coaxial or fiber optics from there.

Transmissions are either broadband or baseband. Baseband transmission uses discrete (digital) signals to carry information. Repeaters are usually placed along the route of the signal to overcome deterioration since as the signal travels along a channel it gets weaker. This is the most common type of LAN transmission.

Broadband transmission uses nondiscrete (analog) signals. The information is converted to analog waves using amplitude, frequency, or phase modulation of the original signal. This conversion is done by modems at the sending and receiving nodes. The difference between the highest and lowest frequencies that can be carried over the channel indicates the channel's capacity, which is referred to as its bandwidth.

Local area networks allow a group of users to communicate and share data and other resources. For users of different LANs to communicate, the LANs themselves must be interconnected, using the devices discussed in Sec. 5.7, "Network Hardware." LANs can be interconnected directly or through MANs and WANs.

5.5   Enterprise-wide Networks

When an organization connects LANs and WANs, it begins to provide connectivity for the entire enterprise. LAN/WAN connections can be fixed-bandwidth, such as T1 and T3, or bandwidth-on-demand, such as Frame Relay and ATM. Fixed-bandwidth provides point-to-point communication at a fixed speed. Bandwidth-on-demand allows an application to feed data to the network at its desired speed. The first bandwidth-on-demand implementation was Integrated Services Digital Network (ISDN).

5.6   Virtual Networks

A virtual LAN (VLAN) uses software to create logical networks out of the physical infrastructure and provide all the benefits of physical segmentation on the logical network segments. These software-defined groups of nodes communicate as if they were on the same LAN segment, even though they are distributed across different segments of the network. Packets sent between stations in the VLAN are switched only between ports within the same VLAN, thus reducing traffic and congestion on the network. VLAN functionality is embedded in LAN switches so Ethernet, token ring, FDDI, or ATM switching must be used in order to implement a VLAN.

VLANs are attractive because they remove the physical constraints of networking and more closely resemble the way organizations are now structured. Any group, no matter how physically dispersed, can maintain its group identity. And since changes in the configuration mean changing a software switch, administrative costs when employees move or change groups are greatly reduced. VLANs also offer better security than more traditional topologies because of the microsegmentation of the network. Microsegmenting reduces the network to small pieces, making security control easier by allowing organizations to build firewalls to protect the network.

VLANs support easier management of network traffic and alteration of the network configuration. VLANs address the administrative expense of client moves, adds, and changes by automating many of the configuration tasks and placing management control of these changes centrally. No longer does an organization have to recable or do hub reconfigurations. When a user moves, the network address remains the same, and if a user joins a different workgroup, the network address is reassigned to the new VLAN by changing the user's subnet address.

Two years ago, only a handful of LAN switch vendors offered VLAN capability. Today there are more than 15, and the number is growing. But the lack of VLAN standards means that each vendor has implemented its own VLAN concept. Vendors are working toward standards for VLANs, but those standards are not expected until 1998.

VLAN implementations use either OSI Layer 2 information (the Data Link layer) or Layer 3 information (the Network layer). Layer 2 VLANs are simpler to design and administer, although moving users may require physical reconnection to a LAN switch. Layer 3 VLANs allow network managers to segment a large network into VLANs, and different VLANs can be defined for different protocol groups. However, Layer 3 VLANs require more processing in the switch.

However, standardization is becoming a key issue for VLANs. LAN emulation provides a standards-based transport mechanism for transporting virtual LANs from existing LANs to ATM. There is no standard for transporting VLANs across shared LANs such as FDDI. Most vendors use proprietary encapsulation schemes, which locks the user into a single vendor.

Management tools for virtual LANs have been slow in coming. When there are VLAN standards and management tools for VLANs in the marketplace, VLANs will become a strategic option for most organizations.

5.7   Network Hardware

LAN hardware includes the actual cabling and the infrastructure—the internetwork connections. Servers must be able to access other servers, and users must be able to access information anywhere in the network. In client/server environments, servers send fewer packets per request than in other environments because only the results of requests are sent back to the client. However, this may not ultimately decrease network traffic because client/server environments usually support more users than mainframe-oriented networks.

There are seven ways to interconnect LANs:

- Repeaters
- Bridges
- Routers
- Network hardware gateways
- Intelligent hubs
- LAN switching hubs
- Backbone networks

The methods are listed in order of increasing functionality. Backbone networks are connecting networks, not pieces of hardware that connect networks. The characteristics of the LANs to be connected determine which device should be used, as illustrated in Fig. 5.6. OSI levels referred to in the figure were discussed in Sec. 5.3.1, "OSI model."

If the physical characteristics of the LANs are the same—the same hardware and software transporting bits between nodes—a repeater can be used. If the implementations of the Physical layer are different but the Data Link layers and those layers above them are the same, a bridge can be used. If the implementations of the first two layers of the LANs are different but the software used to handle the upper layers is the same, a router can be used. If the LANs use totally different implementations, a gateway must be used.

5.7.1   Repeaters

As a signal travels along a cable, it loses strength. If communicating stations

	Repeater	Bridge	Router	Network Gateway
Physical characteristics (OSI Layer 1)	Same	Different	Different	Different
Access and transmission control (OSI Layer 2)	Same	Same	Different	Different
Other functions (OSI Layers 307)	Same	Same	Same	Different

Figure 5.6 Comparison of network hardware

are at great distances from one another, repeaters can be used to restore the signal to its original strength. A repeater can also be used to extend the reach of a LAN.

Repeaters can be used only when the LANs on both sides of the repeater are identical. They must have the same physical transmission characteristics and use the same protocols.

5.7.2   Bridges

Bridges are used to connect LANs with different physical transmission characteristics and protocols. For example, a third-party bridge might be used to link multiple Ethernet LANs, each supplied by a different manufacturer. Bridges temporarily store messages forwarded to another network in case retransmission is required. However, they do not handle large amounts of broadcast packets very well. A bridged network is illustrated in Fig. 5.7.

Bridges are a simpler technology than routers. Bridges are devices that use Data Link layer routing information and physical addresses to connect LANs. Bridges pass frames from one segment of the LAN to another based on the MAC addresses of the sender and receiver network interface cards.

All addresses, even across networks, must be unique and of the same format because bridges do not convert addresses. There can be only one route to each station because a bridge does not make routing decisions. Bridges use a fixed path scheme and cannot reroute traffic if a node is down.

Bridges do not have to be configured. The forwarding database of a bridge

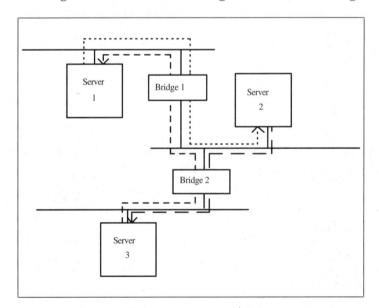

Figure 5.7 Bridged network

is built and maintained automatically. Since routers base their decisions on a higher-level addressing scheme, they are more flexible than bridges. However, they are more difficult to configure because they require specification of selected protocols, network addresses, interfaces, and management facilities.

Protocols that do not support internetworking, such as NetBIOS, must be bridged.

Routers make efficient use of all available links in the internet by using them concurrently. Bridges depend on the IEEE 802 Spanning Tree protocol to manage redundant links and paths.

Bridge traffic must be monitored for heavy load periods, called choking. Additional network processing or additional server hardware may be required to rectify the situation.

Bridges used to be faster than routers. Because of 32-bit CPUs, higher-speed buses, and software performance improvements, routers are now as fast as or faster than bridges.

5.7.3   Routers

A router is a hardware device that manages the route selection for data packets to minimize traffic loads on linked LANs. Routers link logically separate LANs, permitting them to share traffic loads and prevent the choking that occurs in bridged LANs. Multiprotocol routers segment the network, access WANs, support diverse protocols, provide better routing capabilities, provide high network performance, and control the network.

Routers use protocol-dependent routing information to interconnect LANs, or two different networks. Routers create and maintain dynamic routing tables of the end nodes they are aware of. Routers can redirect traffic when a node is down. Each network may have been implemented independently and so may include stations with the same address. If a LAN message is intended for another network, the router accepts it. Each individual router understands the entire internet's topology. After a router determines the best route for a message, the message is passed along with two additional addresses, the address of the next node along the route and the address of the final route.

Routers are typically used with protocols such as TCP/IP, IPX/SPX, APPN, XNS, AppleTalk, and OSI. Router products from IBM, Digital, Bay Networks, Inc., Cabletron Systems, Inc., Cisco Systems, Inc., and Proteon, Inc. can encapsulate IPX/SPX, NetBIOS, AppleTalk, and SNA to allow a single protocol to run on a backbone, usually IPX/SPX, APPN, or TCP/IP.

External routers require a micro, two or more network interface cards, and router software. They support a local interface, remote interfaces, and protocols; and can handle concurrent communication among different LAN access methods, such as Ethernet, Token Ring, and FDDI. However, only nodes that use the same protocol can be linked. For example, a router can provide communication between a NetWare (IPX) user on an Ethernet LAN and a NetWare (IPX) server on a Token Ring LAN. It cannot provide communication between that NetWare user and a UNIX (TCP/IP) server.

Because routers use the Network layer address (OSI's third layer), they can determine the best internetwork path between any two nodes. "Best" could be determined by the cheapest, the most cost-effective, the least congested, the one with the highest data rate, the one with the least number of hops between end nodes, or a path with some combination of these factors.

The path between routers is decided by interrouter communications protocols. The most popular are the following:

- **Router Information Protocol** (RIP) is a simple, vector-based, hop-count metric (how many jumps from node to node are required). All routers broadcast their entire RIP database across the internet every 60 seconds, whether there are changes or not.
- **Open Shortest Path First** uses a link-state algorithm that allows a router to dynamically monitor the status of each link and broadcast status changes immediately.
- **Interior Gateway Routing Protocol**, developed by router vendor Cisco Systems, Inc., is an enhanced proprietary version of RIP.

The supported network management protocols must also be considered. Most routers support the Simple Network Management Protocol (SNMP) and a management information base (MIB), and provide some MIB extensions. A MIB is a database listing of manageable objects in the internet. Support may also be provided for IBM's NetView and Digital's DECmcc Director.

Routers can usually be managed via SNMP, even in a geographically dispersed internet. A console interface connected to a terminal is used to configure the routers and provide a remote access point for service.

Some routers, such as those from Cisco Systems, NCR Corp., and Proteon support the virtual terminal features of TCP/IP Telenet utilities. Routers from vendors such as Cisco Systems, Proteon, NCR Corp., 3M Corp., and UB Networks (formerly Ungermann-Bass, now a subsidiary of Tandem Computers) also integrate LANs with IBM's SNA protocols (by encapsulating SNA traffic within TCP/IP or other routable packets), and in some cases with NetBIOS and DECnet Phase V protocols as well.

Because each individual router understands the entire internet's topology, a router can automatically pick up a failed device's traffic load, thereby rerouting traffic around the failed router. This network partitioning also means that the separate LANs can still function as local communication paths. A routed internet is more secure than a bridged LAN because a communication device has access to the router's addressing capabilities only when they are needed.

Router reliability is measured in mean time between failures. High-end multiprotocol routers offer redundant power supplies, hot-swappable components, and fault-tolerant bus architectures.

Router performance is typically rated by the same two variables used for bridges: filtering rate and forwarding rate, both measured in packets or frames per second. However, these do not take into account the complex process the router must go through to convert the frames of dissimilar LANs. Each LAN type uses a different frame size and frame structure. A router backplane can support virtually anything thrown at it today. However, LANs operate at a set speed (Ethernet at 10 Mbps, Token Ring at 4 or 16 Mbps, and FDDI at 100 Mbps), regardless of the speed of the interconnecting routers.

Routers come in a variety of chassis sizes and corresponding capabilities. A small chassis has a fixed configuration with one or two interface slots. A medium chassis is modular and has four slots. A large chassis is also modular and has 8, 12, or more slots.

Bridge/routers, which are single devices that can perform both bridge and router functions, are more popular today. Hybrid bridge/router software can handle both functions. If the software cannot identify the protocol for a packet-routing request, it simply bridges the packet.

Because Digital's Local Area Transport and IBM's NetBIOS do not contain routing information, they will not work (as is) with routers. Some router vendors offer bridging or encapsulation options for these protocols, but bridges are simpler to install and maintain and cost less.

Internal bridges included with such LAN operating systems as Banyan VINES, NetWare, and LAN Manager can be used for routing functions. Internal bridges require a network interface card in the file server and must notify the LAN operating system of their existence. Each network interface card in the file server supports a different logical network.

Remote office routers are beginning to appear on the market. These routers can handle a few protocols and perform Frame Relay access device (FRAD) functions. These features allow an organization to take different types of traffic and send them over one Frame Relay network.

The most commonly mentioned advantages and disadvantages of bridges and routers are listed in Fig. 5.8. As is usually the case with competing technologies, some of these points are disputed by advocates of each technology.

The future role of routers hinges on the creation of virtual LANs in switched architectures because they provide the communication between logically defined work groups configured as virtual LANs. They also provide virtual LAN access to shared resources within the network and connect the user to other parts of the network that either are logically segmented using traditional approaches or require access to remote sites across wide area network links.

Advantages
Bridges • Easy to install requiring minimal configuration • Inexpensive with good price performance • Transparent to a variety of high-level protocols • Flexible and transparent to users **Routers** • Support for all topologies • Determine transmission path based on availability • Can perform load-splitting • Provide security through logical segmentation of subnetworks

Disadvantages
Bridges • Cannot handle all network problems and delays • Cannot prevent broadcast protocols from flooding every node • Can preclude some applications from running on the network • Limited functionality, such as no load-splitting • Limited support for fault isolation **Routers** • Protocol-dependent • Slower and more expensive than bridges unless compression software is used • Can be difficult to configure and install • May require additional connecting hardware for protocols that are not routable • Relocation of subnetworks requires the assignment of a new network address

Figure 5.8 Advantages and disadvantages of bridges and routers

5.7.4   Network hardware gateways

Routers can connect networks whose Physical and Data Link layers are different, but whose upper-level layers are the same. Network hardware gateways are used to connect networks that are entirely different.

Hardware gateways are devices that perform translations between protocols. They are used when a backbone can support only one protocol and all other protocols must be translated to it.

Network gateways perform all the conversions necessary to go from one set of protocols to another, including:

■ **Message format conversion**. The gateway converts messages of different formats, sizes, and character codes into those formats, sizes, and codes appropriate for the destination network.

- **Address translation**. The gateway translates the address information to the structure of the destination network.
- **Protocol conversion**. The control information sent with the message must be replaced with the appropriate control information for comparable functions in the destination network.

While network hardware gateways provide great flexibility in connecting networks, they are also the most complex and expensive means of doing so.

5.7.5   Intelligent hubs

An intelligent hub combines the features of a wiring hub, a multiprotocol router, and a network management station. These smart hubs are designed to integrate heterogeneous networks and workstations from multiple vendors. They are based on open and scalable platforms that are physically linked to the smart hub. Smart hubs centralize the support and administrative functions for communication services and increase platform security.

5.7.6   LAN switching hubs

LAN switching provides the ability to replace shared LAN capacity with bigger, dedicated pipes to each desktop. It also eliminates bandwidth bottlenecks in backbone networks. Support for Ethernet, Token Ring, and FDDI networks is currently provided. LAN switching hubs allow an organization to mix and match nodes from different LAN segments to create a virtual LAN. (See Sec. 5.6 for more information about virtual LANs.) Router software is being added to switching hubs, along with the capabilities for remote access, LAN-to-host links, and Token-Ring switching.

Stand-alone hubs are ideal for small networks with few management needs. They're inexpensive and easy to use. You just plug them in and let them run. Chassis-based hubs are a larger commitment. They offer the capability to condense a variety of network devices, such as Ethernet hubs, remote access, and routers, into a single manageable enclosure. But they're pricey and they're more than is needed for small environments.

Stackable hubs are a type of 10BaseT Ethernet hub that can be expanded by daisy chaining additional hubs together. These units are designed to stack vertically. Stackable hubs combine the ease of use and cost-effectiveness of stand-alone units with many of the added features found in the chassis-based solutions, at a much lower price.

LAN switching hubs are scalable. It is the expansion capabilities that attract network managers to intelligent hubs and LAN switching hubs.

5.7.7   Backbone networks

Many organizations are now providing connections between LANs using backbone networks. As illustrated in Fig. 5.9, the users are not attached directly to the backbone network; instead they are attached to a LAN, which is connected to the backbone.

Backbone networks are of a higher quality than the connected LANs and usually use microwave-based links or fiber distributed data interface (FDDI) cabling. Fiber networks can span greater distances than LANs. An FDDI may be run vertically in a building to connect the LANs on each floor. An FDDI could also be used to connect office buildings or buildings on a campus.

A backbone network requires a high bandwidth and the ability to transmit long distances with high reliability (because the network covers such great distances, faults are sometimes difficult to locate and repair). Backbone networks are usually built with leased wideband circuits, such as T1 or T3 links operating at 1.5 and 45 Mbps, respectively.

FDDI uses two counterrotating optical fiber rings, in which two networks actually run on one set of cables. One ring is set up as the primary ring, and the other ring is the backup ring. If the primary ring encounters a problem, the other remains in operation. The backup ring wraps around, isolating the failure, as illustrated in Fig. 5.10.

A backbone network allows the individual LANs to operate in parallel, for optimum processing efficiency and reliability (each LAN can continue to operate no matter what goes down in the rest of the network, including the backbone). The individual LANs are connected to the backbone with a bridge, router, or gateway.

5.8   LAN Access Methods

The two most widely installed local area access methods are Ethernet and token ring.

5.8.1   Ethernet

Ethernet connects up to 1,024 nodes at 10 Mbps over twisted-pair, coax, and

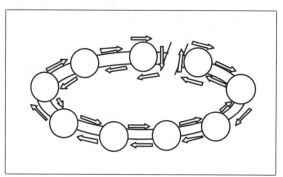

Figure 5.10 Failed FDDI network

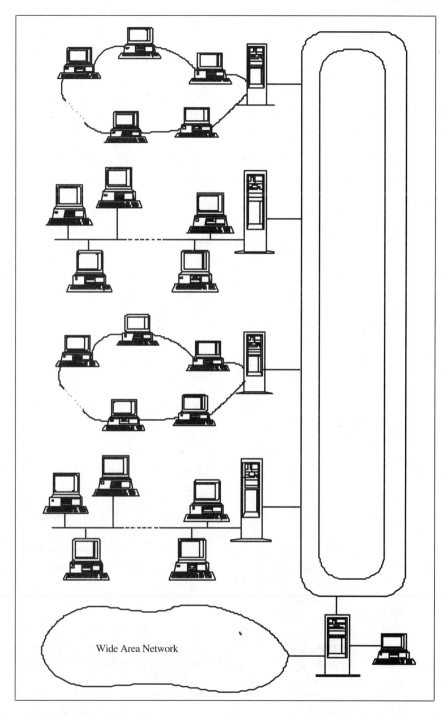

Figure 5.9 Backbone network

optical fiber cabling. Faster Ethernets are emerging: Switched Ethernet gives each user a dedicated 10-Mbps channel, whereas Fast Ethernet runs at 100 Mbps shared.

Ethernet uses the broadcast method of transmission. When a station is ready to send, it transmits its data packets (called frames) onto the network. All stations "hear" the data. The station that matches the destination address in the packet responds to the broadcast; all others ignore it.

Ethernet is a data link protocol and functions at the Data Link and Physical layers of the OSI model (layers 2 and 1). The theoretical limit of Ethernet, measured in 64-byte packets, is 14,800 packets per second. By comparison, the limit of the token ring is 30,000 packets per second and that of FDDI is 170,000.

Ethernet uses CSMA/CD access method and conforms to the IEEE 802.3 standard. CSMA/CD, Carrier Sense Multiple Access with Collision Detection, is a technique for sharing a common medium, such as cabling, among several devices. When two devices attempt to broadcast at the same time (a collision), the node on the network that detects the collision alerts the other nodes by jamming the network. After a pause, the sending nodes each try again.

5.8.2 Token ring

With a token ring system, when a station wishes to transmit, it captures the token and transmits the frame of data onto the ring. This frame is then copied by the receiving station, but it continues to circulate around the ring until it is removed by the transmitting station and checked for verification. The transmitting station then puts the free token back onto the ring for another station to use.

Token ring LANs can be wired as a circle or as a star, with all workstations wired to a central wiring center or to multiple wiring centers. The most common wiring scheme is called a star-wired ring, in which each computer is wired directly to a device called a multistation access unit (MAU). These units are usually grouped together in a wiring closet for convenience. The MAU is wired to create a ring between the computers. If one of the computers is turned off or breaks or if its cable to the MAU is broken, the MAU automatically recreates the ring without that computer. This gives token ring networks great flexibility, reliability, and ease of configuration and maintenance.

Despite the wiring, a token ring LAN always works logically as a circle, with the token passing around the circle from one workstation to another. The advantage of token ring LANs is that problems like broken cables can be fixed easily because they are easy to isolate.

Token ring LANs can operate at transmission rates of either 4 Mbps or 16 Mbps. The number of computers that can be connected to a single token ring

LAN is limited to 256. Large installations connect multiple token ring LANs with bridges.

5.9   Connectivity Services

Connectivity has been defined as the ability of a network operating system to simultaneously communicate over multiple protocols.

The network must support the exchange of information between clients and servers as well as synchronize the actions between two or more components. Semaphones, monitors, or message passing can be used for synchronization.

Connectivity can be connectionless or connection-oriented. Connectionless services handle each message transaction independently. An example is a datagram where the user is not able to respond to the message. Datagram services are used for broadcast messages.

Connection-oriented services maintain a relationship between the sending and receiving nodes and have three phases of operation: establishment, data, and termination. Flows can be unidirectional or bidirectional. Bidirectional implies a return message and the need for synchronization in response to the initial request—the very method used by client/server architectures.

5.10   Client/Server Interconnections

There are a variety of networking systems used to handle the switching on the network.

5.10.1   Frame relay

Frame relay is a high-speed packet switching protocol used in WANs which provides a connection-oriented frame transport service. It has become popular for LAN to LAN connections across distances. Frame relay is faster than traditional X.25 networks because it performs less rigorous error detection. Frame relay was originally viewed as a stopgap technology for organizations waiting for ATM to mature and come down in price.

Frame Relay is an interface standard defined under OSI and ISDN with high-bandwidth potential. It operates at the protocol layer (Layer 2) of OSI; conventional packet switching operates at Layer 3 (the Network layer). Because it operates at a lower layer, it offers fewer services and is therefore faster.

Frame relay provides low-overhead packet switching at speeds of up to 2 Mbps. Frame relay sends variable-length packets. Access to frame relay networks is provided at multiples of 64 kbps or T1/E1 speeds. Frame relay provides cost-effective, high-performance bandwidth-on-demand and can be used to provide point-to-point virtual circuits on networks like ATM. The protocol allocates logical channels to obtain additional bandwidth, allowing users to use variable-rate channels over a fixed-rate T1/E1.

Frame relay is suited for data and image transfer and is very efficient at handling high-speed, bursty data. However, because of its variable-length packet architecture, it is not the most efficient transmission for realtime voice or video.

Frame relay relies on today's high quality phone lines to minimize errors. It does some error checking. If errors occur, the frame causing the errors is discarded; problems are not resolved by the transport software. Error recovery is the responsibility of the end node, not—as is the case with the error control mechanism found in network protocols such as X.25—the intervening network components. By off-loading error recovery to the end points, Frame relay can realize higher performance levels.

5.10.2 SMDS

Switched Multimegabit Data Services (SMDS) provides high-speed cell switching using the same 53-byte cells selected for ATM but emphasizes the transmission of bursty traffic over a short period of time. SMDS looks like a LAN but operates over a wider area. A user buys an access interface to an SMDS network for connection to remote locations.

SMDS uses the public telephone network to connect LANs and WANs, eliminating the need for carrier switches as a call path between two transmitting nodes. SMDS access devices pass 53-byte cells to a carrier switch, which interprets addresses and sends cells over any available path.

Because there is no fixed connection, there is no need to predict traffic flows. Data in an SMDS network can travel over the least congested route.

Both SMDS and frame relay are targeted toward the LAN-to-LAN interconnectivity market.

SMDS works at higher ranges than frame relay, T1/E1 to T3 versus 64 kbps to E1. SMDS is used more by local telephone companies and therefore provides metropolitan coverage rather than the more national coverage provided by frame relay (because it is promoted by the long-distance service providers). SMDS is a connectionless, cell-based service similar to ATM. Frame relay is connection-oriented and is compatible with X.25.

5.10.3 ISDN

Integrated Services Digital Network (ISDN) is designed to carry both voice and data messages on the same line. ISDN is implemented as either two 64-kbps circuit-switched channels or a 116-kbps packet-switched channel.

Many organizations are beginning to see the benefits of an ISDN-to-frame relay protocol. ISDN provides high-speed dial-up capabilities. Frame relay is being used to link their LANs.

ISDN is supported in Windows 95, which means that a Windows 95 system will automatically recognize ISDN hardware—plug-and-play ISDN connections.

A second-generation ISDN standard, known as broadband ISDN or BISDN, uses fiber-optic cables to obtain speeds of 155 Mbps and higher. The bottom three layers of its implementation make up ATM (asynchronous transfer mode), and as ATM begins to win favor, so should BISDN.

5.10.4 FDDI

Fiber Distributed Data Interface (FDDI) uses two counterrotating optical fiber rings, in which two networks actually run on one set of cables. Tokens can travel on either of the two rings and use either of two station connections.

One ring is set up as the primary ring, and the other ring is the backup ring. If the primary ring encounters a problem, the other ring remains in operation. The backup ring wraps around, isolating the failure, as illustrated in Fig. 5.10. This process provides a very reliable system.

Features of FDDI include:

- **High capacity**. The capacity is currently 100 Mbps in each direction for a dual-fiber cable.
- **Minimal signal loss**. A typical segment can extend for several kilometers without requiring a repeater.
- **Low noise**. The light-conducting fiber is virtually unaffected by external magnetic and electrical interference.
- **High security**. It is difficult to tap into an FDDI network without being detected.

FDDI uses a Physical layer protocol that specifies transmission details such as line state and rules for encoding and decoding data. It uses a media access control standard to define the FDDI token rules, packet frame formats, and addressing conventions. A station management feature of FDDI handles monitoring, managing, and configuring the ring and connections.

The most common use of FDDI is as a backbone that connects departmental LANs, wide area networks, large systems, and LAN servers. However, FDDI costs are still high. The prices of the hardware (adapters, concentrators, and hubs, for example) are coming down, but the fiber optic cable is still expensive to buy, install, and maintain.

5.10.5 ATM

Asynchronous transfer mode (ATM) is a sophisticated switched networking system that hosts an active application at each end that can run on WANs, backbone networks, and desktops. Although ATM breaks data into 53-byte "cells," it is not a packet-switched or routed network architecture. For each stream of data that is sent, ATM creates a virtual circuit among two or more points and does this at high speeds (45 to 155 Mbps) with a minimum of delays. Advances in the next few years will see speeds from 1 gigabyte per second (Gbps) to 10 Gbps.

ATM uses fixed-length packets called cells, each of which consists of a header and information fields. The header specifies the path. The fixed cell length minimizes switch delay. Variable-length packets such as those used by X.25 and frame relay are effective for data transmission but increase the complexity of the network switches and create switching delays.

What makes ATM so attractive is the ability to manage bandwidth. ATM adapters can establish multiple connections at a variety of speeds and guarantee applications that bandwidth will continue to be available. Once an ATM circuit is established, the computers at either end can communicate at the agreed-upon speed regardless of how much other traffic comes over the network.

A connectionless protocol would allocate bandwidth dynamically from 1 to 5 Mbps, but current ATM switches do not support this feature. Instead, bandwidth is divvied up as if ATM were a connection-oriented protocol. ATM was designed to carry voice, data, and images, but ATM switches are able to work with only one type of transmission, mostly data.

ATM is more secure than other network options because the communications are point-to-point and eavesdroppers must tap into a fiber backbone—no easy task.

ATM hardware that supports ATM service at the desktop machine is beginning to appear on the market. Using ATM adapters, stackable ATM switches, and the appropriate software 25 Mbps of ATM bandwidth can be delivered at the desktop.

However, the virtual circuit architecture of ATM doesn't work well with the drive-mapping techniques used in today's LANs. ATM-aware applications initiate connections to named resources and computers, not drive letters. ATM switches with LAN emulation can be used to build a transparent bridge between network packets and ATM connections.

One other hurdle in migrating from LANs to ATMs has been the limited number of performance management tools. ATM networks can support dozens to hundreds of traffic routes through a single ATM permanent virtual circuit between two ATM switches. The monitoring system for ATM networks must be able to manage switched virtual circuits and add in debugging packets as well. Network General's ATM Sniffer Network Analyzer can also spot problems on all seven layers of the OSI model as they pertain to traffic over point-to-point ATM connections.

ATM wide area network services are available in only a handful of locations with nationwide service predicted for 1999. In addition, most carrier equipment can support only 45 Mbps, not the promised 155 Mbps for

ATM. LAN emulation must be used to connect Ethernet and token ring networks to an ATM network.

At the other end of the connections, the desktop, IBM is pursuing 25-Mbps ATM links to the desktop.

The other question IT organizations have to ask themselves is whether the promised boost in network performance will offset the expense of implementing an all-ATM approach. They also need to weigh the option of an all-at-once enterprise ATM rollout against an incremental one—which is less painful and still effective. ATM promises to simplify the world, but until it gets there, there is going to be a lot of pain as organizations introduce a whole new technology into their networks.

One stopgap measure is to segment LANs with bridges and routers or upgrade to higher-speed shared-media LAN protocols such as FDDI or Fast Ethernet. Another migration path from shared LANs to switched LANs is through the use of intelligent hubs and the more recently announced switching hubs. These products offer integrated bridging and routing functions for LAN segmentation, full LAN management capabilities, and the ability to move to higher-speed switching, possibly to ATM technologies.

5.10.6   Fast Ethernet

ATM, SMDS, ISDN, and Frame Relay are primarily WAN technologies. Fast Ethernet, a fairly new technology, is aimed at the LAN market. The need for faster transmission support results from the trend toward moving large amounts of data in a single burst, such as desktop published documents, computer-aided designs, images, and multimedia applications. Like regular Ethernet, Fast Ethernet is a shared-media LAN. All nodes share the 100-Mbps bandwidth. (Today's Ethernet runs at 10 Mbps.)

FDDI has offered 100-Mbps speed for several years but was too expensive to support communications at the desktop. Fast Ethernet presently costs about a tenth of an FDDI installation. To upgrade to Fast Ethernet, an organization does have to replace hubs, network interface cards, and drivers with 100-Mbps-capable equipment but should be able to use existing cabling.

Two separate groups are working on specifications for Fast Ethernet.

100Base-T

This specification is an extension of the existing IEEE 802.3 Ethernet standard. This specification is backed by the Fast Ethernet Alliance of 40 companies, such as Intel Corp., 3Com Corp., Sun, and Digital.

100Base-T uses the same access method as Ethernet, CSMA/CD, with some modifications. 100Base-T is completely compatible with today's common 10Base-T. Organizations can use 100Base-T LANs to connect 10Base-T LANs.

100VG-Anylan

This specification builds on products created by IBM, Hewlett-Packard, AT&T, and others. 100VG-Anylan avoids the traffic collision methodology employed by standard Ethernet. While 100Base-T handles only Ethernet traffic, 100VG-Anylan will ultimately handle Ethernet and token ring transmissions.

100VG-Anylan uses all four pairs in the 10Base-T twisted pair wiring scheme to transmit or receive, rather than today's system of using one pair to transmit and one pair to receive. 10Base-T is an Ethernet standard that uses twisted wire pairs (telephone wires).

To provide high speeds over existing cabling, a new protocol was designed. The demand priority protocol is a frame-switching technique that is controlled by the hub. The hub looks at the destination address and provides the connection.

Under CSMA/CD, it is not possible to predict how long a device will wait to send a packet. The demand priority protocol can predict this length if the number of workstations in the network is known. This protocol also provides some built-in security that is not available in CSMA/CD, as well as being able to prioritize traffic, giving time-critical applications high-priority access to the network.

The viability of Fast Ethernet is questionable. Using switched Ethernet, each network node can handle speeds up to 10 Mbps, and each user is given a dedicated 10-Mbps channel on demand. ATM at 25 Mbps will compete with Fast Ethernet and is faster and more scalable. The success of Fast Ethernet will most likely be determined by price—Is it cheap enough?

6

Server and Network Operating Systems

In today's client/server software offerings, it is getting harder and harder to draw hard lines between the servers and the networks. The robust server operating systems of today are also network operating systems in their own right. Thus, this chapter is devoted to operating systems, be they server, network, or hybrid.

6.1 Operating System Requirements for Servers

A server operating system is supposed to serve multiple clients who need to "share" the resources owned by the server. The server waits for client requests, which arrive in the form of messages. Requests arrive as communication sessions, which must be tracked, and integrity must be maintained. Servers should always be available and able to serve client requests regardless of network traffic, and should respond quickly regardless of how many client requests are being served at one time. The server operating system should be able to handle different service priorities. OLTP clients should have a higher priority than a batch job, for example. In addition, a server operating system should be able to run background tasks.

In order to provide all these services server operating systems must include:

- Semaphores
- Interprocess communications
- Multithreading
- Multiprocessing

- Preemptive multitasking
- Intertask protection
- Disk arrays
- Memory subsystems
- Memory management
- Memory protection
- Redundant components
- High-performance file systems

In addition, server operating systems must provide additional services to support network connections and data access.

6.1.1   Semaphores

Server operating systems need to keep concurrent tasks separate when accessing shared resources. To do this, they use semaphores, which are hardware or software flags used to indicate the status of some activity. A message is sent when a file (or segment of a file, depending on the level of lock-out) is opened to prevent other users from opening the same file at that time. Its purpose is to preserve the integrity of data while a user is using it.

It has also evolved into the name given a shared space for interprocess communications (IPC) controlled by "wake up" and "sleep" commands. The source process fills a queue and goes to sleep until the destination process uses the data and tells the source process to wake up.

6.1.2   Interprocess communications

IPCs are used by independent processes to exchange and share data. Server operating systems should support both local and remote IPCs. An application should not be aware that an interprocess call is being made to a remote process over the network. This extension across machine boundaries is key to the flexibility of client/server architecture where resources and processes need to be easily moved across machines.

6.1.3   Multithreading

A thread is the smallest unit of execution that the system can schedule to run—a path of execution through a process. Each thread consists of a stack, an instruction pointer, a priority, the CPU state, and an entry in the system's scheduler list. A thread may be blocked, scheduled to execute, or executing.

Threads communicate by sending messages to each other, and they compete for ownership of various semaphores, which govern the allocation of computing resources among the individual threads. A thread asks the system for an instruction to carry out. If no instruction is ready, the thread is suspended until it has something to do. If an instruction is ready, the thread performs the task and then makes another request to the system for work.

Older operating systems achieve multitasking by creating multiple processes, which creates a great deal of overhead. In a multithreaded environment, a process is broken into independent executable tasks (threads). These threads then collectively perform all the work that a single program could execute, allowing applications to perform many tasks simultaneously. The separate threads complete their tasks in the background and allow continued operation of the primary assignment. The challenge is to break the application up into discrete tasks that can become threads.

An ice cream parlor is an example of a multithreaded process. As demand increases, more counter help is added. Each additional person shares the floor space and the equipment (the ice cream, the cones and dishes, the scoops, the cash register). In an environment that is not multithreaded, each additional person would have his or her own equipment and floor space. At some point, even though shared resources are being used, it may make sense to add a whole new environment to service the additional demand. Hence, a new ice cream parlor opens up one mile away. In IT terms, a larger server machine is added to the environment.

Tightly coupled processes that execute concurrently require programmers to push problem abstraction further than they have in the past. A *thread of execution* is a new conceptual unit that performs the work in the system by moving from one instruction or statement (thread) to the next, executing each in turn.

The greatest adjustment required by multitasking may be in users' work habits. Users are accustomed to taking a break or staring at the screen after issuing a command. Under multithreading, users need to adjust to the idea that they don't have to wait after issuing a command—they can switch to another task.

6.1.4 Multiprocessing

Vendors are including multiple processors in their hardware to increase processing speed or productivity. Multiple processors permit servers to do either symmetric or asymmetric multiprocessing.

With symmetric multiprocessing, processors within the same system share all processes as well as disk input/output (I/O), network I/O, memory management, and the operating system. All the processors function as a single resource pool and dynamically take on whatever tasks need to be processed next, as illustrated in Fig. 6.1. Processing resources are maximized. A processor does not sit idle if there is work to be done. However, this capability has to be supported by either the network operating system or the server operating system. The application software must be able to support multiprocessing as well.

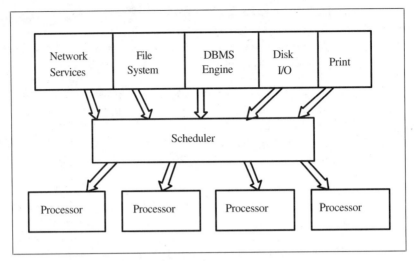

Figure 6.1 Symmetrical processing

With asymmetric multiprocessing, processors in the same or different systems are permanently assigned a set of tasks, such as disk I/O, network I/O, or memory management, as illustrated in Fig. 6.2. Consequently, one processor (usually the I/O processor) may sit idle while another is overloaded. Processors offload these tasks from the main system's CPU, freeing it up to run the operating system. Each processor usually has its own dedicated memory. With the newer massively parallel processors, each processor could be assigned a particular program or part of a program to execute during a session.

A special form of multiprocessing is called bus mastering. Add-in boards called bus masters can process independently of the CPU and are able to access the computer's memory and peripherals on their own. This frees up the CPU for other processing tasks.

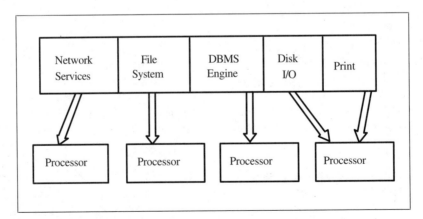

Figure 6.2 Functional multiprocessing

Multiprocessing supports multithreading, the concurrent execution of multiple tasks. However, applications—and also operating systems and network operating systems—must be written to be multithreaded (as discussed above), to allow parts of the application to run as different tasks on different processors.

Multiprocessing hardware platforms are discussed in more detail in Sec. 4.6, "Multiprocessing Systems."

6.1.5 Preemptive multitasking

Multitasking allows a server to allocate resources and time among multiple tasks evenly or based on a set of priorities. Preemptive multitasking allows one task (typically of a higher priority) to interrupt another task when necessary. Windows 3.x uses cooperative multitasking, where one application gives up control to another application.

Windows 95 and Windows NT use a time-slice priority-based preemptive multitasking algorithm for scheduling threads. Both are also preemptively multitasked with fixed time slices.

6.1.6 Intertask protection

The server operating system must protect tasks from interfering with one another's resources. A single task must not be able to bring down the entire system. Protection should also extend to the file system and calls to the operating system.

6.1.7 Disk arrays

Fault-tolerant disk arrays, which are referred to as redundant arrays of inexpensive disks (RAID), are standard on superservers and optional on other platforms. Multiple drivers are treated as a single logical drive by the server operating system.

RAID implementations have three attributes.

- RAID is a set of physical disk devices that are viewed by the system and the user as a single logical device.
- The user's data is distributed across the physical set of disk drives in a defined manner.
- Redundant disk capacity is added so that the user's data can be recovered if one (but no more than one) drive fails.

Redundant disk arrays can transparently recover from the failure of any single drive and allow a failed drive to be replaced while the server is on-line. As illustrated in Fig. 6.3, data is actually broken into chunks and simultaneously written to multiple disks, a process called striping. If a disk fails, the data can be reconstructed by reviewing the remaining pieces of data. Server performance is degraded slightly while the reconstruction

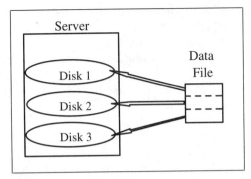

Figure 6.3 Redundant disk arrays

process is going on, but the self-healing process is otherwise transparent to the user.

RAID systems are categorized by where their "intelligence" lies: in the software or in the hardware. Software solutions, such as those built into Microsoft's Windows NT, are competent but can take away CPU cycles if a drive rebuild is necessary.

Hardware-based RAID systems provide more flexibility in terms of which operating systems are supported and tend to be more reliable and faster, but, of course, are more expensive. The RAID firmware can reside in the host controller or in the RAID cabinet, which is often called SCSI-to-SCSI. In a controller-based system, the RAID intelligence (a microprocessor and specialized firmware) is on the controller card that fits into one of the expansion slots of the host system. A SCSI-to-SCSI RAID system puts the intelligence into the disk array cabinet and attaches to the host system via a standard SCSI controller, with the disk array appearing as a large drive to the operating system.

The most common RAID implementations are RAID 0, 1, and 5. RAID 0, known as data striping, places data block-by-block across multiple disks. The parity data is also spread across multiple disks. This process is very fast but provides no fault tolerance. RAID 1, known as disk mirroring, mirrors one set of disks with another set of similar size, but the operating system uses only the capacity of one set. RAID 1 is also fast and provides a high level of fault tolerance, but at a price.

RAID 5 is the most popular implementation today. The data and a parity value are striped over a minimum of three disks. If one disk fails, the system will still remain operational. If a drive must be reconfigured, the system must read data from all the drives in order to compute the correct value of the requested data.

Usually provided with RAID systems, although not in the RAID specifications, are support for an on-line spare drive and the ability to hot-swap drives. The on-line spare drive remains idle until one of the drives in the array fails, at which time it takes over for that drive. The data on the failed drive is re-created on the on-line drive, using the data and parity values on the remaining two drives. Hot-swapping allows the operating system to remove and add drives while the disk array and the operating system are on-line.

The cost of RAID systems used to be prohibitive for small businesses but prices have come below $1,000 and the downward trend will probably continue. In addition, the software supplied with the RAID systems is providing more features, such as graphical displays of controller statistics, alarms that sound when failures occur, and support for network information standards such as SNMP.

6.1.8 Memory subsystems

Error-correction code (ECC) memory and parity checking (often including automatic recovery) are used to prevent corruption of data traveling within the server. ECC memory is a memory subsystem design that automatically corrects single-bit errors and detects multiple-bit errors.

Each time data is written to the disk array, an ECC is written to an extra disk in the array or to a primary storage disk. The actual code for the ECC is calculated by applying an error-correction formula to the data written to the other drives. If one drive fails, the lost data is reconstructed from the ECC, the intact data on the remaining drives, and the formula.

Many physical faults can be tolerated by a system memory that is designed with ECC. However, the physical faults must be within the error-correcting capability of the ECC. The ECC method uses the conventional one-bit-per-chip design and stores each bit of a codeword in a different chip. Failures can thus corrupt only one bit of codeword.

Intel's 430HX and 430VX chip sets (formerly the Triton II chips) are Pentium chip sets that supports ECC. They also support more memory, a higher data throughput rate, and two processors, which allows for the construction of low-end multiprocessor servers. The 430HX is aimed at business micros with support for 512 Mbytes of main memory and for dual processors. The 430VX is aimed at micros used at home and in small businesses. The 430VX differs from the 430HX in that it supports only 128 Mbytes of main memory.

During the second quarter of 1996, Intel released the 440FX (code named Natoma), which replaced the prototype Mars chip set which was scrapped because of technical difficulties. A chip set for the Pentium Pro, the 440FX, offers a high level of data integrity and supports two processors.

6.1.9 Memory management

The operating system must efficiently support very large programs and very large data objects. Programs and data objects must be easily swapped to and from disk in small granular blocks.

The operating system must be able to store data and programs in memory, keep track of them, and reclaim the memory space when they are no longer needed. In traditional minicomputers and mainframes, it comprises virtual memory, bank switching, and memory protection techniques.

Memory management has become a major issue with micros, because managing memory in a micro means managing conventional memory, the upper memory area, the high memory area, extended memory, and expanded memory.

6.1.10 Memory protection

Memory protection is a set of techniques that prohibit one program from accidentally clobbering another active program. Using various different techniques, a protective boundary is created around the program, and instructions within the program are prohibited from referencing data outside of that boundary.

Memory also needs to be protected from leaks. A memory leak is a reserved section of memory that has not been freed up and turned back over to the general memory pool. When an application allocates memory, it should deallocate it when the memory is no longer used. Some operating system can determine when what is in memory is no longer required and deallocate it. This routine, called garbage collection, searches memory for program segments or data that is no longer active and reclaims the space.

6.1.11 Redundant components

Redundant server components, such as disk drives, power supplies, and fans, and automatic recovery features are options on micro/servers and standard on superservers. Some servers offer mirrored processors and include remote alarms that immediately warn of network trouble.

The goal of the organization should be to provide a fault-tolerant environment. Fault tolerance is the ability to continue nonstop when a hardware failure occurs. A fault-tolerant system is designed from the ground up for reliability by building multiples of all critical components, such as CPUs, memory, disks, and power supplies. In the event that one component fails, another takes over without skipping a beat. Fault-tolerant machines are designed to detect the failed component and automatically switch to another system. High-availability systems are fault-tolerant to some degree, but there isn't an automatic switch over. The software is required to resubmit requests when the second system is available.

True fault-tolerant systems are the most costly, because redundant hardware is wasted if there is no failure in the system. High-availability systems usually are more inexpensive because they provide reduced capacity after a failure.

Tandem and Stratus are the two major manufacturers of fault-tolerant computer systems. However, vendors of most servers now provide some level of fault tolerance as either standard or optional equipment.

6.1.12 High-performance file system

The file system must support multiple tasks and provide locks to protect the integrity of the data. Server operating systems typically work with many files at the same time. The file system must support large numbers of open files without deterioration in performance.

Analysts say that a file system that abstracts an application's components from their actual location is essential to distributed computing.

6.1.13 Extended services

As more architectures become distributed and network-centric, server operating systems will need to extend their services to support the network and provide flexible access to the data on the network. In addition, the operating systems will need to become easier to manage and maintain. Some of the services that will become base services within the next few years are:

- **Ubiquitous communications**. By providing communications protocol stacks, a server will be able to communicate with a large number of client platforms as well as other servers if services need to be distributed.
- **Binary large objects** (BLOBs). Images, video, graphics, and database snapshots are examples of BLOBs. Their movement within the architecture requires robust message handling on the part of the operating system, storage and accessibility on the part of the database systems, protocols for exchanging them across systems, and programs that know what to do with them when they get one.
- **Global directories and network yellow pages**. Client processes need to be able to locate servers and their services, using a directory similar to the yellow pages in our phone books. Servers should be accessible by name and should be able to dynamically register their services with the directory service.
- **Authentication and authorization services**. Clients should be able to prove to servers that they are who they claim to be. Servers should be able to determine if an authenticated client has authorization to obtain a remote service.
- **System management**. Operating systems should be more closely integrated with network and system management services, as discussed in Chap. 12, "Managing the Client/Server Environment."
- **Uniform time**. Clients and servers should be able to synchronize their clocks using some universal time authority.

6.2 Operating System Requirements for Networks

As networks become more sophisticated, they need operating system software to shield application programs from direct communication with the hardware. A network operating system manages the services of the server in the same way that an operating system manages the services of the

Network Operating System	Upper-Layer Software
NetWare	Novell proprietary Third-party links to NetView, SNMP, proprietary
LAN Manager	Proprietary NetView Alerts SNMP
VINES	Third-party links to NetView, SNMP, proprietary
OS/2 LAN Server	NetView Alerts

Figure 6.4 Network management software links

hardware. Today's leading network operating systems offer the reliability, performance, security, and internetworking capability once associated primarily with mainframe and midrange computers.

A network operating system exists at the Session and Presentation layers of the client machine's network management software and provides links to upper-layer network management software, as shown in Fig. 6.4. GUIs are an overlay to the network operating system.

When an existing network is used to support a basic client/server application, no new software should be required. Care must be taken, however, to ensure that the resulting network traffic does not bring the network to its knees.

Traditional network operating systems are file-server centric—the user logs into a file server. Since a particular file server handles its own logins, high-throughput servers are required to handle a large number of login authentications—high throughput, not necessarily processing power, is key for a successful implementation.

Developed as server-enablers, LAN operating systems have evolved into network management tools, enablers of other software packages, and a platform for GUIs and other presentation standards. These operating systems have evolved into robust network operating systems with the following characteristics:

- Scalable and more reliable
- Communicate easily over multiple protocols
- Offer extensive security because they expect to be handling geographically dispersed networks
- Offer directory services to improve the interoperability of directories in operating systems and applications.

Network operating systems are now making the transition to being network-centric—the user logs into the network, not into a specific file server. In addition, their services are being tightly entwined with operating system software.

6.3 Hybrid Operating Systems

The popular server operating systems manage the server hardware as well as the services required by the network. They are multiuser and multithreaded and support preemptive multitasking. The popular operating systems today include:

- Windows NT Server
- OS/2 Warp Server
- UNIX

6.3.1 Windows NT Server 3.5

Windows NT Server was designed as an application-server platform and is aimed at network-centric multiserver networks. NT Server includes SMP support, preemptive multitasking, and virtual memory. It provides some fault tolerance because it is built on a microkernel architecture.

Windows NT Server performs at C1-level security and is compatible with a broad range of platforms, including PowerPC and Digital's Alpha. It provides file and print services for the Macintosh, a NetWare gateway, built-in disk mirroring and RAID 5 support, and directory services.

Windows NT Server 3.5, released early in 1996 as the successor to NT Advanced Server 3.1, allows systems administrators to choose from an extensive range of network protocols, including:

- Access to NetWare file and print services
- NetBEUI (NetBIOS Extended User Interface) for peer-to-peer communication with Windows for Workgroups and LAN Manager environments
- Data Link Control (DLC), the protocol used for accessing IBM mainframe computers
- TCP/IP for communicating on UNIX networks, heterogeneous networks, or the Internet
- Dynamic Host Configuration Protocol (DHCP) and Windows Internetwork Name Service (WINS), which support dynamic IP address assignment and name resolution for large IP networks.

Windows NT networks are built and managed around the concept of domains, which are groups of servers that function as single systems. All the NT servers in a domain use the same set of user accounts. The Configuration Registry is a database that contains information about the operating system, the computer, and the users who have logged on in the past. User Profiles (user preferences and settings) are used whenever the user logs on at any Windows NT computer—the profile follows the user.

Remote Access Service

NT Server 3.5 includes a Remote Access Service (RAS) that allows remote users to dial into the network to access file, print, and application servers. The RAS connection is transparent to the clients and network applications.

The NT Server RAS also offers Point-to-Point Protocol (PPP) for asynchronous serial (dial-up) connection between remote clients and the RAS server. RAS can handle the IPX/SPX, TCP/IP, and NetBEUI protocols, which allow remote clients to use RAS to access LAN Manager, LAN Server, NT Server, and NetWare servers as well as NT Workstation, UNIX, and Windows for Workgroups peer notes. The NT Server RAS can handle 256 connections and supports modems with data compression.

File and Print Services for NetWare

File and Print Services for NetWare (FNPNW) allows Windows NT to emulate a NetWare 3.12 file server. With no changes on the client machines, the Windows NT server looks just like their NetWare 3.x and 4.x file servers, although it is a little slower than a native NetWare server. FNPNW does not work with NDS, and users cannot load NLMs (NetWare Loadable Modules) onto the Windows NT server. FNPNW is compatible with different versions of the NetWare shell requestor. FNPNW is aimed at those organizations that want to add a Windows NT server to their NetWare network but don't want to replace their NetWare servers.

Security

Security is provided through such options as dial-back, data encryption, and NT Server logon and domain validation. Support for ISDN and X.25 WAN is also available.

6.3.2 Windows NT Server 4.0

Microsoft began shipping Windows NT Server 4.0 in the fall of 1996. Many of its features are those that were expected in the version code-named Cairo (see the next section). The only things that keeps Windows NT 4.0 from being Cairo are plug-and-play capabilities, and object support for the file system.

The new features in Windows NT Server 4.0 include:

- A Windows 95–like interface that will include all of the Windows 95 features, except as plug-and-play capabilities.
- Administrative Wizards, which simplify setup processes such as connecting printers and creating sets or groups of users

- Enhanced diagnostic tools that report, in graphic format, information on network usage and system resources
- Task Manager, a tool to manage applications and measure Windows NT performance
- Internet Information Server (IIS) Version 2.0, Microsoft's NT-based Web server as well as a peer Web server that can be used to set up a workgroup intranet for up to 10 users
- Microsoft Internet Explorer 2.0, a Web browser
- FrontPage 1.1, a Web authoring tool
- Index Server, a search engine with automatic indexing for documents of any type
- Distributed Component Object Model (DCOM), which can be used to design software as a set of components that reside on different machines on a network
- A multiprotocol router which allows Appletalk, IPX, and TCP/IP protocols to be routed on a single network
- Support for Novell's NetWare Directory Services
- Bandwidth aggregation, which can be used to combine multiple connection pipes to increase throughput

6.3.3   Cairo, the next Windows NT Server

The next version of Windows NT, code named Cairo, was expected to ship sometime late 1997 or early 1998 (depending on who you believe!). Microsoft shipped Windows NT 4.0 as an interm version. Cairo, expected to be released as Windows NT 5.0, is expected to include an updated distributed security system based on Kerberos (a security system developed at MIT that authenticates users but does not provide authorization to services or databases—it establishes identity at logon, which is used throughout the session), as well as the following enhancements.

New file system

Distributed File System (DFS) has been one of the most hotly anticipated parts of Cairo, and is expected to be Microsoft's answer to NDS (NetWare Directory Services) and be competition for directories from IBM and Banyan Systems Inc.

DFS will replace the Microsoft Directory Service, the domain directory in the current version of Windows NT. Like Novell's NDS, DFS is meant to track the location of objects within applications regardless of the objects' location. It currently looks as if the Distributed File System will be based on technologies inherited from Microsoft Exchange's mail directory engine and not on new technologies. DFS will be built on the Exchange engine to carry the X.500 messaging extensions in the Exchange's directory into the new Cairo directory.

Microsoft also will support the DNS (Domain Name System) standard, shelving plans to create a global directory that links filenames and directory service information in a unified object-oriented storage system called the Object File System.

Microsoft's new unified naming system will resolve DNS-style names, as well as other names, and will also use DNS for some name storage. DNS is an Internet service that converts readable names, such as www.babson.edu, to the cryptic number-filled IP addresses used by the Internet.

New directory services

As operating systems move into the next century, they will need a robust directory architecture that conforms to the X.500 directory services specification to share resources and exchange messages across enterprises. X.500 is a set of ITU-T (International Telecommunications Union) protocols for accessing, distributing, and managing directory data in a client/server environment. For example, networks with an X.500 directory service can support single-point log-ons, which give access to all network resources with one log-on; location-independent network resources, which are network resources (such as a user's home directories) that are not tied to a physical location; and a way of extending the database to incorporate advances in network design.

On its own, NT doesn't support X.500. Instead, it offers services such as single-point log-on and, to an extent, location independence (by letting users move around the network, from home office to remote site), thereby matching some basic X.500 services. Although transparent to users, NT's way of providing these services creates a lot of work for LAN administrators: To move a network resource from one server to another, for instance, an administrator must manually enter all changes to NT's directory and to the affected user accounts.

Microsoft Exchange Server adds X.500 services to NT Server. Microsoft Exchange Server will use NT's current user database and extend it by adding user data, such as e-mail addresses. This extensibility is key to building directory services into NT 3.51 and will benefit not only NT, but Microsoft's BackOffice applications as well. For instance, Microsoft System Management Server will be able to employ the enhanced user data these extensions provide to install international versions of an application across a worldwide corporate net. But there is true only if Exchange is running on the server. Otherwise, there is no X.500 support.

Microsoft Exchange is also expected to include support for Lightweight Directory Access Protocol (LDAP), which is an emerging Internet standard intended to serve as a universal mechanism for locating and managing users and network resources across disparate directories. LDAP is a simplification of the X.500 Directory Access Protocol. Microsoft expects to add LDAP to its next version of Microsoft Exchange, expected to be released by the end of 1996, and include it in Windows NT Server itself beginning with Cairo.

Currently, Banyan VINES' StreetTalk and Novell NetWare's NetWare Directory Services offer stronger, easier to manage X.500 directory services that are far more elegant than NT's—that is, until Cairo arrives, with its full-blown, ground-up deployment of X.500 and its object-based directory services.

Trust relationships within domains

NT's directory services use a linear domain model to build and manage networks. This linear model is clumsy for managing large networks with many neatly defined domains because before one domain can share resources with another, you need to create explicit trust relationships between them. Fortunately, Cairo will improve NT's domain model by supporting implicit trust relationships, meaning that if A trusts B and B trusts C, then A will trust C intrinsically.

6.3.4   OS/2 Warp Server

IBM's OS/2 Warp Server 4 adds the best features of LAN Server 4.0 to OS/2 Warp Connect, the workstation operating system. OS/2 Warp Server is a 32-bit preemptive multitasking operating system with an integrated file, print, application, and database server. Warp Server interoperates seamlessly with other network operating system environments, such as NetWare and Banyan VINES. Warp Server can connect natively to NT networks and to a NetWare environment through Requestor software. It has real-time network management, remote access, and dynamic domain named services. The product is still weak on security and crash protection, but because of this, it requires less memory on the server (16 Mbytes) and on the workstation (8 Mbytes).

OS/2 Warp Server can run DOS and OS/2 applications and will work with 16- and 32-bit Windows applications. Warp Server can back up data using storage devices attached to NetWare or Windows NT servers.

OS/2 Warp Server includes TCP/IP features that are collectively called Dynamic IP, which consists of Dynamic Host Configuration Protocol (DHCP) and Dynamic Domain Name System (DNS). DHCP centralizes the network configuration information, such as IP addresses, and the parameters of network-aware applications, such as World Wide Web browsers. Dynamic DNS maintains this information at each client, eliminating the need for administrators to manually maintain the data. However, Dynamic DNS support is limited to OS/2 Warp clients, which leaves out the Windows clients that dominate the desktop.

Microsoft's counterpart to Dynamic DNS is Windows Internet Name Service (WINS), which performs the same functions and supports Windows NT, Windows for Workgroups, and Windows 95. Warp Server's DHCP support for NT is offered in the Windows NT Resource Kit, available free of charge on the Internet. Novell expects to add DHCP and Dynamic DNS support to NetWare but has not specified a time frame.

OS/2 Warp Server includes the following:

- IBM **LAN Distance Remote** for remote node support, which allows users to log in via high-speed modems and ISDN lines as network nodes
- IBM's **Distributed Console Access Facility** for remote systems management, which lets systems managers remotely monitor or manipulate workstations
- IBM **Networking Solutions** backup and recovery tools, which combine IBM's Personally Safe 'n' Sound product with its AdStar Distributed Storage Manager backup facility
- **Advanced printing** capability and support for bidirectional printers
- **Client support** for Windows 95, Windows NT, Windows 3.x, DOS, OS/2 Warp, and the Macintosh
- IBM's **Internet Access Kit and Web Explorer**

Some missing features include:

- **Missing directory services**. It is difficult to compete with NetWare as a file and print server without directory services.
- **Missing high-level security** features
- **Missing Internet server products**. It cannot function as an effective Internet server without Internet server products such as Spyglass Inc.'s WebServer and Netscape Communications Corp.'s NetSite server.

These missing features are offered as part of IBM Software Servers, code-named Project Eagle, bundle, which is discussed in Sec. 12.2.2, "System Management".

OS/2 Warp Server's file system is based on the faster HPFS (High Performance File System) 386 used in LAN Server Advanced rather than on the original Warp file system. The HPFS 386 file system has its own cache-allocation program and a different I/O method.

OS/2 Warp Server Advanced 4 also includes HPFS, which lets hard drives more easily handle data transfer on large networks, as well as disk mirroring and duplexing.

OS/2 Warp Server SMP was released in late 1996. It will scale to as many as 16 processors but is focused on four-processor systems. Warp Server SMP also includes high-performance memory-tuning optimization and expanded virtual memory support.

A PowerPC version of OS/2 Warp Server was released in March 1996. This was the first released microkernel-based version of OS/2 Warp, and as such is a portable version. The microkernel manages all the hardware-specific tasks of the operating system, including memory management and device drivers.

6.3.5 Merlin, the next OS/2 Warp Server

The next version of OS/2 Warp, called Warp 2 or code name Merlin, is due for release in early 1997. Merlin is being built on the PowerPC, and IBM expects it to be relatively easy to bring the features back to Intel.

Merlin is expected to include the following features:

- A redesigned user interface (Workplace Shell)
- An OpenDoc-based, customizable, network-aware user interface which resembles Windows 95 integrated with the Plus Pack themes and Lotus Development Corp.'s Infobox technology, and is network-aware, making connections automatically as the user needs them
- Improved multimedia support, including IBM's DIVE (Direct Interactive Video Extension) and features such as CD autoplay, Win/TXV applet support, and real-time Musical Instrument Digital Interface support
- Enhanced plug-and-play and input queuing
- A DOS-Warp toggling feature called Trap Door
- Support for Microsoft's Windows 95 file allocation table that will allow Warp users to work with long filenames
- Speech recognition capabilities using IBM's VoiceType technology, which will allow users to navigate the interface and dictate data entry without using the keyboard
- Support for Object REXX and PowerSOM (Object REXX is the object-oriented version of REXX, a powerful procedural language and an SAA standard; PowerSOM, which stands for System Object Model, is an object architecture from IBM that provides a full implementation of the CORBA standard)
- C2 security extensions
- Built-in Developer API Extensions which will allow software developers to write Windows 95 and OS/2 Warp applications simultaneously
- A Java-enabled version of IBM's Web Explorer browser and Java support integrated into the operating system itself
- OpenDoc run-time support, which will enable developers to use OpenDoc components in their applications and users to embed OLE 2.0 information in OS/2 Warp documents.

6.3.6 UNIX

UNIX has been ported to a wide range of hardware platforms, including SMP and MPP machines. UNIX provides National Computer Security Center C1- and C2-level security and is POSIX-compliant. The interface to UNIX is command-driven. UNIX is often pointed to as an open system, even though the many variations of UNIX are to some degree different.

Because of its maturity, UNIX's strengths include established standards conformity, scalability, high availability and reliability, and multiprocessing support. There are also UNIX-specific performance acceleration tools available on the market. Its greatest liability is its many variations. Efforts by vendor alliances such as the Common Open Software Environment (COSE) and standards proposed by the IEEE Portable Operating System Interface for UNIX (POSIX) should help to ensure source-code portability across hardware and operating system platforms.

UNIX comes in many variants, such as AIX from IBM, Digital Ultrix from

Digital Equipment Corp., HP-UX from Hewlett-Packard, and Solaris from SunSoft. The "base" version is AT&T UNIX System V (Release 4.2), usually referred to as AT&T UNIX SVR4.2. However, since The Santa Cruz Operation (SCO) bought Novell's UNIX business and AT&T's UNIX System V, SCO now provides the UNIX source code used by the vast majority of all UNIX vendors. SCO's tactical acquisition has placed the small company in control of the source code used by 90 percent of all UNIX suppliers. SCO currently licenses UNIX products to hundreds of companies.

The UNIX operating systems' interoperability falls short in five critical areas: applications portability, security, systems management, network management, and object-oriented technologies. For example, a program written for IBM's AIX does not automatically run on Hewlett-Packard's HP-UX.

UNIX vendors are trying to remedy the situation. They have announced plans to unify UNIX around two standards: a graphical front end called the Common Desktop Environment (CDE), which is discussed in Sec. 3.5.2, and a set of APIs known as the Single UNIX Specification, formerly called Spec 1170 and now generally referred to as UNIX 95. Hewlett-Packard released the first UNIX 95 branded operating system in early 1996. This version of HP-UX (10.10) is among the first UNIX systems to receive the X/Open (now Open Group) UNIX 95 brand. This version is also compliant with the CDE standard.

In August of 1995, UNIX suppliers took another step forward and announced industry-wide support for a 64-bit API for future releases of their operating systems, working toward the X/Open Single UNIX Specification (Spec 1170), UNIX95 branding, and the Common Desktop Environment (CDE).

SCO plans to integrate SCO UNIX and UnixWare into one platform. At the same time, Hewlett-Packard and SCO will share technology as Hewlett-Packard develops a 64-bit UNIX operating system that combines HP-UX and SCO's versions of UNIX.

The new UNIX will run on Intel's IA-64 Merced chip (formerly referred to as P7), the combined RISC/CISC microprocessor successor to the Pentium Plus, which is P6, and is based on an advanced three-dimentional architecture (3DA). The Merced chip, being developed jointly by Hewlett-Packard and Intel for release in 1998, uses a 64-bit instruction set. SCO and Hewlett-Packard promise that the new platforms will comply with emerging UNIX standards, such as CDE, UNIX 95, and the 64-bit API. The new three-UNIX-in-one operating system will compete with IBM's AIX on PowerPC, Digital's UNIX on Alpha, and SunSoft's Solaris on Sparc.

SCO expects to release a new version of UnixWare, code named Eiger, in early 1997. Eiger integrates Novell's NetWare Directory Services (NDS) and NetWare file and print services. Eiger will add support for NetWare 4.0's APIs, network clients, NetWare Directory Services (NDS), and utilities, as well as file, print, and administration services. Eiger will be compliant with UNIX 95 specifications.

A release of SCO's own Intel-based UNIX offering, SCO OpenServer, is planned for late 1996. Code named Comet, this release will add high-availability features and improved scalability. Comet will add support for Intel Corp.'s P6 chip and increase the amount of RAM support to 4 gigabytes.

A third release—code-named Gemini, which was beta-released in mid-1996 and has a planned ship date of mid-1997—will merge UnixWare with SCO OpenServer to provide a single migration path to a 64-bit operating system. Gemini will combine the existing code base with a high degree of scalability, letting SCO continue selling to its traditional small-business customers while offering such capabilities as clustering and fault tolerance to attract enterprise customers.

All of this push to standards with UNIX 95 has actually redefined what can be called UNIX. A system will not have to be based on UNIX source code to be called UNIX. Rather, any system that complies with the specification—comprising more than 1,000 APIs (1,170, to be exact—hence the name of the specification) gathered from the top 50 UNIX applications—can carry X/Open's UNIX brand. (Yes, Novell gave up the UNIX brand name!) So ultimately even Microsoft's 32-bit Windows NT could be called UNIX.

As wonderful as 64-bit operating systems are, the reality is that there are few 64-bit applications currently available, which makes the hardware and operating system running at 64-bits meaningless. Intel also needs 64-bit operating systems and applications if it expects to sell its future 64-bit chip.

The biggest hurdle for UNIX is still interoperability with Microsoft systems. Few UNIX systems ship with built-in support for Windows applications, and Microsoft's operating systems don't support most UNIX standards, including NFS (network file system). Third-party products are filling the Windows-to-UNIX interoperability void.

6.4 Network Operating Systems

Not all organizations benefit from operating systems that handle both server requirements and network requirements. Many organizations need a robust file-oriented network operating system.

6.4.1 NetWare

Novell's NetWare is a file and print server network operating system that is optimized for I/O operations but is able to support application services through NetWare Loadable Modules (NLMs). NetWare supports up to 250 users per server, and can handle up to 32 Tbytes of virtual disk space and 10,000 concurrent open files. It adjusts the amount of memory needed at each stage of file transfer for optimum caching.

NetWare can handle up to 64 LAN adapter cards in server and support tunneling of SPX and IPX packets over TCP/IP backbone networks. NetWare features built-in read-after-write verification, hot fix, disk mirroring, disk duplexing, and resource tracking.

NetWare offers excellent security through packet signatures and public encryption key technology. NetWare does not include preemptive multitasking or virtual memory but does support UNIX clients.

NetWare 4.0 is traditionally installed in a file server-centric single-server network. Both IBM's LAN Server (which is now a part of OS/2 Warp Server) and NetWare 4.0 are essentially equivalent in the following areas:

- File and print services
- Disk duplexing
- Disk mirroring
- Uninterruptible Power Supply (UPS) support
- Multiserver domain administration
- Audit trails
- Alerts
- Security features
- Login scripts
- Multiple adapter support
- Named Pipes support
- Remote IPL capabilities for DOS, Windows, and OS/2 clients

NetWare has fault tolerance through replicated servers, and has X.500-based directory services, burst-mode technology, and file-by-file compression. NetWare's file system allows files to be stored as if each was in its own file system. LAN Server has a file replication service, a network time service, multiprocessing, and remote execution of commands. In addition, any OS/2 software package can be used to program for the LAN Server environment.

The newest version of NetWare, code-name Green River and released as NetWare 4.1.1, is expected to ship by the end of 1996. Green River includes the NetWare Web Server, as a NetWare Loadable Module, which provides intranet and Internet gateway and routing technology, a NetBasic scripting tool for creating intranet applications, and Novell's InnerWeb Publisher suite. Green River has improved NetWare Directory Services and administration tools and built-in IP support. However, NetWare 4.1.1 is not expected to support NT.

6.4.2 Banyan VINES

Banyan VINES (VIrtual NEtworking System) integrates the entire suite of enterprise network services with its UNIX-based network operating system. DOS, OS/2, Windows NT, and Macintosh clients can share information and computing resources with each other as well as the server resources. VINES supports each client type's native file storage environment and performs file access through the user's native client interface. The network operating system defines and controls user file and directory access and provides fine-grained security, expanded printer support, and high-capacity disk support.

In the race with Windows NT, users of VINES point to VINES' StreetTalk, its global naming service that supports domains across extended networks, and Intelligent Messaging services, but note that these have been duplicated by Microsoft's Domains and NDS services.

Banyan VINES supports TCP/IP connectivity and SNMP through a SNMP Server Agent. The latest release also supports a dial-in remote node.

Banyan VINES 7.0 is due in 1997 and will have enhanced StreetTalk directory capabilities and improved ease of use. It is expected to update the UNIX core to the UNIX System V 3.x kernel (Banyan VINES sets on top of UNIX) and eliminate VINES 2-gigabyte file size limit, support long file names, offer improved performance, and eliminate hardware-based server keys in favor of a software-based licensing method.

Banyan is also working on BeyondMail 96, a code name for a BeyondMail release that will support rich text formats, which will enable users to cut and paste documents and pictures into E-mail messages without losing their text formatting.

Chapter

7

Data

Data should be approached from a modular point of view—a data model. A data model can be used by multiple applications and if necessary expanded to include the requirements of a new application without affecting the applications that already use the data model.

Data should be logically separated from the business rules that use it. If the data is part of a business rule, then the only applications that can use that data are those that use that business rule.

Modularity provides the foundation for reusability, flexibility, and consistency. Data with a consistent definition will be understood by all applications (and their developers). This allows an organization to reuse existing data and data concepts within the enterprise. The organization still maintains the flexibility to expand the data concept without affecting those applications that already use the data.

In addition, modularity allows an organization to more easily distribute its data as the need arises. This feature is becoming more and more critical as organizations are beginning to include EDI and mobile clients in their IT portfolio.

Data is what all client/server applications are trying to get to with their requests. The data may be on the server the client is directly connected to or on some other server in the environment. Chances are, the data structure will be relational.

7.1 Relational Database Structure

A relational data model views all data as organized in tables made up of rows and columns. The rows represent records, and the columns represent

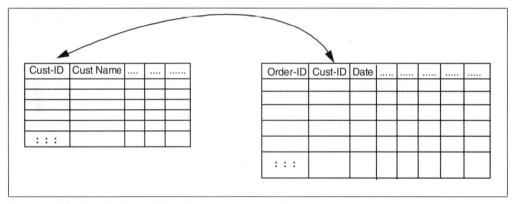

Figure 7.1 Relational tables and their links

fields in the records. The order of the rows is not significant. Each row has a key field which makes that row unique. A table can contain a field that contains the value of a key field in another table. This field is called a foreign key and links the two tables for processing.

It is this ability to link tables that provides the relational model with the ability to maintain data integrity. Consider a table of customer information and a table of orders, as illustrated in Fig. 7.1. The database contains both tables. The Customer table is related to the Orders table via the link between the Cust-ID as a primary key in the Customer table and Cust-ID as a foreign key in the Orders table.

Because of this link, values cannot be entered as customer IDs for orders unless they already exist in the Customer table. Customers cannot be deleted if they have an opened order. This type of integrity is called referential integrity.

The power of relational technology is in its access language, Structured Query Language (SQL). SQL provides a 4GL access to relational databases. The user needs to deal only with the "what I want" and not with "how to get it."

SQL is discussed in more detail in Sec. 7.9.

7.2 Distributed Data

As organizations flatten and disperse and functions and locations are decentralized, the notion of a corporate database—one very large database in a central location that serves the entire organization—has outlived its usefulness. This is partly due to the changes in responsibility for data—who creates it, who owns it, who uses it. In the age of knowledge workers, organizations must provide fast and reliable access to data. And organizations must provide access to more than just the transactional data: users need to analyze data and they need to mine the data (see Sec. 17.8 for more on data mining).

The idea behind data distribution is to distribute the data among multiple nodes to provide more efficient use of the environment but to keep the fact that the data is distributed transparent to the user.

This approach allows an organization

- To place the data nearest to its source, which is usually the most frequent user of the data as well
- To eliminate a potential single point of failure by placing multiple copies of critical data at different locations
- To provide for load balancing
- To provide scalability.

With all these benefits come the drawbacks of complexity and potential for loss of data synchronization.

7.2.1 Types of distribution

Data can be distributed in a number of ways:

- Data files can be maintained at a central source, available to be copied by users or procedures as needed. This is referred to as a manual extract even though the data is actually copied.
- Data can be distributed automatically at set intervals. The data for the snapshot is specified by the user, as is the frequency. This provides an easy, automatic method for distributing static data that changes infrequently.
- Data can also be replicated.

A distributed database management system that supports replication can

- Create and maintain copies of a given table at multiple locations
- Maintain consistency among all replicas, either synchronously or asynchronously

Clearly, creating copies is not a complex task, but maintaining consistency among all the copies is. If a company is maintaining replicated versions of its customer tables to facilitate customer service, any action relating to a table must appear almost instantaneously in all copies of that table, not just the copy at the node accessed by the person who happened to enter the change.

In addition, since location is supposed to be transparent to the process, a program should not care (or even know) which copy it is actually using. It could be that the server the "ideal" copy is on is down, and so the environment passed the request on to another server that also had a copy of the table. If changes are made to the table at this point, when the "ideal" server comes back on-line, its copy must also be updated.

Fragmentation distributes particular rows and columns rather than entire tables. There may be a "virtual" copy of the entire database on a central server but the actual pieces reside on nodes throughout the organization. Tables can be fragmented horizontally or vertically.

7.3 Fragmentation

Distributing parts of the data (fragmentation) is a more complex method of data distribution and is handled by distributed DBMSs. Relational tables can be fragmented horizontally along row boundaries, vertically along column boundaries, or both.

For example, a human resource application has a table of employees for a company with three divisions which are all in separate locations. Each division is responsible for maintaining the information on its own employees. The company must generate a variety of reports that summarize information about all its employees.

As illustrated in Fig. 7.2, the actual table would be in four segments: headquarters plus one for each division. To the human resource applications running at headquarters, the four segments would be treated as one entity. The applications at each node would treat the segment of the table at that node as a complete entity.

The main drawbacks of fragmentation are the complexity of its implementation and the lack of transparent access by other nodes. Somehow the fragmented data must be viewed as a single table at a single site. Fragmented data distribution is best handled by a distributed DBMS.

In our example, when applications must treat the four segments as a whole, processing time increases. The access would be transparent to the user and the application because it is handled by the distributed DBMS, but response time would be affected. If a user at one division wished to query the information at a company-wide level—perhaps looking for an employee with a particular skill set—the entire table (all four segments) would have to

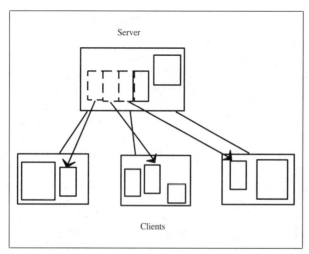

Figure 7.2 Fragmented database

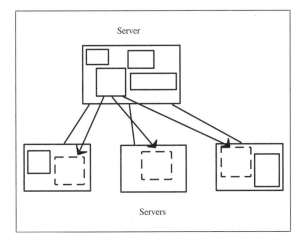

Figure 7.3 Replicated database

be "reconstructed" before the query could be executed. Another disadvantage is the overhead required to provide reliability. If the segments are to be treated as one and one node is down, alternative procedures must be in place to ensure that the application handles the situation correctly.

7.4 Types of Replication

The reason for intentionally placing copies of data (called replicas) at multiple sites, as illustrated in Fig. 7.3, is to improve performance. When two groups of users at different nodes of the infrastructure both routinely access the same data, it may be beneficial to replicate it at both nodes.

Replication sounds great, but organizations must keep some of the risks in mind as they explore replication as an option. One of the major risks is unsychronized copies—for some nanosecond replicas are out of synch. While a nanosecond or two doesn't seem like a long time to us, it's long enough for an application to access a database and pull out records. If replicas are to be updated, rather than restricting updates to the source or master copy, there are no automatic conflict-detection routines available (yet). But replication does solve many of the problems associated with distributed DBMS while providing some of the benefits. The best advice is planning carefully and proceeding cautiously.

7.4.1 Extraction

One of the simplest approaches to replication is to allow users to make their own copies of a dataset from a central location. This process is called extraction. When the users require more recent copies of the dataset, they copy the new data to their nodes. An alternative to user intervention would be an IS-initiated process. The weakness in this approach to replication is its reliance on human intervention.

7.4.2   Snapshots

A more reliable alternative would be to use a distributed DBMS's capability to generate snapshots (copies) of the data and distribute those snapshots. The timing of the snapshots could be specified by the user. The distributed DBMS automatically builds the snapshot copy of the original data at the times specified and handles synchronization of the multiple copies of the data. Snapshots are usually restricted to read-only access because typically no provisions are made for transferring updates made to snapshot data back to the original source. Snapshots can be updated with a full refresh (a complete new copy) or simply sent the changes (called a differential refresh).

7.4.3   Multiple simultaneous updates

Another distributed DBMS-managed alternative is the capability to replicate data and handle simultaneous updates at multiple locations. A relational database might use row or table replication. When a request for the data is made, a query optimizer takes into account all locations of the data and accesses the node that minimizes communication costs and response time.

The tradeoff is the overhead required to keep all copies of the data consistent and to maintain the consistency in a way that is transparent to the user.

7.4.4   Capture and transmit changes

There are two main approaches for capturing and transmitting changes. One uses the recovery log that every DBMS should keep (although micro-based products generally do not). Any changes made to a database that is replicated are copied to a staging area. Changes are transmitted from this staging area. The other approach uses procedures that propagate the changes as they occur. As soon as a change is made, it is sent out to the replicas. This creates network traffic as well as server resource use but is necessary if data must be "instantly" refreshed.

7.4.5   Publish and subscribe

This method of replication is hierarchical. The primary database, referred to as the publisher, contains the master copy of the database. The database is copied to other database servers, called the subscribers. Subscribers receive updates from the publisher at scheduled intervals. Subscribers can also be publishers with their own sets of subscribers, which allows for the establishment of a hub-and-star replication system.

7.5   Replication Techniques

The replication architecture is illustrated in Fig. 7.4.

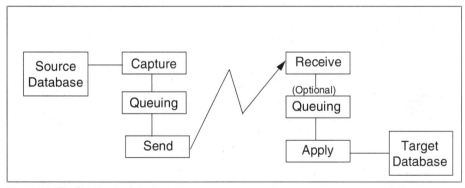

Figure 7.4 Replication architecture

From the point of view of the data source and the data target, replication is implemented as a full refresh or change propagation model. A full refresh model uses the entire source file to create replicas at remote sites. The change propagation model accepts only changes to the source data and propagates those changes to defined target databases.

There are two types of replication techniques. Peer-to-peer replication (also called symmetric or bidirectional replication) allows any server that holds a replica of the data to change the data. At replication time, those changes are reflected on other copies of the data.

Publisher/subscriber replication (also called master/slave) relies on one central copy owned by the publisher, called the primary copy. Changes made to the primary copy are then replicated to subscribers at specific times or upon the occurrence of specified events.

Replication can be synchronous or asynchronous. Synchronous replication adheres to the change propagation model—changes are propagated at or near real time. Asynchronous replication uses the store-and-forward principle—changes made to the data are logged and then applied at predefined intervals. Both full refresh and change propagation models can be supported by asynchronous replication.

Replications can be tightly consistent (all copies are 100 percent consistent at all times) or loosely consistent (they may not be consistent at any given time but are 100 percent consistent following replication).

Either changes for replication are captured in the DBMS log or triggers and/or stored procedures are used within the SQL statements that perform the changes.

Actual replication techniques vary among the major database vendors and are enhanced often in response to customer requests and high-performing hardware capabilities. Those techniques include the following:

- IBM's **propagation model** is based on a primary site update–only model, with asynchronous updates propagated to read-only targets.
- **Sybase Replication Server** from Sybase is credited with starting the replication revolution. The product moves data from a primary site to

read-only targets, using the changed row information to create an SQL statement which is sent to the target site.

- When Oracle Corp. released **Oracle7**, it contained an extract utility called Table Snapshots which relied on user-written code for replicating transactions. **Oracle7.3**, released mid-1996, includes Replication Manager, a visual utility that allows for the graphical representation of replication procedure. **Oracle8**, expected in early 1997, adds Symmetric Replication which can support synchronization of full copies of tables as well as updatable snapshots.

- Computer Associates International Inc. offers **CA-Ingres/Replicator**, which uses triggers to update replicas. When a table is registered for replication, the triggers are automatically created and stored as part of the source database.

- **SQL Server 95** (for Windows NT) from Microsoft made replication an integral part of the DBMS. Replication is based on a primary site strategy in which the source is the only updatable copy and targets are read-only. Using a publish-and-subscribe framework, the database server acts as a publication server making data available for replication. The published data is sent from the log to a staging table, which then distributes the changes to subscribers, which are database servers requesting the data in a replicatable table.

- **Lotus Notes** from Lotus Development Corp. (now part of IBM) is a database that specializes in documents. Copies of a Lotus Notes database may exist at multiple sites, with one site acting as the master. All changes made to the other copies flow through this copy to the rest of the replicas. After a period of no update activity, the copies will converge to the same contents. This approach is well suited for document databases but not for record-keeping databases.

- Platinum Technology Inc.'s **InfoPump** is a snapshot program for extracting data from one data source and inserting it into a target—it is not intended for transaction propagation. InfoPump supports a wide range of source and target databases and is designed for bulk data movement. InfoPump is really a client application that uses the capabilities of the internal database to extract the data and route it to the targets. Sybase has a partnership with Platinum to integrate the InfoPump product into Sybase's suite of data distribution mechanisms.

7.6 Distributed Databases

Distributing a database requires increased functionality from the DBMS architecture and special considerations in the logical and physical design of the database itself. A distributed database must

- Maintain data integrity by providing local and global locking mechanisms and by supporting commit/rollback transaction integrity.

- Automatically detect deadlocks and perform transaction and database recovery.
- Be able to optimize data access for a wide variety of application requests.
- Be capable of taking advantage of high-powered platforms, especially shared-memory SMP, loosely coupled clusters, and shared-nothing distributed memory MPP processors, as discussed in Sec. 4.6, "Multiprocessing Systems."
- Be able to tune the DBMS engine and I/O subsystem to achieve high data throughput.
- Be able to optimize disk space.
- Be able to support database security and administration for distributed locations, preferably from a centralized location.

One fundamental problem with distributed databases is how to distribute the data. Should it be fragmented onto different machines so that there is only one copy of any one item at any one time? Or should the data be duplicated, either as a whole or in fragments? Some of the questions that need to considered are:

- Is the data being accessed for read-only or is it to be written to?
- Who owns the data and who has access to it?
- Is there a high degree of data availability and integrity?
- Where does the processing take place: locally or on a server?
- Are there constraints on network traffic?

There is no easy solution. If the database is replicated, the replicas must be refreshed regularly. If the database is fragmented, there will be network and processing overhead when the pieces need to be considered as a whole. With either replication or fragmentation, there is some node independence because if some other node goes down, the access to the data at the user's station should be unaffected.

7.7   Distributed Database Architecture

Distributed data management, where data and the DBMS are dispersed among multiple systems, is often required in client/server applications. Organizations can spread enterprise data over multiple systems. Access across the network must be transparent to end users.

But data cannot be distributed without planning. There are some simple rules of thumb for distributing data:

- Every item of data should have a single point of update.
- Distributed updates should be kept to a minimum.
- Distributed data should be as close as possible to the processors that are likely to use it.
- Applications should use location-transparent code.

Some of these issues are being addressed by emerging industry standards such as ANSI SQL3, X/Open's XA architecture, and Remote Data Access from ISO. Most DBMS vendors, most notably IBM, are also involved in distributed data management and have developed their own solutions.

7.7.1   IBM's Distributed Relational Database Architecture

Distributed Relational Database Architecture (DRDA) will provide access to distributed relational data in IBM operating environments—MVS, VM, OS/4000, OS/2, and AIX—and in non-IBM environments that conform to DRDA. It provides the necessary connectivity between relational DBMSs and can operate in homogeneous and heterogeneous system environments. DRDA is a set of communications and interface protocols that if followed will provide access and interoperability among applications and one or more remote relational databases.

DRDA provides a common protocol that supports distributed data and client/server environments using the following IBM architectures:

- Distributed Data Management Architecture (DDM)
- Logical Unit type 6.2 (APPC/LU6.2) Architecture
- SNA Management Services Architecture (MSA)
- Formatted Data Object Content Architecture (FD:OCA)
- Character Data Representation Architecture (CDRA)

DRDA provides the formats and protocols required for data access in a distributed database environment but does not provide the APIs for applications accessing data in a distributed relational DBMS environment. The formats and protocols supported by DRDA depend on the type of distributed database processing supported by the distributed database system.

Within DRDA, the four types of distributed database processing (as described in Sec. 8.5—remote request, remote transaction, distributed transaction, and distributed request) are called degrees of distribution and have been summarized into three degrees:

- **Remote unit of work**. This includes remote request and remote transaction types of distributed database processing and is described in the current level of DRDA.
- **Distributed unit of work**. This is equivalent to the distributed transaction type of processing.
- **Distributed request**. This is equivalent to the distributed request as discussed earlier and is the highest degree of distribution.

Within the framework of the remote unit of work, an application uses SQL to access relational data at a remote system. The SQL request is provided to and executed by this remote system. Any commit/rollback process is confined to one machine.

With the higher degrees of distribution, the commit/rollback process needs to be coordinated among multiple units of work executing at multiple locations. The coordination may be handled by a transaction manager or by one of the participants in the unit of work. DRDA defines the responsibilities of the participants in the distributed unit of work or request as well as the formats and protocols required by a transaction coordinator.

Since it is limited to relational data, DRDA uses SQL as the common access language for defining logical connections between applications and relational DBMSs. Subsets of data managed by a relational DBMS can be connected separately from the entire database.

7.7.2 ISO's Remote Data Access

Remote Data Access (RDA) is the ISO protocol for multisite transaction processing. It is not an all-encompassing framework or architecture; it is a communications protocol optimized for heterogeneous data access. RDA fits into the OSI seven-layer model at the Application layer and is viewed by some as an extension of OSI.

The RDA standard is made up of the Generic Model, which defines a common transfer syntax and a database access protocol, and specializations, which tailors the Generic Model for use with specific data models or languages.

In the DRDA environment, an application is connected to one database at a time. Under ISO's RDA, an application can be connected to more than one database at a time. However, the RDA approach has not completely sorted out the problems related to updating multiple databases, such as failures during updating and coordinating recoveries.

DRDA and RDA are compared in Fig. 7.5.

7.8 Transactions

A transaction is one or more operations that are performed together to complete a task. A postal address change is a simple transaction. A slightly

IBM's DRDA	ISO's RDA
Performance-centered	Portability-centered
Based on SNA	Based on OSI
Each server uses its native SQL	Only a common subset of SQL is supported
Maximizes support for existing applications	Minimizes the effort to port tools to different servers
Focus is on IBM interoperability	Focus is on multivendor, heterogeneous database interoperability
IBM, plus nine other vendors	Every major DBMS vendor except IBM

Figure 7.5 Comparison of DRDA and RDA

more complex transaction is a banking transaction that debits one account and credits another. An even more complex transaction is "taking" an order for items, one of which is not in stock—generate an order transaction, reduce inventory for the items being shipped, generate a picklist for the items being shipped, generate a credit card transaction for the items being shipped, generate a purchase order for the item out of stock (following prescribed rules), and generate an order transaction for the out-of-stock item that is tied to the original order.

For a transaction to be considered successful, **all** operations must be performed. If **any** operation of a transaction cannot be completed, the operations that have taken effect must be undone, a process called *commit and rollback*. While executing the steps of a transaction, the system keeps a log of the work, including before and after images of the data. When the transaction is successfully completed, the system commits all the changes permanently. If the transaction is not successfully completed, the system uses the log to restore (roll back) the database to its state prior to execution. This function is mandatory for transaction processing systems to keep the database in a consistent state between transactions.

In distributed transaction processing, transactions have the following traits (known as the ACID test):

- **Atomicity**. The entire transaction must be either completed or aborted. It cannot be partially completed.
- **Consistency**. The system and its resources go from one steady state to another.
- **Isolation**. The effect of a transaction is not evident to other transactions until the transaction is committed. But any data that a transaction in progress needs is locked to prevent other transactions from changing it.
- **Durability**. The effects of a transaction are permanent and should not be affected by system failures.

To understand the process, consider a banking transaction. A customer transfers $500 from a savings account to a checking account. The transaction has two operations—debit the savings account $500, and credit the checking account $500. For this transaction to be complete, both operations **must** occur. If the debit is handled first and the credit doesn't occur, the savings account will reflect the $500 withdrawal, but the checking account will not reflect the deposit. The table for this transaction may be on the same server or on different ones.

7.9 SQL

SQL (Structured Query Language) has become the standard language for data access in client/server applications, but each vendor's implementation of SQL is slightly different. In order for applications to be portable, developers must be able to write SQL on one hardware/software platform and port it without change (except system-related modifications) to another hardware/software platform.

Structurally, SQL includes

- **Data definition language**, which defines data structures and relationships
- **Data manipulation language**, which moves and updates data
- **Data control language**, which defines access and security constraints

SQL processes data in sets. This allows multiple records—and only those records that satisfy the request—to be transmitted to a client using a single call. When records are retrieved for update purposes, exclusive locks are used, resulting in possible contention for access and bottlenecks.

In addition, SQL can be used to create a results table that combines, filters, and transforms data before transmitting results to the client. Only necessary rows and columns of data are sent over the network, resulting in considerable savings of data communication time and costs.

The assumption is made that most data for client/server applications is stored in relational data structures. The interface software on the client builds an SQL query that is sent to the server relational DBMS. The server executes the query and returns the requested data to the client. Vendors of client/server tools are recognizing that some data needed for client/server applications reside in nonrelational structures. Gateways to non-SQL databases and other data sources are now available. Whether SQL or gateways are used, the process should be transparent to the user; however, some tools are more transparent than others.

Server software must provide all of the data management services typically handled by mainframe systems, such as backup and recovery, rollforward/rollback mechanisms for transaction processing, and testing and diagnostic tools. In addition, the server software should be platform independent to facilitate machine upgrades.

SQL was initially intended to solve problems associated with database interoperability. Although vendors maintain their support of SQL-provided application portability, their proprietary extensions—intended to enhance SQL's functionality—have hindered this interoperability.

7.9.1 SQL92

The initial release of SQL is referred to as SQL89. SQL92 was ratified in 1992. Standards defined for SQL92 are a superset of SQL89. SQL92 has standardized many of the features that were previously left up to the implementor's discretion. Some of the key features that were added include

- **SQL agents**, which are programs or interactive users that produce SQL statements.
- **SQL client/server connections**. SQL92 supports concurrent connections but only one can be active at a time.
- **Standardized catalogs**. A catalog is a collection of SQL schemas that

describe one database, using SQL tables that describe the structure of base tables, views, and privileges, for example.

- **Embedded SQL support** for C, Ada, and MUMPS.
- **Support for dynamic SQL**, including cursors that are used to generate SQL code at run time.
- **Support for new data types**, such as BLOB, VARCHAR, DATE, TIME, and TIMESTAMP.
- **Support for temporary tables**, local and global, that are used as working storage and dropped at the end of the session.
- **Standardized error codes** and diagnostics.

Most analysts feel that bringing the current relational DBMS software up to SQL92 code is a major undertaking. To assist in the process, a program, called a flagger, was written that examines the source code and flags all SQL statements that do not conform to SQL92.

7.9.2 SQL3

Even before most vendors have started the upgrade process to SQL92, ISO and the American National Standard Institute (ANSI) have begun the review process for a third standard for SQL, still called SQL3, which is expected to both close the rift between SQL and programming languages commonly used to develop relational DBMS applications and compete with technologies such as OLE DB and DCE (Distributed Computing Environment).

The SQL3 draft includes Object SQL features, including encapsulation, methods, user-defined data types, and inheritance. The specification refers to these functions as MOOSE, which stands for Major Object-Oriented SQL Extensions.

SQL3 is addressing standards for stored procedures, triggers, and user-defined functions. It will probably include a revised version of the X/Open SQL Call Level Interface (CLI), which supports stored procedures. Persistent Stored Modules (SQL/PSM) deals with stored procedures and offer tight control over data manipulation, and abstract data types that consist of attributes and routines accessible through the dot operator. SQL3 will offer standardized control statements, recursive unions, and roles that are similar to groups and can have access permissions assigned to them.

As more and more applications are including multimedia, SQL3 is developing specifications for multimedia SQL (SQL/MM), which will recognize and handle multimedia data such as full text, audio, video, and BLOBs. SQL/MM will use abstract data types to define the operations supported on each multimedia object type.

A draft of SQL3 is expected to be available in mid-1997.

7.9.3 Call level interface

In 1990, SQL Access Group took the lead in developing an SQL-based call level interface (CLI). The SAG CLI is an API for database access, offering an alternative invocation technique for embedded SQL that provides essentially equivalent operations. The interface would enable client/server applications to access data stored in heterogeneous relational and nonrelational databases. The interface would be platform, vendor, database, and language neutral. SQL Access Group and X/Open published the CLI Snapshot Specification in 1992 as a "work in progress," and it was adopted for use in commercial software products.

Microsoft helped define the X/Open CLI specification and became the first company to commercialize the CLI specification by shipping Open Database Connectivity (ODBC) 1.0 for Windows in 1992. To create ODBC, Microsoft extended the CLI specification and created a three-layer specification in which the "core" layer corresponds to the SAG CLI. Over the next two years, the CLI specification underwent several transformations, reemerging in 1994 as an X/Open Preliminary Specification. Also in 1994, Microsoft released ODBC 2.0, whose core functionality was still aligned with the SAG CLI. In early 1996, Microsoft announced that ODBC 3.0 (to be released in early 1997) will be fully aligned with both ISO's CLI standard and SAG's CLI Specification.

In March 1995, after the SQL Access Group merged with X/Open, the CLI was published as an X/Open Common Application Environment (CAE) specification. CAE specifications are adopted by consensus and are the basis against which suppliers brand their products.

Under CLI, SQL statements are passed directly to the server without being recompiled.

7.10   Database Access

As relational data structures have become the de facto standard for data storage within client/server computing, SQL has become the de facto standard data access language. SQL queries are generated by the client and executed on the server. Some SQL queries may be stored on the server as stored procedures and called by a client application for execution on the server.

7.10.1   SQL interface

How the user accesses the data on the server depends on the tool used to generate the interface. Ideally, the user should not have to know SQL to build an SQL query. Some interfaces use graphics to lead the user through every step of the building process. For example, two scrollable boxes would appear on the screen. One box lists the names of the tables that the user can access. As the user scrolls through the list, the other box displays the data fields in the highlighted table. As the user clicks on choices from the list of fields, that table is automatically selected for the FROM clause. If more than one table is chosen, the interface lists the fields from two tables at a time and asks the user to indicate how they should be joined. The interface then prompts the user for criteria for the selection.

Intelligent SQL interfaces can determine the join patterns when multiple tables are selected and can optimize the retrieval process when criteria are given.

7.10.2 Extended SQL

Most vendors of relational database products have their own versions of SQL, which extend ANSI SQL to include some proprietary extensions. While these extensions may make the products more attractive, they reduce the openness of that particular relational DBMS. If an SQL query includes extensions and must access another version of SQL to complete the query, one of two things will happen. Either the query will not be accepted by the other version of SQL, or the results could be faulty.

If an organization is striving for openness and portability, generated SQL queries must be as close to ANSI standards as possible. One way to ensure this is to use a development and production tool that can generate the appropriate SQL code for the target data source.

7.11 Server DBMSs

Server databases must be able to handle high-volume, multiuser, concurrent access environments. They should support some type of distribution. The databases should be moving in the direction of supporting at least SMP and possibly clusters. MPP support requires more effort and is not as readily available among the major DBMS vendors yet.

7.11.1 Microsoft SQL Server

SQL Server is a client/server relational database aimed at high-volume multiuser network environments. SQL Server was developed jointly by Microsoft and Sybase, but in 1994 the two companies severed their relationship. Microsoft SQL Server and Sybase's SQL Server System 11 both have similar versions of Transact-SQL language, stored procedures, triggers, user-defined data types, and validation rules. Both products support DB-Lib and require modest resources for users.

Microsoft SQL Server 6.x takes advantage of features within NT (in fact, it runs only under NT), has built-in replication capability, and is the center of Microsoft's BackOffice suite. (See Sec. 12.2.3, "System Management," for a discussion of BackOffice) Microsoft SQL Server also addresses improved scalability, manageability, and integration with legacy applications. It has support for SQL89 and SQL92 standards and support for declarative referential integrity, which determines what happens to records in a child table when the corresponding row is deleted from the parent table.

To support replication, Microsoft SQL Server uses a publish-and-subscribe metaphor with a drag-and-drop management interface. It supports snapshot and log-based synchronization strategies, and uses NT security to control data distribution.

This version supports databases of sizes in excess of 100 Gbytes and takes advantage of symmetric multiprocessing hardware, which gives it a speed boost. Other performance enhancements include asynchronous read-ahead and parallel database operations. SQL Server 6x can spawn multiple threads to divide and reattach database tasks. These enhancements make SQL Server a viable choice for on-line transaction processing applications which was not the case with earlier versions.

Enhancements were also made to the desktop side of the software. The software has server-based support for backward and forward scrollable "fat" cursors that can be used to pull back multiple records. To balance network loads, developers can set the number of records that can be pulled across for each query.

Microsoft SQL Server has built-in support for major LANs, OLE Automation, ODBC, MAPI, SQL client APIs, and third-party gateways for connections to external data sources and processing operations. Microsoft is looking for third-party deals to hook SQL Server into the enterprise.

SQL Server 6.5, released mid-1996, includes support for bidirectional data replication from external databases, and the IETF's relational DBMS SNMP Management Information Base through a translation component for converting Windows NT events into SNMP format. This feature allows administrators to monitor SQL Server remotely from network-management consoles.

Microsoft SQL Server 6.5 integrates with such NT services as security, event logging, performance monitoring, threading, and asynchronous input/output. One of this version's most promising enhancements is the Distributed Transaction Coordinator which offers transparent two-phase commit between databases and supports transactions over multiple physical databases. In addition, this version has built-in support for Internet applications and the SQL Server Web Assistant for publishing Microsoft SQL Server data on the WWW.

A new locking architecture called dynamic locking is also included in SQL Server 6.5. SQL Server chooses the right level of lock—row, page, table, or database—to maximize both speed and concurrency of the access.

Microsoft SQL Server 6.5 also includes a system administration model called SQL Distributed Management Framework (SQL-DMF) with three main components.

- **SQL Enterprise Manager**, a graphical tool for administering servers from a single console. Tasks include configuring servers, monitoring their activity, backing up and restoring data, and analyzing queries. It provides active notifications such as alarms or E-mail and uses built-in Simple Network Management Protocol (SNMP) monitoring agents. An

OLE-based three-tier architecture allows users to build automated maintenance procedures.

- **SQL Executive**, a Windows NT applications that uses a SQL Server database to track scheduling, begin tasks at appointed times, and manage events, alerts, and tasks.
- **Distributed Management Objects** (SQL-DMO), over forty 32-bit OLE objects with interfaces that can be invoked from a language such as Visual Basic, Visual C++, or any language that supports OLE.

7.11.2   Oracle

Oracle offers three DBMS products: Oracle7 (and soon Oracle8), with its parallel query offerings for decision support and database administration for very large databases, Oracle Workgroup Server for workgroups, and Personal Oracle7. Workgroup Server and Personal have all the features of the Oracle engine except parallel query, distributed database, and replication features. Oracle runs on over ten platforms including NetWare, Solaris, NT, and Macintosh.

Oracle's replication is a read-only implementation using snapshots. This requires additional programming if it is running in an occasionally connected environment.

Oracle Objects for OLE is an alternative to ODBC and the Microsoft JET engine and Oracle Power Objects.

Release 7.3 of Oracle7, referred to as Oracle's Universal Database and shipped mid-1996, includes analytical query processing capabilities, parallel execution technology, support for new data types (such as video and audio), and advanced replication capabilities, as well as an improved GUI and a WWW server. Data warehouse technology—including support for star schema—is also integrated into 7.3.

Oracle7 includes the following tools:

- Security Manager, for setting up users
- Enterprise Manager, for creating databases and tables and for managing Oracle servers
- Schema Manager, for creating table definitions
- Data Manager, for loading data

Oracle8, an object-oriented version of this popular product, is scheduled for release in 1997.

7.11.3   Sybase

At the core of its System 10 product, Sybase packages a DBMS engine and system administration services for small LANs. Options include

- **Replication Server** for managing copies of data
- **Enterprise SQL Server Manager** for administering large networks of servers

- **Navigation Server** for massively parallel computers
- **OmniSQL Gateway** and **Turnkey Gateway** for access to heterogeneous data sources
- **Open Client/Open Server** interface for integrating heterogeneous clients and servers

In the System 10 family of Sybase SQL Server, Sybase enhanced the core server product, added new data types, built in compliance for SQL89 and SQL92 standards, provided support for declarative integrity constraints, and added new server-based cursors for both applications and stored procedures. Sybase also released a modernized version of its API library, called CT-Lib, but is continuing to support DB-Lib.

The newer System 11, primarily a performance release, runs on a variety of platforms including Digital Unix, HP-UX, IBM AIX, Sun Solaris, and Windows NT. Sybase redesigned the database engine to make better use of hardware and processing cycles by maximizing the use of idle time and multiprocessor computing.

The System 11 DBMS family of products includes SQL Server 11 as well as the following add-ons:

- **Sybase IQ** is an extension of SQL Server 11 that supports interactive query processing for data marts. Sybase claims that IQ is faster and requires less disk space than competing relational DBMSs.
- **Sybase SQL Anywhere**, formerly Watcom SQL, is a database for individuals and workgroups that is compartible and interoperable with SQL Server and uses SQL Server's stored-procedure language. SQL Anywhere's executable requires less than 1 Mbyte of memory.
- **Sybase MPP**, another extension of SQL Server, supports large-scale parallel processing architecture for data warehouse applications. Sybase MPP, formerly known as Navigation Server, currently available for the AT&T Global Information Solutions NCR3600 and IBM's RS/6000 platforms, supports large-scale warehouses that exceed the size of a single SMP (symmetric multiprocessing) computer. Sybase MPP includes Configurator, which analyzes information about parallel systems and predicts performance and response times, recommends the best way to spread data across disk drives, and analyzes the impact of growth.

Sybase's systems management tool suite includes

- **Backup Server** to coordinate backup and restores of multiple SQL Servers across a network
- **SQL Server Monitor** to provide stats for tuning SQL Server

These two together perform functions equivalent to those executed by Microsoft's SQL Enterprise Manager.

To address very large enterprise environments, Sybase built Enterprise SQL Server Manager (ESSM), which allows a single database administrator to create and manage database objects, such as schemas and tables, across several Sybase databases. ESSM, based on the Tivoli Management

Framework, is an object-oriented graphical product for managing and automating administrative tasks through an object request broker that complies with OMG's CORBA. Using ESSM, administrators can configure databases and monitor database status. ESSM also provides services for configuration management, scheduling, transaction control, and security. ESSM uses an alerter to notify systems administrators of important events. Multiple servers can be administered simultaneously with single drag-and-drop operations.

7.11.4 DB2/2

The DB2 family of relational DBMSs from IBM include its legacy mainframe version as well as server versions that run on IBM's AS/400; under AIX, HP-UX, Solaris, OS/2, and Windows NT. All versions of DB2 are based on DB2's Common Technology, which refers to millions of lines of C/C++ code that is common across all DB2 platforms.

DB2/2 for OS/2 from IBM was recently updated to version 2.1. It uses the thread-based architecture of OS/2. IBM improved the product's cost-based optimizer, introduced stored procedures, and added trigger support. DB2/2 for OS/2 also includes replication, text and image manipulation, and strong DBA support with administration tools such as DataHub and end-user tools such as Visualizer.

DB2/2 for Windows NT is the cornerstone of IBM's Database Server component of its software server suite. Database Server provides a graphical interface to DB2 for NT's command prompt interface. Database Server also includes Web Connect, which is a programming interface that connects databases to Web servers, and Database Director, which administrators can use to manage databases, table spaces, log-ins, and backups.

7.11.5 Informix Online Workgroup Server

Informix's Online Dynamic Server supports unstructured and object-relational data as well as relational databases. Online Dynamic Server offers functionality which includes storage and retrieval of data, images, audio, and video. User can develop and deploy next-generation applications that utilize a variety of data types. The product uses Dynamic Scalable Architecture foundation, which is a parallel database technology.

7.12 Data for On-line Analytic Processing

On-line analytic processing (OLAP) is a relatively new buzzword for the industry. In its former life, the structure was known as multidimensional cubes, and the tools that used the structure were marketed as decision-support system (DSS) tools. Vendors have repackaged the concept, expanded its functionality, and positioned it as the technology for doing flexible analysis (which it always has been able to do).

Multidimensional analysis involves representing data as user-defined dimensions, not as tables. The data in these "cubes" is typically summarized, but not always.

Dimensions are usually related to the reporting hierarchy of the organization. A multidimensional database could have multiple hierarchies. The most general are time, geography, and product. For example, a sales analysis database might organize data by product, customer, and time. Each customer belongs in a particular territory, each product belongs to a product group, and each time element (such as weeks) belongs to a higher, more summarized time element (such as months). Because of these additional hierarchies (or roll-up aggregations), the data in the sales analysis database could be analyzed in a variety of ways, as illustrated in Fig. 7.6.

Multidimensional analysis involves extracting data along particular dimensions and roll-up aggregations. Users may manipulate the results of the analysis (usually a tabular display) by reviewing the detail ("drilling down"), rolling up into higher levels of detail, or modifying the slice under review. OLAP analysis also usually involves ranking, moving averages, period-to-period comparisons, cumulative statistics, and other financial and statistical calculations.

OLAP data is bulk loaded from other data sources on a periodic basis. The data sources could include ASCII data files, SQL databases, legacy files, and spreadsheets.

OLAP tools emphasize interactive use and many tools use agents to

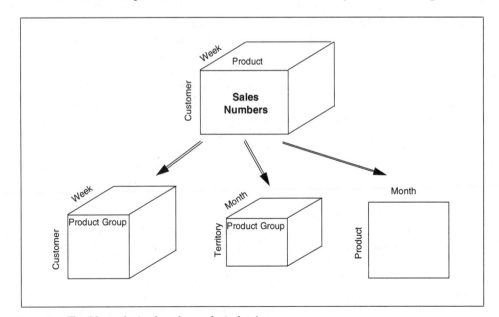

Figure 7.6 Flexible analysis of a sales analysis database

automate tasks without direct user intervention. Agents run in background, either at scheduled times or when triggered by an event. Since agents are in effect programs, they are limited to what the user thinks should be analyzed and how it should be analyzed. The next set of features will no doubt include some intelligent data mining techniques.

Relational DBMSs are ill-equiped to handle these requirements. However, the OLAP products, with their GUI front ends, specialized languages, and structures, are specifically geared toward solving these problems. Products offering true OLAP include Essbase from Arbor Software Corp., Commander series from Comshare Inc., Oracle Express product family from Oracle (formerly IRI Software), Pilot Decision Support Suite and Pilot Discovery Server Pilot Software Inc. (a subsidiary of Dun and Bradstreet), and SAS System from SAS Institute, Inc.

To address the need for analytic processing along dimensions without resorting to OLAP, organizations use query tools that provide multi-dimensional analysis by creating a layer between the application and the relational DBMS. These tools use metadata repositories to store definitions of dimensions and their mapping to the relational tables, hierarchy relationships between the dimensions, and formulas and calculations.

The client software generates the request and sends it to the server software. The server software translates the request into SQL queries, obtains the results of the queries from the relational DBMS, performs the multidimensional analysis, and returns the final results to the client.

The primary advantage of these intermediaries is that there is no initial loading or periodic updating of OLAP data. In addition, the results are always against real-time data. The downside is defining and creating the megadata repository and modifying table structures to facilitate this type of access, as well as high resource use and response times while the request is being translated.

Products that offer this kind of support include BusinessObjects from Business Objects, Inc., DSS Agent from MicroStrategy Inc., MetaCube from Stanford Technology Group Inc., Holos from Holistic Systems, Inc., and BrioQuery from Brio Technology.

Tools marketed as OLAP tools range in capabilities. Some, such as CrossTarget from Dimensional Insight Inc. and DecisionSuite from Information Advantage Inc., extract data from relational and legacy data sources and place the data into proprietary multidimensional databases. The companies offer additional products to support exception reporting, to combine databases as a virtual data store to allow the users to analyze larger amounts of information, to provide agent technology, to export data to spreadsheets, and to add filters to the data.

7.13   Data Warehouses

The concept behind data warehouses is to give any authorized user access to the latest data, efficiently organized and ready to go. With a data warehouse, the organization decides what data is of interest and therefore should be in the warehouse. The data comes into the data warehouse from a company's production systems. It is cleaned up, broken down, combined with other data, and placed in the warehouse to wait for a user to access it. It sounds so simple—which should be the first clue that it isn't.

A data warehouse is a repository of data from production systems that is summarized or aggregated and possibly translated. The basic idea behind data warehouses is to separate the operational data, the real-time transaction-based data, from the historical data used to analyze business trends and produce historical "what happened" reports. As transaction data accumulates, it is transferred to the warehouse—once an hour, once a day, once a week, or monthly. The data is aggregated, calculations run against it, and/or it may be restructured into a format that supports ad hoc query, analysis, and reporting. In most cases, the data warehouse is on a separate machine from the production applications that produce the original data

A data warehouse can be centralized or decentralized; the latter are sometimes referred to as data marts. Data marts are discussed in Sec. 7.13.2.

OLAP vendors are big proponents of data warehouses. They feel that multidimensional databases complement the relational databases stored in the warehouses. One is aimed at fast retrieval of data, and the other at multidimensional analysis aimed at a particular problem set.

Any discussion of data warehouses would not be complete without mention of resources. Consultants predict that to build an enterprise data warehouse could take as long as two to three years and cost between $2 and $3 billion.

7.13.1   Metadata

But what about that data? How does an organization ensure that it is accurate and that every one is using the same language? An organization has to determine what the data is, what it means, how it relates to other data, who uses it, and how do they use it. Routines need to be developed to take copies of the data from the production systems, scrub it, and insert the clean data into the right place in the data warehouse. In addition, the organization needs new tools to get to this uniquely structured data.

The glue that makes a data warehouse work is its metadata (data about data). It tracks the information about the data: what it is, where it is, what it means, how it is accessed, and who updates it (and how). Currently, all metadata implementations are proprietary. The Metadata Council was formed in 1995 by Arbor Software Corp., Business Objects Inc., Cognos Corp., Evolutionary Technologies International, Platinum Technology Inc., and Texas Instruments Inc. The council was created to define a vendor-independent API for metadata which would allow organizations to define metadata once and have it be shared by different tools.

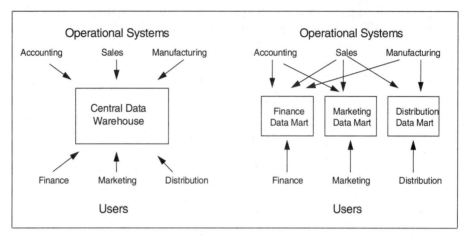

Figure 7.7 Centralized data warehouse and data marts

In late 1995 the Metadata Council proposed a standard for the exchange and storage of metadata called the Metadata Interchange Initiative. The first phase released in early 1996 creates a standardized ASCII file format which vendors can use to import and export metadata. The second phase, scheduled to appear in 1997, will consist of a standardized API through which vendors can directly and automatically exchange metadata. However, it is too early to tell when products compliant with these standards will be market-ready.

7.13.2 Data marts

Data marts are subsets of a larger data warehouse schema. Instead of an enterprise data warehouse that serves everyone's needs at once, organizations are working on data marts that serve the need of a highly focused business group. By limiting the size and scope of the project, companies can get the data into the hands of the users in a fraction of the time and at a reasonable cost. They also allow a company to prototype or pilot a larger data warehouse.

The data is selected and organized for a particular set of usage requirements. The focus may be on a single functional area such as sales or inventory, or based on organizational boundaries or geography, such as sales in the eastern region. These mini–data warehouses serve as distributed data sources. For comparisons of the two approaches, review Fig. 7.7.

A data mart is easier and faster to implement because there are fewer subjects to model, fewer users to support, and less data to transform and store. Data marts can often be built using existing hardware, databases, and networks.

One danger associated with data marts is that each entity creates its own data mart without regard to a unified, global view of data that is necessary to run the corporation as a strategic entity. In effort, creating legacy systems of tomorrow which may be more costly to integrate than legacy systems of today. There needs to be a balance between the short-term tactical requirements to get data in the hands of the users and a long-term architecture to provide a unified view of corporate data.

Most of the DBMS vendors offer products that support the building of data marts. Some offer a wider range of functionality than others—and with each new release, the range gets narrower and narrower.

7.13.3 Implementing data warehouses and data marts

Data warehouse and data mart implementation requires five steps.

- **Identify the data**. This sounds like the easy step, but it actually turns out to require a great deal of time and human interactions. As discussed in Sec. 13.2, "Data Quality", the data that is to be stored in the data warehouse must be reviewed for consistency and accuracy. How the data should be presented in the data warehouse must also be determined: detailed or summarized, if summarized, how—along what lines, using what rules?

- **Assemble the data**. The bridges and access routines to the various primary data sources must be built and tested. These data sources could be relational or nonrelational and from heterogeneous platforms.

- **Transform the data**. The captured data must be converted into its warehouse form. This transformation includes aggregation, data type conversion, data reformatting, and translation.

- **Distribute the data**. This step takes the results of the transformation and populates the files in the data warehouse.

- **Access the data**. Users need to be provided with front-end tools to access and manipulate the data in the warehouse.

8

Middleware

Designing client/server applications is fundamentally different from building traditional mainframe or macro-based micro applications. Programmers should be isolated from network intricacies and given easy access to server and network functions.

Middleware does just that. It is viewed as the glue that holds together all the disparate components in a client/server (or distributed computing) environment. The middleware software sits between the client and the server—hence the name "middleware"—and supports the communications, data access, and run-time facilities that are required for a client request to be serviced. A visual picture of middleware's capabilities is presented in Fig. 8.1.

Middleware provides the integration between the application programs and other software components in the environment which allows resources to be shared, processing to be distributed, and interaction between heterogeneous systems, nodes, and networks to take place. Since middleware sits on top of the communication protocols, it eliminates the need for client applications to know about low-level communication protocols.

The need for middleware has been driven by the diversity of the components that are being connected in the enterprise network. Data is being distributed throughout the network on an as-needed basis; mainframe data is being accessed by client/server applications. Heterogeneous solutions are the norm, and such solutions require interoperability across network and data access protocols, DBMSs, and operating systems.

However, little progress has been made toward standardizing the various functions that are delivered as APIs (application program interfaces). It is

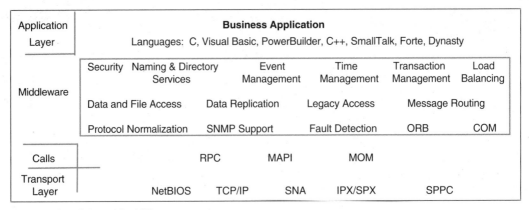

Figure 8.1 Capabilities of middleware

unlikely that middleware functionality from different vendors operates or interoperates identically.

Middleware is used to fill three major application requirements: distributed-system services, application-enabling services, and middleware management services.

Distributed-system services sit above the network layers and provide communication and program-to-program services. The communication services include RPCs and message passing and message queuing. Program-to-program services include directory and naming services, consistent time reference, and security.

Among **application-enabling services,** data management services provide access to files and databases distributed over the network and the functions necessary to maintain operational integrity and application availability. Application cooperation services provide high-level application-oriented functions which reduce the amount of intelligence that must be built into the distributed applications themselves. E-mail is also an application-enabling service. Transaction monitors provide an API for development of transaction applications and a facility for more efficient execution. User interface services manage the communication sessions between the user and the distributed applications and services.

Middleware management services are still something of a wish list. They would enable applications and system functions to be continuously monitored to ensure optimum quality of service from the distributed application network. These functions include configuration and change management, and operation and performance management that would monitor all events that occur, respond to abnormal events, and provide statistics that could be used to tune the system.

8.1 Functions of Middleware

Middleware services are sets of distributable software services that exist between the application and the operating systems and network services on the system node in the network. The middleware services provide a simpler and more functional set of APIs than the operating system and network services.

The middleware services allow an application to

- Transparently locate services within the network and interact with another application or service.
- Be independent from network services.
- Be reliable and available.
- Scale up or down in capacity without losing function.

8.2 Middleware Models

As illustrated in Fig. 8.2, middleware can be used to support all of the styles of distributed computing.

Middleware handles the splitting of logic between the server and the workstation when application logic is distributed. This link is provided by the APIs generated by the middleware software.

Data management middleware handles the connections between an application or DBMS on one node and a DBMS running on another node. The target DBMS could be a relational database within the client/server environment or legacy data residing on a mainframe that is linked into the environment. This type of middleware supports remote data management and distributed DBMS environments. This link is provided by tools such as EDA/SQL, SQL, and software that is compliant with standards such as ODBC, DRDA, and OLE DB.

Middleware can also be used to route service requests. In some cases, middleware is used to route a service request to the server that can handle it most quickly. In other cases, requests are broken up and routed to specific servers (when a particular server has a predefined role in the process) using some specified rules.

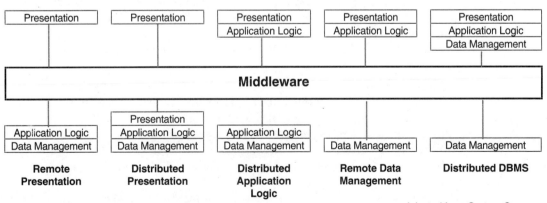

Adapted from Gartner Group

Figure 8.2 Middleware in all styles of distributed computing

8.3   Connecting Clients to Servers

Connecting clients to the servers in the enterprise-wide network is the responsibility of middleware. It is the tough part of multitier architectures.

There are two main categories. One type provides data access connections for heterogeneous data sources. Database APIs and gateways such as Microsoft's ODBC and Information Builder's EDA/SQL provide this type of connection.

The other category is client-to-server and server-to-server. This type of connectivity is based on four types of related technologies:

- Remote procedure calls
- Message queuing
- TP monitors
- Object request brokers

The first two are discussed in Sec. 8.9, "Connection Services." TP monitors are discussed in Sec. 11.4.2, and object request brokers in Sec. 17.1.1.

8.4   Distributed Presentation

The presentation portion of an application is usually not distributed. All presentation functions are usually done by the client machine. In the case of mobile users, however, the idea of breaking up the presentation into two pieces makes some sense. The front-end of the presentation component is the actual services: GUI, color, font, and mouse/keyboard interactions. The back end performs some presentation logic.

8.4.1   Legacy screen scrapers

Some products are designed to add value to existing host applications by building graphical front ends to existing applications. These tools are called frontware or screen scrapers. Their chief advantage is that they capture 3270/5250 data streams and provide routines for developers to use to convert them to CUA-compliant graphical presentations. No changes in the host application code are required.

Some of the common capabilities of screen-scraping products include the following:

- Multiple host screens can be combined on one display panel.
- Support for the Windows DDE interface allows data from Windows programs, such as Microsoft Excel or Lotus 1-2-3 for Windows, to be placed into windows on the display panel or data to be downloaded to Windows programs.
- Supported GUI objects include file folders, fields, tables, icons, action bars, drop-down menus, radio buttons, dialog boxes, and check boxes.
- GUI objects have predefined characteristics that can be customized.

Major benefits of using the screen-scraping option include the following:

- It gives the legacy system a new boost and a longer life.
- It gives the users (and developers) experience with GUIs.
- The legacy system can be moved to a client/server environment with a minimum of disruption.
- Business processes can be improved and simplified.
- Heavily used screens can be reengineered to improve user productivity and effectiveness. Menu choices can be replaced by a drop-down Windows menu. Color can be used to distinguish required fields from optional ones. Function keys can be replaced with mouse clicks on Windows objects.
- Workflow can be improved so that users are able to navigate more easily through the application.

Other Windows-like enhancements include hot lists, which are pull-down menus of common entries for some field in the application, and hot spots, which allow a user to use the mouse for faster operation.

However, this is not as easy as it sounds. The developers need to understand the business process, the host applications, and the technology platform. A business analyst should be called in to improve the existing process. One-to-one screen mapping isn't always possible because host screens may have more data on them than can efficiently be placed on one GUI screen.

Screen scrapers are also being used to present information from multiple host applications without having to integrate the applications. This software is being called legacy extension software and is discussed in Sec. 10.4.3. Some organizations are looking to OLE to build data links between the desktop and host applications and to graphical development environments such as Visual Basic to produce the screens.

8.5   Distributed Access Methods

When data is distributed, all or part of the data management logic accompanies the data. The services should be provided in such a way that users and applications do not even know that the data is distributed. The four types of distributed data access are

- Remote request
- Remote transaction
- Distributed transaction
- Distributed request

The terminology of client/server computing will be used to illustrate the individual processes. For example, a client (micro or server) requests data from a server.

8.5.1   Remote request

In a remote request, an application issues a single data request that can be processed from a single remote site, as illustrated in Fig. 8.3. This is also referred to as a logical unit of work or a processing transaction. The

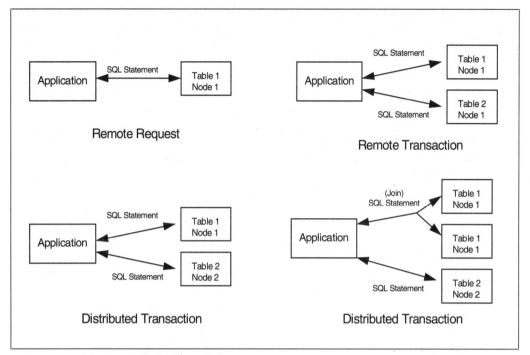

Figure 8.3 Four types of distributed data access

application must know the physical location of the data. Remote requests can be used to perform the manual extract method of data distribution.

8.5.2   Remote transaction

A remote transaction contains multiple data requests, but all the requested data resides on the same node, as illustrated in Fig. 8.3. This is also referred to as a remote unit of work. For example, using the relational model, a remote transaction could contain two or more SQL statements that refer to data on a single node. The application must know the physical location of the data. For the transaction to be successful, *all* statements in the transaction would have to be successful.

8.5.3   Distributed transaction

A distributed transaction contains multiple data requests that refer to data residing on multiple nodes, as illustrated in Fig. 8.3. In the client/server model, a client can request data from multiple servers in a single processing transaction. The application must know the physical location of the data. For the transaction to be successful, *all* statements in the transaction would have to be successful.

8.5.4   Distributed request

A distributed request is a transaction consisting of multiple requests that can be processed at multiple sites, as illustrated in Fig. 8.3. Each request can reference data residing on multiple sites. All actions performed by a distributed request are considered one logical unit of work—one processing transaction. An application does not need to know where the data is physically located.

8.6   Types of Access

If IT organizations could get all their users to work only at their desks, access would not be a problem.

Local access is getting into the network through an internal line. It is very straightforward and a mature process.

Remote access is using dial-in access to gain entry into the network. Remote access technology is broken down into two categories: remote control connections and remote node connections.

8.6.1   Remote control connection

In remote control connections, the micro is in effect a dumb terminal with a monitor, keyboard, and mouse. The dial-up telephone line connects these components with the computer at the host site that can log on to the network. The remote micro performs no processing operations beyond executing the remote control software itself, which simply updates the display and sends keyboard and mouse input to the host. The network exchanges are at the Application layer of the network operating system.

The principal problem with remote control solutions for organizations is their expense. A host computer with a network interface, modem, and telephone line and a remote micro and modem must be dedicated to every remote session. If the host machines are distributed among different offices, providing security and technical support becomes a big issue. Logged-in machines distributed throughout the building with no local users are a security risk. Also, finding someone to physically reboot crashed host machines is a problem.

Organizations that wish to take this route can use chassis- or rack-based systems of host computers on plug-in boards. These systems enable network managers to install a high density of remote-session hosts in a central and controlled location and provide additional features such as remote rebooting and remote management. While the costs of these systems are higher than those of individual stand-alone micros, the reduced support, management, and administration costs will offset some (if not all) of the price difference.

Some of the popular remote control programs are Symantec's Norton pcANYWHERE, Microcom Inc.'s Carbon Copy, and Traveling Software Inc.'s LapLink for Windows.

8.6.2 Remote node connection

Remote node sessions need only a dedicated modem and a serial port. Multiple sessions can readily share a single processor and network interface. A remote network server is a router (or sometimes a bridge) that translates frames on the serial port to a frame layout that the LAN can accommodate and then passes them along. The processor is required only to route or bridge incoming and outgoing traffic. Since a 10-Mbps Ethernet link can handle a large number of ISDN sessions and more than a thousand 9,600-bps asynchronous connections, supporting a few remote nodes doesn't require a high-end microprocessor.

Remote node services can be provided using a number of hardware options. Processing can be handled by a product sold as a router or bridge, on a processor in a dedicated box, on a communications server, or on a file server which is also functioning as a communications server. The options are almost endless. Stand-alone modems may be mounted on an external rack and plugged into serial ports. Internal modems may be installed on plug-in boards. Multiple serial ports may be built into a dedicated access box or mounted on boards that plug into the communications server or file server. ISDN ports may be supplied on plug-in boards for servers, on modular boards for dedicated servers, or on digital modems (terminal adapter boxes) that connect to a serial port.

Remote node servers can be purchased with built-in modems or with serial ports that can be connected to external modems or to other wide area links such as ISDN lines.

Dedicated remote access boxes are generally the easiest way to provide network access to remote users. Configuration problems are few, as most of these products are just about at plug-and-play levels. However, they are not the least expensive option, and they offer little or no flexibility for upgrading and expanding. If an organization has standardized on routers and bridges, they may provide the most effective remote node solution. Except for the fact that the modems or ISDN attachment equipment must be configured, most devices designed specifically for remote access are as easy to set up as a dedicated box.

Micro servers that function as remote node servers require the most configuration. The software and all the ports that attach to the dial-up lines need to be configured.

Some software vendors are offering a single package that combines remote control and remote node support. These products allow an organization to match the access method to the applications instead of having the applications adapt to the access method.

Dedicated access boxes such as those from Shiva Corp., Telebit Corp., and 3COM Corp. run their own routing software. IBM's LAN Distance software allows a portable computer or remote micro to access a LAN as if it were on the network. LAN Distance also filters and directs WAN traffic.

Novell's NetWare Connect provides remote-node access, remote-control connections, and dial-out connections for NetWare, AppleTalk, and LAN

Workplace clients on NetWare 3.x and 4.x networks for DOS, Macintosh, NetWare, or Windows clients.

Windows NT includes Remote Access Server. Attachmate's Remote LAN Node (RLN) software supports DOS, Windows, and ARA clients. RLN allows all remote users to have the same access and functionality as locally connected LAN users—the remote micro views the LAN as an extension of its own environment.

Early remote node applications used a proprietary interface for remote client–to–remote node server sessions. Today, most products use Point-to-Point Protocol (PPP), which supports most ordinary LAN protocols. PPP encapsulates common Network layer protocols in specialized Network Control Protocol packets—for example, IPCP (IP over PPP) and IPXCP (IPX over PPP). PPP is a variant of the High-level Data Link Control protocol and is a slower alternative to Ethernet or token ring at the Data Link layer. PPP can work with Physical layers (modems, and analog and ISDN telephone links). The use of PPP provides interoperability among products from multiple hardware and software vendors.

8.6.3 Comparisons

Remote node access is appropriate when the remote client machine has applications installed on it and the connection is necessary for the transfer or manipulation of data in small doses. Applications that use shared directories on a LAN for data storage are ideal for remote node access. It is best to avoid transferring even files "only" as large as 100 kbytes, as the transfer will be extremely slow.

With large data files and when applications are installed on the host, remote control provides a huge performance advantage. Because the processing is local and the files move across local links, the connection pipe doesn't become a bottleneck.

Remote E-mail is an exception to the rule. The remote clients provided by most E-mail vendors connect using an application-specific remote node connection. The remote E-mail software posts the mail to the "main" post office and downloads new messages. It does not necessarily display old messages or other material that would appear locally. For full-featured E-mail access to a single, complete in-box, remote control is the best choice.

The availability of ISDN connections and advances in compression techniques (which make files smaller) have slowed down the demand for remote control access. That and the fact that remote node connections are less costly! However, as programs continue to get bigger and multimedia (whose files are very, very large) continues to play a more important role in applications, remote control is not going away any time soon.

8.7 Distributed Data Access

Access to data has to be provided even if the data is distributed throughout the network. More importantly, access to heterogeneous databases is necessary. In a homogeneous database environment, the DBMS would take care of the access. In heterogeneous environments, organizations look to middleware.

8.7.1   APIs and formats

An application programming interface (API) is a set of programming routines used to provide services and link different types of software. APIs have been written to access data sources and network services, and to pass control and data back and forth between software. APIs can be used to access resources and software that are not directly supported by the language used for development.

APIs define how data is presented to other components of a system, such as a server, a database, or an E-mail application. APIs are receiving a great deal of attention, as organizations use them to provide the connections between their existing heterogeneous equipment and software, thus creating an open system.

FAPs (format and protocols) are the format of the message and the handshake between the client and the server. They are the set of rules that specifies the format, timing, sequencing, and/or error checking for communication.

8.7.2   Database gateways

Database gateways act as interface translators that move data, SQL commands, and applications from one type of database to another, as illustrated in Fig. 8.4. Database gateways must know the details (syntax, data format, data types, and catalog naming conventions) of the products to be accessed and be synchronized with software releases of the data sources. The price of this accessibility is speed, because it is necessary to translate the client request and the server results.

Database gateways sit between the client application and the target mainframe database. The client, gateway, and server can reside on the same

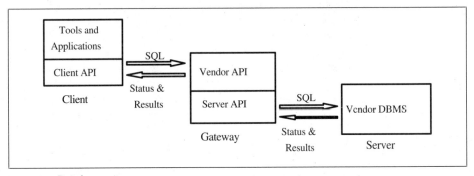

Figure 8.4 Database gateways

platform or different ones. This allows gateways to connect clients and servers running on dissimilar networks. They are ideally suited to bridge network protocols, such as TCP/IP, OSI, and SNA, while acting as the transportation interfaces for moving data among database platforms. They do not create an actual file of the data.

A server-based database gateway can act as a concentrator providing gateway services for several workstations in a workgroup. This is a more cost-effective solution and off-loads communications work from the workstation.

Database gateways have the following functions:

- Accept statements specified by a well-defined grammar (usually SQL) from a client application.
- Translate the statements to a specific database format.
- Send the statements to be executed against the database which may involve translating LAN protocols to WAN packets.
- Translate the results back into a well-defined format.
- Return the data and status information to the client.

To appear transparent to the user, a database gateway must also include log-in validation, a cancel/interrupt/error handler, and data-type conversions, and must be able to emulate the defined security. It must also be flexible enough to allow users to activate various modes of operation, such as pass-through and debug/trace modes.

EDA

Enterprise Data Access (EDA), from Information Builders, Inc. (IBI), is a family of client/server products, based on an open architecture, that provides SQL-based access to relational and nonrelational data sources on a networked multivendor system.

EDA provides a uniform, relational view of data, regardless of the storage structure. The operating environment and file location are transparent to the user. EDA can access over 60 relational and nonrelational data sources and support over 35 different operating environments.

Using a variety of end-user tools, the user develops SQL requests, which EDA distributes and processes against local or remote data, returning the results to the end-user tool. Users can join relational and nonrelational data sources. EDA can directly update relational databases and uses RPCs to update nonrelational databases. EDA can also be used by applications written in third-generation languages to send and receive SQL requests from anywhere in the network.

The family of tools includes

- **EDA/SQL Server**, which processes SQL requests against relational and nonrelational data and enables data warehousing by permitting users to access, store, migrate, and retrieve data

- **API/SQL,** a call level API which allows third-generation languages to address local or remote data via SQL calls
- **EDA/Link,** a modular system of communication interfaces
- **EDA/WebLink**, which links common gateway interface (CGI) scripts to more than 60 databases and formats and allows access from a corporate Web page to corporate EDA-accessible data via a Web browser
- **EDA/Extender** products, which are direct interfaces that allow many existing products immediate entry to Information Warehouse framework

EDA/Start, which combines IBI's EDA with Open Environment Corp.'s Entera distributed application, links Distributed Computing Environment applications to the EDA/SQL gateway. EDA/Start accesses SQL databases and relational and nonrelational databases in a three-tier environment and provides DCE applications with asynchronous RPC support.

Information Builders plans to include MOM (message-oriented middleware) from Momentum Software Corp. in the Version 4.X release of its EDA middleware slated for announcement in early 1997. Momentum's X*IPC will add messaging, queuing, and the guarantee of delivery services to EDA, thereby expanding its functionality to include asynchronous connections. With asynchronous connectivity supported, messages such as SQL queries can be either stored and forwarded or delivered instantly. X*IPC guarantees message delivery.

Database Gateway

Database Gateway, from the InfoCONNECT division of Sybase (formerly from Micro Decisionware Inc. [MDI] which was acquired by Sybase in 1995), resides on a server platform and accepts SQL transactions from client stations. The SQL transactions are redirected to DB2, SQL/DS, AS/400, Oracle, or Teradata DBC/1012 databases for processing. The client stations can be running DOS, Windows, UNIX, OS/2, or Mac. Database Gateway is available for VSE, AS/400 running DB2 or SQL/DS with DRDA, Windows NT, and Teradata DBC/1012.

Database Gateway includes two components.

- One component runs on the LAN under the OS/2 Communication Manager and handles communications to and from the client applications and the host.
- The second component is the host portion that links the gateway to DB2, SQL/DS, or Teradata DBC/108.

Communication between the front end and the gateway is achieved using Named Pipes, the interprocess communications mechanism used in SQL Server. The gateway will therefore run on any network that can support Named Pipes (such as NetWare and VINES). Communication between the gateway server and the IBM host is then achieved via IBM's APPC protocol.

Database Gateway supplies a data compression algorithm, which transfers data between the client and the server at a fast rate because of the compression. It also permits retrieved data to bypass temporary storage within CICS, transmitting the data directly to the client application.

InfoPump

InfoPump, from Platinum Technology, allows organizations to schedule periodic data extracts from a variety of data sources and directly output the requests to a local database server, such as Oracle or Sybase. InfoPump pumps data and metadata and allows data to be manipulated enroute.

InfoPump includes a scripting language used to specify the data sources, data targets, and schedule. It connects to a mainframe database via IBI's EDA or Sybase's Database Gateway, or to local database servers via direct drivers.

InfoPump 2.2 provides bidirectional replication of data between more than 30 heterogenous data sources on multiple platforms. This version of InfoPump supports 32-bit implementations of HP-UX, Sun Solaris, AIX, Windows NT, and OS/2, as well as Lotus Notes 4.0.

8.8   Distributed Processing

Communication gets trickier when an application needs to communicate between clients and servers and between servers and servers, with some of the servers being dedicated servers.

8.8.1   Distributed transaction processing (DTP)

Distributed transaction processing is the result of the evolution from centralized transaction processing to distributed processing. The definition of distributed transaction processing is that there are two or more programs residing on different machines that cooperate in order to perform certain required functions of a transaction.

In distributed transaction processing, a business transaction that is executed across a network of systems is broken into "local" transactions. Each local transaction is executed on its own system under the control of a transaction manager. Communication between the local transactions is synchronous—one-way. Each transaction is designed so that its processing depends directly on the results of the processing performed by the other local transactions.

The actions of the local transactions must be coordinated so that all changes made to local or remote resources can be committed or rolled back synchronously.

8.9   Connection Services

Middleware products provide a mechanism for distributing program logic across a LAN or WAN. Each has its strengths. RPCs work effectively in synchronous communications and are the most appropriate for bidirectional, real-time communication, but lack scalability and adequate support for security and maintaining speed. Message-oriented middleware offers a complete environment for creating and running distributed applications. Transaction monitors, which are discussed in Sec. 11.4.2, maintain transactions across multiple servers.

8.9.1   Interprocess communication (IPC)

An IPC is a mechanism that allows threads and processes to exchange and share data among themselves, whether they are within the same computer or over a network. IPCs can also be used to offer services to and receive services from other programs. This implies a protocol that guarantees a response to a request.

IPC mechanisms include semaphores, signals, pipes, queues, shared memory, and dynamic data exchange.

IPCs are performed automatically by programs. For example, a spreadsheet program could query a database program and retrieve data from one of its databases. A manual example of an IPC function is performed when users cut and paste data from one file to another using the Windows clipboard.

8.9.2   Remote procedure calls (RPCs)

RPC mechanisms were one of the earliest program-to-program communications methods available that allowed programmers to call a remote procedure the way they would a local subroutine. A client process calls a function on a remote server and waits for the result before continuing with its processing. Therefore, an RPC is a connectionless mechanism—the connection exists only for the duration of the call.

A simplified version of how RPCs work is illustrated in Fig. 8.5.

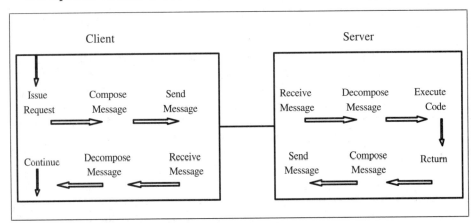

Figure 8.5 Remote procedure call

The details of the transport mechanism used by the RPC are hidden from an RPC user. An RPC tool may support one or several different transport mechanisms. The key to a successful RPC implementation is the ability of a requester to find a server on which the subroutine resides. A subroutine could reside on more than one server for optimal response time for the users.

RPCs, which are APIs layered on top of a network IPC mechanism, allow servers to communicate directly with each other. They allow individual processing components of an application to run on other nodes in the network. Distributed file systems, system management, security, and application programming depend on the capabilities of the underlying RPC mechanisms. Server access control and the use of a directory service are common needs that can be met with RPCs.

RPCs also manage the network interface and handle security and directory services. The paradigm of using high-level languages to call procedures is not new. To the programmer, a remote procedure call should look and act just like a local procedure call. The idea is to spread work and data over the network to optimize resources.

The client and server pieces of an RPC are called stubs. Stubs are automatically generated from the information the programmer supplies, using a nonprocedural language called the interface definition language (IDL). The RPC code (the stub) is generated for both the calling program and the called program by running the IDL code through an RPC compiler. Data required by the remote procedure must be sent as part of the call.

The stub on the client acts as a substitute stub for the required server procedure. The server stub substitutes for a client. The stubs are needed to copy arguments to and from RPC headers, convert data if necessary, and call the RPC Runtime.

The RPC generator gathers and packages the parameters to be passed. This process is called marshaling. The receiving procedure unpacks the message and uses it. RPCs also provide data translation services. One of the key differentiators among RPC products is how easily and how well they can marshal data and translate data.

Up until now, RPCs were processed only synchronously. A calling process had to wait for a remote procedure to complete its task before it (the calling process) could do anything else. Newer RPC packages provide easy-to-use asynchronous mechanisms that allow the calling program to continue processing while waiting for the remote procedure to complete its task. In addition, many RPC products are moving beyond TCP/IP to support other protocols, such as Novell's IPX.

Most RPCs assume that the programmer knows the location of the called procedure, which is a valid assumption for modest-sized applications. For larger applications, naming services such as those from Open Software Foundation's Distributed Computing Environment (DCE) are necessary. Naming services provide a directory of RPC services and their locations, which enables developers to use RPC names rather than locations. The extra overhead for resolving location information is far outweighed by the improved scalability of the enterprise-wide architecture.

RPC tools usually include

- A language and a compiler that can be used to produce portable source code
- A run-time facility that makes the system architecture and network protocols transparent to the application procedures

Although RPC implementations are roughly the same, RPCs from different vendors are usually not compatible.

The RPC Runtime performs the actual transmission functions and should have the following features:

- Transparency and independence from the underlying network protocols
- Error detection and recovery from network failure
- Support for network naming, addressing and directory services
- Ability to handle multiple requests simultaneously
- Portability among various systems

Sun Microsystems Computer Co. offers its general-purpose Transport Independent Remote Procedure Call (TI RPC) toolkit, based on source-code generation technology from Netwise (now a division of Microsoft). The software allows software developers to create a single version of a client/server application that will run unmodified across a range of operating systems, hardware bases, and networks such as TCP/IP, OSI, and NetWare's IPX/SPX. TI RPC includes a compiler, translator, and libraries.

Microsoft's Netwise offers TransAccess Application/Integrator, which provides procedural access to mainframe resources and integrates applications running on disparate platforms including micros, UNIX servers, and MVS mainframes. The access to mainframe data can be used by host-based applications and transaction monitors such as CICS and IMS. TransAccess supports two- and three-tier architectures.

NobleNet's product, EZ-RPC, analyzes the client and server application programs and automatically generates the client and server stubs. EZ-RPC automatically converts C APIs to Windows DLLs. It supports the industry standard distributed computing model ONC/NFS.

RPCs have one major limitation: They typically require synchronous connections. If an application uses an RPC to link to a server that is inoperable or busy, the application will wait for the data rather than moving to other tasks.

RPCs have become quite commonplace in applications built with Visual Basic and PowerBuilder from Powersoft. Building distributed applications across Windows 3.x, Windows NT, OS/2, and UNIX environments is no longer only for those who are not faint of heart.

8.9.3   Message-oriented middleware (MOM)

Message-oriented middleware is based on a specific middleware communications model. It provides a single, standard API across hardware and operating system platforms and networks. It lets developers code to the API and not the network protocol, as is true of all middleware options. Message-oriented middleware guarantees that messages reach their destination.

Messaging products are application-oriented and establish a reliable message path from one application to another. The established pipe can be used for bulk data transport or can be used interactively. Messaging products are aimed at application developers, shielding them from network programming. Using a MOM tool, a developer writes an application that opens a connection to exchange information between two applications, such as inventory and purchasing.

The two models used by MOM products are process-to-process messaging and message queuing. Process-to-process messaging requires that the sending and receiving processes be active in order to exchange information. Message queuing puts messages in a queue for delivery, using a store-and-forward mechanism and therefore does not require that the receiving node be active as the sending node releases the message. Queuing is the ideal choice for decoupled distributed processing. Another advantage of queuing is that it consumes less network bandwidth.

MOM products handle message queuing in one of three ways.

- **Nonpersistent queuing** stores queuing information in volatile memory, which boosts performance but is vulnerable to equipment failure and other interruptions. An example is PeerLogic's PIPES.
- **Persistent queuing** uses a more secure disk-based queuing, at the expense of speed. Examples are Covia Technologies's Communications Integrator and NetWeave Corp.'s NetWeave.
- **Transactional queuing** builds on disk-based queuing with a means of verifying that messages are received and responded to. These are high-end products that are very appropriate for business-critical applications and may overlap in functionality with transaction monitors. Examples are IBM's MQSeries and Momentum's X*IPC.

The very basic concept behind all connectivity is the exchange of messages between applications in a network-transparent fashion. Message-oriented middleware accomplishes this task through the use of messages. A message consists of a message ID, a message type, logical source and destination name, and data, which could be an SQL query. The developer programs the recipient of the message to process the data contained in the message, depending on the message type.

Message processing is asynchronous because the source doesn't wait for a reply.

A message can pass through multiple nodes before getting to its destination, using a store-and-forward methodology. When sending a request using an RPC function call, the requesting application must wait until the request is completed before it can continue to process. This time delay is called blocking the application because it cannot do work while it is waiting. Message-oriented middleware provides unblocking because the application continues to process and is notified when the request is completed. This becomes very critical when applications are using diverse platforms and slower methods of communication to complete a task.

Asynchronous message queuing differentiates itself from other forms of client/server communications in the following ways:

- **Time-independent**. Since messages wait on a local queue to be picked up by the remote system, the communicating programs can run at different times.
- **Flexible structure**. Messages can be sent to one queue or a list of queues.
- **Shielded from underlying communications mechanisms**. Like RPCs, message queuing shields applications from the details of the transport method. A simple API is used to send and receive messages.
- **Reduced number of necessary networking connections**. By generalizing the network connections, organizations can reduce the number of networks that must be supported and simplify application development.

Messaging actually facilities the event-driven model used by client/server applications. Because messaging is asynchronous, a client can send a message and then immediately respond to other events. Also, the messages are self-defining. Each message carries a description of what it is, which lets the invoking procedure remain independent of the remote procedure. This also makes it easy to add new events.

The server cares only about the message, not about the program that sent it. This provides greater interoperability among applications running on heterogeneous platforms and/or written in different languages.

Messages may be buffered between the sender and the ultimate destination with a message queue. The message is sent to the queue, and the destination queue pulls messages out of the queue when it is ready to execute them. More than one program can put messages into the queue and more than one program can take messages out of the queue.

One of the advantages of using a queue is that the client and destination processes do not have to run simultaneously. Another advantage is load balancing. If several computers are configured to support a message queue, the next available computer can take the message and execute the request.

Messaging is more flexible than RPCs in that the messages are sent to named locations (a naming service is used) transparent to the sender. In addition, messages can be broadcast to multiple targets, unlike RPCs, which are point-to-point.

The disadvantage of messaging middleware is that the programmer must gather the data needed by the remote program and perform the data translation services. This makes the programming for both the client and server more complex.

Both messaging and RPCs are excellent methods for building multitier client/server applications, bearing in mind that each has its own strengths. RPCs are best suited for well-defined client/server relationships. Messaging is well suited for complex architectures with peer-to-peer exchanges and dynamic connections. However, neither typically provides transactional integrity and database connectivity, although there is talk about movement in this direction. For transaction support and other connectivity features, transaction processing monitors must be employed.

MOM is one of those technologies still waiting for its "killer app." It has been ready to explode for a few years but just doesn't seem to get enough momentum. MOM vendors are competing with RPC and TP vendors, ORB vendors, database middleware vendors, and relational DBMS vendors, as well as among themselves.

Those who believe that objects will some day soon be the way of the world see MOM as a transition to that day.

8.9.4 Transaction processing monitors

TP monitors manage transactions across multiple servers. Transactions are two-way communications. They ensure that a given communication has a desired result or alert the application if it does not. TP monitors such as Tuxedo from Novell, Encina from IBM subsidiary Transarc, and TOP END from NCR (formerly AT&T GIS) provide an environment for creating and controlling transaction-based applications (as well as messaging and RPCs, if needed) across multiple platforms and operating systems.

Transaction processing monitors are discussed in great detail in Sec. 11.4.2.

8.9.5 Object request broker (ORB)

Object request broker architecture is a newer technique for enabling objects to extend messages within a single system or across distributed computers. The object orientation provides a higher level of abstraction for connecting objects than an RPC, messaging, or TP monitor approach.

An ORB takes a message from a client program, locates the target object class, finds the object occurrence, performs the necessary translation to allow the invoking and called objects to communicate, and passes back the result. The underlying connections are usually performed by a synchronous RPC or messaging system.

Some industry watchers predict that distributed objects (objects located on different machines and possibly using different object models) is the way client/server applications will be built in the future. But for now, the technology is still in its infancy, with many technological problems yet to be solved.

One problem is how to ensure that the objects' connections work well and do not overload the network.

Another problem is how to make objects that use different models work together. The proposed CORBA 2 (Common Object Request Broker Architecture) addresses interoperability among CORBA-compliant ORBs only, which eliminates non-CORBA-compliant objects such as Microsoft's Component Object Model (COM). Different object models do not understand each other's messages or data types.

Using distributed objects does not address the need for transactional support and integrity. Either the ORB or the TP monitor must provide these functions. ORBs are also discussed in Sec. 17.1.1.

8.10   Interoperability Tools

The goal of middleware is to provide the integration necessary for two processes within an environment to exchange data or services. Most middleware is aimed at one piece of the puzzle: the data, the network messages, or the processing. Newer products on the market are addressing all three in one product. WOSA is one of the first.

8.10.1   WOSA

Windows Open Services Architecture (WOSA) provides an open architecture and a consistent standardized set of APIs to provide interoperability between Windows workstations and services available in heterogeneous environments.

The vendor-independent APIs are organized into a layered architecture that is placed between Windows applications and service providers, as illustrated in Fig. 8.6.

WOSA connects front-end applications to back-end services. They don't need to speak each other's languages to communicate as long as they can speak WOSA's interface.

WOSA uses a Windows dynamic link library (DLL) that allows the software components to be linked at run time—applications connect dynamically to WOSA services. The application needs to know only the definition of the interface, not its implementation. A system-level DLL defined by WOSA provides the common procedures necessary for that service. Applications call system APIs to access services that have been standardized within WOSA. The API routes the calls to the appropriate service provider and provides procedures and functions that are used in common by all providers.

The services provided by WOSA APIs are divided into three groups:

- Common application services
- Communication services
- Vertical market services

Common application services include

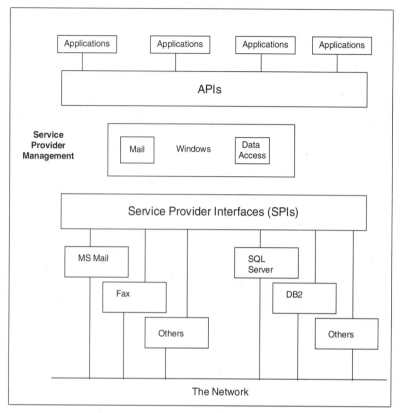

Figure 8.6 WOSA architecture

- **Data access**. The Open Database Connectivity (ODBC) API provides WOSA data access to relational databases. ODBC is based on the SQL call level interface defined by the SQL Access Group. ODBC already has wide industry support.
- **Messaging.** The Mail API (MAPI) provides mail and scheduling functionality and supports mix-and-match mail front-end applications and services. Extended MAPI adds an additional API set to handle complex messaging-based applications that require large and complex messages in large numbers and sophisticated addressing features.
- **Licensing**. The License Service API (LSAPI) provides license system independence and isolates an application from the licensing policy.
- **Telephones**. The Telephony API (TAPI) defines and establishes a telephony interface standard to support visual call control; integrated messaging with E-mail, voice mail, and fax; and voice and micro integration.

Communication services include

- **Windows Sockets API**. The Sockets API provides a single interface for

Windows applications to communicate with sockets-based applications, such as those running on UNIX.

- **Windows SNA API**. The SNA API provides an SNA interface for Windows and Windows NT environments and supports all major SNA protocols (HLLAPI, APPC, CPI-C, and LU0).
- **Windows RPC API**. The Windows RPC API supports the OSF DCE RPC protocol and provides an intercommunication mechanism for Microsoft.

Vertical market services include WOSA extensions for financial services such as the banking industry and for real-time market data.

WOSA is also being extended to include new services in distributed security and systems management.

8.11   E-Mail

Since E-mail is one of the common productivity tools available in a client/server environment, organizations are looking for ways to tie in application processing to their E-mail systems. Applications that use E-mail capabilities fall into two categories:

- **Mail-aware** applications send messages. These may be forms that need to be processed, alert messages, or reports.
- **Mail-enabled** applications require full access to all messaging services, such as the address book or directory and transport function.

Several industry initiatives are under way to define standard interfaces to these E-mail capabilities. One, called the Common Mail Calls (CMC) interface, offers a simple interface to basic mail services and is appropriate for implementing simple mail-aware applications. The other is Microsoft's MAPI (1.0), which allows mail-enabled applications to more fully manage large volumes of complex messages and addressing.

Client/Server Approach

The basic premise behind the second generation of client/server computing is that process execution and data should be placed on nodes within the enterprise network that provide optimal user response while still providing efficient use of resources.

The use of multitier environments is a response to that premise. Multitiered implementations have their own problems and management requirements, such as serialization and currency. A multitier architecture is often the solution for links to legacy applications. Some organizations are using RPCs to link to legacy applications; others are "wrapping" the applications.

An organization has to decide how to distribute data and then where the distributed data should reside. Distributed data has its own set of currency issues. Once data is distributed, it is harder to manage—it is, after all, in more than one place and those locations could be geographically separate.

Transactions are no longer confined to one LAN or one data source. Transactions could require data from any node in the enterprise network, and these requirements could involve heterogeneous data sources. In order to ensure that all tasks within a transaction do occur, transaction managers monitor their progress and provide recovery routines in the event that a task cannot be completed and the transaction must be rolled back. In addition, these requirements don't have to be text and numbers; they could be a bitmap, a graphic, or voice!

Applications should be partitioned when appropriate, and those pieces of executable code should be distributed to support efficient use of resources as well as integrity for the application. This requires that all components of the environment be reliable and accessible.

Testing applications in today's environments takes on a life of its own, just as the applications do in the hands of the users.

Managing the network has become the critical task for most organizations. The network is monitored for performance, traffic jams are identified and data rerouted, underutilized paths are identified, and traffic patterns are adjusted to even out resource utilization. Network addresses must be assigned.

But the organization needs to go beyond managing the network; it needs to manage the environment, and manage the system. Data sources should be manageable from remote sites. There should be automatic backup and recovery, transparent to the user. The organization should develop metrics for measuring the performance of the system. Diagnostic tools should be used to measure performance against these metrics.

9

Applying the Client/Server Approach

The client/server computing approach requires that an organization plan its environment carefully. Data is not on one machine—and there may be copies on multiple machines. Processes may reside on one machine and be executed on another. With this distribution, some key considerations arise:

- Clients and servers must be able to find each other within the network.
- Clients and servers must be able to share data and processes across the network.
- Clients and servers must be able to synchronize their processing despite the fact that they are on different platforms and may have different data structures, network architectures, and operating systems.

9.1 Key Technical Alternatives

The downside of flexibility is having so many choices. Picking the right ones during the design stage is critical.

9.1.1 Peer-to-peer operations

Peer-to-peer computing is the ultimate in distributed processing. Every node can request services from every other node. A single node (machine) can be a client for other servers and a server for other clients, including itself. This allows a machine to ask any other node (client or server) that isn't busy to perform business logic for its application.

9.1.2 Remote service access

For frequent and stationary users of the applications within a client/server environment, access is local. Their machines are wired into the network; their applications have access to the resources they need to accomplish the users' tasks.

In today's business climate, more and more applications are being used by remote users—users who dial into the network. These users range from workers using computers at home to those using laptops and dialing in from anywhere (hotel rooms, airports, client locations), using a regular phone line or a cellular phone.

The client portion of the application is on the mobile machine. By dialing into the network, the mobile client should have all the capabilities of the "stationary" client with regard to accessibility of resources. The mobile user should see no difference in functionality because of the mobile rather than hard-wired connection.

Some organizations that are early adapters of new technology are taking the idea of mobile access and the strengths of client/server segmentation one step further. In these organizations, workers may be dialing into their desktop machine—which then acts as a server—for applications and data on that machine, as well as for access to resources on the network.

9.1.3   Transparency considerations

Transparency is in the eye of the user. The user's view of any application is its interface. What happens after a user clicks on a button or makes a menu choice should be transparent to the user—although sometimes using an hourglass to show the click was recognized but that the process might take a little bit longer than normal is a great idea!

If a server goes down, the system should be able to reroute processes to another application server. If a network node is down or is experiencing heavy traffic, the network management software should be able to detect the situation and reroute traffic. If a database server is down, the system should be able to automatically kick in its backup copy. On-line backups of databases should not affect users' access to the data. All of these actions should be transparent to the user. A small, barely noticeable increase in response time should be the only indication to the user that something unusual is happening.

9.1.4   Matching task and processor capability

With the flexibility of client/server technology, an organization can match the requirements of a task with the capabilities of a processor. That's the theory behind putting the presentation services and logic on the client machine. Not only are the resources required by only that machine, these machine resource–intensive functions would overload network traffic if they occurred anywhere else. The theory is now being used for adding dedicated servers into a network: The server is optimized for the tasks it will perform, such as data access, computations, or transaction processing.

The flexibility also works on the other side of the equation. If the processor needs more capacity because the user base is growing, the applications are expanding, the number of applications is increasing, etc., then a new processor can be added to the system or an existing processor upgraded to support the new requirements.

9.2   Intelligent Databases

Client/server applications demand more than just management of data—more than data storage, data integrity, some degree of security, and recovery and backup procedures. Client/server applications require that some of the application logic be stored with the data in the database. The logic can be stored as an integrity check, a trigger, or a stored procedure. When the logic is defined in the database, it is written once and used when the "protected" data is accessed.

Most server-stored logic is vendor-dependent. The stored logic will execute only with the server database software. Some client/server application development products that are not tied to server database software allow developers to compile and store vendor-neutral logic.

The server database software should handle referential integrity, which ensures that related data in different tables is consistent. If a *parent* row (for example, a customer) is deleted, the rows related to that parent row in the *children* tables (for example, accounts such as savings, checking, and loans) should also be deleted. This centralizes the control of data integrity, ensures that the rules are followed no matter what node accessed the data, and frees the developers from having to code integrity rules into the front-end programs.

Business rules should be enforceable centrally, as well. Rules can validate data or be associated with data. A rule might use a range check or require a match against a particular pattern or against an entry in a specific list. Rules can be associated with a particular column, a number of columns, or all columns of a particular data type.

A special type of check is called a constraint—a passive check that returns only error messages. A constraint might be, *If a customer's title is "Mr.," then the sex must be M*.

In addition, there may be procedural logic associated with the data and allocated to the server, rather than the client, for execution. This might be done for reasons of load balancing or speed.

9.2.1   Stored procedures

Stored procedures are a collection of SQL statements that are compiled and

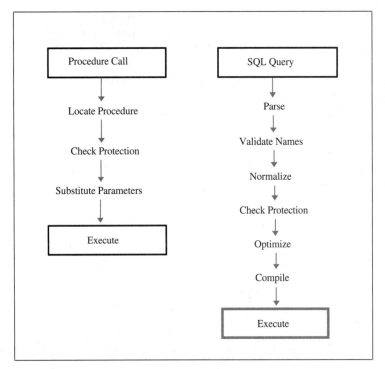

Figure 9.1 Stored procedures and interactive queries

stored on the server database. When an SQL command is sent to the server database, the server parses the command, checks the syntax and names used, checks the protection levels, and then generates an execution plan for the query. The comparison with interactive queries is illustrated in Fig. 9.1.

Stored procedures allow developers to code queries and other groups of statements into stored procedures, compile them, store them on the server, and invoke them directly from applications. The stored procedures are parsed and checked for syntax the first time the procedure is called. The compiled version is stored in cache memory. Subsequent calls to the procedure use the compiled version in cache.

Since they are stored as compiled code, stored procedures execute quickly. They are automatically recompiled when changes are made to the objects they affect. Since stored procedures accept parameters, they can be used by multiple applications with a variety of data. Stored procedures can be nested, and remote calls can be made to procedures on other systems.

Stored procedures can also be used to enforce business rules and data integrity. In the case of the banking transaction used earlier as an example, the logic for the debit and the credit and a validity check to ensure that the debited account has enough funds to cover the transfer could be coded into a stored procedure called *transfer-amt*. This procedure could be used by any transaction that transferred money between accounts. The parameters used when the procedure was invoked would specify which accounts.

To comply with federal reporting requirements, this procedure could be modified to include an operation that recorded all transfers over $10,000 in a special table. The change would have to be made to the specific stored procedure only. Subsequently, any transfers made using the procedure would be checked against the $10,000 limit and recorded, if necessary.

9.2.2 Triggers

Triggers are special stored procedures that are automatically invoked by server database software. Stored procedures are explicitly called; triggers, which are associated with particular tables, are executed when attempts are made to modify data in those tables. Triggers and rules are both associated with particular tables, but rules can perform only simple checks on the data. Triggers can perform complex checks on the data, since they can use the full power of SQL.

Triggers can be used to enforce referential integrity. In the banking example, a *delete-customer* trigger could be written to check all the open account tables for the customer number and refuse to process the delete request if any exist. The *delete-customer* trigger would be fired when a request to delete a customer from the customer table was received.

Triggers can also be used to cascade a change through related tables in a database. If a customer number is changed, all references to that customer number must also be changed. A trigger could be written to fire whenever the customer number was changed in the customer table. This trigger would check all the open account tables for the customer number and change them all to the new number.

Depending on the relational DBMS, a trigger can access other databases over a network via remote procedure calls. This allows a developer to implement a referential integrity check between two or more separate databases over a network.

Business rules can be enforced through the use of triggers as well. A trigger in an order entry system might refuse to accept a new order from a customer with an outstanding balance. A trigger in a banking system might refuse to increase any credit limit more than 20 percent.

Triggers can be used to maintain summary data. Whenever an order is placed in an order entry system, a trigger could update a sales-to-date field.

9.3 Transaction Processing

Transaction processing places additional requirements on the server database software. Transactions are generated at the client and sent to the server for processing. Very often these transactions affect two or more data tables which could reside on different machines. When the system crashes (and it will!), the server database software must be able to roll back the transactions that were in process (and therefore not committed) and roll forward those transactions that were committed before the crash but were not reflected in the last backup of the database.

As discussed in Chap. 7, a transaction is one or more operations that are performed together to complete a task. For a transaction to be considered successful, all operations must be performed. If any operation of a transaction cannot be completed, the operations that have taken effect must be undone, a process called *commit and rollback*.

If the transaction is not successfully completed, the system uses the log to restore (roll back) the database to its state prior to execution. When the transaction is successfully completed, the system commits all the changes permanently. The commit and rollback function is mandatory for transaction processing systems to keep the database in a consistent state between transactions.

Commit and rollback facilities are aimed at recovering from data errors or software malfunctions. Safeguards for hardware malfunctions, such as power outages or hardware failure, should also be considered. Some typical safeguards are an uninterruptible power supply and disk mirroring, in which data is copied to a second disk so that if one disk fails, the other can be accessed.

To understand the process, consider the processing of applying a payment, let's say $200, to a customer's accounts receivable balance. The transaction has two operations: Debit the accounts receivable balance by $200 and credit cash by $200. For this transaction to be complete, both operations **must** occur. If the debit is handled first and the credit doesn't occur, the accounts receivable balance will reflect the $200, but the cash on hand balance will not reflect the payment. The tables for this transaction may be on the same server or on different ones.

9.3.1 Two-phase commits

A two-phase commit ensures data consistency and completeness for transaction processing when a transaction uses more than one table. The client application designates one server as the commit server (the record keeper) to decide to commit or roll back a transaction.

The two-phase commit process is illustrated in Fig. 9.2. In the first phase, each server involved in the update process performs its portion of the transaction and informs the commit server that it is ready to commit its work. In the second phase, the commit server broadcasts a commit message to the other servers and records the transaction. Once this happens, the transaction is committed, regardless of subsequent failures. If any server fails during the second phase, the commit server cancels the entire transaction and instructs the participating servers to roll back their work.

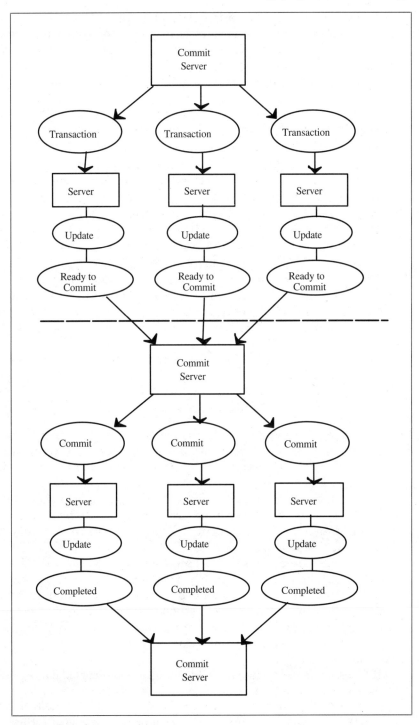

Figure 9.2 Two-phase commit

IBM's Customer Information Control System (CICS) is an example of a mainframe-based transaction processing monitor that supports distributed transaction processing. Using a master/slave tree approach, the request starts the front-end transaction (the master of the tree), which initiates a communications session, specifies the remote system, and then initiates a back-end transaction.

The front-end transaction allocates a conversation with another remote transaction (its slave), which then initiates its slave, and so on. The tree master coordinates the following tasks:

- Identifies all participants involved in the transaction
- Sends prepare-to-commit (PTC) requests to all participants
- Ensures that all participants acknowledge the PTC request
- Logs the fact that all participants are prepared
- Sends the commit request to all participants
- Ensures that all participants acknowledge the commit request
- Logs the fact that all participants have committed

If any participant does not commit, the master sends an abend to every other transaction in the tree, and all transactions are backed out.

Most database products aimed at the client/server market include two-phase commit capabilities. In addition, transaction managers also provide two-phase commit between heterogeneous platforms. This important feature allows the software to handle transactions that span multiple data sources as well as multiple machines.

9.3.2   Locking schemes

Transaction processing applications also require the use of locking schemes to ensure that the database record a user is accessing is protected while it is in use. When a transaction locks a record, that record cannot be updated until the lock is released.

Data transmissions handle data in blocks. To allow a client to update the transmitted data, the server must prevent an update by another application after the data is sent to the client. To maintain this concurrency control, the server locks the result data.

Figure 9.3 summarizes the locking rules used by most DBMS products. A shared lock allows more than one transaction to read the same data. An exclusive lock is granted when a transaction wants to update data. When an exclusive lock has been granted, other transactions cannot obtain any type of lock on the data and therefore cannot access the data at all. An exclusive lock can be obtained by a transaction only if no other transaction currently has a lock on the data.

If blocking is used, the entire block (all rows/records) can be locked or the block can be locked one row at a time as data are fetched by the client application. If blocking is not used, a row could be locked as it was sent across the network. Data would be transmitted one row at a time.

Asking for	Current Lock		
	Unlocked	Shared Lock	Exclusive Lock
Unlocked	OK	OK	OK
Shared Lock	OK	OK	NO
Exclusive Lock	OK	NO	NO

Figure 9.3 Locking rules

Another alternative is to use optimistic concurrency control. This method, based on the premise that records are usually updated by only one application at a time, checks for update collisions at commit time. If the record has been read by other applications, they are notified of the impending update.

9.3.3 Transaction logs

These files are used when a database needs to be restored after a failure, such as a system crash.

A well-designed transaction processing environment should include a history log that records committed transactions. The loss from a brief power outage can be restored using the transaction log and a simple redo procedure.

To recover from a hardware failure, transactions must be re-created from an archive so that the database can roll forward. Some DBMSs, such as Sybase SQL Server and Oracle, provide such functionality. If failure recovery is not built into the DBMS, it must be coded into the application or automatically generated as part of the application code by a development tool.

9.3.4 On-line transaction processing

On-line transaction processing (OLTP) applications have the same characteristics, whether they are host-based or client/server-based. They have

- Large number of relatively short interactions
- Many users
- Large shareable databases

Since most OLTP applications are business-critical, they require high availability and recoverability and transaction management.

In the host-based environment, these requirements are built into the software typically used in that environment. Capacity issues become the traffic within the network from the dumb terminals to the host, the number of simultaneous users the host can support, and the throughput of the host itself, in terms of both compute cycle times and data access.

In client/server environments, meeting these requirements needs to be part of the planning process. Software that can help manage the system and the network is critical for reliability. Transaction managers will ensure the integrity of the transaction processing.

First-generation client/server development tools, software, and architectures are not robust enough to support OLTP. Many of the early client/server failures were due to the fact that the organization tried to build an OLTP application in a first-generation environment, which just couldn't support it. Organizations must look to second-generation client/server technology for robust support.

When planning for OLTP applications, keep these guidelines in mind:

- Attempt to reduce overhead per interaction and per user.
- Provide resource shareability.
- Use high-performance DBMS.
- Prioritize transactional activity.
- Ensure reliability, integrity, availability, and security of transactions.

9.4   User Interfacing

Many users have been hearing about client/server technology—that their company is going to begin to use it, that it's easy to use, and that it will make their life easier. For many, it's their first look at a windowing GUI, their first exposure to an event-driven environment, and their first experience with a mouse.

Developers need to keep their audience in mind and plan the interface accordingly. It may be necessary to design two interfaces for the same application: one for the experienced Windows users and one for those low on the learning curve. The appropriate interface comes up based on the ID.

In addition, developers need to understand what "easy to use" means to their audience. Going from keyboard to mouse is awkward and takes time. Designing the interfaces to minimize the frequency of this switch will increase users' comfort with the interface.

Developers need to have users involved in testing interfaces very early in the development process—not so much to test how they work as to test how they are to work with. Remember, the interface is the users' view into the application and into the environment. If they don't find it easy to use, they will balk at using it.

9.5   Determine Data Location

After designers have determined how data will be distributed, they must decide on the location of the data—on which node(s) the data will reside. For data with only one group of users who are connected to the same server, this is an easy decision. But since most data is shared across LAN-imposed boundaries, it is harder to decide which node to place shared data on. A rule of thumb has been to put data on the node that updates it, the rationale being that updating creates most of the network traffic and is more open to possible failures (a server or network goes down). However, data that is updated at one node and often accessed by another node might be better placed at the accessing node if users at that node are accessing it often enough.

Designers must try to simulate the impact each placement decision will have on the entire enterprise environment. This can be done manually by determining the number of calls that will be made, the size of the data traveling on the network, and the number of hops the data would need to take. The other network activity would also have to be factored in.

Some software products that can simulate this process are beginning to appear on the market.

Either way, an effort must be made to determine the effects of data placement *before* the application is placed into production. Fine-tuning data placement once an application is in production is expected; a major overhaul is not.

9.6   Determine Process Location

After the data has been attended to, designers must decide on the location of processes—on which node(s) the process will reside. Determining process location is very similar in nature to determining data location.

A process may be accessed by many users across multiple nodes and use data from multiple nodes, as well. Designers need to determine a location for the process that optimizes its access time—both for the user and for needed data—and minimizes network bottlenecks and server overload. The impact of each placement decision must be analyzed.

As is the case with data placement, the effects of process placement must be examined before the application goes live. Doing a major overhaul of process locations after an application is in production is the result of poor planning.

The use of stored procedures is one way to put some of the business logic on the server. The business logic might be placed on the server because it is too complicated for stored procedures or because the database being used does not support stored procedures.

One of the benefits of application partitioning is minimized network traffic by moving the database access application logic onto the server, which off-loads work from the workstations. As application processing becomes more complex, it is more economical to upgrade a server and move some of the application processing to it than it is to upgrade hundreds of client workstations.

Partitioning applications is not without risk. Partioned applications are more difficult to design and maintain. If an application is to be partitioned, the decision must be made before the application is designed and coded so that logical break points for splitting the pieces can be built into the application before it reaches full-system testing or, even worse, production.

An application that is split into many pieces operating on different platforms has more points of failure. Identifying a point of failure and rectifying the situation without affecting the rest of the application becomes difficult.

9.7   Application Development

There are two sides to client/server development tools. One side supports the developers (developing the application), the other side the users (the delivered application).

Available tools for developers include CASE tools for specifications, 3GL-based development, 4GL tools, and canned, delivered solutions. Regardless of the tool used, the development environment should be a highly visual one, allowing user interfaces, database manipulations, and application logic to be developed graphically in a windowing environment. The development environment should also allow a developer to augment the graphically created application with code for complex applications and should provide a high-level programming language.

An organization must be careful not to assume that because a development tool can provide links across heterogeneous platforms, its own environment can support those links.

Object-oriented development tools are touted as the wave of the future. Indeed, the benefit of reusable code is hard to argue with. However, be careful to separate object-oriented development from object-oriented applications. Most businesses are not ready to think in terms of objects.

9.8   Partitioning Application Execution

When client/server applications distribute their logic, applications are broken into modular pieces that can be ported among multiple client and server platforms. This is true for display, data, and application logic. Developers need to think carefully about what the components of an application are and how can they be broken down into independent modules that can work together.

Many organizations are restructuring their application logic as sets of modular application services (some might argue that these are objects!). These services can then be repeated or used in different situations and on different platforms. For example, an application service module could come off the server and onto the client. Or a module could come off a client and onto a mobile client. The modularity of the logic allows an organization to react to platform changes as well as changes in the business.

Modular application logic can also be useful for increasing performance. A module can be moved to a node closer to the data, thus reducing network traffic and increasing response time.

Deciding how to break application logic successfully into modules requires skill and the right tools. Some of the development tools discussed in Chap. 14 automatically enforce modular programming concepts and build the communications layer between the application modules automatically. This frees the developer from thinking about where the code is going to be distributed while he or she is writing it. Other tools are much more free-form and therefore require much more discipline and greater attention to the links between the modules.

As many organizations are discovering, the tool chosen for developing client/server applications is very often the overriding determining factor in the quality of the development effort. Some tools can repartition an application at runtime.

Modularity should also be considered when developing the client side of client/server applications. Most would agree that the presentation service and logic belong on the client. However, there is a tendency to include application logic on the client as well, very often interfacing directly with the graphical window manager and using platform-specific functionality. This locks the application logic with the display logic, and therefore locks it to the current client platform. This denies the organization the flexibility to move the application logic off the client platform and also leaves the organization at the mercy of the GUI/platform vendor.

To decide how to partition the execution of an application, some general rules of thumb provide some guidance:

- The presentation services and presentation logic belong on the client.
- Application logic that is screen-related, such as editing, should be on the client as well.
- All common and shared application logic and business rules should be on a server.

An organization needs to review how the data is actually accessed, how many users are accessing it, and where those users are. This allows an organization to consider replication or fragmentation.

When considering the feasibility of dedicated servers, an organization has to weigh the flexibility of common access against the increased network traffic and costs.

Partitioning requires a solid understanding of the real-time requirements of the application. Where does the data to be created, read, or updated reside? How many users are expected at peak times? What are the expected (and accepted) response times? What is the amount of data access for each transaction?

To effectively partition an application, the developers must be aware of two distinct views of the application: logical and physical. The logical view divides the application into three functions: presentation, data access, and logical processes. The presentation function is handled by the client. The data access function is handled by data servers and includes both data access and validation. The logical processes are the business rules that the application executes. The physical view is where all of this happens. The users will intuitively know about the logical view. Because of the transparency of client/server technology, the users should be aware of the physical side of the application. They interface with a screen, they click on buttons or menu choices, and they get their results.

The business logic can be physically partitioned as well. First-generation applications execute all the business logic from the client and issue data calls to the server. These are now referred to as "fat clients and thin servers." The clients are in fact sharing the resources of the server. This is an acceptable solution for applications that are SQL-based with low transaction volume and a network robust enough to handle the large amounts of data that will be shipped back and forth between the client and server.

The first partitioning of business logic occurred when organizations started to implement business logic as stored procedures and triggers on the databases being accessed by the applications. The business logic is written in the proprietary stored procedure language of the DBMS vendor. This is typically compiled and can provide good performance and moderately high transaction rates in a well-designed system.

Stored procedures are a solution if your data reside in one vendor's DBMS and the business logic can be expressed as a function of database calls. The downside is the introduction of another development language and being tied to a particular solution (and vendor).

Application servers are used to execute all the business logic. By using application servers and separating the presentation and data access completely from the business logic, organizations end up with flexibility, responsiveness, and performance. The physical partitioning is straightforward—put the processing where it fits best—and takes advantages of the capabilities of each tier of processing.

For example, an application could be split along these lines: The presentation and local business rules reside on the client. The server attached to the client has application logic on it that can access multiple databases from a database server, performs the necessary calculations on the data returned from the data requests, follows the relevant business rules, requests services from other devices, and finally returns the appropriate response to the client, where the presentation logic and services take over and display the results.

Application servers can support high volumes of transactions but are the most difficult approach to implement. The DBMS vendor is no longer responsible for the communication between the client and the server. Applications can update multiple databases residing on different servers, and so two-phase commits for transaction processing become a must. What communication protocol is used becomes a more important issue.

Partitioning is more than just deciding what runs where. It requires an understanding of the business and technical issues surrounding the application. Such a powerful and flexible architecture is the most complex to implement.

Once an application enters production mode, application partitioning becomes a system-management task, not a development task. To optimize performance and reflect changes in the system resources, system administrators need to be able to move application components at run time. The application can't come off-line and there isn't time to return the application to the developers to have it repartitioned and dynamically switch to the new version.

An ideal situation would be one in which developers could specify application requirements without regard to where the application will ultimately run. After the application is designed, it can be split into separate partitions that execute on different machines in the network. It can be further partitioned if the environment changes. In order for this to be effective, developers have to view an application as a set of logical objects that are snapped together to form the application.

The location of these objects can be determined at compile time or be assigned dynamically at run time. At compile time, the application notes the location of the elements within the application, and those locations become part of the compiled version of the application.

Dynamic assignment looks at a resource directory each time the application is run and uses those assignments for that particular execution of the application. The resource directory is updated as resources change (are either added, moved, or off-line for some reason) and are built and maintained separately from the development tool. The directory is available to each server's operating system.

For example, if a client application makes a request to an application server that has crashed, the client application can then search for another server that contains the business logic the client application needs.

Some of the focus is beginning to be on further refining the application into object components. Objects could represent presentation, business logic, or data entities, or smaller elements within each of these components, such as a radio button on a GUI or a "funds transfer" command in a bank teller application.

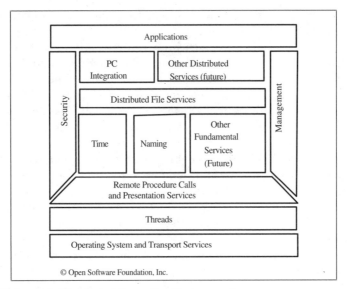

Figure 9.4 Distributed Computing Environment

9.9   Standards

Adherence to standards facilitates linking client/server components. Standard specifications for newer technologies take a long time to develop. Organizations need to decide how important the new technology is to them strategically and decide to forge ahead or wait for the standard and standard-compliant software.

9.9.1   DCE

Distributed Computing Environment (DCE) from the Open Group, an organization formed from the merger of Open Software Foundation, which specified DCE, and X/Open, provides a framework of services for distributing applications in heterogeneous hardware and software environments. DCE is illustrated in Fig. 9.4. The details of the basic services are hidden from end users. DCE is an open system that can run on any platform or operating system. It is not restricted to UNIX.

The DCE model provides an integrated approach to distributed processing. Its layered architecture provides flexibility to include future technologies. Each layer provides its own security and management.

DCE supports OSI standards and protocols and Internet standards, such as TCP/IP transport and network protocols, the Domain Name System, and Network Time Protocol; and uses standard interfaces, such as POSIX and X/Open. DCE can be ported to OSF/1, UNIX System V, AIX, Ultrix, HP UX, and SunOS and adapted to VMS and OS/2.

DCE provides two sets of services:

- **Basic distributed services** allow developers to build applications.
- **Data-sharing services**, which require no programming by the end users, include a distributed file system, diskless system support, and micro integration.

DCE services are deployed in administrative units called cells. A cell can include one host or thousands of hosts in a single network or in an internetwork. The hosts in a cell do not have to have the same physical topology. A cell contains a single security datase and a single Cell Directory Service (CDS) namesake so all users and applications within a cell are subject to the same administrative rules and resources are more easily shared within the cell than between the cell.

The tools provided by DCE as basic distributed services are

- Remote procedure calls
- Distributed Directory Service
- Threads Service
- Time Service
- Security Service

Remote Procedure Calls

DCE's remote procedure calls (RPCs) allow an application's programs to execute on more than one server in the network, regardless of the other machines' architectures or physical locations. Because information transfer is transparent between different platforms, the use of RPCs allows heterogeneous operation.

The DCE RPC standard is based on the Network Computing System from Hewlett-Packard and Interface Definition Language (IDL) compiler-generated C-program files, which handle the interfacing of clients and servers. Its specifications include special semantics for network transport independence and transparency.

A DCE RPC can specify communication with a specific file server or with any file server offering a required service. The integration with DCE's Threads Service component allows clients to simultaneously interact with multiple servers. Servers are identified and located by name. Developers use the IDL to specify server-to-client operations. Integration with DCE's Security Service provides communication privacy and integrity for distributed applications.

Because DCE's RPCs support connectionless and connection-oriented transports, an application does not have to be rewritten to use different transport services. DCE's RPCs can also efficiently handle bulk data for large data-processing applications.

The RPC syntax, semantics, and presentation services represent the major differences between OSF's DCE and SunSoft's Open Network

Computing (ONC) architecture. These differences are discussed in the ONC section later in this chapter. Remote procedure calls are discussed in more detail in Section 8.9.2.

Distributed Directory Service

This service provides a single naming model throughout the distributed network. Users locate and access servers, files, or print queues by name, not by their physical location. Users use the same name even if the network address changes. The Directory Service uses a local cell directory service and a global directory service. Global names can reside in the X.500 standard directory service or Internet Domain Name System name space.

The Directory Service can accommodate large and small networks and is easily modified to incorporate expansion. Using transport-independent RPCs, DCE's Directory Service can operate in both LAN and WAN environments.

The Cell Directory Service maintains a database of objects within a DCE cell and maps their names to their identifiers and locations. The Global Directory Service maintains a database of objects that exist anywhere in the internetwork and enables DCE programs to access objects outside the cell.

The directory services is integrated with other DCE components, such as the Security Service and the Distributed File System.

Time Service

This software-based service synchronizes system clocks of all hosts in a cell with each other and, optionally, with an external time source. It provides an accurate timestamp for application development files that must be stored in sequence.

The Time Service supports time values from external services used for distributed sites using the Network Time Protocol. The Time Service is integrated with other DCE components, such as RPC and the Directory and Security Services.

Threads Service

DCE requires threads for operation. The Threads Service allows multiple threads of execution in a single process and synchronizes the global data access. One thread can be executing an RPC while another processes user input. Applications do not need to know whether threads are executing on one or several processors.

The Thread Service is used by RPCs; Security, Directory, and Time Services; and distributed file system. The Thread Service conforms to Draft 4 of the emerging POSIX standard for multithreaded programs.

Security Service

Data integrity and privacy are provided by three facilities:

- **Authentication** is based on the Kerberos Version 5 standard from MIT. It verifies a user through a third server.
- Once users are authenticated, the **authorization** facility decides if they should have access to the requested resources.
- A **user registry** facilitates the management of user information. The registry ensures that user names are unique across the network. It also maintains a log of user and log-in activity.

Distributed file system

Distributed file systems allow users to access data on another system via the network. In DCE's DFS, the user's system is the client and the system where the data is stored is the server.

When data is accessed, a copy of it is cached (stored) on the client system, where the client can read and modify it. Modified data is written back to the server. DCE's DFS uses tokens to keep track of cached information. Tokens (read or write) are assigned by the server when data is cached. To modify data, a client requests a write token. When a write token is assigned, the server informs other clients that a write token for that data has been assigned. If other clients cached the same data with a read token, the server notifies them that the data is no longer current and voids their tokens.

DCE's DFS, based on the Andrews File System from Transarc Corp., provides the following advanced distributed file system features:

- **Access security and protection**. Security is enforced through user authentication and an access control list.
- **Data reliability**. To ensure a client's ability to process, DCE's DFS supports replication of all network services. If one of the servers fails, the system automatically switches a client to one of the replicated servers.
- **Data availability**. Routine maintenance of the server, such as backup, can be done in real time.

DCE's DFS works with Sun's Network File System (NFS), the current de facto standard, but differs in the following areas:

- DFS has **integrated support** for LAN and WAN networks. NFS supports only LAN networks.
- DFS uses a **global file space**, where all network users see the same paths to accessible files. Global names are used to ensure uniform file access from any network node via a uniform name space. In NFS, each network node has a different view of the file space.

DCE's DFS supports diskless workstations with general-purpose protocols. The DFS cache manager can cache files in the diskless client memory instead of on a local disk. This gives organizations options. They can purchase less expensive diskless micros to be used as client machines or specify that micros use server disk space instead of more expensive local disk space.

Desktop support

DCE supports the distribution of network processing power among a large number of computers and allows interconnected clients to work with other DCE-compliant systems and to access files and peripherals.

DCE RPCs allow low-end systems to work with other architectures and share applications with other systems in the network. They can use Directory Service to access information and compute resources anywhere in the enterprise network. Micros and Macintosh computers can view and copy files to and from systems running UNIX-based and proprietary operating systems.

DCE Client/Server Model

DCE is more than just a server software package. As illustrated in Fig. 9.5, DCE components are placed between applications and networking services on both the client and the server. The interaction between the layers is transparent to end users.

DCE Version 1.2.1

The Open Group released Release 1.2.1 of DCE mid-1996. This release includes enhancements in four major areas:

- **Ease of programming** the Interface Definition Language. DCE supports C++ and C++ features such as inheritance and object references.

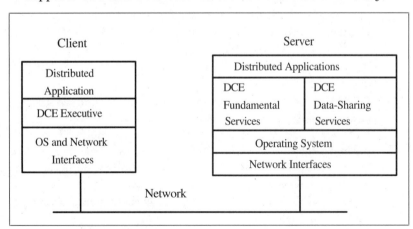

Figure 9.5 DCE's integration with frontend and backend software

This support also includes adoption of any object model or class hierarchy.

- **ONC co-existance.** DCE's NFS protocol gateway has been extended to support NetWare and ONC environments and provides file-sharing services.
- **Multiple distributed file system** (DFS). Enhancements to DCE's DFS include replication implementation and a backup utility for stackers and jukeboxes.
- **DCE administration**. DCE Control Program has added extensions and administrative functions over the Release 1.1 capabilities.

DCE and Internet Technology

Mid-1996 the Open Group began shipping its DCE Web technology which is available in Gradient's Web Crusader and DASCOM's IntrVerse product suites. Vendors including IBM, Digital, and Hewlett Packard plan implementations as well. DCE-Web is designed to provide basic distributed-environment capabilities like DCE security, naming, and integrity services to the World Wide Web.

DCE Web is made up of several components:

- **Multiprotocol Server** provides secure access to sensitive enterprise data and to public Web data.
- **Secure Local Proxy** provides secure DCE-WEB access using standard off-the-shelf browsers.
- **Secure Gateway** integrates DCE-Web with other secure Web protocols.

The Open Group expects to ship its Jade (**J**ava **a**nd **D**CE **e**nhancements) technology, which will allow Java applets to talk to the DCE infrastructure. Jade provides secure communications between Java clients and Web servers by tapping into the Kerberos-based security of the DCE RPCs. Jade also makes the standard DCE API available to Java applications through a set of native classes. Jade is expected to be released mid-1997.

9.9.2   OMA and CORBA

Object Management Group's Object Management Architecture (OMA) combines distributed processing with object-oriented computing. It provides a standard method for creating, preserving, locating, and communicating objects, which can be anything from entire applications to pieces of applications such as graphical screens or complex number-crunching algorithms. Using this mechanism, cooperative-processing applications can be supported within a heterogeneous, distributed, networked environment.

In late 1996, the Object Management Group (OMG) announced an interface between Microsoft's Component Object Model (COM) and OMG's

Common Object Request Broker Architecture (CORBA). The purpose of the COM-CORBA interworking is to specify bidirectional communication between CORBA objects and COM objects. The goal is that objects from one object model could be be viewed as if they existed in another, and key object functionality would be visible to the clients even if the application was using another system.

The OMA performs as a layer above existing operating systems and communication transports that support standard RPCs such as SunSoft's Open Network Computing (ONC). The OMA has of four main components:

- **Object Request Broker** (ORB), the interface that must be used and the information that must be presented if an object is to communicate with another object.
- **Object services**, utilitylike objects that can be called on to help perform basic object-oriented housekeeping chores and provide for consistency, integrity, and security of objects and the messages that pass between objects.
- **Common facilities**, functions commonly used by applications, such as printing and spooling or error reporting.
- **Application objects**, applications or components of applications, which are created by independent software vendors or in-house software developers.

To link to the other OMA components, the Object Request Broker uses its Interface Definition Language (IDL), an OMG-developed language with its roots in C++. Mappings between the IDL and common programming languages such as C (currently the only mapping specified) or COBOL are provided which allow developers to write to the ORB interfaces.

The ORB also specifies features for managing the interobject messages. These features include name services (similar to an object directory) and exception handling. ORB allows objects to communicate dynamically or via a set of faster, preprogrammed static facilities.

CORBA is discussed in more detail in Sec. 17.1.2.

9.9.3   OLE

Microsoft's Object Linking and Embedding (OLE) is a set of APIs for implementing object-oriented "compound document" features for business applications. A compound document is created in one application but is made up of sections created in other applications or maintained in other sources. The sections are called objects and can be almost any data type, such as text, spreadsheet, graphics, video, bitmap images, or even voice annotations.

When viewing a compound document, the user should be unaware of its source. The user can browse and manipulate the data without switching from application to application. The presentation services and logic stay with the document as it becomes part of the compound document. OLE supports dynamic binding, so the functions provided by an interface can be determined at run time.

The objects can be linked (reference the creating application) or embedded (physically maintained as part of the compound document). It is possible to edit an embedded object in place or within its own container because the compound document includes a copy of the original embedded object and all of the information needed to manage the object.

OLE is not just for compound documents any more. OLE has evolved into a set of object-oriented interfaces and services that provide a framework for building reuseable, integrated software components. Component technology provides the benefits of object technology (reuse through encapsulation, polymorphism, and inheritance) to developers (vendors and in-house) using development tools that support component software. By using the standard OLE interfaces, software developers can create their own components which can plug into other components such as applications and software packages. OLE can be used for compound documents, custom controls, inter-application scripting, and data transfer.

OLE is built on Microsoft's Component Object Model (COM), which is discussed below. COM, which handles object creation and local/remote transparency services, is the foundation of OLE technology.Sometimes the term COM is used interchangeably with the term OLE.

The client application (that contains the objects) is called an OLE container. When an embedded object is clicked, the application that created the object, known as the OLE server, is launched in order to edit the object. The server application appears to run within the container application.

If an object is linked, the OLE container does not hold the object; it holds a pointer to the object. If a change is made to a linked object, all documents that contain the link are automatically updated the next time the document is opened. Linked objects can also be treated as embedded objects to edit the object.

OLE implements a standard set of protocols for performing a variety of data-transfer operations, including drag-and-drop, clipboard control, and compound document processing. Uniform Data Transfer simplifies data transfers and change notification. OLE custom controls (OCXs, now referred to as ActiveX components) are Windows controls that provide data-binding capabilities that make them particularly suited to database work.

OLE lets developers encapsulate rules in objects that are accessible to PowerBuilder, Visual Basic, and other OLE-enabled applications.

Microsoft also will incorporate ODBC 3.0 into OLE as part of the company's strategy for enterprise computing. The entire ODBC API will become a subset of OLE DB, which is scheduled to ship in early 1997. In addition, ODBC's driver manager (Kagera) will also include modifications that conform to the OLE specification.

Microsoft considers OLE a precursor to Cairo, its next-generation operating system that will treat operating system services as objects. Cairo will compete with IBM's System Object Model (SOM), OpenDoc, OMG's CORBA, and SunSoft's Neo (renamed from Distributed Objects Environment or DOE).

OLE DB

OLE DB, formerly code named Nile, is Microsoft's solution for data access. ODBC would be used to access relational databases, and OLE DB would be used for nonrelational data and application data linking. OLE DB provides a database architecture that allows applications, compiler, and other database components efficient access to Microsoft and third-party data stores. OLE DB uses COM to define the interfaces between OLE component objects, in this case data sources, and other components such as applications.

OLE DB is an extension of the ODBC model, and aligns ODBC with the SQL-92 CLI, the current SQL standard. The transition to OLE DB should have minimal impact on the application architecture. Microsoft plans to offer a translator (code named Kagera) between OLE DB applications and ODBC drivers. OLE DB integration of data access into the OLE will free application developers from the details of data location, structure, and even technology.

OLE DB will use ODBC to let applications access data from a larger variety of sources, not just databases. For example, OLE DB will allow queries across databases, spreadsheets, and word processing documents simultaneously.

Any component that directly exposes functionality through an OLE DB interface is an OLE data provider. For example, Microsoft could build a data provider that knows how to access and manipulate data stored in Microsoft Excel spreadsheets. Applications could use this data provider to retrieve data stored in an Excel spreadsheet.

OLE DB component objects can be built to implement more advanced features than those provided by the data providers. These components, called service providers, can be used to expose more sophisticated data manipulation and navigation interfaces on behalf of the data providers. These features could include query processors or report builders. Service providers can also be used to span different data storage types without bringing data locally to the client.

Component Object Model

Component Object Model (COM) is a core technology for creating shareable binary components. COM supports the creation of components by providing a standard for component interoperability and a single programming model for components to communicate within the same process as well as across process and network boundaries. COM allows for dynamic loading and unloading of components and for shared memory management between components.

COM is programming-language-independent and is available on multiple platforms including Windows, Windows 95, Windows NT, Macintosh, and many varieties of UNIX. COM uses proxies and stubs to support object location transparency. It generally supports technologies which focus on the GUI single-user desktop. A network version, originally called Network OLE and expected to be released as Distributed COM, is expected to be available in early 1997.

OLE provides more than basic component object management; additional features built upon COM include Structured Storage, Monikers, Uniform Data Transfer, Drag and Drop, Linking, Embedding, and Automation.

Distributed Component Object Model

Distributed COM (DCOM), formerly known as Network OLE, adds new interfaces related to remote objects. DCOM is an open, platform-independent technology.

With DCOM, Microsoft intends to support partitioning to enable applications to use local remote components. COM provides location transparency. DCOM is the foundation of ActiveX technology (see Sec. 18.5).

DCOM, expected to be released in early 1997, is based on OLE and any OLE-enabled application will work with it. DCOM will operate across networks to connect components on different machines. DCOM uses the DCE RPC mechanism as a means of communication between OLE objects in a process or system or across a network.

9.9.4 OpenDoc

OpenDoc is OLE's competition. A consortium of Apple, IBM, Borland, WordPerfect, Novell, Oracle, and Xerox produced a nonproprietary OLE superset   that is CORBA-compliant and has greater cross-platform interoperability.

OLE is thought of as an application-linking mechanism. OpenDoc was designed as a cross-platform technology, platform independent, and to interoperate with other similar architectures such as OLE. OpenDoc is available on Macintosh, Windows, and OS/2.

OpenDoc has application linking and supports OLE but is a superset of the features in the current OLE technology. Any OpenDoc part (an OpenDoc object) can be linked to an OLE container and any OpenDoc container can be linked to an OLE server application. When an OLE object is embedded in an OpenDoc container, it is unnecessary to register it with the OpenDoc shell, only with OLE.

Comparisons of OLE and OpenDoc usually focus on the compound document architecture: OpenDoc's ability to operate across multiple process spaces or the need to distribute parts viewers for compound documents.

In later 1995 IBM took over all development efforts for the OpenDoc for Windows software development kit. The OS/2 and Windows implementations of OpenDoc offer a type of wrapper component that can reroute method calls between containers and embedded components. A distributed 32-bit OpenDoc kit that allows OpenDoc developers to use any ORB that complies with the OMG's CORBA 2.0 and uses IBM's Distributed System Object Model is expected to be released in late 1996.

9.9.5 ODBC

Microsoft's Open Database Connectivity (ODBC) is a core component of WOSA (see Sec. 8.10.1) and Microsoft's strategic interface for accessing data in a heterogeneous environment. The ODBC API permits applications to communicate with relational and nonrelational data sources. ODBC is compared to proprietary DBMS access in Fig. 9.6.

ODBC provides an open, vendor-neutral way of accessing data stored in a variety of propriety data sources, thus eliminating the need for independent software vendors and corporate developers to learn and use multiple APIs. ODBC drivers allow developers to write Windows-based applications that transparently access the data sources supported by the drivers.

ODBC is based on the SQL Access Group's Call Level Interface (CLI)

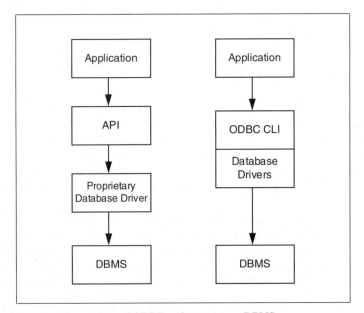

Figure 9.6 Comparison of ODBC and proprietary DBMS access

specification (see Sec. 7.9.3), which has broad industry support. ODBC is SQL-based but can also support non-SQL databases. This communications protocol–independent API consists of the SAG CLI specification plus enhancements for data typing, error handling, scrollable cursors, and performance optimization.

Each application uses the same code as defined by the ODBC API to talk to many types of data sources through DBMS-specific drivers. A Driver Manager sits between the applications and the drivers and provides information such as a list of available data sources to an application, loads drivers dynamically as they are needed, and provides argument and state transition checking. The application calls ODBC functions to connect to a data source, send and receive data, and disconnect.

A single application can make multiple connections, each through a different driver, or multiple connections to similar sources through a single driver.

The advantage of ODBC is the ease of adding additional data sources to an application. All that is required to access a new DBMS is to install the driver for that DBMS. However, if application developers use native DBMS calls, the applications is not portable from one DBMS to another.

ODBC 3.0, released in 1996, aligns ODBC with the SQL-92 CLI and supports SQL3 locators, which are 32-bit run-time token values that provide access to large binary and character objects. In addition ODBC 3.0 also adds support for Unicode, the 16-bit encoding standard that uses double-wide characters to support international character sets and enhanced facilities for describing data, handling errors, and uninstalling component.

9.10 Testing

Testing client/server systems and the applications running on them require testing (and ultimately managing) multiple platforms, multiple network configurations, multiple operating systems, and multiple layers of the application (logic, business rules, middleware, DBMS, GUI, etc.). The testing process itself should be part of the planning process and should be in the forefront of the developers' minds as they design and implement. Testing cannot be an afterthought.

The entire system—the hardware, all layers of software, and all the nodes in the network—must be tested as a whole, using well-thought-out and published processes, the final results of which can be quantified. There must be processes that are standard throughout the organization. Procedures that test the whole system are run before a change and after a change to ensure that no area of the system has been adversely affected by the change (regression testing).

Quality needs to be built into the application as it is being designed and developed. Adding in quality after the fact is difficult with client/server systems and their applications. There are just too many pieces. And a seemingly minor change in one piece could have a major impact on a seemingly unrelated piece—an impact such as increased response time, increased network traffic, or application failure.

Testing applications in today's interactive, event-driven, user-controlled environment is much more difficult than testing applications in host-based, program-controlled environments. Testing today goes well beyond evaluating pieces of code to see if they work according to their specifications. The testing client/server applications can be broken into five separate areas: formal planning, data quality assurance, application testing, load balancing and ongoing monitoring.

9.10.1   Formal Planning

Testing today's application cannot be an afterthought or be considered a trivial task. It should be thought of not as a last step, but as an ongoing process. Study after study indicates that the reason many client/server applications fail is that they were not adequately tested. How an application is going to be tested must be determined as the scope of the project is being planned, and expanded as the details of the project begin to play out. Software that would support this effort must be identified and, if necessary, purchased, installed, and training scheduled. Organizations must plan on taking almost as long to adequately test an application as to develop it, and, in many cases, maybe even more time. The biggest hurdle is not finding the software, or even scheduling the time. It's convincing management that testing is critical, that the success of the project rides on it.

The literature has made a point of convincing its readers that client/server development is fast and efficient. What is barely mentioned, if at all, is that planning must be done before development begins: planning the data and data structures, planning the screens, planning the events, planning the interfaces between screens, planning on-line help, planning the testing procedures, etc. This planning takes a lot of time. The better the planning, the better the (quickly developed) final product.

9.10.2   Data quality assurance

Most of today's client/server applications are based on data that is maintained somewhere else. An application might be using middleware to access legacy data or using data maintained by another client/server application. Or an application might be using data that resides within a data warehouse. In these cases, the data and its definitions have been determined by another group of people (and another application) within the organization. Consequently, it becomes critical that the users of an application understand what those definitions are and either buy into those definitions or refine their own data requirements to ensure that the data they are getting is actually the data they want and need.

The quality of the data feeding into the application must be tested long before the users are shown a prototype of the application. If the data does not match the users' data requirements perfectly, their reactions tend to be that the application is not right, not working, a failure, etc. This negative image is difficult to overcome. For that reason, it is important to separate the data feeding the application from the workings of the application itself. As soon as the data requirements have been determined, use some sort of extract facility against the data sources to pull out the data for the users' review. Do this simultaneously with design development. It is important to have the data requirements, sources, and any massaging that must be done firmly identified before the actual development of middleware links and application coding begin.

9.10.3   Application testing

Since so much of the movement within an application is under the control of the user, application testing is tricky. The IT group that developed the application and the users who worked with that group should be the first set of testers. Their charter should be to try to break the application. They might try things like doing tasks out of sequence, miniaturizing the application while in the middle of entering data, closing out the application while in the middle of something, and turning the machine off in the middle of the application.

The second set of testers should be the ultimate users who understand the process but weren't involved in the requirements specifications. Their charter should be to just use it. This will help the developers understand how the application will really be used and will uncover other problems.

Testing software that can log the uncovered problems and track their resolution is critical. This step of testing cannot be treated lightly. If 100 problems are detected, they must all be resolved before the users are given another shot at testing the application. You can guarantee that a user will try to redo the process that didn't work the first time, and it had better work this time—or IT will have *Image repair* to add to their list of things to do.

As these problems are solved, care must be taken to ensure that the fix did not break some other part of the application. There should be documented testing procedures to be followed to ensure that the fix doesn't create more problems.

9.10.4 Fine-tuning load balancing

Load balancing involves testing the effects of the application on the resources within the environment. It is important to simulate the effects of the application on the network and the servers. This needs to be done before the application is rolled out into production.

One of the easiest ways to simulate load balancing is to run scripts. A script is a set of keystrokes that is executed under the control of testing software. Scripts should be carefully developed to test all aspects of an application, such as updates, create new, deletes, queries, and reporting.

The testing software can run the same script over and over again from one station or simulate the effect of having the script run on multiple stations as if there were users simultaneously pressing the keys. The testing software should be able to run scripts unattended at off-peak hours, but still be able to simulate peak conditions. Snapshots of the resource load statistics can be stored and the results reviewed for network bottlenecks, server bottlenecks, memory leaks, or unacceptable response times.

The results of these tests may cause the developers to rethink how an application is partitioned. If network traffic becomes an issue, more work could be done on the server so that fewer data is sent to the client. If the application server is near capacity, a different server might be used for the application, a new server added to the environment, or more work done on the client. If the database server seems to be the bottleneck, the database could be replicated or distributed.

An additional advantage of developing scripts that accurately represent the application is that they can be used to test the application when changes are made either to the application or to the environment. The results can be compared to previous results to ensure that no degradation in services has occurred: this is called regression testing.

Most of today's testing software has the capability to run scripts. They differ in their scripting languages, how the effects of the execution of the scripts are captured, and how closely they can simulate fully loaded applications.

9.10.5 Ongoing monitoring

Once the data going into an application has been reviewed, and the application has been tested and balanced, the focus becomes real-time. This focus goes beyond monitoring the health of the environment, such as whether a node is down or a server's disk capacity is nearly full. The health of the application itself needs to be reviewed. Now that the application is being used, what are the resource implications? Are there bottlenecks? Are response times unacceptable? Do things get worse at certain times of the day? Do they get worse when another application has a heavy load?

Solutions may be as simple as rerouting network traffic to improve the situation. Other solutions that aren't nearly as simple include adding another server to the environment, replicating or distributing databases, and repartitioning the application itself.

At this point, changes can be made to the environment and load balancing routines rerun to determine if the problem has been corrected without negatively affecting the application or other applications in the environment.

The words "testing an application" give the impression that there is a beginning and an end. In host-based environments, there is a beginning and an end to the testing process. In client/server environments, there is no end, because we are not testing, we are evaluating, and reevaluating, how well an application is serving its purpose. The process begins as the design work on the application begins and ends when the application is phased out.

10

Two-Tier and Multitier Environments

One of the newest debates for client/server architectures is two-tier versus three-tier (and multitier) designs. This book will use the term multitier to include three or more tiers.

10.1 Two-Tier Architectures

The earliest implementations of client/server architectures (two-tier) were based on the idea that most of an application's resources were tied up in the presentation logic. To separate the presentation logic from the rest of the application needs (retrieving data and business logic and rules) required two separate platforms, hence the term two-tier.

The client application requested data from the server, and the server sent it back. All logic (presentation and application) was executed on the client station. All data services were provided by the server. This definition is still used by many to describe client/server computing.

Organizations that were early adopters of the client/server paradigm were willing to risk using the new technology to gain the promised benefits. The user productivity gained through the use of point-and-click interfaces justified the cost and learning curve of development software and the hardware costs for the LAN, the client stations, and the server.

10.1.1 Fat clients and thin servers

A "fat client" is the term used to describe a client/server architecture in

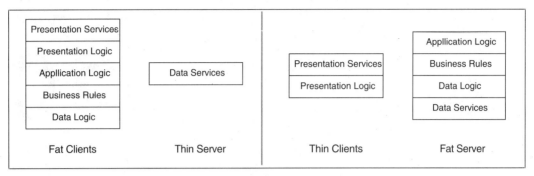

Figure 10.1 Fat clients and thin servers and thinner clients and fatter servers

which most or all of the application processing is done on the client and little or none is done on the server (a "thin server"). This early implementation of client/server technology relied on servers as data repositories. The client side of the application formulated an SQL request, which was sent to the server and the results returned to the client, where the returned data records were processed according to the application and/or business rules and logic.

10.1.2 Thinner clients and fatter servers

This "fat client" model started to evolve as the applications that organizations were implementing became more complex and/or began to cross application boundary lines. Some application logic began to be executed on the server, as illustrated in Fig. 10.1. Some of the first implementations used the stored procedure and trigger features of the database software that resided on the server. This allowed business rules and logic to be executed on the server at higher speeds and consistently across all applications that used the data elements themselves. After all, the data was shared by multiple applications, and having business logic residing in every client station meant multiple updates when the rules changed.

Organizations then began to expand this further by actually coding the applications themselves so that some of the application logic was executed by the server. First implementations hard-copied the application so that the server always executed a particular piece of code. Eventually, the software became more robust and the code could be executed on any platform, anywhere in the network, that was "free." Some obvious examples were statistical routines. Instead of sending all the data samples to the client station to be analyzed, the analysis is done at the server level and the results sent to the client station. This also saves network traffic.

The next step in the evolution was dynamic partitioning, which allowed developers to determine at installation time which parts of the application would run on the clients and which on the servers. This has continued to the point where the decision can be made by the application itself at the point of execution. The data services are still executed by the server.

Through all of this evolution, organizations were still dealing with two tiers. What started to change was the environment organizations needed to exist in. A two-tier architecture is perfect for homogeneous environments where all the DBMSs on the servers are the same and for applications whose business logic is not very complex. A two-tier architecture continues to be the right choice for such applications.

10.2 Three-Tier Architectures

Three-tier architecture grew out of organizations' need to extend their client/server architectures into the organization (hence the name enterprise-wide client/server computing). Organizations also began to realize that while stored procedures were great for off-loading client processing to the server, they were very limited when expressing complex business logic. In addition, using stored procedures hindered future scalability. Two-tier architectures do not scale well. An organization can't just put another server in the network to accommodate an increased number of users for one particular application.

In a three-tier client/server architecture, the functions of an application are separated into three distinct components: graphical user interface (GUI), application business logic, and data access functions. Each component resides on a dedicated platform. The GUI resides on the client station, and the other two pieces reside on high-end micros or midlevel servers such as UNIX systems.

Three tiers allow organizations to connect heterogeneous database servers, standardize on an application language, mix processing requirements (such as batch, reporting, on-line transaction processing, and EDI) while still balancing workloads, and provide a scalable and maintainable environment.

Three-tier (and for that matter multitier) architectures take the ideas behind two-tier architectures one step further. There are still servers and clients; the difference is that by expanding the number of nodes used to process the applications, organizations can take advantage of a mixed set of servers and clients and gain instant scalability.

Employing a three-tier (or multitier) architecture requires that the organization focus on both aspects of such an architecture. One is the application architecture: The three components of any application are its presentation requirements, application logic and related services, and data handling. In two-tier architectures, presentation is handled by the client, as are most, if not all, application logic and related services. Data handling is the job of the server.

Figure 10.2 Three-tier architecture

The other aspect is the physical configuration of the computers on which the application runs. In a two-tier architecture, the client portion of the application runs on the client and the server portion runs on the server that the client is connected to—two platforms, two tiers. A typical three-tier architecture puts a server in the middle of these two tiers, as illustrated in Fig. 10.2.

The server in a two-tier architecture is used primarily for responding to data requests. Little or no application logic is performed by the server. In a three-tier architecture, the client still handles the application's presentation requirements, the server that the client is connected to handles application logic and services, and the back-end server (the server that server is connected to) handles the data requests.

If one considers that applications are broken into three components (presentation, application logic, and data handling), then it's easy to see how well three-tier architectures fit with client/server applications. Organizations can begin to share logic among applications because the logic is not on the client; it's accessible by all clients on a server. These servers can be optimized for application processing. The back-end server can be optimized for data retrieval, since that is its only job, unlike the situation in two-tier architectures where the server needs to do both data retrieval and some application processing.

Two-tier architectures are not dead. They are still very valid for certain applications, especially those that are departmental in nature or that are very independent in nature. If all the application needs is data from some other platform and it makes sense for the processing of that data as well as the presentation of the results to be on the client, then there is no need for more than two nodes for that particular application. Departmental applications that have a few homogeneous databases, uniform clients, and simple business logic continue to be ideal candidates for two-tier architectures.

In addition, two-tier architectures are very appropriate for organizations that are just getting into client/server computing. They reduce the complexity of the architecture and make the pilot application for client/server computing much more manageable. However, organizations should keep in mind that the pilot may not accurately represent the true impact of client/server technology on the organization, or its true costs or savings.

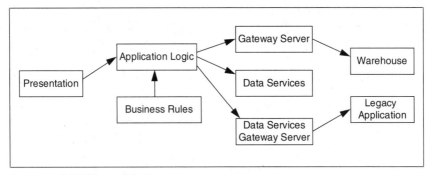

Figure 10.3 Multitier architecture

10.3 Multitier Architectures

Most of the literature suggests and discusses three tiers, but reality suggests a multitier design with dedicated machines for data warehouses, functional servers (as opposed to servers that are used to execute a variety of applications), gateway servers to legacy data, database servers, and transaction processing servers, as illustrated in Fig. 10.3. In addition, application logic could be spread among nodes in the network. These types of specialized servers are discussed in Sec. 4.9.

The move to multitier architecture truly allows organizations to develop a flexible, evolving enterprise-wide information systems architecture. The most interesting point of all in this evolution in client/server architecture is that it is still based on one of the original premises of client/server computing: to put the right processing on the right machine at the right time.

10.3.1 Decomposing the application

For a multitier architecture to be successful, applications running on it must be decomposed into separate and independent modules. The application must first be decomposed into its three component parts (presentation, application logic, data handling) and then each of these must be decomposed if the processing is to be distributed at a finer level. This allows the organization to modify each module or replace it entirely without affecting the other modules.

Most mainframe applications and early client/server applications are difficult to decompose. Application components are not easily extracted and ported to another platform or changed without affecting other parts of the application.

The popular GUI builders such as Powersoft's Powerbuilder and Sybase's SQLWindows link presentation and application logic in the portion of the application that runs on the client and rely on the server to store and manage data. Application screens arc developed with GUI objects such as buttons and dialog boxes. Scripts are then attached to each object. Clicking on the object activates the script—in effect, runs a program. Therefore, the logic is tied to the GUI. Changing the logic requires rewriting the script and relinking the script to the appropriate GUI object.

With the presentation and the logic separated, the presentation can run on the client and the logic can run on any server in the network. Updating the logic is also easier because it resides in one place rather than on hundreds of clients.

How can organizations decompose applications? Currently there are three ways. One is to use a programming language to segment the application into callable procedures. Another option is to link the presentation, application logic, and data handling components via common interfaces such as RPCs and APIs. The third way is to build the components from autonomous objects. Interfaces to connect these objects range from Microsoft's ODBC and Sybase's DB-Lib to RPCs to vendor-proprietary APIs.

10.3.2 Interfaces

The challenge for multitier architectures is getting all the clients and all these servers to cooperate. Middleware is the glue that holds a multitier architecture together. There are three types of middleware, as was discussed in Chap. 8. One type provides data access connections to heterogeneous data sources. This category of middleware includes database APIs and gateways. Another type of middleware is the central player in getting clients to communicate with server programs and server programs to communicate with database server programs. In this category are three related technologies: remote procedure call mechanisms, message queuing, and TP monitors. The third type of middleware uses an object request broker architecture, which is discussed in Sec. 17.1.1.

Open Environment Corp. has done a great deal of education regarding multitier environments. Its tools enable developers to build interfaces between application components using a proprietary RPC or OSF's DCE RPC. However, building RPC interfaces between all application components pays off only when an organization is working in enterprise-wide environments in which large numbers of clients need to access a large number of distributed services.

A more common approach is to leverage vendor interfaces to link components. For example, Magna Software Corp. offers a transactional API on Windows clients that allows developers to link GUI programs such as those written with Powersoft's PowerBuilder to the 4GL Magna code residing on the server. Magna also provides an API to execute transactions on relational DBMSs. Most relational DBMS vendors now offer APIs to access data stored in their database structure.

Developers can create an application entirely in modules using a single programming language, given enough up-front planning and discipline. The code is segmented into callable procedures that at a later date can be ported to another platform and connected back via an RPC. However, as procedures are ported out of the original platform and often modified at their new platform, the application itself runs the risk of losing its ability to separate components.

Treating the application as a group of objects requires that the application be decomposed into much finer detail than with other design alternatives. The objects can represent complete components of the application or smaller elements within each of the components. For example, an object might be a radio button used in more than one application or a process used in more than one application.

Because objects encapsulate their implementation and are accessed via a generic interface, moving objects from one platform to another requires no modification to the rest of the application's objects. In addition, an object's actions can be modified by changing the methods of that object without requiring changes to the rest of the application's objects.

10.3.3 Dedicated servers

Multitier architectures allow an organization to leverage its hardware. Since all the application components are independent and linked via an interface, developers can deploy the components on optimal platforms.

For example, applications with computation-intensive functions such as statistical routines might be better off having this compute function calculated on a high-performance supercomputer that is optimized for scientific calculations. This optimizes the resource utilization as well as response time and allows the calculation to be used by other applications that may need the same function.

Servers can be added to the architecture whose purpose is to provide services or functions shared by many applications. A function or service is written once and made accessible to all applications requiring it by placing it on a server accessible by those applications.

The recent interest in data warehouses has prompted organizations to add a data warehouse server to their client/server architecture. Specific mainframe data is extracted and downloaded to a dedicated server within the client/server network. This moves the data closer to the users who use it and reduces network traffic between the client/server network and the mainframe. Data warehouses are discussed in more detail in Sec. 7.13.

Dedicated servers can also be used to support the interfaces discussed in the previous section. A dedicated server could run a database gateway such as Information Builders' EDA, giving transparent access to data stores across the network. EDA translates the client API calls to the appropriate syntax for the remote data source and handles all the underlying communications. This relieves developers of the need to know the details about the remote data and how to navigate to access them.

This location transparency also provides for migration transparency. If the data moves or is converted to a new data structure, only the database gateway needs to be changed to reflect these changes. No changes are required in the applications themselves.

Organizations are also using dedicated servers as transaction monitors which manage the flow of requests to resources such as relational database engines. When these capabilities are placed on a single machine, all aspects of the client/server interaction within the network can be optimized, such as load balancing, recovery and rollback services, and redirecting requests when a server fails.

Core services such as security could run on dedicated servers rather than being built from scratch for every new application.

10.3.4 Developing multitier applications

Developers can create multitier applications using the best-of-breed approach. The best tool for generating each of the application's components is used to create that component. Developers snap the pieces together, using interfaces supported by the different tools. Obviously, manually integrating the components is more difficult than using one tool to generate all the components, but it keeps the organization from getting locked into a single vendor's proprietary scripting language, communications engine, or services.

Second-generation, object-oriented client/server development tools are designed to develop multitier applications. Such tools include Template Software's SNAP, Forte Software's Forte, Magna Software's Magna X, and Dynasty Technologies' Dynasty. They are designed to build all types of applications, not just database applications. The designs for the application components are stored in a shared repository with version control capabilities. They usually contain a GUI toolkit, a proprietary 4GL for writing business logic, and a point-and-click interface for defining services. They generally support a Windows development environment and generate code for a range of platforms, databases, networks, and database gateways.

Three key features of the high-end development tools that support multitier environments are their support for partitioning, concurrency, and serialization.

10.3.5 Built-in application partitioning

Many of the premier development tool vendors provide some degree of application partitioning and support for three-tier topologies. These tools include Oracle's Developer/2000 and Designer/2000, Informix Software's NewEra, and Unify Corp.'s Unify Vision. PowerBuilder 5.0, released in

1996, supports application partitioning and three-tier topologies. as well as DCE and TP monitors and distributed object computing. Centura technology from Centura Software Corp. (formerly Gupta Corp.) supports application partitioning and three-tier scalability using DCE and Tuxedo, as well as RPCs to several DBMSs. The high-end products such as Forte from Forte Software and Dynasty from Dynasty Technologies are also designed to take advantage of three-tier partitioning.

10.3.6 Concurrency

It is important that a dedicated server that is being accessed by multiple clients, often for the same resources, be able to process multiple requests simultaneously; this is referred to as concurrency. Servers must be optimized for throughput speed and maintain adequate response times for users.

In two-tier architectures, concurrency is handled by the database manager. In multitier applications, the business logic is separate from the data and so concurrency must be handled some other way. In most cases, it is provided by a transaction monitor or a sophisticated operating system both of which can thread multiple requests within a single process.

10.3.7 Serialization

Concurrency also needs serialization, which ensures that applications access resources one at a time. Serialization prevents conflict and contention for shared resources and ensures data integrity. Database managers provided serialization with lock management. Transaction monitors can also be used to enforce serialization. In addition, other tools that provide serialization capabilities can be made available to applications.

What does this mean for organizations that need to build enterprise-wide client/server applications? It is possible—the tools aren't vaporware—but such applications require greater skill and resources. A solution can be built from multivendor components with in-house-built client-to-server connections.

Connecting the application server to the database server is straightforward, especially in a homogeneous environment. Transaction monitors can be used to link heterogeneous data sources. Client/server tool vendors have announced support for application partitioning (to one degree or another) and three-tier support using RPCs and transaction monitors. But the process is not for the faint of heart.

10.3.8 Application services

Multitier architectures require robust services to reliably integrate all components of the application and to ensure data integrity and adequate performance. These services include transaction, directory, security, messaging, time, and data management services, as well as application management.

Transaction services

Transaction services must include support for two-phase commit, rollback, and recovery services. Most organizations look to transaction monitors for these services.

Directory services

Directory services are required in order to locate application resources for routing messages. Robust directory services store aliases and can dynamically route messages along optimal paths to improve performance.

Security services

Most organizations rely on the security services of the underlying operating system, database, or transaction monitor. Many are planning to integrate with DCE's security system which provides interapplication security. DCE's security system is discussed in Sec. 9.9.1.

Messaging support

Messaging support goes beyond just application exchanges. Multitier architectures need to be able to translate between data constructs employed by different platforms. Some platforms represent time and data differently. There needs to be some way of translating data between proprietary formats and some neutral format such as XDR or ASN.1.

Time services

Time services provide a means of representing time on different platforms in different time zones as well as different countries. This allows processes to keep in synch despite their differences.

Data management services

Data management services are usually provided by a database gateway tool that uses standards-based data access APIs such as Microsoft's ODBC or SQL Access Group's Call Level Interface. The services also rely on native relational DBMS APIs to achieve higher throughput and their additional features. The object-oriented tools can map objects to relational tables and vice versa.

Application management

Multitier architectures also need robust application management. If an application fails, an administrator needs to be able to determine whether the failure was caused by the application, the client, a server (and if so which one), or the network (and if so, where). OSF's Distributed Management Environment (DME) was designed for this purpose but never materialized. Tools moving in the direction of application management include Legent, Tivoli, Computer Associates, and Open Vision.

10.3.9 Communication modes

The communication requirements in a multitier architecture are more complex than those in a two-tier environment. Two-tier architectures need only support straightforward client/server interactions. The client initiates a session with the server by sending SQL statements across the network. The server responds. This mode of communication takes place across a single network protocol and is handled by an RPC.

Multitier applications involve multiple network protocols, platforms, and resource servers. As such, they need to support multiple modes of communication. The client/server modes are

- **Datagrams**. These are one-shot, one-way messages. The client sends a message but does not expect a response.
- **Synchronous mode**. A client makes a request and waits for the response before continuing processing or issuing another request. Synchronous communication requires an active connection between the client and the server.
- **Asynchronous mode**. The client makes a request but then continues processing while waiting for the response. The client may make multiple requests (of one or more servers), and can field them in whatever order they return. Asynchronous communication requires an active connection only when there is actual messages being sent.
- **Conversational mode**. Clients and servers issue multiple requests and responses in serial fashion within a single network connection session. Conversational protocols are IBM's CPI-C and APPC.

Server-to-server communication is supported by RPCs, MOM, and ORBs.

Remote procedure calls (RPCs) were used by early client/server implementations to tightly couple the client and the server and to handle synchronous communications. The RPC establishes communications code and handles data translation transparently to developers. Newer RPCs use threads to support asynchronous and conversational communications. RPCs are vulnerable to network and system outages and loads. RPCs are discussed in Sec. 8.9.2.

Message-oriented middleware (MOM) works best with loosely coupled applications that don't require real-time messages and can operate with asynchronous communication. MOM sends messages between applications using queues that are holding areas for hundreds of messages. Applications check the queues for their messages and then respond to the messages. MOM is discussed in Sec. 8.9.3.

Object request brokers (ORBs) deal with objects rather than communication modes. ORBs can run on RPCs or MOM or directly on top of network interfaces such as TCP/IP. ORBs are discussed in Sec. 17.1.1.

Most of the development tools mentioned in this section use message queuing to provide interapplication communications. Others, such as Template Software's SNAP, Forte, and Expersoft's PowerBroker family of products, provide their own communications infrastructure. Others, such as Magna X and Dynasty, provide hooks to transaction monitors to support client/server communications. Most of these tools also support standards-based communications services such as OSF's DCE and OMG's CORBA.

10.4   Linking to Legacy Applications

Legacy applications are "old" applications that are still being used. They may be using old technology, but they aren't broken, so it's difficult to justify replacing them. And any investigation into the cost of replacing them usually results in very high numbers for time and dollars. They are too massive, complex, and/or poorly documented.

However, legacy applications often provide the data or processes needed for the newer client/server applications. So organizations are usually looking for ways to link into these legacy applications.

One method being used is to "wrap" the application with a software layer that insulates the legacy application from the client/server applications and deals with the transfer of control from one to other.

The term wrapper is used in different ways:

- A **database wrapper** surrounds legacy data only, thus bypassing legacy code.
- A **service wrapper** surrounds system services like printers, E-mail, and transaction managers.
- An **application wrapper** surrounds a complete legacy system, both the code and the data, thus tricking the legacy application into thinking it is interfacing with an end user sitting at a character terminal.

10.4.1   Database and service wrappers

Databases and services work well if an object-oriented access is used. The object orientation encapsulates the data access or service, providing an easy yet controlled interface to the database or service.

Digitalk offers PARTS, an object-oriented visual-programming tool based on Smalltalk. PARTS runs on a client to transaction processing servers on IBM mainframes, thus providing an interface to IBM's CICS transaction manager. Hewlett-Packard offers an object wrapper called Object-Oriented DCE that packages DCE functions as C++ objects.

To compensate for the mismatch between presentation logic written in Smalltalk and data logic written in SQL, Hewlett-Packard offers Odapter. Data logic is written in OSQL, a superset of SQL with object-oriented extensions. Odapter then generates C++ or Smalltalk classes which can be easily accessed on the client. On the server, Odapter maps OSQL to Oracle7, All-Base/SQL, or legacy databases via Information Builder's EDA.

10.4.2 Application wrapper

When an application is surrounded by an application wrapper, no changes in the application are required. The object-oriented layer that wraps the business logic and/or data—the wrapper—converts the character stream issued by the legacy application to a call (RPC, API, ORB, transaction manager, etc.). The client/server application interacts with the legacy application via this call mechanism.

Each application wrapper is different because each legacy application is different; each has different screens and functions. What this means is that application wrappers must be built; they cannot be bought. But don't despair, there are products available that can aid with the programming, terminal emulation, and screen recognition.

Application wrappers are similar to screen scrapers (see Sec. 8.4.1), which allow organizations to build GUIs to legacy applications. However, screen scrapers convert the character stream generated by the legacy application to a GUI: the application wrapper converts the application and, therefore, its logic, to a call, allowing the logic itself to be accessible without being constrained to the coded interface to the application.

Most of the time spent developing wrappers is spent in tuning and debugging them. Every character sequence generated by the legacy application must be tested.

Application wrappers have the same inherent flaw that screen scrapers do: Underneath the technology that the user sees is the legacy system itself, which continues to age and is unlikely to ever include new functionality. The business processes it uses and the design of its data and transactions will not change. Sooner or later, it will have to be rewritten. Application wrappers and screen scrapers extend the life of the legacy system but they don't change the system itself.

Enterprise/Access from Apertus Technologies and CL/7 from Century Analyses are examples of tools that can be used to build procedural application wrappers. They provide a library of procedures for interacting with 3270, 5250, or VT100 terminals and a scripting language to program the conversion. They also provide a facility to define legacy screens and fields and map these to the parameters in the API.

10.4.3 Legacy extension software

Legacy extension software is more complex and functional than the screen scrapers discussed in Sec. 8.4.1. Emulation software from such companies as Attachmate Corp. and Walker Richer and Quinn Inc. provides cut-and-paste capabilities for the transfer of data and generating the screen.

External Presentation Interface

IBM's legacy extension product, External Presentation Interface (EPI), enables new technologies to be placed in front of existing 3270 CICS applications without requiring the programmer to alter the application. The client software also provide a terminal emulation function to run CICS 3270 transactions. Basically, EPI is the CICS implementation of screen-scraper technology.

GUISys/400

Client/Server Technology Inc. offers GUISys/400 for AS/400 applications and GUISys/3270 for converting IBM mainframe applications. The development kit offers developers the ability to generate GUI interfaces from character-based applications. The conversion essentially scans screens from the host system and translates the screens' text and fields into Windows GUI controls. The original screen elements are first categorized into pattern definitions that are compiled in a knowledge base.

GUISys/400 also provides multiple session support and windows layout facilities.

STAR:Flashpoint

STAR:Flashpoint, from Sterling Software Inc., is an icon-based design tool used by developers to add a front end to existing 3270/5250 screens and perform data validation. Independent software vendors are using the product to revamp the interfaces to their mainframe products.

STAR:Flashpoint converts 3270/5250 screens by accessing their data streams and parsing the screens. Fields are mapped from their position on the host screen to their position on the display panel, and a direct link is established between the two. Modifications to a display field do not break the link with the host screen field.

Developers can improve the panels by moving fields, deleting unnecessary fields, and adding field headers, and can also combine several related host screens into one panel or add new panels.

Because STAR:Flashpoint supports DDE, Windows DLLs, and SQL commands, panels can be tailored to allow users to display and work with information from a single or multiple remote and local sources.

GUI/400

A fairly new product, GUI/400, from Seagull Software Systems Inc., allows micro users running Windows or OS/2 and attached to an AS/400 to run existing AS/400 applications with graphical screens. No changes in the AS/400 code or micro programming are required. GUI/400 goes through the AS/400 code and identifies screens, which it automatically converts into GUI screens with multiple fonts, icons, pushbuttons, mouse support, and business graphics. Tools are provided for screens or portions of screens it can't convert. At run time, GUI/400 code builds the GUI screen from the AS/400 screen. The resulting application is not really event-driven, but users can navigate with a mouse and populate fields by picking from lists or choosing functions off a menu bar.

11

Managing the Data

The price of flexibility and quick response is an increased need to manage the environment. All aspects of the environment must be carefully monitored and managed. Managing the data in the environment is as critical as managing the hardware and network but often the last area considered.

11.1 Management of Distributed Data

As was discussed in Chap. 7, entire tables of data or a subset of a table can be replicated or fragmented. Fragmentation involves splitting the data horizontally, vertically, or both. The resulting subtable is stored at the appropriate node. The distributed DBMS recognizes that the table is fragmented and how it is fragmented and maintains the integrity of the fragmented data. The local distributed DBMS treats the subtable as a complete table. The central distributed DBMS has control over and can access all the subtables as needed. There is no complete copy of a table that is fragmented.

Data is replicated (copied) for performance reasons. If multiple clients within the infrastructure routinely access the same data, it may be beneficial to replicate it at the client's nodes.

Data replication is accomplished by allowing users to make their own copies of a data set. When the users require updated copies of the data set, they copy the new data to their nodes. An alternative to user intervention would be an IS-initiated process. For example, a batch job, executed each time the data set changed, would copy the new data to each user node on an approved list. The weakness in this approach to replication is its reliance on human intervention. Users have to remember to execute the copy instructions. The approved list must be kept up to date. The batch job must be submitted and its results checked to verify that every out-of-date copy of the data was rewritten.

A more reliable alternative would be to use a distributed DBMS's capability to generate snapshots of the data and distribute those snapshots. The timing of the snapshots could be specified by the user. Most distributed DBMSs do not support transferring updates of snapshot data back to the original source.

Some distributed DBMSs have the capability to replicate data and handle updates at multiple locations. Using this advanced data distribution method, the distributed DBMS can

- Create and maintain copies of the data at multiple locations.
- Maintain data consistency among all copies, using synchronous or asynchronous processing.
- Provide location transparency to the applications accessing the data.

The tradeoff for replication is the overhead required to keep copies of the data consistent and to maintain this consistency transparently to the user. One approach for managing this process is called the master/slave technique, where one database is designated as the master (primary) database and the others as slave databases. The distributed DBMS at the primary site is responsible for maintaining the integrity of the slave sites. If a slave site is unavailable when the distributed DBMS is attempting to update the replicated data, the distributed DBMS will keep trying that site until it is available and the task can be completed.

The other approach is called two-phase commit. One site is designated as the coordinator. When an application is ready to update replicated data, the coordinator sends a request to every affected site to prepare to locally commit (make) the update. If all respond as ready, the update is made to all sites. If one site responds as not ready, the update is not performed. Two-phase commit is discussed in more detail in Sec. 9.3.1.

Fragmentation is a more complicated method of distributing data. Relational tables can be fragmented horizontally, vertically, or both. The management of fragmented tables should be the responsibility of a distributed DBMS. It is a complex implementation. The table segment on each node should be treated as a complete entity by that node. At a central node, the virtual joining of the table's segments must be transparent to the user.

Various methods for distributing data are discussed in Sec. 7.2.1.

11.2 Issues for Distributing Data

When data is distributed, a portion of the distributed DBMS as well as the data itself reside on the node. Data is usually kept local to the site that uses it the most (usually the site that updates it) while transparent access to that data from other nodes in the environment is provided.

Distributing data among multiple sites offers the following benefits:

- Data is closer to access locations, resulting in quick response times.
- Data access is more efficient.
- Data traffic on the network can be minimized.
- Resource balancing occurs at its most critical resource—data access.
- Multiple copies of critical data can be stored at different locations to eliminate a single point of failure.
- Distributed applications are easier to expand as the user community grows and application complexity increases.

But data cannot be distributed without careful planning. Some rules of thumb for distributing data are:

- Every item of data should have a single point of update.
- Distributed updates should be kept to a minimum.
- Applications should use location-independent code.
- Distributed data should be as close as possible to the processors that use the data the most.

An organization must also define who is authorized to see what data. Rather than an entire table being replicated, rules could be used to define what portion of that table should be replicated and to what group. For example, out of the entire orders table, replicate orders to customers in the east region to the server designated as the east region's server.

11.2.1 Technical issues for distributing data

Among the many technical challenges designers of distributed data applications face, two stand out. These challenges are:

- **Synchronizing distributed databases**. Maintaining the integrity of the data is perhaps the most challenging technical issue designers face. Databases containing the same data must be changed in tandem, ideally using a two-phase commit protocol (see Sec. 9.3.1). This capability should be a feature of the DBMS and not be coded into the applications themselves.
- **Optimizing queries**. A query optimizer must be able to determine the fastest and most efficient steps to handle a query, even if it may require moving data from one node to another to perform a join. The query optimizer needs to know the sizes of the databases, the speeds of the networks, the capabilities of the computers, and the workloads of the nodes.
- **Managing backup and recovery.**
- **Ensuring system and data availability.**

11.2.2 Database administration

To maintain high availability of the database, a distributed DBMS should support remote administration and on-line administration. Database administration includes managing disk storage, creating and managing database objects, controlling database/table access, managing database users and their permissions/privileges, providing database security, performing backup and recovery procedures, monitoring and tuning system performance, and determining and solving system problems. In a distributed environment, these tasks may have to be done at each database location. Remote database administration allows these tasks to be performed from any location (preferably a centralized one for control reasons). The options of having trained database administrators at each node in the architecture or sending administrators to nodes as the need arises (which could be often) are not economically feasible.

In addition, performing these administration tasks should not require that the database be taken off-line.

Other administration headaches include doing such tasks as backups, recovery, modifications to remote sites, change and version management, and creating or deleting database objects without taking down a node—any node—when nodes are all working together.

If the administration of the distributed DBMS is done by local DBAs, the efforts of the individual DBAs must be coordinated, and the organization has high personnel costs for all these DBAs. On the other hand, a central DBA can't travel to each remote site when DBA intervention is needed. Software is beginning to appear on the market that will allow a DBA to monitor the health of the database and handle more administrative tasks and remotely.

11.2.3 Security

Data security is defined as protecting data from deliberate or inadvertent disclosure, modification, or destruction. Standard data security techniques include access control, assigning user privileges, password protection, and data encryption.

In a distributed environment, data security requires the cooperation of data administrators, security administrators, and network managers. If a table is fragmented, for instance, is a user allowed to access only one part of the table, or the entire table? If the user is allowed to access the entire table, then the user must be able to access all three nodes and have access privileges to all three table fragments. All three nodes would have to be able to recognize the user's password.

Another security issue is ensuring that data that should not be downloaded to a workstation is not downloaded. To provide this type of security, security procedures, rules, validations, and checking are usually placed on the server itself. The most often quoted security levels are the government standards of C1, C2, and B1 levels of security.

11.2.4 Currency control

Currency means that all related databases are consistent relative to a version or data/time. If a server goes down, any transactions that were using that server are rolled back. However, if the server is the repository of transaction logs from other servers, any updates to the functioning servers must be captured and reapplied to the crashed server once it is brought on line.

11.3 Distributed Data Management

Distributed data management facilitates the distribution of data to multiple network nodes (sites) and the access to that data. Distributed data management also handles keeping data current among the sites.

There has to be a global or centralized knowledge of the entire data set within the environment. This knowledge includes the structure and location of every file, database, table, and column, and their possible replicas. If the database is fragmented, how and to whom must also be documented as part of this knowledge.

Organizations are capturing and using this knowledge in three "documents."

- A database **dictionary** is already generated and used by each individual database. It keeps all the information about the entities, attributes, rules, and indexes for the data in that database. With a distributed database, the dictionary also includes references to remote data, control information about the network, and its nodes' characteristics.

- Database **directories** hold data location references, so that as a data element is referenced, its location (i.e., its database, node, etc.) can be quickly determined.

- A **catalog** contains all the information about the internal, relational systems tables which contain the information about the relational objects.

If these documents are centralized, they become a bottleneck for all data requests and a single point of failure. Consequently, these documents are themselves distributed. All copies must be kept in sync as data locations and network node characteristics change. As the distributed DBMS software improves, we can expect this synchronization to be handled automatically.

11.3.1 Centralized or distributed database

A centralized database ensures that all users always see exactly the same data. However, a centralized database of transaction data does not perform well as a query and analysis database. Centralized databases do not scale well, nor do they support geographically dispersed users without generating network delays and network problems.

Distributed database technology puts pieces of a database on separate nodes (that also have copies of the DBMS software), creating a "virtual" database. It allows an organization to place pieces (fragments) of the database on the nodes closest to the users that do most of the updating and reads. This minimizes network traffic and maximizes data access times for those local nodes.

However, distributed DBMSs are not the right solution for applications that require multisite access or update. They also require a great amount of administration—maintaining the distributed data dictionary, fine-tuning to take into account multiple network paths and speeds. Since the data is in only one location, if that node is inoperable, the data is inaccessible. In addition, since a distributed database should appear to both the users and the applications as a single, logical database, one database engine is assumed. Most of today's organizations have not standardized on one database engine, let alone one platform, and therefore need to build a single-system image from heterogeneous sources.

Replication, keeping copies of the same data in different locations, addresses many of these problems. There is no wide-area connectivity or network traffic to deal with. Response time is machine-dependent, and scalability is easy. The biggest hurdle is keeping the copies synchronized and determining what is the acceptable interval for them to be out of sync.

These options are discussed in more detail below.

11.3.2 Data management software

Most of the major vendors of server data management software offer a complete package of services: client software, network software, and server software. Organizations can develop vendor-supplied or vendor-neutral solutions.

Vendor-supplied solutions offer some advantages. The products are tightly integrated. When problems do crop up, support should be excellent. However, vendor-supplied solutions violate the concept of openness and wide-reaching data access.

With vendor-neutral solutions, more work may be required to integrate all components of client/server architecture. However, these solutions do support openness and allow the organization to customize the architecture.

Host-based processing client/server applications require no new server software because they interface directly with an existing application, and all of the integrity and logic for the application is built into its code. Since these applications are using the host environment, they access the facilities of the host operating system.

Most other types of client/server applications require the server software to handle data integrity and security.

Organizations can choose between integrated data management software, which provides data management capabilities integrated with front-end tools and a 4GL, and data management software designed for the client/server environment, which provides data management capabilities only.

Server data management software products should have the following common features:

- Triggers, discussed in Sec. 9.2.2
- Two-phase commits, discussed in Sec. 9.3.1
- RPC support, discussed in Sec. 8.9.2
- Stored procedures, discussed in Sec. 9.2.1

11.4 Managing Transactions

Business-critical applications are usually transaction-based applications. If these applications are implemented in a client/server environment, the transaction processing will usually be distributed within the network. The system must maintain consistency and be sure that a transaction can pass the ACID test, as introduced in Sec. 7.8:

- **Atomic**. The transaction works or it doesn't.
- **Consistency**. The system is always left in a correct state after the transaction is executed or the transaction is aborted.
- **Isolation**. A transaction is not affected by other transactions currently being executed.
- **Durability**. A committed transaction can survive system failures.

If a transaction's actions affect only one table or multiple tables in the same database, the ACID test and all transaction management can and should be handled by the DBMS itself. In today's environments, these actions could require resources from a variety of data sources which could reside on multiple geographically dispersed servers—hence the new term distributed transaction processing.

The first solution to the distributed transaction was the use of two-phase commits. A two-phase commit is usually used to ensure that transactions pass the ACID test—that there is data consistency and completeness—when a transaction uses more than one table. In the first phase, the commit server sends out a message that a transaction piece is to take place. The receiving server locks the necessary records, performs its portion of the transaction, and lets the commit server know that it is ready to commit. In the second phase, if one or more of the participating servers cannot commit, the commit server broadcasts a cancel message. If all participating servers indicated that they are ready to commit, the commit server broadcasts a commit message to all participating servers and records the transaction. If something happens during the second phase (the commit phase) so that a participating server cannot successfully commit its portion of the transaction, the commit server broadcasts a rollback message to all participating servers. Two-phase commit is discussed in Sec. 9.3.1.

Distributed transaction processing also needs to handle serialization. As long as a transaction in progress depends on certain information, this information is locked to prevent any other transaction from changing it.

When designing applications that access data on multiple nodes of the infrastructure, developers have to provide procedures that will preserve the integrity of the data, something that is taken for granted in mainframe-based environments. These procedures can be written by the developer or provided by middleware.

As discussed in Chap. 8, middleware sits between the application and the operating system. Transaction managers, a form of middleware, are used to ensure the integrity of the data sources. As discussed earlier, updating data in distributed environments is more complex because the data required for a transaction might span many nodes and be in many formats. Transaction managers oversee the process to ensure that the database is always in a consistent state. If one portion of the transaction cannot be completed, then no portion should be completed.

Transaction managers must

- Support transactions that affect multiple distributed databases.
- Manage the flow of transactions and distribute the workload.
- Send and receive messages between nodes in the network.
- Deal with resource managers, such as DBMSs, using standard interfaces.
- Provide a flexible and powerful system administration facility.

A transaction must either succeed or fail; there is no middle ground. The system cannot be left in an unstable state, nor can a database be left corrupted. The idea of commit or abort ensures that clients and servers are in the correct state. TP monitors maintain the ACID properties for all transactions, regardless of whether they access a single or multiple DBMS, heterogeneous or homogeneous DBMSs, or non-DBMS data.

11.4.1 Categories of software that manage transactions

The software used to monitor and manage transactions is referred to as TP-Lite, OLTP monitors (or TP monitors), and transaction managers. TP-Lite implementations are integrated into the database software. Because of multithreading, architectures can use their own scheduler for tasking services. Instead of each client getting its own process address space on the server and its own pipeline into the database, the requests are funneled through the TP-Lite software, and one pipeline is built to the database.

Transactions can also be monitored through the use of stored procedures. Because a stored procedure is a transactional item, the procedure cannot participate in global transactions. Because it is under the control of the database, it cannot commit resources outside the database or resources not managed by the database.

OLTP monitors, also called TP monitors, perform the required message passing between the components to ensure that the individual actions are executable. They then commit all the actions to execute (the two-phase commit). TOP END from NCR Corp. (formerly AT&T Global Information Services) is an example of an OLTP monitor.

Transaction managers perform message passing as well, but also provide transaction integrity, security, and workload balancing. Transaction managers take the idea of multithreading even further. They assign the execution of transaction tasks to individual threads, but balance the workload between the threads on a server. If the number of incoming client requests is greater than the number of process threads in the server class, the transaction manager can dynamically start new ones.

To be able to coordinate applications that were probably developed with different tools that don't interoperate, transaction managers require adherence to standards to perform their functions. Accepted standards are OSI for message protocols and X/Open's Distributed Transaction Processing (DTP) specification. Applications that adhere to OSI and X/Open DTP can communicate with a transaction manager. However, transaction managers use proprietary languages. While applications can communicate with them, they cannot communicate with each other. Familiar transaction managers include CICS from IBM, Encina from Transarc Corp., a subsidiary of IBM, and Tuxedo from Novell.

For simplicity's sake, and because OLTP monitors are adding more and more features that recast them as transaction managers, this text will use **transaction manager** to refer to both OLTP monitors and transaction managers.

11.4.2   Transaction managers

Transaction managers manage processes and coordinate services; they divide complex applications into smaller units called transactions. Transaction managers control transactions from their starting point, usually a client, to remote resource managers, usually a database server, and back again.

In host-based environments, this was a straightforward task assigned to software like CICS. In the client/server world, transaction managers route transactions across heterogeneous systems, provide load balancing and thread control to ensure performance, and restart systems and transactions when a failure occurs. Transactions can be assigned an execution priority or can execute according to a predefined schedule. Transaction managers can control transactions from one to many servers and coordinate transactions with other middleware layers.

Transaction managers were originally developed to support interactive terminal processing and to manage transactions.   Today's transaction managers can be used to build large-scale, multitier client/server applications that support heterogeneous transaction integrity. Transaction managers are built on top of RPCs or a messaging and queuing base that provides the communications infrastructure. As such, transaction managers provide a higher level of abstraction.

Transaction managers provide an environment for applications by adding such tasks as load balancing, name services, transaction integrity, security, prioritization, and systems administration. They also improve the scalability of database servers by allowing multiple transactions to share a single database connection and by allowing application logic to be dynamically moved to the application server.

Transaction managers go beyond transaction management. They also provide guaranteed delivery of application-to-application messages across similar or dissimilar operating systems, synchronous and asynchronous message delivery, reduced server workload by managing client transactions, and automatic scalability with application replication.

They also simplify system administration because of their built-in capability to balance workload, collect system statistics, and monitor performance and throughput. They can be used to provide application and DBMS recovery and restart. They also insulate developers from knowledge of low-level synchronous and asynchronous middleware software such as APPC, RPCs, and message queuing.

Like other middleware products, transaction managers receive requests from an application program and route the requests to a server application, which updates the target database. Their special capabilities support the management of large distributed applications. Transaction managers guarantee that the application request is delivered to the target database server platform by utilizing disk-based message queues that are not lost with system failure. They include built-in logging to recover transactions that were in process but not completed when a system failure occurs. They also support heterogeneous database updates with two-phase commits.

Transaction managers provide an operating environment in which application code can run. They can be used to provide business rule processing. This service is similar to the features of stored procedures and triggers in a DBMS, which is why the use of stored procedures and triggers is called "TP-Lite." The advantage of transaction managers is that they are DBMS-independent.

A more important advantage is the ability to manage transactions to balance the processing load of a database server. Organizations can increase the number of clients supported by the server without increasing the power of the server. The transaction manager funnels client requests to shared server processes managed by the transaction manager. If the number of client requests increases, the transaction manager simply starts new shared processes. Since DBMS software for servers is usually priced on a per user basis, using a transaction manager can save money, because the number of users is only the number of shared processes set up by the transaction manager, not the actual number of client machines sending requests to the TP monitor.

Transaction managers can also route requests around server and network problems, thus providing high reliability. Transaction managers can sense when an application server has failed and automatically redirect requests to the remaining available servers, thus providing a high availability of system resources. They can also enforce a prioritization scheme in which high-priority requests are given immediate access while low-priority requests are throttled back. This prevents ad hoc SQL requests from bogging down on-line transaction systems.

Transactions work through a two-phase commit which guarantees their completion. If all the work performed by the participants of a transaction is not completed successfully, all work is automatically rolled back, the environment cleaned up, and the transactions returned as failed transactions.

Transaction managers communicate via remote procedure calls, distributed dynamic program links, interprocess communications, and message-oriented middleware. Yes, it's middleware using middleware.

In the Windows world, access to transaction managers exists as a DLL (dynamic link library) that contain several transaction manager functions. The application loads the DLL and invokes functions that access services running in the transaction manager. The client makes calls to the transaction manager, which in turn talks to the database server. The developer is responsible for writing the client application and the transaction manager services that access the database. The client application is decoupled from the database server, creating a three-tier architecture. The client talks to the application server using a transactional remote procedure call. The application server, in turn, talks to the resource managers using the proper protocol, such as SQL for a relational database server.

A transaction manager is worthy of consideration when the number of clients on the client/server system approaches 200 or more or if your architecture requires more than two tiers. The transaction manager will provide the control needed to move information around from server to server. Its ability to manage database requests to maximize load balancing will allow the organization to increase the number of clients without upgrading the database server hardware. In addition, most transaction managers provide built-in recovery services, security, and integrity checks as part of their base services.

The downside is the cost of the additional tier, the cost of the transaction manager software itself, and the complexity of application development. In addition, there is no clear definition of what functionality a transaction manager should provide, and no two transaction managers manage transactions the same way. All transaction managers are proprietary, and code written for a particular transaction manager works only with that transaction manager. However, for large-scale, mission-critical client/server applications, transaction managers are well worth the money and the trouble.

11.4.3 X/Open DTP Reference Model

The DTP Reference Model is incorporated in the X/Open Portability Guide (XPG4). The standard interfaces employed by a transaction manager include

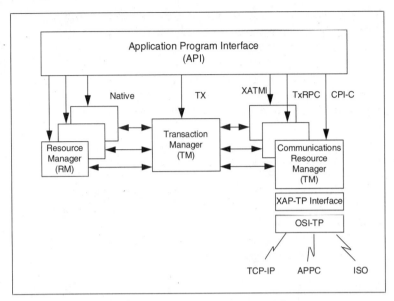

Figure 11.1 Components of X/Open's DTP reference model

X/Open's XA and TX interfaces for communication with resource managers and application programs.

As illustrated in Fig. 11.1, the components of the DTP reference model are

- An application program
- Resource managers (RM) such as databases that provide access to shared resources
- Transaction managers (TM) that assign global identifiers to transactions, monitor their progress, manage the transaction integrity, and recover from failures
- Communication resource managers that controls the communiations between distributed applications

The XA specification handles the interface between a transaction manager and resource managers. The XA specification uses such constructs as "transaction begin," "transaction commit," "transaction abort," and "transaction end." XA also includes the concept of global and branch transactions. A global transaction is the unit of work as seen by the application. A global transaction can be broken into branch transactions, each performing a particular function.

11.4.4 CICS

IBM's Customer Information Control System (CICS) was designed to support on-line transaction processing and real-time communication between the users, computer programs, and data resources. The CICS API allows developers to build applications for a distributed transaction processing environment. The documented API is provided on all supported platforms, allowing developers to write applications that are portable across all supported platforms.

CICS systems that run in the same host are located in different address spaces to communicate with each other. Communication between systems residing in different locations uses a communication access method to provide the necessary communication protocols. This intersystem communication is an implementation of IBM's Systems Network Architecture (SNA), thus it is a proprietary solution.

CICS Intersystem Communication (ISC) provides the following intercommunication facilities:

- **CICS function shipping**. This facility allows an application program running in one CICS system to access a resource owned by another CICS system. The remote resource could be a file, database, data queue, or storage queue. Application programs are designed and coded as if the resources were local to the system in which the application is to run.
- **Asynchronous processing**. Support for asynchronous processing enables a CICS transaction to distribute processing between systems by initiating a transaction in a remote system and passing data to it. Since the reply does not have to be returned to the task that initiated the remote transaction, the communication is asynchronous.
- **CICS transaction routing**. This facility enables a terminal that is owned by one CICS system to initiate a transaction that is owned by another CICS system. As with Function Shipping, the communications are handled by CICS itself.
- **CICS distributed transaction processing**. This is the CICS feature that actually implements System Application Architecture (SAA) distribution. It allows a CICS transaction to communicate with a transaction running in another system for the purpose of distributing the required processing between two or more systems.

11.4.5 Tuxedo

Tuxedo, from Novell, provides interface specifications for applications and resource managers. The Application Transaction Manager Interface (ATMI) supports

- Location transparency
- Load balancing
- Transparent data format conversion
- Context-sensitive routing
- Priority processing
- Network independence

In addition, Tuxedo uses UNIX System V Transport Layer Interface to provide access to underlying network technologies, such as TCP/IP, NetBIOS, OSI protocols, and APPC/LU6.2.

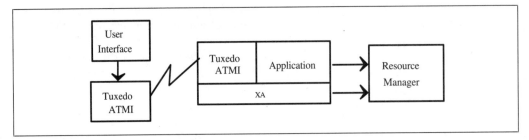

Figure 11.2 Components of Tuxedo

As illustrated in Fig. 11.2, the Tuxedo transaction manager and resource manager components use standard interfaces to communicate with the systems' resource managers. The Tuxedo ATMI treats transactions that involve more than one resource manager and more than one physical location (also called global transactions) as one logical unit of work. For a global transaction to be successful, all local transactions must be successful.

In 1995 Novell released Tuxedo Enterprise Transaction Processing, which consists of the following:

- **System/T** is the base TP monitor, which includes Name Server, Communications Manager, Transaction Control, and Operations, Administration, and Maintenance (OA&M) to control client/server interactions.
- **System/Q** is the queuing service enhancement to the monitor.
- **System/WS** supplies APIs that allow Windows, DOS, OS/2, and UNIX stations to be Tuxedo clients.
- **System/Host** provides a framework for building gateway servers between legacy mainframe applications and UNIX products.
- **System/D** is a proprietary TP-oriented data management system which includes server applications and their interfaces for database access and access to remote applications.

Novell turned control of Tuxedo over to BEA Systems Inc., which was founded last year by former executives of Sun Microsystems and Pyramid Technology Inc. and specializes in distributed computing and middleware technology, in an effort to improve customer support and increase product interoperability. BEA will assume the role of developer and master distributor of Tuxedo on all non-NetWare platforms, including UNIX and mainframe operating systems. Novell will retain the rights to develop and integrate Tuxedo within NetWare. Full integration is expected in 1997.

11.4.6 TOP END

TOP END, from NCR Corp. (formerly AT&T Global Information Services), is based on X/Open's Distributed Transaction Processing environment and uses XA (the X/Open Resource Manager) interfaces to UNIX-based DBMSs. As illustrated in Fig. 11.3, TOP END divides the transaction processing into

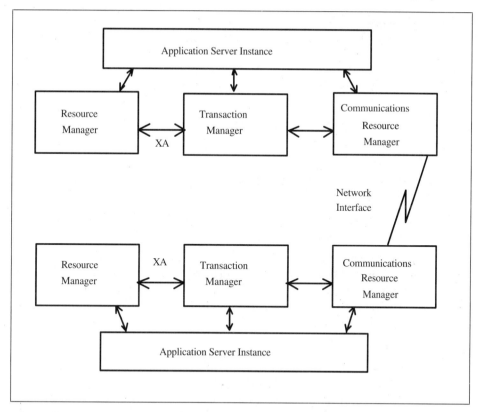

Figure 11.3 Components of TOP END

modules that can be distributed across the network for efficiency and flexibility. TOP END keeps track of their distribution and uses the information to do dynamic load balancing. A two-phase commit protocol, which is transparent to the user, ensures global transaction integrity.

TOP END is similar in architecture and functionality to the older Tuxedo. The major differences are in the following areas:

- **Administration**. In TOP END, resource definitions can be created interactively and stored in a repository. Tuxedo uses the UNIX editor to create definitions and the UNIX file system to store them.
- **Communications**. TOP END has direct support for major UNIX network protocols. Tuxedo uses UNIX Transport Level Interface only.
- **Security**. TOP END supports MIT's Kerberos security system. Tuxedo offers little authorization security.
- **Workload balancing**. The workload balancing performed by TOP END is dynamic and network-sensitive. In Tuxedo, it is predefined.

In late 1996, NCR released a Java client for TOP END. This Web-specific version of TOP END is designed to take advantage of the Internet and bypass weaknesses in standard Internet protocols. NCR has rewritten the

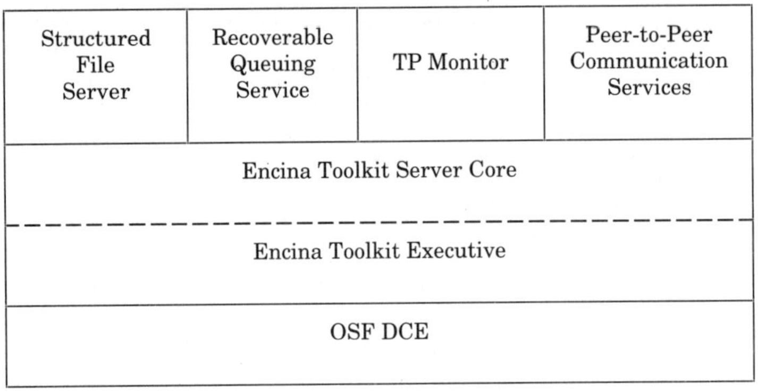

Structured File Server	Recoverable Queuing Service	TP Monitor	Peer-to-Peer Communication Services
Encina Toolkit Server Core			
Encina Toolkit Executive			
OSF DCE			

Source: Transarc Corp.

Figure 11.4 Components of Encina

TOP END client code, which runs on micros and can sit inside automated teller machines and cash registers, as a set of Java class libraries. This new software will also let users deploy point-of-sale applications over the World Wide Web. NCR expects to deliver an ActiveX client for TOP END by 1997.

11.4.7 Encina

Based on the technologies of X/Open Consortium and Open Software Foundation's Distributed Computing Environment (DCE), the Encina product line from Transarc Corp., a subsidiary of IBM, provides highly reliable and easy-to-use transaction management software for distributed environments. Encina, released commercially in the first quarter of 1993, combines DCE's strengths, such as communication and management tools, resource location transparency, and security, with application development tools. Encina has its own multithreaded environment and supports nested transactions. Encina uses a two-phase commit for distributed transactions and a local two-phase commit for nondistributed transactions.

As illustrated in Fig. 11.4, Encina is based on a two-tier strategy, which is designed to support full-featured transaction processing (TP) managers, resource managers, or other distributed systems. The first tier sits on top of DCE and expands the DCE foundation to include services that support distributed transaction processing (the Encina Toolkit Executive) and the management of recoverable data (the Encina Toolkit Server Core).

The second tier consists of TP services based on facilities provided by the first tier. These tools, developed by Transarc, include:

- The **Encina Monitor**, a full-featured TP monitor, provides an easy-to-use development environment, a reliable execution environment, and an administrative environment.
- The **Encina Structured File Server** is a record-oriented file system which provides high performance and full transactional integrity, and can participate in two-phase commit protocols across multiple servers.

- The **Encina Peer-to-Peer Communication Services** support transactional CPI-C peer-to-peer communications over TCP/IP and LU6.2 (for IBM's SNA) transports.
- The **Encina Recoverable Queuing Service** provides queuing of transactional data. It provides multiple levels of priority and can support large numbers of users and high volumes of data.

One of the key features of Encina is the extension of RPCs into transactional RPCs. With transactional RPCs, applications can use DCE's RPC facility to invoke transactions on a network as if they were local. All necessary transaction processing, including state information, is delivered over an existing client/server RPC connection that is totally transparent to users and applications. Another important feature is the transactional RPC use of DCE authentication and security down to the RPC level.

In late 1995, Transarc released Encina 2.0, which was designed for three-tier, enterprise-wide client/server environments. Version 2.0 provides users with Encina++, for object-oriented development of Encina and DCE applications. Version 2.0 also includes Encina Console, the first Encina graphical administration tool, to let users manage servers, communications, and other processes from a single workstation.

Encina++ is a distributed object development environment, supporting application development and reuse of Encina code through C++ class libraries. With Encina++, developers are shielded from the underlying complexities of client/server computing.

For DCE users, Encina++ reduces the programming effort required for underlying DCE communications. For example, Encina++ automatically establishes DCE security mechanisms and object location services without additional code generation. Encina++ provides an interface to the Object Management Group's (OMG) Object Transaction Service (OTS), the OMG standard for business-critical transactions.

In early 1996, Transarc introduced DCE Encina Light (DE-Light,) a new transaction processing client that supports DCE, to reduce client overhead and simplify software development. DE-Light extends the reach of Encina to all Windows platforms and Java-compatible Web browsers. It moves the DCE client off the desktop and onto an intermediary workstation to reduce client resource requirements. Client machines contain only enough code to generate transactional requests, but include nearly all DCE capabilities. DE-Light runs over slow-speed dial-up lines.

11.4.8 Development tools

Developers must create the client application as well as the TP monitor processes and the links to the database. The client and application server services can be built using traditional 3GLs or 4GL tools that can work with TP monitors, such as Transarc's EncinaBuilder, an integration of PowerBuilder and Encina for Windows; Prolifics's JAM 7/Transaction Processing interface (JAM 7/TPi); and Microsoft's Visual Basic.

EncinaBuilder from Transarc

EncinaBuilder is an integration of PowerBuilder Enterprise application development environment and Encina for Windows. It lets developers build Windows applications that can access any Encina applications services. EncinaBuilder's Service Browser can be used to select an Encina service to add to a PowerBuilder application. EncinaBuilder automatically creates custom user objects, including data windows, transaction objects, and dynamic link libraries.

JAM 7/TPi from Prolifics

Prolifics provides a TP monitor–ready version of JAM 7 for Novell's Tuxedo. JAM/TPi for Tuxedo provides easy 4GL OLTP applications construction on the client as well as with the TP monitor. The client portion links JAM with the client facilities of Tuxedo. This link allows developers to construct Tuxedo clients that can run on Windows and UNIX/Motif. The server portion links Tuxedo to the scripting language and database interface capabilities of JAM, including the ability to specify database interaction graphically. Prolifics expects to deliver similar capabilities with JAM 7/TPi for Encina, and JAM 7/TPi for CICS in 1997.

12

Managing the
Client/Server Environment

Managing the client/server environment requires that the applications themselves, the system, and the network all be monitored and managed. Each impacts the other and must always be reviewed together rather than independently.

12.1 Managing the Applications

Before system management tools (as discussed below) became available, network and system managers would write their own scripts to monitor and identify application performance bottlenecks. They quickly realized that not being able to manage the many disparate technology components of an enterprise-wide client/server system was totally inacceptable.

They also quickly realized that application monitoring needs are driven by the site and as such are used for different purposes. Application monitoring usually falls into one of four categories:

- **Resource manager**: Monitor the performance of a business-critical application.
- **Service-level manger**: Monitor response times to determine if service-level agreements (SLAs) are being meet.
- **Performance manager**: Do proactive troubleshooting and problem management.
- **Capacity manager**: Provide better understanding of what is on the network for capacity planning.

To accomplish these tasks, organizations need to focus on managing the system and managing the network.

12.2 Managing the System

An effective strategy for managing a client/server environment requires dealing with multiple vendors, network topologies, operating systems, and applications. The strategy must also be flexible enough to support an ever-changing environment.

The terms bandied about are production, system, and network management. Systems management is used as a catch-all phrase. Let's set out some definitions:

- **Production management** focuses on keeping applications available when unplanned events happen without notice and immediate action is needed.
- **System management** reaches out to planned events that are achieved on a scheduled basis from a systems administrator.
- **Network management** is the management of the network infrastructure and is typically done through network information standards such as SNMP.

Lately the scope of network management has expanded to include computer hardware as well as network devices. Production management differs from the others in that the database, system, and network are looked at on a synchronized basis and not in an isolation fashion.

12.2.1 Production management

Reducing the support costs while increasing overall system availability is the goal of production management. By reacting to critical events immediately, organizations can reduce the impact of these events on production systems. A corrective action can be initiated immediately when an unplanned event occurs.

But before a problem can be identified, what is normal has to be identified. That requires collecting data for analysis and capacity planning, performance, and resource accounting and archiving the data to be used to identify system performance bottlenecks. This information is also used to teach a production management tool what it must react to.

12.2.2 System management

Not all applications have to have subsecond response time. System managers need to ensure that resources necessary for business-critical application are made available as they become needed.

Many resource problems are due to the fact that many enterprise networks have grown haphazardly. Servers were not placed for optimal network traffic, message routing may be inefficient, and applications that are not business-critical may be taking more than their fair share of the valuable resources. Performance tools can help an organization pinpoint where these areas are and redesign the enterprise network so that it better supports the organization.

Some of these same tools have scenario capabilities so that system managers can test the impact of moving a server, increasing the bandwidth on a network segment, or increasing the numbers of users per application, or (more often the case today) the impact of users browsing on the World Wide Web.

System management software should include capabilities for

- **Problem detection, analysis, and resolution**. Administrators should be alerted when a device or application fails, and should be able to determine what went wrong and how to resolve the problem, even if it occurred on a remote site.
- **Asset management**. There should be automated inventory discovery and software auditing.
- **Security management**. The software should include profile definition, verification, authorization, and authentication.
- **Backup and recovery** of distributed data and applications.
- **Software distribution, configuration, and change management**. In addition, the software should also support inventory management, version control, security, and software distribution.
- **Performance management**. The software should include performance trend analysis and threshold event management. Administrators should be able to pinpoint sources of performance degradation and tune the system to acceptable levels of performance.
- **Remote database management**. The software should be able to manage remote databases from a single central console, including user setup, performance monitoring, backup and restore, and integration with network management platforms such as Hewlett-Packard's SNMP-compliant OpenView and Tivoli Management Environment (TME).

To satisfy the requirements for system management, an organization can

- **Install individual products to solve individual problems**. While the functionality of each product may be very rich, the task of managing and supporting so many disparate tools from different vendors is expensive and difficult.
- **Install large, complex applications that combine the functionality of individual products**. While this might be effective, the applications tend to be difficult to manage because of their size, and the organization is locked into one vendor.
- **Install individual products that comply with a management framework**. Framework solutions are usually based on a set of well-defined APIs that glue the management applications together. A variation on an API-based framework is a repository-based framework

where a relational database is used to integrate the systems management applications.

Software vendors are beginning to address this issue. Here is just a sampling:

- **Tivoli Systems** has a program that invites application and application-development tool vendors to join forces with Tivoli to provide performance monitoring hooks from Tivoli's Tivoli Management Environment (TME) into their products. SNMP alerts from OpenView and other network management platforms are integrated through Tivoli's Enterprise Console.

- **Platinum Technology**'s database and systems management tools architecture, POEMS (Platinum Open Enterprise Management System), provides a single platform for managing databases and includes querying and development tools.

- **Landmark Systems Corp.**'s PerformanceWorks includes performance management software called SmartAgent that can monitor, manage, and report on operating systems, databases, and end-user applications.

- **OpenVision Technologies Inc.**'s OpenV*Event Manager includes event libraries for Oracle and Sybase databases and agents that can actually take corrective actions in response to events. Event libraries for more data sources are under development. OpenV*Perform provides a single screen shot of multiple devices and lets a network technician set event thresholds. OpenV*Trend collects historical performance data.

- Patrol from **BMC Software Inc.** has built-in automatic procedures to monitor and control machines (include Net servers), databaes, networks, and applications. It operates as an event-driven management tool, uses independent server-based software agents, and provides automatic notification and recovery actions.

- CA-Unicenter from **Computer Associates International** includes disk and tape backup, event and help desk, report distribution, and security features, and provides status information via a centralized console. CA-Unicenter TNG (The Next Generation) uses Jasmine, an architecture based on CA's object-oriented database to store and monitor information about resources. Unicenter TNG manages all components from one console regardless of the platform.

- **Compuware Corp.**'s EcoTools includes intelligent agents for monitoring and analyzing the network, the databases, and the servers. The tools provide an early warning system.

  EcoNet, originally called CoroNet Management System from CoroNet Systems before CoroNet was acquired in 1995 by Compuware, monitors the network from an application perspective using data collected from software-only monitors. The data can be used to show which applications are creating traffic and which parts of the network are most affected. End-to-end performance data across multiple network segments and through routers can also be captured for analysis. EcoNet also accepts application monitoring data from network-measurement instruments such as Sniffer from Network General Corp.

- Optimal Networks Tool Kit from **Optimal Networks Corp.** consists of Optimal Surveyor, a multiprotocol network discovery and analysis tool, and Optimal Performance, a network modeling application, both of which are Windows-based. Surveyor uses SNMP to discover and graph the topology of the network as well as the logical connectivity of bridged and switched networks. A topology browser lets network administrators view specific IP or IPX segments, router WAN and LAN interfaces, subnet addresses, all routers that are enabled for IP traffic, and all switches and users on each segment.

Optimal Performance accepts data from network-measurement instruments but does not collect any of its own. It adds analysis and modeling capabilities. It creates an integrated model of network traffic that is stored in a relational database. A traffic browser supplies multidimensional views of network traffic by protocol or applications. Optimal Performance also has "what-if" simulation capability to evaluate the impact of potential network design changes. The software also features intelligent algorithms that generate recommendations for LAN segmentation, switch deployment, optimal server and application positioning, and capacity requirements for WAN links.

12.2.3   Distributed System Management framework

X/Open's Systems Management Work Group defines a systems management framework as cohesive and object-oriented, enabling and promoting the development of interoperable management applications. The Distributed System Management framework has multiple-level services and interfaces that include

- Management applications
- Managed objects
- Services such as communications, data storage, security, OMG object services, and management services (scheduling, collections, customization, policy)

An object request broker is at the center of the Distributed System Management framework and provides the mechanisms that allow objects to make and receive requests regardless of their locations. ORBs are discussed in Sec. 17.1.1.

This framework is the foundation of Tivoli Management Environment (TME) and Sybase's Enterprise SQL Server Manager (ESSM).

IBM Software Servers

IBM Software Servers (code named Project Eagle), released in late 1996, is a series of seven cross-platform applications and enabling servers. It consists of software and middleware that sit above the operating system. The IBM Software Server functions include communications, database, directory and security, Internet connection, Lotus Notes, SystemView, and transaction processing. The seven applications—which will be packaged separately—will be capable of running on AIX and OS/2 Warp as well as Windows NT. Eventually support will be expanded to HP-UX and Solaris.

Although sold separately, Software Server applications will give customers the benefit of an integrated suite. The applications will support the same clients, feature similar installation and documentation, and share common technical support services. IBM has bundled new features into its servers including intranet support and Windows 95 client support.

IBM Software Servers are based on the IBM Open Blueprint, which incorporates industry and de facto standards in an effort to ensure compatibility with projects from multiple vendors and have open APIs for linking to other vendors' products. The Servers are

- Internet Connection Server, as a base server or a secure server
- Database Server, which is based on DB2
- Lotus Notes Server
- Communications Server, which is built on IBM's Communication Manager and AnyNet and supports Systems Network Architecture (SNA) and TCP/IP
- Systems Management Server, which is based on IBM's SystemView
- Transaction Server, which combines CICS and Encina technologies to provide a transaction-processing infrastructure
- Directory and Security Server, which is based on DCE

The Windows NT versions of these last four Software Servers will not be available until 1997.

BackOffice

Microsoft's BackOffice (1.5), marketed as an enterprise suite of client/server infrastructure applications, is a combination of Microsoft Systems Management Server (1.1), Microsoft SNA Server 2.12, Microsoft Windows NT Server 3.51, Microsoft SQL Server 6.0, and Microsoft Mail Server 3.5, which will be replaced by Microsoft Exchange Server. To ensure interoperability, Microsoft created a set of BackOffice standards that are being picked up by several software vendors, from Oracle to IBM to SAP to Digital.

Certification (called Logo Certification by Microsoft) means that the product will be ready for the Cairo technologies when they are released in 1996. These include a new Object File System, new iterations of OLE that incorporate Transaction OLE and OLE DB, and a new directory service called Open Data Services Interface (ODSI), or alternatively OLE Directory Services Interface. The products will also be ready for the Microsoft

Exchange Server (the workgroup replacement for MS Mail) and BackOffice for the Internet, in addition to application development tools specially created and tuned for building BackOffice-based applications.

Microsoft has priced BackOffice such that all five products come for the price of three. An additional incentive is the fact that Microsoft is promoting BackOffice to VARs and resellers as an easy-to-manage infrastructure for departmental client/server applications. This strategy is expected to generate a new set of NT Server customers. Microsoft is also promoting BackOffice to large corporate users as the centralized management structure for all an organization's client/server systems. This approach works best with organizations that expect to be true Windows shops. But the promise of being able to control everything in the enterprise from a single console is appealing.

BackOffice is priced in client or server versions. However, a BackOffice license for all five server products cannot be divided up among several servers. All five BackOffice applications must run on the same server.

BackOffice 2.0, released mid-1996, includes intranet and Internet capabilities and improved integration with network and client applications, and is capable of coexisting with most network environments.

12.3 Managing the Network

As noted above, it is difficult to truly separate the management of the applications from the management of the network. And indeed, managing the network provides the same kinds of challenges as managing applications does.

Managing the network requires managing the physical aspects of the network, such as managing the LAN connections, analyzing LAN protocols, and monitoring LAN devices. Software is used to monitor and manage the physical devices. Network management software is discussed in Sec. 12.4.

For client/server systems to work at all, organizations have to ensure that the physical network is working. If it is not functioning, there is no need to manage applications, because they won't be running anyway. When an organization thinks of its physical network, it must realize that every piece of the network—LAN segments, cabling, routers, hubs, switches, and even protocols—is a potential failure site and as such needs to be managed.

However, there currently exists a variety of tools that can aid network administrators in cutting through dissimilar products to fine-tune network performance, reduce downtime, and reduce the need for network consultants. These products fall into four categories:

- Protocol analyzers and monitors
- Intelligent wiring hubs
- Network management software
- Network performance monitors

12.3.1   Protocol analyzers and monitors

Protocol analyzers and monitors allow network administrators to watch and inspect the packets of a particular protocol within a specific architecture. The functions of protocol analyzers (capture, view, analyze) are divided between the software in the monitor attached to the LAN and the manager software running at the operator's machine.

Protocol analyzers can be dedicated, portable, or remote. Remote analyzers plug into a particular segment of the network and allow the data to be read from another location on the network. These are sometimes referred to as *sniffers*.

The products currently in the marketplace range from the software-based LANwatch from FTP Software Inc. to hardware/software products from Novell (LANalyzer), Hewlett-Packard (LanProbe II), and Network General Corp. (Sniffer).

12.3.2   Intelligent wiring hubs

Intelligent wiring hubs, also called smart wiring hubs, allow the network to be segmented into manageable chunks, making it easier to isolate problems, track configuration changes, and enforce security. Hubs can be run from local consoles or central management stations.

The major vendors of intelligent hubs are Cabletron Systems Inc., Bay Networks (formed when SynOptics Communications Inc. merged with Wellfleet Communications Inc.), and the UB Networks subsidiary of Tandem Computers (formerly Ungermann-Bass, Inc.).

Network operating systems are appearing as components in smart wiring hubs, which reduces the hub cost because the server's CPU runs the hub management software. In addition, wiring hubs allow vendors to ship ready-to-run networks with preconfigured file servers. Novell's Hub Management Interface bundles low-end hub cards into its servers, integrating the wiring hub and the file server into a single device.

12.3.3   Network management software

Network management software allows network administrators to monitor the entire network including remote workstations, servers, and the network cabling from a central point. Network management software is discussed in Sec. 12.4. Vendors of network operating systems are beginning to integrate network management features into their products.

Central Point LANlord, from Symantec Corp., manages and controls resources across multiple heterogeneous LANs. Hewlett-Packard's PerfView is based on HP's OpenView framework, which supports the management of heterogeneous networks from one location and was accepted by OSF as part of DME. OpenView focuses on managing network resources; PerfView focuses on managing the performance of distributed systems across a WAN.

12.3.4   Network performance monitors

Physically connecting the pieces is in itself challenging, but managing the change is more difficult. If a port in a hub has a problem, the network administrator needs to be able to remotely turn that port off and have the network adjust for the changes.

Network performance monitors allow a network administrator, from a central location, to analyze network performance and reconfigure resources to bypass problems and bottlenecks.

Think for a moment about what happens when a client makes a request of a server. The request goes from the client application to the operating system to the network software to a hub to a router and then to a T1 or frame relay line. When it is received at the server site, it goes through a router to network software to the operating system to possibly a transaction monitor to a DBMS and finally to the server portion of the application, if there is one.

In order to monitor this environment, it is necessary to be able to trace and measure each link. On a system management software console, each link is a little box on the map. As the applications become more business-critical, network and system managers need to know more about these little boxes than where they are.

Products such as the Sniffer family from Network General Corp. are used to analyze network activity. They proactively identify network problems on distributed networks and can manage multiple network segments from a central site. They report their findings using one of the network information standards discussed below.

12.4   Software for Managing Networks

Network management software allows network administrators to monitor, manage, and control resources across multiple heterogeneous networks from a single point, giving administrators much more functionality than that provided by network performance monitors. Like performance monitors, network management software can analyze operations at remote workstations and servers as well as the network cabling. The software also maintains a topological layout of the network.

Network management is usually looked at as a framework of several building blocks. Software agents are components that reside on the managed systems and interact with the network system manager software, which is the heart of the network management system. Vendors of network operating systems are beginning to integrate network management features into their products.

Software is used to support the following network functions:

- **LAN administration**, which includes adding new users, applications, and peripherals, as well as configuring LAN servers.
- **Monitoring LAN devices**, which includes fault, configuration, and performance monitoring of routers and bridges.
- **Transmission link management**, which includes wide area leased lines, X.25 switches, and WAN switches such as T1 multiplexers.
- **Performance management**, which includes measuring response time and should automatically reroute network traffic.
- **Fault management**, which should detect and isolate problems in the network protocols, cabling, or devices.
- **Security management**, which protects against unauthorized modifications of data and eavesdropping on the network.
- **Accounting**, which includes billing, budgeting and accounting verification.

A key requirement of network management is the gathering and displaying of information from devices on the network. Information is gathered by MIB (Management Information Base) browsers for SNMP, CMIP, IP discoverers, and event monitors. SNMP and CMIP are discussed in the next section.

12.4.1   OpenView

Hewlett-Packard's OpenView is an SNMP-based network manager. Its Network Node Manager (NNM), a distributed version of OpenView, provides a client/server architecture that separates its processor-intensive GUI from its server-based discovery, mapping, event handling, and data storage functions.

NNM version 4.0, released in early 1996, is a more resource-efficient management system, and will distribute polling, discovery, and event-handling features across various workstations. Version 4.0 manages twice as many nodes as version 3.3. Network Node Manager 4.0 is the first phase in HP's future framework code named Tornado.

HP is expected to merge its Network Node Manager with the OpenView problem-management component, OperationsCenter. The combination will decrease the number of agents needed on a monitored device, potentially improving its performance while reducing memory requirements. In addition, OperationsCenter will eliminate redundancies between the OpenView components found in the GUI and event-handling capability, as well as possibly providing OperationsCenter developers an easy avenue to port their applications to the more prevalent Network Node Manager.

Hewlett-Packard is also expected to make OpenView Network Node Manager Web-enabled and to add embedded Java support to the product.

12.4.2   NetView

IBM's NetView was one of the first products aimed at distributed system management at the enterprise level. NetView uses the concept of *manager of managers* to oversee the entire enterprise. It creates a single system image using a three-level hierarchy of management elements:

- Entry points, at the lowest level, collect management information and send it upward.
- Service points, at the middle, act on the information from the entry points and send the rest upward.
- Focal points, at the top, maintain a central database of management information and present a unified view of all distributed resources.

NetView is a component of Digital's PolyCenter Manager, which is limited to Digital environments, and IBM's SystemView (see Sec. 13.12.3).

12.5 Network Management Information Standards

Standardization is one of the critical success factors for networking. Most of the public data networks rely on open system standards, such as X.25 packet switching. Most of these open system standards refer to the lower layers of the OSI model. More important standards developments are occurring at the upper layers. X.400 electronic mail, X.500 directories, and EDI plus file transfer standards for intervendor communication have been accepted and used by the industry in recent years.

In order to manage different networks as one enterprise network, network variables must be tracked. The interface between a device or software in the network and the management system is called the manager-agent interface. For each device or software component involved, there is an agent that collects information for the management system and executes management controls. Management information flows in both directions. To work together, the manager and the agent must use the same management information protocols.

The major protocols for network management information are Common Management Information Protocol (CMIP), Simple Network Management Protocol (SNMP) and an improved version of SNMP (SNMP-2), Remote Network Monitoring (RMON), and XMP and XOM from X/Open. There is also a new standard, the Desktop Management Interface (DMI) from the Desktop Management Task Force.

The most popular management standards are SNMP and CMIP. SNMP's approach is simple and straightforward, and CMIP's is more powerful and complex. SNMP-2 expanded on SNMP, and the protocol is now anything but straightforward.

Both SNMP and CMIP use object-oriented techniques to describe the information to be managed. Each resource to be managed is called a managed object and can represent anything that needs to be managed— from an entire server to a single variable. A management information base (MIB) defines a structure collection of managed objects. The structure of the management information (SMI) defines the model, notations, and naming conventions used by a particular protocol (SNMP or CMIP).

A MIB is a form of a hierarchical database and as such needs tools, such as

- A MIB compiler that converts a file to a format that can be used by the management station
- A MIB browser that displays the MIB tree graphically and allows an administrator to search for objects by groups or attributes
- A MIB report writer, which is a visual interface for producing reports of the managed data

Most MIBs are integrated with other tools, such as an agent discovery tool which can display the location of the agents on the network and whose data can be assessed by the MIB query tool.

A management agent is a program that gathers information and forwards it to a management program. An intelligent agent not only gathers information and reports when queried, but also makes intelligent decisions. It may filter information, determining what is relevant and what the problem is, and it may automatically fix the problem.

A midlevel manager can do the same things as an intelligent agent. But instead of managing a single device, it manages a domain by communicating with agents. For this reason, it is also referred to as a domain manager or super agent. Agents in managed devices are called embedded agents.

Midlevel managers can be used to construct management hierarchies that provide multiple levels of data consolidation and analysis. This means that local problems can be addressed locally, while broader problems can be investigated and analyzed at appropriate higher levels.

Intelligent agents for network management have been slow in coming, probably because of the wide acceptance of SNMP. SNMP agents aren't supposed to be intelligent; they're supposed to gather statistics and report to higher-level managers when they are requested to do so. They're not supposed to analyze or solve problems—that's the job of the higher-level managers.

The managed resources are represented by managed objects, and all managed objects are stored in the MIB. This MIB is made visible to managers by the agent, which is typically a management station or an application program. The agent's job is to receive management protocol operations from the manager and to map the operations on the conceptual managed objects (as "stored" in the MIB) to the physical system resources. Agents can be configured to constantly send information, which creates a lot of network traffic, or to send information as the result of exceptions, pieces of real-time information that are outside of the stored allowed range of values. For example, an agent could send the number of packets received on a network interface every 3 seconds so that the manager can decide if the network is overloaded, or an agent could check the number of packets every

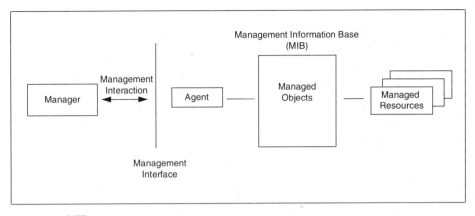

Figure 12.1 MIB management agents

3 seconds and send the number of packets only if it is greater than a pre-specified number. Figure 12.1 illustrated this process.

MIB-II adds additional groups of managed objects. Objects are defined by their hierarchical location in the tree. The concept of a group provides a way to organize management objects according to the functions they provide. All objects within a group must be supported for the group to be MIB-II compliant. All devices that claim to be Internet managed nodes must implement the MIB, but not all functions need to be present on all nodes.

The architects of SNMP also discouraged agents from sending "trap" or alarm messages. They designed SNMP on the assumption that the higher-level manager would usually take the initiative to poll the agent. Therefore, agents don't need any intelligence.

SNMP is an older standard. Intelligent agents are newer technology and at some point the two should converge. Intelligent agents are a natural for LAN management. They can off-load the central console and minimize traffic, make corrective actions even when the network is down, and be used at remote offices where links may be too slow for effective remote management.

Equipment vendors have been among the first to implement intelligent agents on PC LANs. Bay Network is one example. If the agent embedded in this supplier's hubs sees excess traffic on a port, it can "wrap" (disable) that port. Only an agent embedded in the hub can efficiently do this because excessive traffic will probably prevent remote access to the hub.

Embedded agents are not the answer to everything, however. For one thing, they're not well positioned to perform certain functions, such as global topology mapping or fault correlation for multiple devices. Also, intelligent agents require processing power and other resources, such as memory and storage. Because one embedded agent is required per device, the cost of these agents must be kept at a reasonable level. Vendors must achieve a balance between agent capabilities and cost considerations. Some vendors who have been making intelligent agents for UNIX environments are now offering agents for LANs. Legent and Tivoli are among the most successful.

SNMP wasn't designed with intelligent agents or midlevel managers in mind. It doesn't provide a way to define faults or corrective actions. An agent can query the MIB, come to conclusions about faults, and take appropriate actions. But faults and actions would be defined in the agent, not in the MIB. SNMP provides no shared repository or format for defining faults or actions.

Today, faults and actions are defined at the central SNMP console. Even if the definitions are programmatic, they're still proprietary. If the intelligent agents' and midlevel managers' functions are to be standardized, these proprietary, console-based fault and action definitions will no longer suffice.

The solution may lie in a new interface called the Desktop Management Interface (DMI).

12.5.1 Simple Network Management Protocol

Simple Network Management Protocol (SNMP) is based on TCP/IP standards and provides a common format for network devices to exchange management information with the network management station (or stations). The station controls the network through agents located in the different pieces of equipment on the network. The network management software polls each SNMP agent module installed on each network component for status information. This data is stored in the MIB.

In effect, SNMP defines a standard MIB that will allow any network management station to work with any agent and its MIB. However, vendors provide extensions to the information reported by their equipment. Management software looking for these extensions cannot provide the same level of information about other vendors' equipment, and software that cannot read the extensions provides erroneous results.

One of the first network management information standards, SNMP has some major limitations in terms of support for today's enterprise networks. These limitations include the following:

- There is a lack of security features. Passwords are passed across the network in a single, unprotected packet.
- It assumes the end device is dumb and so there are a limited number of tests that can be run on it.
- It is unable to collect network management data in bulk.
- It supports only TCP/IP networks. However, vendors, such as Novell and Apple, are beginning to modify SNMP to run on other network platforms.

But SNMP is suitable for what it was designed for: handling simple tasks such as allowing network administrators to monitor remote hubs, switches, bridges, and routers.

12.5.2   Simple Network Management Protocol, Version 2

The Internet Engineering Task Force (IETF), the standards-setting body for SNMP, released the Simple Network Management Protocol, Version 2 as a new standard to replace SNMP. Unlike SNMP, the new version, referred to as SNMP-2, supports the management of applications on hosts and micros and offers secure communication between the management systems and the managed network devices.

SNMP-2 supports manager-to-manager communication, which allows a central management station to delegate tasks to subnetwork managers. Transport mappings are provided for multiple protocol stacks, including AppleTalk, IPX used in Novell's NetWare, and OSI, as well as TCP/IP. SNMP runs only over TCP/IP.

SNMP-2 provides utilities that can be used to send notifications between SNMP agents and managers. SNMP-2 also has richer error codes. In addition, SNMP-2 can more efficiently retrieve large amounts of data (bulk collection).

SNMP-2 also provides security measures including authentication, access control, and authorization.

Security features include encrypted password transfer, user authentication, and secure remote configuration capabilities.

Another feature of SNMP-2 that has also been implemented in SNMP is the remote monitoring (RMON) MIB. RMON allows active network agents to feed information about the network's health and traffic into the management station without waiting for a request. A single management station can therefore manage a larger number of network nodes. RMON and RMON-2 are discussed in Sec. 12.5.4.

SNMP-2 is backward-compatible with the original SNMP through the use of proxy agents.

12.5.3   Common Management Information Protocol

Common Management Information Protocol (CMIP) and Common Management Information Services (CMIS) permit communication among different networks and network management applications. Based on OSI standards, CMIP and CMIS overcome the limitations of SNMP.

Some of the advantages of CMIP over SNMP for enterprise management include the following:

- CMIP supports peer-to-peer interaction across different network management protocols. CMIP establishes a session with a network device and downloads the information with one command. SNMP centrally polls remote devices for each piece of data.
- CMIP can provide a centralized view of enterprise networks.
- Using CMIP, a remote connection is established with a device, and a single command can implement several actions. With SNMP, it is

necessary to go through several procedural steps to configure a parameter on a device.

- CMIP, in concert with OSI, can guarantee delivery of data. SNMP with TCP/IP cannot. SNMP-2 is supposed to help, but it will not totally solve the problem.
- CMIP uses common object definitions, and object-based systems are viewed as the next wave of integrated network management.
- CMIP automatically updates the various management systems when changes are made in the network's configuration. This is not automatically done in SNMP.

While these protocols offer more capabilities, the tradeoff is in memory requirements. SNMP might need 20 kbytes of memory; CMIP might require as much as 2.5 Mbytes.

However, products that use CMIP have found limited acceptance. The specification is very broad, with room for interpretation, sometimes resulting in differences between different implementations of CMIP. In addition, any changes to the CMIP specifications must wait for OSI's approval cycle, which is currently five years. SNMP modifications take a year or two.

However, CMIP is gaining recognition from critical vendors such as IBM and Hewlett-Packard. It is being recognized as a better option for enterprise network management because it supports peer-to-peer interactions across a variety of management domains. CMIP has shown a greater reliability and ability to provide a centralized perspective on enterprise networks.

12.5.4 RMON and RMON2

An enhancement to SNMP that is closely related to SNMP-2 is the remote monitoring (RMON) MIB. RMON defines a MIB that lets active network monitors continuously feed information about network health and traffic into an SNMP-based console without waiting for a request.

The RMON MIB consists of ten distinct groups of network diagnostics that monitor traffic at Layers 1 and 2 (of the OSI model). Those groups are

- **Statistics**: LAN statistics showing packet counts, error counts, etc.
- **History**: historical views of the statistics
- **Alarms**: user-defined alarm conditions on all variables in RMON
- **Filters**: filtering for Packet Capture group
- **Packet Capture**: buffered capturing of packets
- **Events**: generated SNMP events that can generate alarms and filters
- **Host**: station-specific data showing packets, errors, broadcasts, etc.
- **Host Top N**: hosts table stored by utilization, errors, rates, etc.
- **Traffic matrix**: conversation matrix between stations or pairs of stations

■ **Ring Order Group**, token ring physical station order

However, the RMON agent needs to implement only one of these functions. A single management station can therefore observe and manage a large network with many segments.

RMON-2 was accepted in early 1996. RMON-2 is not a replacement for RMON-1 or a superset; they work side by side. RMON-2 adds higher-level features to RMON to give network managers less raw data and more useful information. RMON-2 monitors all seven layers of the OSI model. It can map Ethernet addresses to MAC addresses and contains mechanisms that can detect address changes.

Because RMON-2 monitors traffic at the network and application layers, network managers can have a better idea of what is causing network bottlenecks or crashes. Switches can be efficiently monitored and virtual LANs created.

Monitoring the volumes of RMON statistics usually means filtering the data to get some useful information. RMON-2 uses a general protocol directory system instead. It allows an administrator to establish which protocols a particular agent employs.

IETF also drafted a specification for a less complex RMON-2 agent that doesn't reach the application layer. RMON-2 Lite can be embedded in a hub or router for monitoring backbone traffic.

12.5.5 Desktop Management Interface

The Desktop Management Interface (DMI) from the Desktop Management Task Force (DMTF) provides a common format for presenting and retrieving management information. It initially addresses only stand-alone desktops. There is no provision for passing that information across the network.

DMI was designed to manage all the components of a micro. When micros are DMI-enabled, their hardware and software configurations can be monitored from a central station in the network.

The DMI agent is a terminate-stay-resident program for DOS and DLL for Windows and OS/2. On demand, the agent loads the code needed to manage a device. After the code is loaded, the DMI software agent collects information in background while other applications are running. The agent responds by sending back data contained in Management Interface Files (MIFs) and/or activating MIF routines.

Static data in a MIF could contain items such as model ID, serial number, and memory and port addresses. A MIF routine could report errors to the management console as they occur, or it could read ROM or RAM chips and report their contents as well.

The DMI can communicate with SNMP and CMIP by loading and unloading different pieces of code on demand. For example, when an SNMP query arrives, DMI can send out the SNMP MIB with data from its MIF.

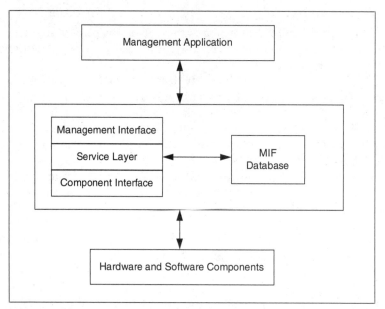

Figure 12.2 The DMI architecture

The DMI architecture, illustrated in Fig. 12.2, consists of four parts:

- The **Component Interface** allows vendors of micro components to register their devices and interfaces with DMI.
- The **Service Layer** provides generic agent services and interfaces to the local MIF database.
- The **Management Interface File** (MIF) contains descriptions of the managed devices. The vendor supplies the MIF and DMI handles the management.
- The **Management Interface** provides a platform-independent API to the DMI services.

The DMTF released a new version of DMI (version 2.0) mid-1996. New features in this release include remote management that provides access to DMI information across the network, and a more sophisticated Event Model for monitoring system alerts and indications, as well as other minor enhancements and updates to the DMI specification.

The architecture is designed to work with any connection, whether it is a LAN over TCP/IP or IPX or a PPP connection over a telephone line. DMI 2.0 allows for events and traps in an architected fashion, rather than as proprietary extensions.

12.5.6 XMP and XOM

X/Open has two APIs, XMP and XOM, that can be used to isolate applications from the underlying management protocols.

The X/Open Management API (XMP) is used for standards-based, process-to-process communications between a managing system and a managed system. XMP defines a set of C API calls that allow access to both SNMP and CMIP. Two different XOM-based products are used for each of the management protocols.

The X/Open Object Manager (XOM) API is used to manipulate the data structures associated with managed objects. The XMP data structures are prepared using XOM API calls. XOM, a general API, is used by DCE in its Global Directory Services.

13

Operating in the Client/Server Environment

Operating a client/server environment requires a lot more care and attention than operating a host-based environment. The client/server environment is a complex environment, compliance with standards is slow in coming, the network is more complex, the workload levels are unpredictable, and the management software is very immature.

System management software can be used to assist the administrators in caring for the client/server environment. System management software manages computer systems in an enterprise and should include some combination of the following: software distribution, version control, backup and recovery, virus protection, printer spooling, job scheduling, and performance and capacity planning. Network management is also becoming an integrated component of system management software.

13.1 Assigning Network Addresses

TCP/IP is the network of choice today: It is open, standards-based, robust, WAN-efficient, and it is the protocol of the Internet. However, TCP/IP is an administrative nightmare. Each device on the network must have a valid IP address, and each IP address must be unique.

All devices on a segment must have the same network number and subnet number and each subnet number must be unique. Communication with nodes on a different subnet or a different network requires a router.

The administrative nightmare? Assigned addresses must be tracked to avoid duplication. This sounds easy. For example, if a node is moved to a different subnet, the subnet portion of the new address must be changed to that of the new subnet. The resulting address must be checked to ensure that it doesn't conflict with the address of any other node on the new subnet.

Reverse Address Resolution Protocol (RARP) and the Bootstrap Protocol (BOOTP) were developed in the mid-1980s to help manage and assign IP addresses.

13.1.1   Reverse Address Resolution Protocol

RARP operates at the bottom of the network stack, at the hardware link level. A RARP client broadcasts a special packet with its network hardware address to some RARP server on the same subnet and receives back its assigned IP address. Most UNIX systems come bundled with a RARP server daemon. Currently the RARP protocol is most commonly used by devices such as print servers that need little more than an IP address to function. Because it is implemented at the bottom of the network stack, RARP is generally not supported by micro TCP/IP vendors.

13.1.2   The Bootstrap Protocol

BOOTP is an alternative to RARP and is used to configure networked micros. BOOTP, first proposed in 1989, uses the network application layer of TCP/IP and can deliver more configuration data in a single packet. BOOTP is commonly used by the TCP/IP stacks on UNIX workstations, X-terminals, and desktop computers to manage and configure TCP/IP parameters such as names and IP addresses from a central location.

BOOTP uses the User Datagram Protocol (UDP) of IP and can be implemented as an application program. Relay agents in routers can forward packets across subnets to a distant BOOTP server. BOOTP extensions have been added and standardized since it was first introduced, with the latest revision dated mid-1995.

BOOTP can provide a large amount of host-configuration data in a single packet exchange but requires an administrator to maintain a centralized database of BOOTP information for each client node based on the hardware address of the network card. When a new host is added to the network, the local hardware address of the installed network card is given to the person maintaining the BOOTP server(s). A unique IP address is assigned manually, and a new entry is added to the BOOTP data file with the associated configuration data.

13.1.3   Dynamic Host Configuration Protocol

BOOTP was designed for a stable environment in which the nodes that have a permanent network connection change infrequently. With the increased use of portable computers, remote access, and wireless networking, it is possible for a computer to move to another location quickly—a situation not easily handled by BOOTP. In addition, a remote node connected through a serial port and modem does not have a unique hardware address.

The proliferation of TCP/IP-based networks, coupled with the growing demand for Internet addresses, has made devising a means of sharing and conserving a pool of TCP/IP addresses critical for corporations that wish to provide Internet access to their end users.

The Dynamic Host Configuration (DHC) working group of Internet Engineering Task Force (IETF) was established the 1989 to develop techniques for configuring hosts dynamically. Their proposed Dynamic Host Configuration Protocol (DHCP) builds on the existing BOOTP protocol and supports all BOOTP vendor extensions. Where it differs from BOOTP is that the BOOTP server merely stores a preset configuration for a BOOTP client and delivers it on boot-up. DHCP doesn't eliminate the need to set up a configuration for the client. DHCP, by contrast, automatically configures DHCP clients, using rules preestablished by the network administrator.

DHCP uses the IETF's recently adopted IP2 protocol, with its longer naming scheme, to support the growing number of TCP/IP nodes. BOOTP, a protocol used on many UNIX systems for dynamically assigning IP addresses, does not support IP2.

Under DHCP, a computer is designed as the DHCP server, and all of the computers on the network that don't have permanent IP addresses are DHCP clients. When the DHCP server is configured initially, it is given a block of IP address numbers that it can dispense to nodes that need IP addresses.

When a new node comes onto the network, it broadcasts a request for an IP address. The DHCP server checks its table of address assignments, selects the next available address, and sends back a response to the requesting node. However, a requesting client must first find a DHCP server! But the protocol is constructed so that a client may negotiate with more than one DHCP server.

A DHCP server could be put in each subnet, or there could be one central DHCP server to which all clients connect to get an IP configuration. The central DHCP approach requires that routers or some other relay agent be capable of forwarding DHCP packets.

The response sent back to the requesting node includes an offer of a specific IP address and a "lease period," which is the length of time the client may use the address. The client software decides which offered IP address to accept (often based on the lease time) and sends its acceptance to the offering server.

DHCP allocates addresses in one of three ways:

- **Automatic allocation**. The DHCP server assigns a permanent IP address (from a pool of IP addresses) to a DHCP client requesting an address.

- **Dynamic allocation**. The DHCP server assigns an IP address for a limited period of time (lease period) or until the DHCP client specifically relinquishes it, whichever comes first. A DHCP client can renew its lease before it expires to continue using the same IP address. Dynamic allocation allows a finite number of IP addresses to serve larger numbers of clients that are only intermittently connected. Leases are also useful for wireless networking, where the remote node will be crossing into a different cell and will need to reconfigure itself.
- **Manual allocation**. The IP address is chosen by the network administrator but the DHCP server is used to convey the assignment to a DHCP client.

Automating the assignment of an initial IP address to the client makes it very easy to add a new client to a network. If a client moves from one subnet to another, DHCP can make the appropriate adjustments to the client's IP configuration. Dynamic allocation lets organization "time-share" a block of IP addresses among many clients, reducing the total number of IP addresses required.

With DHCP, nodes on a network are leased TCP/IP addresses as they log onto the system. DHCP servers from companies such as Competitive Automation, IBM, and Sun Microsystems dole out TCP/IP addresses as users come onto the network.

DHCP is fairly new, with the first RFCs issued in 1993. (A request for comments, or RFC, is a standard or a standard-defining document for the Internet. Individual RFCs define specific aspects of Internet operation.) Several vendors have already adopted it and developed products to support it. Microsoft has built DHCP server capability into Windows NT 3.5 and higher. Windows (3.11) and Windows 95 both have DHCP client capability. Apple's Open Transport includes DHCP client capability. Many of the third-party TCP/IP packages for Windows have DHCP client capability.

The IETF continues to define the DHCP standard, which will eventually give network managers a better method for conserving and sharing Internet addresses. DHCP directs networks to assign TCP/IP addresses to users once they log on to the system. The proliferation of TCP/IP networks and increasing demand for Internet addresses motivated the IETF to design an address allocation system.

The IETF addressed data storage and load balancing problems as it developed the new version of DHCP. Analysts report that the updated version of DHCP should appear in servers from IBM, Sun Microsystems, and others by the end of the 1996.

13.2 Data Quality

A definition of data quality includes such attributes as accuracy, completeness, consistency, timeliness, referential integrity, and context.

Unfortunately, the real world is filled with inconsistent data structures, invalid or missing data, and little or no adherence to existing standards.

As applications evolved and organizations began developing enterprise-wide applications, they were faced with many of the same problems faced by those converting function-oriented applications (such as separate checking, saving, and loan applications in a bank) to an integrated customer-oriented database-based application. The naming conventions in each application needed to be reviewed, and the data structures had to be checked for consistency. Codes needed to be reviewed for overlap, redundancy, and meaning. Business rules and referential integrity were consistent within the application but not necessarily within the company.

With the twenty-first century in sight, data is viewed as an asset, a resource. To leverage the resource, organizations are building data warehouses that hold subsets of extracted data, migrating to client/server architectures so that the processing and the data are closer to the users, generating more reports that require data from multiple applications, attempting to "mine" corporate data to glean information, and reengineering business processes. For many IT shops, the data doesn't hold up to the scrutiny.

Data quality becomes a key issue when existing data is converted to a new format for a client/server application or for inclusion in a data warehouse. With the traditional approach, the existing fields are mapped to the new fields and loaded into the new application. Errors and bad data are corrected in the new application. Alternatively, organizations can use automated data cleanser software or migration and mapping tools to filter out the bad data before mapping it to the new format.

Automated data entry software can then be used to filter the reformatted data before moving it to a new application. Artificial intelligence software can be used to identify bad data that still shows up in the new application. Other tools can then be used for data reconciliation between the files, systems, and interfaces.

Another area affected by data quality is middleware access to legacy data. Any consistency checking, data revalidation, or code conversion must be part of each accessing application, which perpetuates and multiplies the bad data problem. Conversion code becomes part of each application that accesses a particular piece of legacy data, and each piece of data may be converted multiple times.

IT organizations must make sure that they know about the data they are giving their users access to. A data audit is a very good place to begin, as is the development of an enterprise-wide data dictionary and metadata. When data was controlled by and accessed only by or through closed applications, those applications maintained the knowledge about the data. As organizations open up their data stores to middleware access, that knowledge has to be passed along.

13.3   Remote Data Management

To manage heterogeneous database environments, remote data management software must be able to

- Operate from a single central console.
- Perform unattended remote database management functions.
- Provide data replication functionality for full refresh and change propagation.
- Be scaleable from a small to a very large and widely distributed environment.
- Provide data replication functionality for full refresh and change propagation.

The functions that should be available from remote data management software include

- Administration, user setup, and DBA activities
- Operations, including performance monitoring, tuning, backup, and restore
- Advisory tools for analyzing systems and applications
- Integration with systems and network management platforms such as OpenView and TME

SNMP is used for remote database management, but its formats can't handle the complex information flow required by remote database management.

Informix and Sybase designed their products within Tivoli's TME, and Oracle provides event notification through the Tivoli console. Legent's tool integrates database, network, system, and application operations through SNMP-based consoles. Oracle's operations functions are SNMP console–based, and all products can report problems through SNMP consoles.

Benefits of remote database management include that people with data management skills—an expensive resource—can be central rather than being scattered around the organization. Fewer people mean consistent database policies, and integration leads to effective problem resolution.

IBM's suite of database management tools called DataHub uses the concept of software agents resident on managed systems. These agents perform individual checks for database and operating system threshold violation and provide for adjustable threshold value definitions, maintain adjustable timers, and take corrective actions as defined in the DataHub central database. Agent operations are rule-based and can include simple if-then rules, more complex Boolean logic rules, and trends-based rules.

13.4   Interoperability Layers

Ideally, client/server environments are not tied to one vendor. The environment really should support the "best of breed" philosophy when it comes to operating systems, communication software, networking software, and file systems. Interoperability is the ability to operate software and exchange information in a heterogeneous network. With interoperability, Intel-based machines, Macs, Suns, DEC VAXes, IBM mainframes, etc., all work together, with each node allowed to communicate with and take advantage of the resources of another.

Interoperability is possible through the use of common sets of protocols and standards.

Strong network interoperability is also a requirement for any organization. The mix of LANs, WANs, FDDI, ATM, and mobile users within the organization should be able to be managed as a large network with every node accessible (with privilege rights) by every other node, regardless of its network architecture.

13.5 Software Distribution

With 1,000 users (for example) of an application spread throughout the network (notice how references to the network size could almost read as references to the organization!), installing new versions of the client side of the application must be done without manual intervention. The system must be able to download new versions of the application to client machines. This also means that the system must keep track of what version of the application each client machine is running.

The same holds true of vendor-supplied software. Under licensing agreements, organizations have to keep track of how many copies are installed on machines. When an upgrade is made available, the upgrade should be downloaded from a central source and the "inventory" information updated.

Electronic software distribution allows an organization to distribute programs and files. It includes the distribution, configuration, installation, and management of software throughout the organization.

The complexity of electronic software distribution is best understood with an example. A multinational organization has in its enterprise architecture an IBM mainframe, UNIX servers, and client workstations running UNIX, Windows, Windows 95, and Windows NT. The network architecture is a mix of wide area networks and local area networks. Corporate has an upgraded version of a business application that must be distributed to all of the clients as well as the servers. The program will require 15 Mbytes of hard drive to store and must be installed under Windows. The intent is to electronically distribute and install this upgrade.

For this to happen electronically, the distribution software must be able to

■ Determine the configuration of each client workstation, including the amount of available disk space and the drive name where MS Windows is installed.

- Determine the current version of the business application that is installed on the client, so that if the new version does not work properly, the software can restore the correct previous version.
- Schedule the installation when users will not be using the system. This is especially important if changes are made to the CONFIG.SYS file, which requires rebooting the system.
- Provide support utilities to the client workstations if required, such as making backup copies of files.
- Provide security while the software is being distributed to ensure that there is no unauthorized access.
- Use networking protocols for the transport, notification, and optimum network routing selection.

Electronic software distribution software should provide a single view of the distributed environment and support even heterogeneous distributed environments.

There are many tools available today that can maintain hardware and software inventory, distribute software packages, and control license limits for electronic distribution of software.

13.6   Operational Considerations

Operating in a host-based environment was fairly straightforward because of the tools that were available and the intelligence that could be built into those tools. The network was simpler than today's implementations. Applications ran on one platform. Administrators measured throughput, CPU utilization, and storage availability.

Life isn't that easy in client/server environments. And it is easy to understand why it's taking tool vendors so long to develop tools. There is a lot to consider when it comes to the operation of applications in a client/server environment. Should the applications be partitioned differently? Should the network be reconfigured? Will adding a new server help? Would upgrading an existing server be a better idea? Should network traffic be rerouted?

13.7   System Availability and Reliability

For any business-critical application, the environment in which it runs must be there when the user logs in (available) and operate reliably. Available means that the system (or at least the particular parts of the system the user needs!) is running at peak performance and can handle the user's requests. Reliable means that once into the environment, the user does not expect problems to occur, such as crashed disks or inoperable network links.

13.8   Performance Tuning Components

As mission- and business-critical applications are being downsized to client/server platforms or developed on client/server platforms, the reliability of those platforms becomes an integral part of IS planning. Even if these systems seem micro-based, the micro philosophy of "if one goes down, we'll just run it from backups on another machine" does not hold true. This might hold true for the client machines, but certainly not for the server or the network. It is important that IT have alternatives in case a server goes down or the network crashes.

An alternative for servers is built-in fault-tolerant resources. These could include processors, power supplies, and disk drives with disk mirroring. For networks, these could include FDDI-based networks and redundant linking devices, such as routers and bridges.

13.9   Load Leveling

One early premise of client/server computing was that all application logic should be performed on the client machine. Original implementations of client/server computing followed that premise to the letter.

However, as the technology evolved and the impact of earlier practices was felt, the idea of splitting the application logic between the client and the server—if necessary—was adopted for two reasons:

- Maximize throughput and minimize network traffic
- Take advantage of the number-crunching speed of the server, in MIPS

In most instances, developers have to decide where the split between client and server processing should be and code the application logic accordingly. For example, a process that involves data-intensive sorting or multitable joins, but does not require user intervention, could be done faster on the server. Developers must also decide which server will perform which function when two or more servers are involved and how the query should be partitioned.

However, this is not a flexible approach. It does not take into account changes in

- The size of the data being processed
- The power of the client machine
- The power of the server machine
- Fluctuations in server resource availability
- Fluctuations in the network resources

In addition to logic partitioning, placing some user functions on the client machine can also conserve network traffic and server cycles. Two such functions are refreshing (redrawing) a screen when a window is closed and selecting the screen that satisfies a menu choice. Neither should require a network call to the server.

Load-testing software enables testers to test how a system handles any number of users. The software simulates all the users running at the same time, automatically executes an independent test for each user, and collects results for analysis.

On the other hand, performance testing allows testers to define any sequence of operations as a measurable transaction and provides performance data for an individual user or for multiple users that are working simultaneously.

System tuning allows application developers to evaluate such tradeoffs as changes in configuration and system variables to fine-tune systems.

Two sample load-testing packages are discussed below.

Empower

Empower, a load-testing package from Performix Inc., allows an organization to duplicate large environments prior to deployment (or a new version release) to test how many users the system can support and what kind of response time can be expected, and to evaluate the system's ability to perform under varying load conditions.

Empower uses a scripting technology to simulate application performance. Sitting between the micro and the server, the software tracks actual user keystrokes, mouse movements, and SQL requests as they leave the workstation and go to the server. That information is translated into a C language script that is used to represent users and their daily operations. The software then arranges a mixture of scripts—some working heavily on an application and some not—to represent the workflow of the anticipated users of an application.

LoadRunner Client/Server

LoadRunner Client/Server, from Mercury Interactive Corp., bundles LoadRunner/PC, which is a client-load testing tool for Windows-based applications, with LoadRunner/XL, which can simulate thousands of Windows applications transmitting SQL calls on a UNIX workstation. The product enables developers to determine, prior to deployment, the maximum number of users the system can support, the system response time to an end-user request, and the system's ability to perform under varying load conditions. The software is also licensed to Compuware as a component in its Playback for Client/Server product.

13.10 Optimizer

A robust data server software package should provide an optimizer, which analyzes a generated SQL statement and determines the most efficient way to process the request. A query optimizer should take into account local and global factors, including distributed nodes and network characteristics.

Most optimizers available today are cost-based. They analyze the index distribution statistics and table sizes to estimate the cost of the query, using units such as numbers of I/O and/or CPU cycles, number of records needed to satisfy the query, and available indexes, and then factor in other statistics about the data organization. The optimizer then uses the least expensive access path process.

This optimization method becomes trickier when a request needs to join multiple tables that are distributed in multiple locations. The measurements normally used become minor as the network speed, size of each node's tables, and processing and I/O power of each node become the major factors in query performance.

An optimizer must be able to access system directories for information about the nodes themselves and distributed directories for statistics about the remote database. Each additional table or database increases the number of choices for the optimizer.

A good optimizer will check to see if the necessary data is already in cache memory before deciding to use an index. It may also choose to ignore indexes if the selection criteria match a large portion of the rows (one-third or more, for instance). By reviewing the distribution of values in the index, the optimizer can decide whether a complete table scan or a search of the index will result in fewer disk reads.

The optimizer is an important feature of the server database when the SQL queries are generated by the front-end software (instead of being embedded in front-end code). SQL queries can be written in many different ways; for instance, the order of the columns in the WHERE clause or the order of the tables in a JOIN clause can vary. An optimizer analyzes the query and uses statistics and histograms to determine the most efficient execution path.

The amount of data that server database software can realistically handle should also be reviewed. The software should be able to grow with users' requests for additional data and applications (and request they will!). It is important to talk to personnel at other sites using databases equivalent in size to the projected size of the evaluation application. The success of the project rests primarily on the reliability and responsiveness of the server database.

Optimization becomes much more complex when DBMSs are resident on MPP and cluster architectures. This type of query processing is usually called parallel query processing and is discussed in Sec. 17.5.

13.11   Metrics and Measurement Tools

Application   performance   monitoring   was   never   the   major   focus   in centralized systems. The application's performance was monitored by default as the other components—the CPU, operating system, disk space, and memory—were monitored. How to measure application performance (other than "It's running slow") never became an issue.

Organizations need consistent performance measures. A performance measure is a quality measure. Once it is set, the organization has a goal and therefore a direction. But developing application and system performance metrics is not easy. The metrics must be related to a goal, be specific (measurable), and be viewed as important by both the users and management and should address user preferences as well as actual productivity goals. The performance metrics should be included in the development phase as well as the postimplementation review.

Some guidelines to get started:

- Decide what's important by listing the most important products and services you deliver as results to end users. The list should be short and written in specific, plain language.
- Define, in end-user terms, goals for results. Don't jump to numbers yet. Most developers will quickly talk about reliability and performance. While these are noble goals, are they the most important ones for all applications regardless of cost?
- Convert your goals into measures, and be positive. Talk about available time rather than downtime. Don't use trends (10 percent improvement in response time), use actual numbers (response time less than 2 subnanoseconds).
- Validate your measures. Think of as many situations as you possibly can, and make sure that the measure always goes up when things improve and goes down when they get worse. Do whatever fine-tuning is necessary.
- Publicize the results. Send out E-mail, put graphs in the company's newsletters, make a fuss when things improve.

Measurement can be a powerful tool in managing user expectations and maintaining a business-critical application.

Rising in prominence among Oracle and Sybase DBAs is Bradmark Technologies, which makes DB-General, a graphical tool for performance and space management and maintenance. A highly modular system, the product covers the gamut of DBA tasks.

13.11.1 Service level agreements

Service level agreements (SLAs) define users' expectations of a service provider. They also define what vendors expect of users, such as availability of suitable work space and support facilities for the vendor. Both user and vendor can negotiate the type of service to be provided, specific actions to be performed, time frames for response, time frames for completion of repairs, penalties for poor or subpar performance, and even escape clauses that allow users (and vendors) to extricate themselves from unsatisfactory arrangements.

SLAs have long been used between organizations and their external service providers. They are now being used between users and their IT organization, which is, after all, a service provider. SLAs define what the users expect of IT and what IT can expect of the users. SLAs should be jointly developed by the users and IT, with the emphasis on "service first." They are contracts between IT and the users that ensure the provision of specific activities, such as user training, remote diagnostics, acceptable response time, acceptable downtime, and disaster recovery.

Service level agreements require several elements: support from management, commitment on the users' part to SLAs, and an IT group willing to elevate the provision of service to a higher level. Assuming that these are all available, the organization should perform the following steps:

- Define the minimum acceptable level of service for a specific product, professional service, or other defined activity.
- Transform the requirements for service into specific manageable and measurable tasks. This is essential to ensure that defined service levels are being attained.
- Define additional levels of service that are "desirable" but not necessarily mandatory. These can be negotiated as extra-cost items.
- Develop language that spells out specific levels of performance in "normal" and "out of normal" conditions. Define "out of normal" conditions.
- Define penalties for failure to provide service within defined performance levels.
- Develop an agreement between users and IT that clearly spells out the above provisions.
- Execute the agreement, and launch performance measurement activities to ensure that contract service levels are attained—and maintained.

13.12   Monitoring and Diagnostic Tools

One area that still needs attention from server database software vendors is testing and diagnostic tools. Data and generated indexes can be corrupted by system errors (tables sharing disk space) or bad disk sectors. Utilities that can diagnose problems and recover from them are slow in coming, as are SQL debugging tools. Mainframe development environments offer powerful debugging tools with breakpoints and real-time values of variables and support embedding of debugging commands. These types of tools are desperately needed in client/server environments.

Most of the performance monitoring tools use graphs and charts to display their information. To accurately learn the impact of a network application, a system manager needs to get actual response times on a per-application or per-client basis. End-to-end is not sufficient; measurement data from each segment needs to be captured and analyzed.

Organizations need to think about how they plan to monitor the application as it's being developed. The procedures used to testing client/server systems and the applications running on them should be repeatable and have quantifiable results. IT needs to be able to know that the system is working as well after an upgrade as it was before the upgrade. Monitoring requires feedback from multiple platforms, network configurations, operating systems, and layers of the application (logic, business rules, middleware, DBMS, GUI, etc.).

Monitoring should go beyond the health of the environment, such as whether a node is down or a server's disk capacity is nearly full. The health of the application itself needs to be reviewed. Now that the application is being used, what are the resource implications? Are there bottlenecks? Are response times unacceptable? Do things get worse at certain times of the day? Do they get worse when another application has a heavy load?

Solutions may be as simple as rerouting network traffic to improve the situation. Other solutions that aren't nearly as simple include adding another server to the environment, replicating or distributing databases, and repartitioning the application itself.

At this point, changes can be made to the environment and load balancing routines rerun to determine whether the problem has been corrected without negatively affecting the application or other applications in the environment.

Organizations have been slow to deploy comprehensive management tools. Evaluating them and testing their integration takes time. Since the tools are usually workgroup-oriented, a local person within each group is required, making it difficult to manage multiple workgroups across the organization. The tools are expensive and don't scale well. They are too expensive for small offices and too expensive for larger organizations to deploy throughout their operations. But companies do need company-wide management solutions that can address their end-to-end problems.

OpenView and NetView handle tasks such as router management but don't help with log-in problems. Novell offers ManageWise, which combines Novell's NetWare Management System with Intel's LANDesk Manager. ManageWise can be used to manage all aspects of the network, including the routers, servers, hubs, and desktops. Its troubleshooting features include the ability to check the path between two points on a network and to detect faults before they become problems. With its remote control feature, it can look at what a remote workstation is really doing.

IBM is working on a new part (code named Karat) of its SystemView family which consolidates the best of IBM's NetView-based products. Karat will be object-oriented and deployed by CD-ROM, which will contain the software, a common launch panel, a common installation procedure, complete documentation, and up-to-date marketing information. The user will be able to download any product from that single source. This version of Karat is expected to ship in 1997.

13.12.1   Enterprise SQL Server Manager

Sybase's Enterprise SQL Server Manager (ESSM) is designed for efficient control of heterogeneous DBMS environments and allows administrators to perform the following operations on remote servers:

- Start and stop servers.
- Monitor server status and performance levels.
- Manage server space utilization.
- Administer users and ensure security.
- Configure database servers.
- Manage server and database objects.
- Schedule and perform backup and recovery operations.
- Use existing and new database administration scripts.

ESSM can perform these operations on individual servers or groups of servers. ESSM is based on Tivoli Management Environment (TME) and can be used seamlessly with other TME-based third-party tools. ESSM also has provisions to support SNMP and can provide management information to SNMP-based tools such as HP's OpenView and IBM's NetView.

ESSM supports automatic event detection and notification using software agents on each managed system. Agents collect server statistics such as user connections, server status, database lock usage, and segment space available and alert administrators when a defined event has occurred. Events can be handled by agents by triggering predefined responses.

13.12.2   System Management Server

Microsoft's System Management Server (SMS) provides inventory, remote management, software distribution, and network monitoring functions for managing micros in a distributed environment, using a primary site server that requires Windows NT and Microsoft SQLServer 6.0 or higher. The primary site can be connected to target machines directly or via secondary servers over LANs or WANs. SMS supports remote control features including remote reboot, file transfer, and dial-up support.

One component of SMS is Microsoft Network Monitor, which captures network packets of any kind, even from remote nodes, and graphically selects, filters, and displays them. A TCP/IP-like facility is included for testing network connections. SMS network management features include network statistics, SNMP support, job scheduling, and configurable alarms for notification of systems administrators.

SMS's software distribution mechanism requires that each package that is to be installed be defined and then scheduled to be run on a specific platform. SMS performs file compression and stages transmission of software to avoid network saturation. SMS supports full software installs, remote batch editing of INI files, and file update and replacement. SMS also includes software license monitoring and metering functions.

Systems Management Server, Version 1.2, released in late 1996, adds secure remote control of Windows NT, the ability to receive and forward SNMP events, and the collection of inventory data in the background on NT systems. It also adds enhanced network monitoring and protocol support for iNET, Java, and Point-to-Point Tunneling Protocol.

SMS does require a great deal of planning and understanding of the technology of enterprise environments such as network topology. There is also a week-long training requirement.

13.12.3 SystemView

First released in mid-1995, SystemView from IBM includes NetView, which is a network manager (see Sec. 12.4.2), and functions for software distribution, inventory change, and problem management, to name just a few. SystemView allows administrators to manage everything in the system, from the physical network to business procedures, from a single console.

The first offering was SystemView for AIX, which offers problem, change, performance, and configuration management for UNIX-based systems. The product offers a screen-level object integration based on IBM's Systems Object Model (SOM). The interface can be accessed from client workstations, freeing up the SystemView server for processing duties.

SystemView is now also available for MVS, OS/2, and AS/400 platforms. An NT version is expected in late 1996. SystemView for OS/2 is based on IBM's NetFinity desktop management software, which can handle hardware inventory, management, and discovery, as well as software inventory and file transfer. IBM has also integrated software distribution, license management, and its Distributed Console Access Facility (DCAF) remote control software into NetFinity. DCAF allows an operator to take control of a remote OS/2 or Windows workstation and works over a LAN as well as over remote phone lines.

However, with IBM's acquisition of Tivoli Systems, Inc., SystemView's days may be numbered due to the announcement of TME 10, which will be the combination of SystemView and Tivoli Management Environment offerings.

13.12.4 Tivoli Management Environment

Organizations have the option of using a variety of products that are tailored to individual functions and manually consolidating the output or using a third-party tool, such as those discussed in this chapter, that can

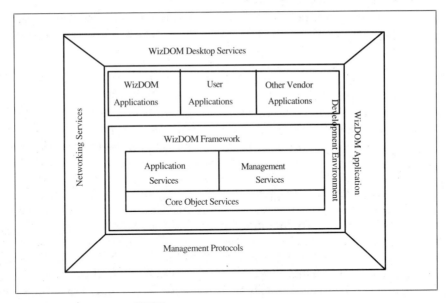

Figure 13.1 Components of TME

manage heterogeneous networks of systems. Another third-party product is Tivoli Management Environment (TME) from Tivoli Systems, Inc., now a subsidiary of IBM.

TME uses an object-oriented framework and provides a GUI interface, resource management, application addressing security, and system configuration. As illustrated in Fig. 13.1, TME consists of the following components:

- **Tivoli Management Framework** uses an object-oriented system management framework (all resources and operations are encapsulated as objects).
- **Tivoli/Works** manages the system resources, including the Management Framework.
- **Tivoli/Admin** simplifies the process of user and system administration and provides centralized control of UNIX and micro systems.
- **Tivoli/Enterprise Console** collects, processes, and automatically initiates corrective actions to events.
- **Tivoli/Workload** automates job scheduling.
- **Tivoli/Print** is a print manager application.
- **Tivoli/Sentry**, an optional package, performs resource monitoring.
- **Tivoli/Courier**, an optional package, manages the distribution of software.
- **Tivoli/FSM**, an optional package, manages network file system relationships. Tivoli/FSM can provide a consistent configuration for related groups of machines and change file system access for multiple machines with one operation.

The two optional toolkits are used for building and customizing applications. Tivoli/AEF is used to customize and extend Tivoli management applications. New management applications are developed using Tivoli/ADE.

The core technology of TME is an OMG CORBA-compliant object request broker. The TME architecture is based on the X/Open Systems Management Reference Model. TME applications interoperate via a consistent interface and present users with a common GUI-based look and feel. TME lets systems administrators manage and control users, systems, databases, and applications from a central location. Users can automate and delegate routine tasks from a central location.

To expand its systems management scope to include distributed applications, in 1995 Tivoli announced an open specification for application management which would include a set of APIs to be used by application developers as well as tool vendors. These Application Management Specifications (AMS) allow TME to handle software distribution, inventory, event monitoring, and administration for applications that incorporate them. Powersoft, in a joint effort with Tivoli, has embedded AMS into the PowerBuilder Enterprise software. As a result, PowerBuilder Enterprise developers can enable TME management functions merely by supplying the required information.

In mid-1996, Tivoli/IBM announced the availability of TME 10, which combines TME and IBM's SystemView. A new TME 10 gateway lets data be passed between SystemView's Resource Object Data Manager (RODM) and the TME 10 database. Tivoli's enterprise console or inventory application will be able to access such information as SNA topology and resource status from RODM for managing mixed-vendor environments from a central TME 10 console or a distributed console.

13.13   Network Security

Desktop machines can access data anywhere in the infrastructure. Unfortunately, micro operating systems and most networking software were not written with security in mind. Yet these two layers of software are major building blocks in distributed environments.

The level of security must be appropriate for the users and the organization, given the way they view the value of data. There are costs and additional steps for users associated with every level of system security. These must be balanced against the cost and inconvenience of unprotected or corrupted data.

Network operating systems are beginning to include security functions such as authentication and authorization. The DBMS products usually offer security features such as authorization checking, often down to the field level. Some server DBMS vendors are extending their products to include government specifications for multilevel data security.

In addition, security products are available for this environment. Some mainframe-based vendors, such as IBM and Computer Associates International, Inc., are porting their host security packages to LAN environments. Others, such as Security Dynamics, SunSoft, and Fischer International Systems Corp., are developing products specifically for LAN environments.

In the mainframe world, security is a given. It is well defined and supported by a robust set of tools. Mainframes typically have full-blown security subsystems and full-time security administrators that use these subsystems to maintain the security of the mainframe. In addition, the software running on the mainframe may have its own built-in security. There is CICS transaction security and internetwork security in the network operating system. All that security tends to breed frustrated users when they need to type in different user IDs and passwords just to get to the software they need to work with to do their job.

Within a LAN-based environment, security is less well defined and not usually considered a major issue. Many client/server systems are LANs that grew up and out. Security within the self-contained LAN was never an issue. The network might have password protection, and security administration required a few hours of effort a week by the person who was most computer-literate (to add user names and change passwords).

In order to identify where security is needed in the client/server environment, an organization needs to identify security checkpoints by identifying the endpoints in the environment—the data and the users—and the paths used to connect those endpoints.

Questions about the users include how they access data (micro, dumb terminal, or both) and whether there is remote data access. Questions about the data include where is it stored, whether it is mainframe-based or kept on a file server or database server, whether there is any replication of data, and how data currency and integrity are maintained. Questions about the paths include which paths require mainframe access and via what routes, whether network gateways are used for translation or are bridges and routers used, where the LAN comes into play, and what paths are there between remote users and data.

Once an organization can picture the structure of the environment (and it is a good idea to draw a diagram of the environment based on the answers to these questions), it can begin to identify where the holes are in its security and work on plugging them.

As a further note on security, what user ID has the right to do backups? In order to back up a database, the user ID needs access to the database and all its underlying table definitions. The user ID should have some level of high security which is detectable, either by the system itself or by the DBMS being backed up.

In the mainframe environment, one person or group was in charge of the security of the environment. In client/server environments, the responsibility for the components of the environment is distributed among many departments and groups. In order for the environment to be secure, this responsibility needs to rest ideally with one group. Closest to that today is two: the LAN administrator who sets up server-level security, and the DBA who controls database- and table-level access.

Security is a funny thing. The more secure an environment is, the more steps users have to take to get to where they need to be in order to do their work. It's a difficult balance: security versus frustration and time loss. But it's one that an organization must struggle with, nevertheless.

Security, usually an afterthought, must be considered at the data level and application level. There should be two levels of security on each processor: direct access via an operating system sign-on and database access which bypasses the operating system by connecting directly to the database manager.

The data-level approach to security is implemented by associating a user with a role or a subschema. A subschema is a profile of allowable data items and operations that is checked by the database engine at data request time. Unlike application-level security, this security is verified at all times, not just when users are within their applications.

However, some relational database products do not have facilities that control access to specific rows or columns within a table.

A role is a collection of predefined table privileges that end users can manage and control independently. With some databases, roles may be assigned to sessions as well as to individual users. When a connection is made to a remote database, the security in the remote database will be applied to the transaction. The security is regulated at the destination, and the privileges at the source are irrelevant.

Application-level security uses access rules that are contained within the application logic itself and lets the application govern data access. This ensures security only when a user is within the application and does nothing to prevent a user from bypassing the application and accessing secured information directly via on-line query tools.

13.14   Backup and Recovery Mechanisms

There are similarities between mainframes and LANs in the areas of backup, recovery, and archiving. The problems for both environments are identical, but the solutions change from tier to tier.

It is no longer a matter of just keeping the mainframe or the network up. Enterprise environments are dealing with multiple servers and multiple networks, all of which must be available at all times.

Databases must be backed up and restored while users are accessing the database. Machines are not brought off-line for backup or restart.

If a disk drive fails, operations staff should be able to swap in a new disk and restore the data without taking the machine off-line. If a server fails, processing should be able to be switched to another processor, either another processor in the enterprise network or a redundant server.

There should be two types of recovery: transaction recovery from a system or application failure and system recovery from a media failure such as disk crash. Transaction recovery means that all committed data must be written to disk, and data affected by the transaction but not yet committed must be recovered (rolled back) to the pretransaction state completely and automatically. The direction of recovery is backward—from point of failure to the point of consistency.

In media failures, restoration of lost data includes using the most current backup and recovery of the data from the point of latest backup to the point of the media failure. Transaction logs are used to store changes to the database and used in the recovery procedures. Transaction logs can maintain before-change images for backward recovery or after-change images for forward recovery. Creating the transaction logs is called database logging. Every change to the database is automatically written to the database log file.

In a client/server environment, backup and recovery mechanisms should be able to operate dynamically while the DBMS continues to operate. A backup of one database should not prevent users from accessing other databases, even on the same physical platform. Ideally, backing up a database should not prevent users from accessing that particular database. Recovery should also be able to be performed on-line.

DBMS should also employ hardware and software measures found in fault-tolerant systems. These measures include duplexing, RAID devices, and disk mirroring. These features are discussed in Chap. 4, "Servers." In addition, some DBMS vendors are providing software-based fault-tolerant features, such as disk mirroring for transaction logs and/or databases.

Network backup software with SNMP capability is beginning to be offered (see Sec. 12.5.1 for details on SNMP). These products allow servers to off-load critical data to remotely stationed tape drives or even mainframes. The SNMP modules, typically OpenView from Hewlett-Packard or SunNet Manager from SunSoft, allow managers to get updates concerning overloaded tapes and failed disk drives. Unfortunately, the notification is after the fact. Network backup software vendors are working on products that will embed the SNMP agent technology into the storage backup products. This will give managers the ability to proactively monitor the backup environment as well.

The options for backups today include tape-based, host-based, and CD-ROM-based backups.

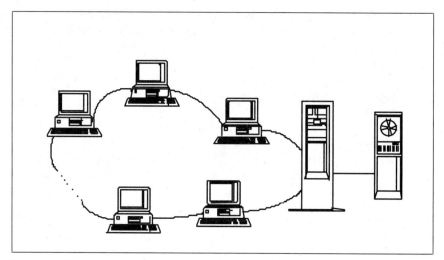

Figure 13.2 Tape backup system

13.14.1   Tape-based backups

A tape backup system, illustrated in Fig. 13.2, continues to be an excellent option for backup and recovery for a number of reasons. The most obvious is cost: To store a megabyte of data on tape costs one-tenth of a cent; on a hard disk, 20 cents; on optical disk, a dollar. Another is reliability. Data is less likely to be unreadable from tape than from hard disk. Finally, tape backup systems are more advanced than simple tape dumps. Most products have menu-driven interfaces, support unattended backups, and offer options as to whether the entire hard disk, selected files, or combinations of files should be backed up.

13.14.2   Host-based backups

Another option is to send the LAN data over the network to a host, where the host system management products take over the storage management. This process is illustrated in Fig. 13.3. This requires adequate bandwidth capabilities to support shipping large amounts of data. It centralizes the LAN data management issue with the other mainframe systems and removes the requirement for backup, recovery, and archiving procedures from the end users.

Organizations need backup devices that can support a heterogeneous network, but backup devices support a specific LAN and workstation operating system. Vendors have been slow in upgrading their backup system products to multiple platforms and in providing the ability to back up interconnected LANs from a central location.

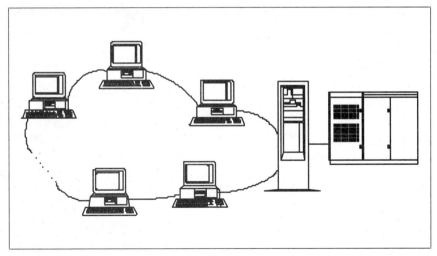

Figure 13.3 Host-based backups

The server database should support dynamic backups so the data can be backed up while the server is in use. This feature minimizes disruptions to the user community and makes it convenient to perform backups. When the backup request is received, the server software checks the transaction logs for any recently committed transactions and writes them to the database. The software proceeds with the backup at this point. The server software keeps a record of which sections of the database have been backed up. When modifications to the database are attempted, the server software can check to see if the affected areas have been backed up. If the area has been backed up, the modification can proceed. If the area has not been backed up, the server software reorders the backup sequence so that area is backed up next. Once the area is backed up, the transaction can be executed.

Backing up transaction logs is straightforward since transactions which are executing during the backup are added to the end of the log.

13.14.3 CD-ROM-based backups

With the availability of affordable write CD-ROM drives, organizations have an alternative to tape-based backups. The speed of writing to the CD-ROM is higher than that to tape. The medium has a longer shelf life and is less likely to have problems being read from at a future time. The ultimate storage requirements will also be less. Hopefully the advantages of write CD-ROM drives and their associated costs will be enough of an incentive to lead more organizations to be more conscientious about doing backups!

4

Client/Server Application Development

Prototyping is an important component of client/server application development. It allows organizations to quickly determine application requirements and build working versions of an application that can be easily modified based on user responses.

Current tools support either a bottom-up or top-down design approach. Bottom-up is appropriate for homogeneous LAN environments. Top-down is appropriate for larger systems and assists in the development of a logical data model as well as application requirements.

Today's client/server development tools run the gamut in functionality. Organizations need to understand their own application requirements before they decide on the development tool for the application. A bad fit between application and development tool puts the success of the project at extremely high risk.

14

Application Development Process

Most client/server application development uses a prototype as a development tool.

A prototype is a working model of the application. It allows users to take part in defining the requirements and deciding how the application will meet those requirements. Working with the users, a series of prototypes can be viewed and revised interactively. The automated products are usually installed on a micro. The number of prototypes can range from several to hundreds. The prototype process is illustrated in Fig. 14.1.

Prototypes can be

- Hand-drawn
- Created with programs such as Apple's MacDraw, Microsoft's PowerPoint, and IBM's PC Storyboard
- Developed using CASE products
- Developed using client/server development products
- Developed using 4GLs

The prototype methodology could be used in many ways, such as

- Development of a more refined prototype
- Development of user requirements that are difficult to define
- A pilot application that is later discarded
- A working version that evolves directly into the final production application

A prototype is usually in constant evolution. Prototyping is best used to

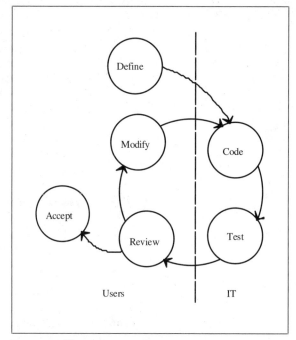

Figure 14.1 The prototype process

develop applications which have components that are not completely understood. It addresses the situation that too often, when what users ask for is not exactly what they want, and what they want is not exactly what they need—unfortunately, they don't recognize this disparity until they begin to work with the finished application. Prototyping allows users to see and react to a working model of the application. The model is rebuilt or refined until users are satisfied with the results.

In many cases, a prototype becomes the working application while developers work on the remainder of the application. Studies have shown that 80 percent of user requirements can be identified with 20 percent of the systems analysis and design effort. Rapid application development can quickly identify the remaining 20 percent. While users work with the resulting prototype, they identify the missing requirements, which can then be addressed by the development team.

14.1 Development Methodologies

The development of event-driven, GUI-based applications is very different from that of their legacy counterparts. The many interactions of the interface evolve the data requirements for the application, which can be very uncomfortable for database personnel who are used to structure (entity-relationship diagrams) and to having the time to generate a logical and then a physical database design.

By following a methodology that has been well thought out, an organization can reduce the risk of making mistakes, especially errors of omission. Traditional methodologies usually impede the development process for client/server applications. Traditional methodologies require extensive modeling prior to the actual design of the application. With current technology, the interface, data requirements, and business logic are all specified as part of the prototyping/development process. Traditional methods focus on providing a great deal of information to the programmers; with current methods, the programmers are part of the prototyping team and do not need a separate document from which to program. In addition, as client/server development tools are object-based, traditional methods cannot take reuse of objects into account.

14.1.1 SDLC

System development life cycle (SDLC) or system life cycle (SLC), as illustrated in Fig. 14.2, is also called a waterfall model. With the waterfall model of software development, each development stage is completed or at least very nearly completed before moving on to the next. Each step is worked on with no thought of returning to a prior phase. Because of this focus on being 100 percent complete, this methodology is time-consuming.

In the analysis phase, the requirements for the new application are identified. In the design phase, those requirements are used to create plans for the new application, such as a data dictionary, data flow diagrams, process specifications, and input and output design forms. CASE tools could be used to aid in these specifications. Prototyping may be used to combine the analysis and design phases. In the construction phase, the hardware is acquired, the programs written and tested, and user documentation developed. In the conversion phase, the organization converts from the old system to the new one.

Each phase in the diagram has a decision point labeled "Return to a

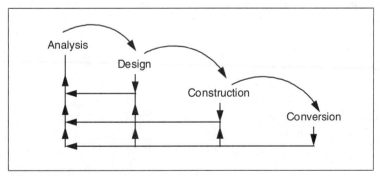

Figure 14.2 System development life cycle

Previous Phase." This is used if at any point during the phase, it is determined that more work needs to be done in a prior phase. Only significant problems should require returning to a previous phase. Clarifications should be expected.

Each phase also has a decision point labeled "Abort Project." If at any time during the process management feels that the future costs outweigh future benefits, the project should be terminated. In other words, at the end of each phase, the original projected cost benefits should be revised and reviewed, resulting in a go–no go decision.

14.1.2 RAD

In today's quickly changing business environments, companies can't always afford the time it takes to do SDLC, such as six months for identifying requirements in the analysis stage. Today's prototyping tools allow developers to begin developing an application without knowing all its details.

Organizations need to be able to deliver something quickly. If it takes longer than six to nine months, the business can change or users lose interest. If more features or enhancements are needed, they can be added in the later part of the project.

Rapid application development (RAD) delivers working pieces of an application incrementally, all the while incorporating feedback from end users. There should be a user run-through of the application to finalize the user interface and navigational paths before any time is spent coding. The sooner users see something, the better they feel. The closer the prototype "design" is to the ultimate finished product, the easier the deployment and acceptance will be. However, if developers know a great deal about the application, the waterfall method may still be the best way to go.

RAD users fall into two camps. Some organizations use RAD to develop the entire application. A typical scenario might be a week of "scoping," some joint application development workshops with users to determine the business logic for the application, followed by six months (or less) of development. Until users actually see something, they don't know what is possible.

The other camp uses RAD in the design phase to quickly prototype the data models and database. The front end and back ends are then coded and first-level testing performed.

RAD developers should still document system requirements to know when a system is complete and how to test it properly. One problem with prototypes is knowing when the development is done because so little analysis is done up front.

Prototyping and RAD methodology have their naysayers. Some feel that software assembled from pieces rather than designed as a whole will have significant problems. The cost of getting requirements is high, and it is essential to get them before coding takes place. Sometimes developers using prototyping as a design vehicle tend to jump into coding without sufficient analysis and design.

Visual tools can be used to move a cross-functional group of users to consensus on the business process and on the look and feel of the application. Their iterative ability can be used to draft a solution—no one should worry about having to do things over.

A major complaint is that RAD lets developers bypass the detailed analysis that well-made systems demand. What they need is a methodology for allowing them to do what they do best while keeping them focused on the problem at hand. These visual tools do have a dramatic effect on how work gets done; they let people see what they need through prototypes rather than by reading textual materials. However, the RAD tools, with their front-end focus, often ignore the larger issues of database design and back-end processing.

14.1.3 JAD

Joint application development (JAD) workshops use a top-down approach to application development. JAD workshops can be used in all phases of development but are especially useful in system analysis and top-level design. IT professionals often misinterpret the users' requirements, and users often view presentations by IT as too technical. The traditional methods used by IT—interviewing users and then returning some time later with specifications in text form—are inadequate. However, users cannot design complex procedures without the help of IT professionals.

JAD workshops require heavy involvement by users in the development of the application. JAD workshops typically have more business end users in attendance than IT professionals.

JAD workshops are usually full-day, consecutive workshops lasting from three to five days, depending on the dynamics of the group and the scope of the problem. By getting away from their day-to-day business operations, the participants can focus on the application being developed during the JAD workshop.

All participants have equal rank. Direct communication among participants is encouraged. Differing points of view are discussed. Users are informed of their options regarding technical issues. Users and IS come to a joint decision that is a strategic and business-supporting resolution.

The key players in a JAD workshop are

- **End users**. They should be easy to work with, well respected, and articulate; understand the business area; and have decision-making authority.
- **JAD leader**. This team member prepares for the workshop and directs it, encourages the members to participate, and keeps the workshop on track toward achieving its goals.

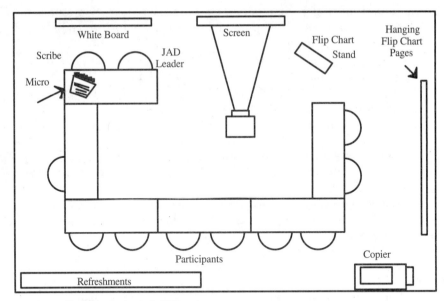

Figure 14.3 Layout of a typical JAD room

- **Scribe**. This participant records the findings of the workshop, using tools to build diagrams, create screen and report designs, extract repository information, and create prototypes.
- **Project manager**. The manager responsible for the project should attend and participate in the JAD workshops but should not be the JAD leader.
- **IT professionals**. There should be one or more IT professionals attending a JAD workshop to ensure that the developed design is good technically.

In addition, there may be visiting specialists who attend on a part-time basis to give advice in their areas of expertise.

A JAD room is usually a separate room configured specifically for JAD workshops. There are no phones or beepers in a JAD room. The workshop is highly visual, as illustrated in the layout of a typical JAD room shown in Fig. 14.3. White boards are used to display designs and dialogues. Flip charts are used, and flip-chart pages can be hung on the walls. A workstation with CASE or client/server software is used by the scribe to record user specifications and build prototypes. The designs and prototypes generated by the software and displayed on the micro's screen are projected on a screen using an LCD display device. The participants take copies of the design with them in the evening and mark them up, ready for the next day's discussion.

The JAD methodology is successful only when there is strong user involvement in the development process. The feeling of ownership of the application that will ultimately be theirs provides a motivation to work with the process and the application and a strong commitment to supporting the inevitable change the application will create. User-oriented development results in better solutions and the users require less training, since they gain a great deal of knowledge during the development process.

An important byproduct of JAD workshops is that IT professionals develop an awareness of what users need in order to be more productive in their jobs, and users get a feeling for what it takes to develop a multiuser application with today's technology. Users can begin to understand the constraints involved in developing applications, whether those constraints are technological, strategic, or financial.

14.2 Development Roles and Infrastructure

Those organizations that have implemented client/server applications seem to agree that success is a function of planning, choosing the right people, building an infrastructure, and following a methodology.

When organizations begin their first client/server implementation, there is usually a lack of GUI development skills, a lack of client/server experience, and a lack of the people skills required to work so closely with users. In addition, there is probably are no client/server-related standards, such as GUI standards and naming standards.

14.2.1 Development roles

People on development teams for client/server applications will be taking some very familiar roles, such as project leader, analyst, and programmer. Because of the heavy reliance on GUI interfaces, there should also be a GUI designer. Because of the separation of business logic and rules from presentation and data access, there should also be a business analyst (for the business rules and logic) and a database analyst (for the data access). Figure 14.4 lists the roles and their responsibilities as defined in the RADPath methodology from LBMS, Inc., which is a Windows-based client/server project process management tool.

14.2.2 Infrastructure

There needs to be a very well-defined set of support roles (the infrastructure) underneath the actual development effort. These roles include quality assurance tester, version controller, standards manager, network communication manager, help (on-line help) writer, systems integrator, and user liaison. (See Fig. 14.4 for more details.)

Successful implementations usually follow internally set standards. These should be created (or selected) and adhered to during the development

Project manager	Estimate resource requirements Monitor project status and schedule Ensure overall success of the project
Business analyst	Conduct user interviews and review processes to gather requirements and determine scope Perform modeling, analysis, and complete design documents
Chief user liaison	Communicate business and user requirements to development team Act as key user in JAD sessions Review prototypes
System architect	Oversee design, procurement, and development of integrated architecture and collection of system components
GUI designer	Design GUI based on user requirements Verify that the design conforms to corporate standards Design iterative prototypes
Features programmer	Implement design of application working with a higher-level tool set Build templates and common components
Back-end programmer	Build and organize APIs to the database server and other low-level coding such as messaging and security
Database analyst	Develop and maintain application data model and write SQL-based code
Infrastructure Coordinator	Develop and monitor services for the development team
Help writer	Develop all on-line help, message-bar help strings, and context sensitive help
Quality Assurance Tester	Develop test cases, scenarios, and scripts to ensure application quality
Development coordinator	Approve coding, monitor bug tracking and supervise testing
Usability tester	Verify application is usable and adheres to GUI standards
Systems integrator	Integrates GUI layer, code objects, and interfaces to other systems across the teams
TQM engineer	Determine how well project development processes adhere to the corporate TQM program

Figure 14.4 Roles and responsibilities

process. The other important factor is the selection of the tools. The tools selected can make or break an implementation.

The technical architecture is critical to the quality and performance of an application. The architecture should fit the size of the application and be as "state of the art" as possible within budget. In addition, it should be flexible enough to integrate with the organization's existing architecture, if necessary, and be scalable.

14.3 Available Design Products

Top-level design, also referred to as user design or conceptual system design, translates the user requirements produced in the analysis phase (the *what*) into design specifications (the *how*). Inputs and outputs are designed. Processes are specified with structured techniques, such as structured English and decision tables. In RAD-based methodologies, the design specification is determined through prototyping of the application.

The design should not be technology-based or developed with a particular technology in mind, if at all possible. If a network is to be designed as part of the application, only its characteristics, such as speed, number of supported users, and estimated traffic, should be determined at this stage, with further specifications of the network topology deferred until the construction phase.

CASE (computer-aided software engineering) products are used to fine-tune data requirements and to facilitate data administration. These products build structured diagrams—data flow diagrams, entity-relationship diagrams, decomposition diagrams, and action diagrams, to name a few—that were familiar to those schooled in traditional development methodologies. CASE products ensure consistency and completeness within the diagrams. Some CASE products do not generate code or program-specific designs.

Client/server development products focus on the end product—the completed application. These products allow developers to concentrate on the application rather than on the GUI APIs (application programming interfaces), access code for relational databases, network protocols, and detailed coding. Client/server development products start with a database schema which is accessible from the development platform. Developers design the graphical presentations and the events that occur in the application.

The output of the analysis stage of application development produces user requirements. The communication media can be either oral, such as user interviews, or written, such as user specifications. The users respond to the specification document, either orally or in writing, the analysts change the specifications and return the entire document to the user for review—and the cycle begins again.

Under the SDLC methodology, the design stage does not begin until all analysis is complete. Many IT organizations are finding that today's environment requires a merging of the various methodologies. They begin the process with structured analysis until most of the application—say, 70 percent—has been specified. Then they turn to prototyping and use CASE products to prototype and define the data, thereby fine-tuning the requirements as they go along. The end result might be a structured design with database schema or an operational version of the application.

14.3.1 CASE products

CASE products formalize communication between developers and users in the early stages of development—analysis. These products have been used by IT professionals to improve the quality of their applications and facilitate the maintenance function.

Structured diagrams that support structured design methodologies are used as a means of communication. High-end CASE products rely on data models, data flow diagrams, entity-relationship diagrams, and functional decomposition diagrams. Many high-end CASE products can also generate skeletons (fragments) of the procedural code (usually COBOL) for processes specified as decomposition diagrams. Low-end CASE products, such as application generators and screen editors, support rapid prototyping and automatic code generation.

A rigorous methodology is required to implement the structured development process used by CASE products. The learning curve for proficient use of a CASE product and the development methodology is usually quite long. Converting to structured techniques and a disciplined methodology generally results in a high degree of cultural change within IT. In addition to the training costs, the high cost of the CASE product itself makes the transition to CASE technology expensive.

Although CASE products can be used to develop decision-support applications, the structured diagrams and complex development methodologies they rely on are overkill for such applications. CASE products are well suited for enterprise-wide applications that require a high degree of integrity.

Support for distributed environments varies among CASE products. While developers can design GUI screens, not all CASE products generate the code for the screen or support multiple GUI platforms. For example, even though it has a Windows-based development platform, a CASE product might not be able to generate the code for any designed GUI screens. If the product can generate code for the screens, it may not be able to generate GUI code for multiple platforms, such as Motif, OpenLook, and OS/2.

Developers are also looking to CASE products to assist in the allocation of processing between the client platform and the server platform. Most of the CASE products that do support client/server computing place all the processing on the client platform. The ability to split the processing between client and server is promised for future releases.

14.3.2   Client/server development products

Client/server development products have no self-contained analysis capability. They start at the design phase, after a database schema has been prepared and installed on the server and business transactions have been defined.

Client/server applications are event-driven. The processes in the application are executed based on user responses, such as entering data and pressing Enter or clicking on an icon or menu choice. To generate client/server applications, developers specify the events that can occur within the application and represent these events in the GUI.

Processes that cannot be handled with the features of the client/server development product may be included in the application during the detailed design phase. Processes are coded in the 4GL provided with the development product, often called a scripting language. Those processes that cannot be completely handled by the 4GL are usually coded in C, the de facto processing language for client/server environments.

Client/server development products do not have an analysis capability and therefore are not well suited for the development of transactional business-critical applications. These products are ideally suited for developing informational and decision-support applications which require transparent access to distributed data.

The transition to client/server development products can be done at low cost and with little cultural change. The products themselves are relatively inexpensive (compared to CASE products). The basic skill required for such products is familiarity with the functionality of a GUI such as Windows.

The more successful client/server development products are object-based. An object—a set of transactions (activities) sharing a common user interface—consists of the definitions of data types, variables, and constants used by the transactions, as well as the definitions for reports and procedures for calculations and data manipulation which can be performed on the object's data. Objects can be organized into class hierarchies and can be reused in multiple applications.

14.3.3 Integration between tools

The traditional CASE vendors are beginning to recognize that their products need to be able to integrate and interact with client/server development products. The client/server development product vendors are building alliances with traditional CASE vendors to support integration of the analysis and development tools. This integration is illustrated in Fig. 14.5.

CASE products focus on analysis issues, such as refining the data requirements and identifying the structure of the application. Client/server products focus on design issues, such as the users' view of the application and breaking the application into events (rather than tasks or process-decomposition diagrams). Since CASE products generate database schemas and client/server products build from a database schema, integrating these two techniques at the database level will shorten the development cycle and manage the database definitions.

The CASE product is used to create a high-level model of the database in the form of entity-relationship diagrams and to generate the physical database for a client/server application. The client/server product is used in a prototyping environment to build the GUI for the application and identify all clickable events. The client/server product is then used to specify the response to each event, using the product's high-level procedural language or C.

CASE products can also generate code for processes. Some can generate the code in C, the production language for many client/server environments. CASE vendors are also evaluating the feasibility of generating the process code in the 4GLs of some of the more popular client/server development products, such as PowerBuilder from Powersoft.

The perfect scenario would support entity-relationship modeling using CASE, generation of SQL statements by the client tool, and automatic incorporation of the SQL into a client application. Currently, no product or set of products can do all three seamlessly.

14.4   Evaluating Design Products

It is important to recognize the strengths and weaknesses of design products

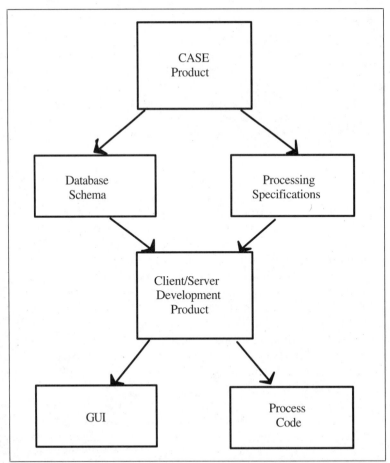

Figure 14.5 Integration of CASE and client/server development tools

and to determine which functionality is best for the application at hand and the IT development staff. Application design and development products generally fall into two categories:

- **Bottom-up**. These products are designed for homogeneous LAN environments and favor quick development over data modeling.
- **Top-down**. These products are designed for larger systems and multiple hardware environments, begin with an analysis of application requirements, and develop a logical data model.

An important feature in any design product is the use of a data dictionary or a repository. The data dictionary and repository facilities should be integrated with the planning, analysis, design, and construction components of the development tool.

14.4.1 Top-down or bottom-up design

The strength of the bottom-up products is in designing and developing client applications that can be quickly designed and built and that maximize the use of windowing operating environments. They feature capabilities for creating windows and managing objects and support Windows interfaces (DDE and OLE). These products include Microsoft's Visual Basic, Powersoft's PowerBuilder, and Centura's SQLWindows.

The strength of the top-down products is support for cross-platform development. Users can mix and match hardware platforms, GUIs, DBMSs, and networks without redeveloping the applications. These products are suitable for designing and developing complex, distributed applications for heterogeneous environments.

The bottom-up products vary in their ability to design and develop complex SQL applications in heterogeneous environments and to build applications from an enterprise data model. Most bottom-up products automate the creation of the GUI but require the developer to write the code for database transactions. The products also differ in their implementation of SQL. Some use a translator to convert queries into SQL; others have no knowledge of the back-end server activities. While most of these products provide access to SQL databases, they do not necessarily support SQL processing as part of the application.

In contrast, the top-down products use SQL as the foundation for all design and development activities, from data modeling to reporting. This allows the product to access multiple, heterogeneous database tables within a single transaction, without requiring the developer to write code. However, the products do not provide the same level of GUI support as the bottom-up products, nor do they necessarily take advantage of the micro operating environment.

With all their differences, there is a place for both types of design and development tools in an organization. For simple applications, the top-down products are overkill. For applications that need to get out the door fast, bottom-up products are the answer. For applications requiring heterogeneous database access with data integrity, top-down products fit the bill.

14.4.2 Use of data dictionaries

As the design phase proceeds, it is important that all designers have access to a list of existing (previously defined) data elements and processes (procedures) via a friendly interface. They should not need to know how to spell the data element name in order to look it up in the dictionary.

It is not productive to provide developers with a long list of all the data elements and processes and expect them to look up items. Looking through such a listing would take too much time. The lookup process needs to be real-time, interactive, and user-intuitive. Hypertext, which provides links between data elements, is very useful for these searches.

Graphical displays that show the layout of relational tables simplify the selection of data elements. These same displays often permit the user to specify relational operatives, such as Select, Join, and Project, without learning a relational database language.

Data dictionaries focus on managing the data about data (metadata). Repositories also manage processes. While reusable code is not a consideration during the top-level design phase, it certainly is during the construction phase.

Data dictionaries provide the meanings of tables (and files) and columns (attributes and fields). A data dictionary can help identify data redundancy—when the same data, often with a different name, appears in more than one place.

Data dictionaries impose naming conventions. Adherence to these conventions and the centralization of the dictionary itself permit an organization to identify and organize its enterprise-wide data and maintain their integrity.

Naming conventions are a set of standard words and abbreviations for naming data objects. The conventions would specify

- How words are to be selected for the name of an object
- How those words should be ordered
- How aliases (abbreviations) can be created

The use of naming standards will improve communication (by the use of a consistent vocabulary), eliminate redundancy, and avoid inventing a new entity when one already exists in a very similar form in the data dictionary. For example, if naming conventions are followed when naming a "new" data element, if the name already existed, the data dictionary would indicate that the data element was not "new."

In addition, naming standards also allow users to search using a standard name. If existing names are developed using the standards and the data element exists, the user should be able to find it.

A dictionary records the links between the data and the processing models. Data dictionaries can be used to analyze the impact of changes to a data structure, which is likely to affect multiple applications.

A data dictionary that is used only by users (developers) is said to be a *passive* dictionary. Typically, its original use is to facilitate the development of the data structures. Any changes to these structures must be made manually to the data dictionary. If the data described in the data dictionary is to be used by an application, the developer must know of its existence and name, then search (usually a sequential text string search) the dictionary and make a copy of the definition.

In contrast, an *active* data dictionary is one that is used by programs (applications). For example, a COBOL program could name a file or a view of a file, and a precompiler would automatically generate the code for the I/O area of the program from the dictionary. A file change would require a recompilation of the program but would not require changing the program.

A *dynamic* data dictionary is one that is accessed at execution. The repository is accessed directly by the operating system or DBMS for information needed to complete the processing. This type of data dictionary is especially useful for prototyping applications and generating queries with 4GLs.

14.4.3 Use of repositories

Repository technology extends the concepts of a data dictionary to include the management of data and process models, addresses, rules, and definitions. A repository stores the diagrams and the meaning represented in the diagrams, and enforces consistency within the diagrams. A repository is an intelligent facility that "understands" the design; a data dictionary does not.

All the design information is entered into the repository of the development product. The information is accumulated first at a high level and then at progressively more detailed levels. The specification process continues until sufficient detail about the design for the application has been accumulated so that the program code can be generated automatically. As illustrated in Fig. 14.6, the repository integrates the front-end planning, analysis, and design components of the product with the back-end code, database, and documentation-generation facilities.

A repository does the following:

- Manages information about repositories.
- Allows the data resource manager to create object views that reflect conceptual schemas.
- Defines the underlying knowledge bases, object bases, databases, and

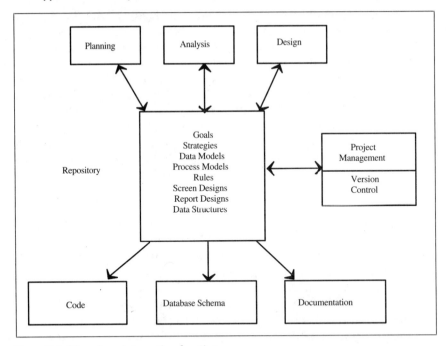

Figure 14.6 Repository integration functions

files; knows where they are, how they are accessed, and how they are modified; and handles interfaces, data transfer formats, and APIs.

- Supports queries of multiple systems for objects and packages the requested data as a single response.
- Runs on any node or combination of nodes and knows which repository facilities are running on the network.
- Runs passively, actively, or dynamically.

Repositories also provide naming services, repository management facilities, such as time services and object management services, and repository administration facilities to install and manage information repositories.

To an application programmer, a repository is a collection of standard and custom objects. For example, processing in an organization might be segmented along primary users: Sales, Manufacturing, Finance, and Human Resources.

At first glance, there is very little overlap of data and processing needs. First, let's look at data and consider the concept of a customer. To the Sales staff, the term *customer* might mean a potential customer, one in the selling cycle, one who has agreed to buy the product, *and* one who has bought the product. To Finance, a customer is most likely only the last of these two—one who has already bought the product.

Now consider processing. Some shareable elements of processing are fairly obvious, such as screens that ensure applications look and feel the same (although adherence may be dictated by IT). Another less obvious element might be preparing mailing labels. Sales most likely has written and implemented such a process. But unless the other departments know of its existence, they might develop their own instead of using the existing procedure.

Repositories are implemented as database applications and, as such, provide standard services, such as data access, data sharing, and data management. In addition, they can also manage

- Data and process models generated by data modeling products
- Processes required for referential integrity
- Reference facilities, such as dictionaries and concordances
- Directories of data addresses and attributes

But the acceptance by IT communities of repositories and repository-based application development has been slow in coming. Reasons for this lack of acceptance include the following:

- There is little integration between repository software. Repositories use custom file systems, provided either by a development product or by repository vendors such as Platinum Technologies, Manager Software Products, Reltech Products, Inc., and Brownstone Solutions, Inc. Third-party software can interface with a repository via import/export facilities, usually provided with the repository software. This redundant information must be kept in synchronization with the repository.
- Very few repository-based development products provide APIs to support an on-line session with the repository encyclopedia and a third-party product. Bridge technology is used to upload repository data to and download it from a third-party DBMS; this also results in redundant information which must be kept synchronized.
- Repository software is expensive and requires a long learning curve for efficient use.
- Migrating existing applications to a repository-based environment can be a major undertaking unless the applications were designed using structured techniques in which the data was carefully modeled, processes were well structured, and naming conventions and shared-copy books were used.

14.5 Define the Data Structure

There are two approaches to identifying data needs:

- The **process-oriented** approach examines all existing input, output, and processing for a given application. This approach does not require heavy user involvement. Data flow diagrams are frequently used for this approach.

- The **data-oriented** approach examines the decisions made in the application and works backward to identify the data required for those decisions. This approach, which requires heavy user involvement, is appropriate when the input, output, and processes are relatively undefined. Entity-relationship diagrams support this approach.

If an application has a component that is well defined and a component that is not fully defined, both of these approaches could be used.

Once the elements of data have been identified, their characteristics must be determined. These characteristics include

- Size
- Type
- Description
- Validation criteria
- Valid ranges
- Security levels
- Access privileges
- Where used

The actual database structure is not designed at this stage; that is done in the detailed design stage.

14.6 Define the Interfaces

Once the data has been determined, designers should begin to focus on the human interfaces, such as GUI screens, input forms, and printed or displayed reports.

Designing screens, input forms, and report formats involves creating a mockup. The process has not changed over the years. How the mockups are generated has. Today designers can use word processing packages, graphic packages, or client/server development products to generate the mockups. Users' changes can be easily incorporated.

GUI screens are best designed with GUI-builder software, ideally a program that can generate precompiled P-code, which can be executed immediately. P-code is pseudocode that is interpreted into the native machine language at run time. The GUI-builder software allows the designer to develop the screen using any of the GUI available features, such as icons, radio buttons, pull-down menus, and multiple window placement. Many designers find that the process is more productive if the first layout of the GUI screen is developed (with the users) as a rough sketch by hand. After a screen is built, users and designers can interactively make modifications to the screen.

Another feature of GUI-builder software is its ability to provide linkages between GUI screens and processes, as well as support for a menu structure.

When defining screens (even in prototype mode), developers should

- Make screens as user intuitive as possible
- Adhere to organization-wide GUI standards
- Ensure that GUIs are consistent across the application

14.7   Define the Events/Processes

If a CASE product is used to develop the user requirements and the top-level design, the application's processes and data model will have been specified in decomposition, data flow, and entity-relationship diagrams.

If the application is a client/server application that is executed from a GUI screen, the designers must identify the events that are to occur within each GUI screen. For example, what happens when the user clicks on the Open icon or clicks on the Update button? These specifications can be provided using the capabilities of the GUI-builder software.

If the event triggers the execution of a process, the code for that process should be specified, at a minimum in structured English and at a maximum in the GUI-builder's 4GL. A notation should also be made if the process cannot be completely handled by the 4GL and will, therefore, require coding in a 3GL.

15

Application Development Tools

Most who have implemented client/server environments would be quick to say that the development tool will determine the success of the project. In order to know what development tool is right for the project, the organization has to understand what the project is and how it fits with client/server technology.

15.1 Client/Server Development Needs

Here are important features that should be present in a client/server development tool. They will not all be in any one tool, and some features are more necessary for some situations than for others. These features are

- Support for application logic
- Support for partitioning
- Portability
- Data access
- Transaction processing
- Security
- Support for teams
- Support for testing
- Support for run-time versions
- Support for interconnections
- Some object orientation

15.1.1 Support for application logic

If the application is a decision-support application, there should be little or no application logic involved. In this case, a client generator such as Powersoft's PowerBuilder or Microsoft's Visual Basic would be fine. Products like these generate client code and SQL calls to the server. Data logic would be written in the stored procedural language of the DBMS.

At the other end of the spectrum are application generators such as Dynasty Development Environment from Dynasty Technologies and Forte from Forte Software. Products such as these capture the logic and generate both the client and the server code.

15.1.2 Support for partitioning

The development tool takes care of the code execution language at the physical level; the developer deals with designing the application using a high-level language. The code can then be partitioned at deployment when the platform is decided. Some tools support partitioning at run time. Each time the application is executed, the software decides on the best distribution for the execution code. For example, if it's a particularly heavy day on a server, the software can put some of the logic on the client.

Partitioning is a useful feature for applications that require a lot of logic execution. Partitioning is now available in most client/server development products to some degree.

15.1.3 Portability

The development tool should support the three popular presentation managers: Windows, Macintosh, and Motif for UNIX. The development tools are usually able to handle the differences in look and feel among these presentation managers but their more advanced features, such as Microsoft's OLE in Windows, are harder to emulate. In order to be competitive, vendors are specializing in one presentation manager (usually Windows) and providing less support for the others.

15.1.4 Data access

No matter how complex the project is, the final application needs to be able to access data. A development tool should support the majer client/server database products (SQL Server, Oracle, Sybase System 11). For support DBMSs, the tool should optimize native SQL code. To connect with other data sources, the tool should support a database gateway such as IBI's EDA (see Sec. 8.7.2) or have a hook into Microsoft's ODBC.

15.1.5 Transaction processing

As more and more organizations use client/server technology to deploy their business-critical applications, which are usually transaction-based, the applications themselves need to be more robust. It follows that the development tool must be more robust and have more features. Some of these features are support for complex locking such as optimistic locking (see Sec. 9.3.2), complex transaction logic, distributed transactions across heterogeneous platforms, nonstop computing, and security.

15.1.6   Security

Security cannot be left up to the DBMS itself because most applications use multiple databases. Security should be enforced across platforms by the application as a single logon.

15.1.7   Support for teams

A development should aid the group of developers working together on a large application. The support is usually through a repository that stores application components that are shared by the developers. The repository should have check-in/check-out capabilities, browsing, version control, and release management. This is often an area that separates the low-end tools from the high-end tools.

15.1.8   Support for testing

An application should be tested in the environment in which it will run. That is rarely the development area! Stopping at a user's station and asking if a developer might use it for a morning or two to test the application (after the developer downloads it, of course!) is not the way to go, either. To facilitate testing, some tools let developers distribute the application to remote machines, be they servers or clients, and test the platforms—the clients, servers, network, middleware, etc. Some of the testing features of these types of development tools can determine the impact the application has on the environment as well.

15.1.9   Support for run-time versions

The idea behind run-time versions is that a translator sits on the client machine and interprets the high-level code generated by the development tool. This allows a tool to partition at execution, since the code has not yet been compiled. However, compiled code runs faster and is portable (the compiled code is usually in C in client/server environments). In addition, vendors usually charge for run-time versions.

15.1.10   Support for interconnections

A development tool should realize that it develops code to run in a changing environment. To accommodate the changes and to help fill any holes they have in their own offerings, development tools have hooks to other products, such as middleware (see Chap. 8) and transaction managers (see Sec. 11.4.2). Support for OSF's DCE is almost a given at this point.

15.1.11 Some object orientation

Object technology is used in varying degrees in client/server development tools. Most are turning to object technology as a vehicle for supporting application partitioning.

Development tools should, at a minimum, support inheritance, which makes them object-based, not object-oriented. Inheritance makes the development of screens much easier, for example. Truly object-oriented tools also support classes and encapsulation. These tools generate C++ or Smalltalk code—another sign that they are truly object-oriented. Some tools, such as Forte's, have their own proprietary object-oriented language.

Object technology is not a necessity. It has a slow and long (read expensive) learning curve. If the application logic has to be written in an object-oriented language, be sure you have seasoned veterans on staff or are prepared to hire some.

15.2 Generations of Development Tools

The first-generation development tools bind the GUI tightly to the logic of an application. All processing occurs on the GUI platform as a consequence of user actions at the screen. The applications are developed by painting screen using a point-and-click and drag-and-drop interface and by scripting GUI events by adding code that was fired when the user clicked on a button or made a menu choice. Database access and integration with other client platforms is accomplished within the scripts.

These tools are not well suited for building enterprise-wide applications, where application size, scope, and complexity require more flexibility in style of development and application architecture. The next generation of client/server applications perform processing independently of the user interface, accept I/O from other than the desktop or database, and do considerable computing, in addition to accessing databases and handling GUIs.

To build enterprise-wide applications which typically run on multitier architectures, a development tool needs to be able to build the GUI separately from the application logic. The logic itself may be partitioned— divided into separate, executable segments and deployed on a different network-accessible platform.

A comprehensive client/server development tool would include a GUI builder for creating one or all of the major GUIs, a fourth-generation language for creating the business logic, an interpreter and/or compiler, and debugging tools. For enterprise-wide client/server development, the tool would allow for application partitioning and the major server environments in order to accommodate the dispersion of business logic onto multiple computers.

The second-generation tools support one of two methods for partitioning. The first is to design and develop a partitioning scheme, with deployment following that scheme. The other is to design and develop the application independent of partitioning, with partitioning happening at deployment. In this case, the partitioning scheme can be changed without affecting application logic. A third option is beginning to emerge: The design and development are done independent of partitioning and the partitioning is dynamically determined at runtime, each time the application is run.

Second-generation tools also require a more formal planning stage before development of a prototype begins. Because the environment is more complex and the screen-painted interfaces represent only one aspect of the application, analysis and design are necessary steps in building enterprise-wide applications.

Since multitier architectures are usually used to implement business-critical applications, the impact is quickly felt if an application goes down. The newer development tools can improve availability through replication and failover. However, most availability will be provided by the platforms on which the applications run.

15.3   New Advances in Client/Server Development Tools

Vendors of client/server development tools are constantly (or so it seems to those who try to stay current on such tools!) upgrading their products' capabilities. If a product doesn't have a particular capability today, it probably will in six months. Some of these enhancements are due to new technologies. Others reflect support for organizations using client/server technology in a new way.

15.3.1   New development tools

One of the interesting trends is desktop versions of client/server application development tools. These products, from vendors such as Powersoft and Centura (formerly Gupta), have the same front-end development functions as their big brothers, but support only desktop data sources. Desktop versions do not support teams of programmers. If an application needed to access a server relational DBMS, even via ODBC, an upgrade would be required.

Micro database products are also calling themselves client/server development products. They loosely fit the definition of client/server computing—the presentation is separate from the logic which is separate from the data services. Network versions of these products do access data from network drives (which could be called servers). They have easy to use design capabilities. They use the prototyping methodology for developing applications. The sticky point is that they usually do not execute SQL against the data on the network drive, the files there are considered extensions of their own hardware and as such as accessed natively.

15.3.2 Robust DBMSs

Relational DBMS vendors are adding more and more functionality to their offerings. Replication is standard in server DBMS products. Support for binary large objects (BLOBs) which are used for storing images, voice, and sound is commonplace. Support for multiple-processor machines improves performance and facilitates application partitioning.

15.3.3 Distributed applications

Distributed applications can have processing or data distributed, or even both. A set of data may be replicated on multiple nodes for quick access by a variety of users. The copies would be kept in synchronization by a distributed DBMS on a coordinating server. A set of data could be split among multiple nodes (fragmented). The coordinating server could make the set of data complete in virtual memory if needed.

Application processing could be distributed by similar methods. A copy of the application could be running on multiple nodes. Updates to the multiple copies would be handled by automated development products and version control utilities. The processing for individual applications could be split among multiple nodes, either by coding the processing destination node into the application itself or by allowing the enterprise system to assign the processing based on run-time resource utilization.

Splitting up application processing is called partitioning.

Not all applications need to be distributed. Applications that share data or processes benefit from distribution. How large a benefit is derived from distribution is a function of the type of application.

15.3.4 Distributed object development

As client/server application development tools turn to object technology, the idea of distributed objects also facilitates distributed applications. Created objects can be distributed throughout the architecture at deployment time. If fine-tuning is required, these same objects can be redeployed on another platform. Key to this assumption, however, is that objects can be coded independently of their execution platform. This requires robust tools and adherence to standards.

15.4 Client/Server Development Tools

Organizations should review development tools by reviewing their support for the development requirements presented in Sec. 15.1. At one end of the spectrum of offerings are tools that simply code the front-end that supports a previously defined database schema and generates ANSI SQL for data access. There is little or no team development, and the user community for the application developed is two or less.

At the other end are tools that could be termed enterprise-strength. Most of the tools at this level look very similar. They are object-oriented, and their prototypes are based on object modeling. They offer a repository-based development environment, a proprietary 4GL, and a toolset comprising a browser, 4GL editor, GUI painter, and partitioning utility. They all offer platform, network, and database portability.

The tools in the middle are moving up, and the tools at the high end are adding more features and functionality. To make sure all appropriate tools are evaluated, just ask the vendor you are considering who its competitors are. If the vendor says it has none, don't believe him or her. And then research the companies the vendor does indicate.

Not all development products are included in this section. The list includes those that are aimed at true development versus cross-platform functionality. In addition, an effort was made to include both the most popular and rising stars—at least at the time of writing. The tools are presented alphabetically.

The reviews of client/server development tools in this section are very brief, and little attempt is made to compare products for the reader. Why? If a product is missing a feature, it will probably be added in the next release, which may be as close as six months away.

The review should give the reader a flavor for the products' strengths and some of their weaknesses. Be mindful of the fact that these reviews are as of mid-1996: the version number is given for each product so that the reader can compare the latest version number with this one. Even if the product has a newer release, the review will serve as a base description.

15.4.1 Dynasty Development Environment

Dynasty Development Environment, from Dynasty Technologies, Inc., was designed to support the development and deployment of partitioned, distributed, and portable client/server applications. The current version (3.0) was released in 1996.

Dynasty is an object-oriented tool. Its development environment is organized around objects, and for application deployment, partitions are built of objects. Dynasty's objects' properties include classes, subclasses, encapsulation, inheritance, instantiation, and polymorphism.

Dynasty objects have attributes, subobjects, methods, and process models. Attributes are references to other objects, to subobjects, and to methods. Subobjects provide an object hierarchy and grouping. Dynasty Window objects have panel and widget subobjects. Methods define the behavior of an object. Process models are another object class that logically groups methods into categories of actions commonly performed in an application.

Dynasty is built around ten primary, predefined object types or superclasses, organized in class libraries and stored in the product's repository. Many of these classes include predefined subclasses that inherit attributes from the superclasses. Developers can create their own subclasses. The ten superclasses are

- **Business objects** define business processes. A business object is the starting point for the development of an application and the implementation of the application's object model.
- **Data objects** represent the values and behavior of data elements.
- **DataManager objects** provide the linkage to relational DBMS servers. They encapsulate the connection from the user to the relational DBMS and the structure of the relational DBMS.
- **DataStore objects** map relational tables.
- **View objects** are the programming interfaces to relational DBMSs.
- **Functions** are methods without objects.
- **Program objects** are collections of all the objects within an application partition.
- **Window objects** make up the Dynasty GUI. They are built of panel and widget subobjects.
- **Panel objects** are groups of widgets. For example, a panel might contain a related group of radio buttons and their labels.
- **Widget objects** are the lowest-level GUI components.

Dynasty has an object-oriented, repository-based development environment. It supports multiple projects, teams of developers, and versions of applications. The repository is the focal point of the Dynasty development environment. The repository contains the class libraries of the objects built by developers, the applications created by assembling objects, and the partitioning, targeting, and generation specifications for those applications.

There are shared repositories and working repositories. Multiple shared repositories can be defined within a development environment—for example, one for each project. Classes and objects are checked out of the shared repository and into the working repository. More than one developer can check out an object.

Dynasty's browser provides easy access to classes and objects using the class structure. The repository is organized hierarchically by the ten superclasses mentioned above. The developer accesses the entries by traversing a graphical tree structure that maps that hierarchy. The Quick Layout tools automatically create all the objects required for database access based on the schema of the database that the application will access.

Dynasty includes automatic mapping between the relational DBMS and Dynasty application objects. The software generates SQL statements to support a range of database operations.

DataManager objects map to relational DBMS servers. Dynasty transfers the database schema into DataManager objects to facilitate object mapping and SQL generation. DataStore objects map to relational DBMS tables. Data objects map to RDBMS columns. View objects create relationships between DataStore objects and correspond to joins and master-detail relationships.

Dynasty allows developers to specify transactions within their applications through the use of a predefined transaction class. Transaction support is then provided through access to external resource managers. Dynasty offers legacy integration through database gateways.

Dynasty applications are deployed through a three-step process

- **Partitioning** segments the application into client and servers. This is a manual process, but it is aided by a graphical partitioning tool.
- **Targeting**, also a manual process, specifies the database, middleware, network, operating system, and GUI environment in which the partitions of an application run.
- The application can then be **generated** by compiling the objects into the C code for each partition on its targeted platform.

Maintaining Dynasty applications requires that only the affected objects be regenerated.

The newest release of Dynasty (3.0) adds the following features:

- Includes a new Services Request Broker which supports failover and load balancing
- Supports the integration of third-party C++ libraries, where before the objects had to come from Dynasty's own environment
- Allows developers to integrate Visual Basic and PowerBuilder client applications into the Dynasty three-tier corporate application environment
- Includes the Dynasty Reusable Components Library, which provides pre-configured components such as LU6.2 connection and IBM MQ Series interfaces, application micro help, and custom widgets
- Capable of partitioning much larger applications than the previous version
- Allows Visual Basic or PowerBuilder client partitions access to Dynasty business objects and network services
- Includes Open-CGI and Open-Java modules, which allows an organization to publish Dynasty-generated shared applications directly via Web servers and Java applets

15.4.2   Forte Application Environment

Forte Application Environment, from Forte Software, is also purely object-oriented. Implemented object properties are classes, subclasses, encapsulation, inheritance, instantiation, and polymorphism. Forte adds events to the attributes and methods that specify each object. Events, in combination with support for multithreading, enable Forte applications to address requirements for asynchronous, real-time processing.

Forte encourages developers to model and build applications in high-level, deployable, and sharable service objects. Service objects implement both business functions and system functions. A system service function might support database access; a business function, the accounts payable function.

Forte provides a set of class libraries that may be used to help developers build application classes and objects. The libraries support database exception handling, database transaction management, GUI building, wrappering external programs, and creating interfaces to CORBA and RPCs.

Forte has a repository-based development environment. A single, centralized repository is shared by all developers. A browser locates classes and objects in the repository and provides developers with the capabilities to add, modify, and extend them. Unlike Dynasty, which supports only Windows as a development platform, Forte supports Macintosh and Motif as well as Windows.

The Forte repository contains both the metadata that define classes and the real objects built from those classes. Developers work on classes or objects by checking them out of the shared repository, which means that they cannot be modified by other developers.

The development environment automatically maps database columns to object attributes and database rows to array variables.

Individual objects may be marked as transactional and/or shared. Forte transparently provides the mechanisms to enforce serialization and transactional coordination of the objects. Forte has integrated its own transaction manager.

External integration with client desktop applications, electronic data input devices, support for database gateways, and support for standards-based middleware are also offered. Legacy integration is done through wrapping, database gateways, and middleware integration.

With Forte, application development is decoupled from application deployment. Developers build "logical" implementation-independent applications that contain all user interface, processing, and data access components. Then application partitions are configured, generated, and distributed to targeted platforms. The client components of Forte applications run interpretively under control of a Forte engine. Server components may run interpretively under the engine or be compiled into C++ code to maximize performance and minimize the footprint. A performance monitor included with the application management tools provides information about message traffic between partitions that can be used to "tune" partition configuration.

In 1996, Forte Software released a new version of Forte, Release 2, which simplifies building and managing distributed applications. The product supports multitier client-server architectures with transparent application partitioning across disparate operating systems, GUIs, networks, and relational databases. Release 2 features open integration with software outside the Forte environment, such as DCE, CORBA, and Encina, and also includes data access through ODBC.

Forte Release 2 fully supports international applications and tight integration with OLE-compliant applications on PC clients. Other new features include repository enhancements, help facilities, application libraries, cross-platform window reusability, user-defined system-management agents, and a global naming service. Release 2 adds support for the Windows NT and Power Macintosh platforms.

In 1996, Forte Software also released Forte Express, a visual application generator for high-end client/server environments. Forte Express is an add-on to the Forte Application Environment.

Forte Express generates the user interface and database access components of object-oriented, multitier applications. The generated default user interface definitions include window layouts, menus, and buttons.

Forte Express has database interfaces to Oracle, Sybase, Informix Online, Microsoft SQL Server, Rdb, and IBM DB2/6000, as well as Microsoft's ODBC, and includes a library of database interactions that generate SQL.

15.4.3 PowerBuilder

When PowerBuilder was released by Powersoft Inc. in 1991, it was one of the first available development tools for client/server environments. As one might expect given that longevity, it has been used to develop more applications than any other tool.

The development version of PowerBuilder included (and still does) a copy of Watcom SQL so that the developer could test against a desktop relational database. Powersoft merged with Watcom in 1993. In 1994, Powersoft merged with Sybase and is now a division of Sybase.

PowerBuilder's DataWindow object is largely credited for the product's success. DataWindow generates SQL from a point-and-click and drag-and-drop interface. PowerBuilder supports DRDA and ODBC and many relational DBMSs.

PowerBuilder's Data Pipeline builds on DataWindow technology to provide graphical data migration and replication. Data Pipeline is an any-to-any conduit for relational databases. Tables from any PowerBuilder-supported relational DBMS are read into one "end" of the Data Pipeline and written to any other PowerBuilder-supported relational DBMS at the other "end." The Data Pipeline also supports graphical filtering, editing, and data conversion.

PowerBuilder offers run-time versions of the product.

In late 1994 Powersoft announced the Powersoft Enterprise Series, which offered new products, new features, cross-platform support, and tight integration of Watcom technology. The Enterprise Series includes the following base products:

- **PowerBuilder Desktop** provides access to common desktop databases via ODBC 2.0. The Advanced Developer Toolkit is a new add-on for PowerBuilder Desktop. It adds multiuser capability via support for NetWare and stored procedures.
- **PowerBuilder TEAM/ODBC** combines the features of PowerBuilder Desktop and the Advanced Developer Toolkit and adds support for data access using ODBC and for team development through version control and configuration management, in addition to the check-out/check-in facilities of previous versions.
- **PowerBuilder Enterprise** builds on the products mentioned above and adds 32-bit support for Windows environments, C++ classes, database connectivity through native interfaces, and cross-platform support. The product also includes InfoMaker.
- **InfoMaker** is a data access and reporting tool. ODBC and native database access to both enterprise and desktop databases are included. InfoMaker allows end users to replicate data graphically and to build and maintain personal data warehouses.

Watcom is bundled into all Enterprise Series products. Watcom supports triggers and stored procedures. Developers can use the database for unit and integration testing of PowerBuilder applications. Single-user and multiuser applications can be deployed against Watcom.

PowerBuilder applications implement remote data or distributed data architectures. PowerBuilder is used to build the client side of the application: all the user interface and programming logic. The servers for PowerBuilder applications are databases which can be accessed via ODBC or native SQL. Networking connections supported between client and server are those supported by the databases.

For applications in multitier environments, PowerBuilder is used to implement the user interface and a portion of the application's logic. The rest of the application logic is implemented on application servers built using third-party tools. Connections between clients and servers are accomplished via RPCs or message passing.

Released in mid-1996, PowerBuilder 5.0 has features that move it closer to enterprise development. PowerBuilder supports a repository of database objects using an Sybase SQL Server database and has these objects accessible to all developers. Powersoft promises that this repository will be opened up to more databases in the near future.

In PowerBuilder 5.0, everything can be compiled. There is no more interpreted code, so things will run faster.

PowerBuilder 5.0 has the capability of outputting a DataWindow or DataStore as HTML.

PowerBuilder version 5.1 are scheduled to ship in early 1997. The new PowerBuilder version will include two new plug-ins:

- The PowerBuilder Window Plug-In will allow PowerBuilder windows developed for LAN-based client/server applications to be dropped into a Web browser for viewing and editing data.
- The DataWindow Plug-in lets the browser read and display a Powersoft report format file generated by PowerBuilder and Optima++ applications.

Distributed Web application server development will also be supported by Optima++ and PowerBuilder. Optima++ is Powersoft's C++ RAD tool.

Powersoft also offers S-Designor 5.1, an application development design toolset with process analysis and data administration capabilities. S-Designor, which is targeted at client/server development teams, spans business process analysis, database development, application generation, and multiuser dictionary functions. The suite's main application, S-Designor DataArchitect, addresses data modeling requirements, including database design, creation, maintenance, reverse engineering, and reporting. The current version added a Windows 95 interface, improved iterative design capabilities, automatic backup of physical data models, improved help functions, and other enhanced modeling and design functions, as well as the capability to generate Visual Basic objects.

The current version also added two components. S-Designor ProcessAnalyst, a module that is integrated with DataArchitect, allows developers to apply standard process modeling schemes to their projects. S-Designor MetaWorks, which is designed to support group and project management for client/server development efforts, facilitates the management of user profile definitions and access privileges; it also includes a data dictionary browser and version control.

15.4.4 SQLWindows and Centura

SQLWindows was released by Gupta Corp. (now known as Centura Software Corp.) at about the same time PowerBuilder was released. Early versions of the product were often described as hard to use. Centura has changed that.

SQLWindows 5.0 has an object-oriented approach with its QuickObjects for building SQLWindows applications. Develoeprs can use QuickObjects to create entire applications extremely quickly by either following RAD techniques or taking the more formal approach of defining an object model for their applications by specializing QuickObject classes.

QuickObjects reduce the time, effort, and skill needed to build database applications. Developers have a head start in three areas:

- Connecting the application to the data source
- Connecting the data to the user interface
- Generating the commands to access and manipulate the data source

In addition to database applications, Centura also provides QuickObjects for Lotus Notes and E-mail applications.

These two supported architectures and the database independence that Centura has may be the two major differentiating features between SQLWindows and PowerBuilder.

TeamWindows, a component of SQLWindows, supports large development teams.

Centura is committed to continuing to enhance and supportSQLWindows even as it delivers its new Centura environment. A new version of SQLWindows is expected in early 1997 with a new Object Compiler, an SAP application generator, and significant performance improvements in its QuickObjects architecture.

Centura environment

Centura has introduced a second-generation, 32-bit application development and deployment environment called Centura, slated for release in late 1996. The Centura product line consists of four products: Team Developer, Ranger, Web Data Publisher and Application Server. The Centura products are based on an enhanced SQLWindows.

Centura Team Developer is a component-based application development environment that provides application scalability and Internet integration. Organizations can build two-tier or three-tier client/server applications that can also be integrated into the Internet. Centura application components are interoperable with those created in languages such as C, COBOL, and Visual Basic.

Centura Ranger provides data replication facilities for synchronizing disparate corporate or mobile databases. Centura builds applications that replicate data across heterogeneous three-tier environments. Ranger provides a "store-and-forward" replication solution for mobile and occasionally connected users. Ranger features GUI drag-and-drop replication management in SQLConsole and client-initiated synchronization using either the Ranger Replication Sync Agent application or an OLE 2 custom control that can be accessed from any application development environment that supports OLE 2 controls. Ranger is included with Team Developer for design and testing purposes, but it is sold separately as a deployment suite.

Centura Application Server allows developers to partition Team Developer applications to execute on different computers. For example, business rules implemented as functional classes can be partitioned to run on a database-independent server, with Application Server managing the network via Remote Procedure Call (RPC) mechanisms.

Centura Web Data Publisher lets companies publish corporate data over the Internet or an intranet. HTML commands are converted into SQL statements and SQL data is returned in a format that the Web browser can display. It lets developers create Web-based applications or forms that access SQL databases without requiring CGI or HTML programming.

15.4.5 Visual Basic

Earlier versions of Visual Basic, from Microsoft, provided an easy-to-use development environment for Windows. Visual Basic 4.0 adds features that are necessary for multitier client/server architectures.

One important feature of Visual Basic is its integration with OLE. All of the Visual Basic controls are based on OLE, and all OLE controls are managed by Windows itself (for Visual Basic 4.0, Windows means Windows 95). Therefore, the Visual Basic controls are easier to find and reuse, and Windows takes care of version control. In addition, Visual Basic is an OLE server, which means that it exposes objects, properties, and methods that applications can use to customize Visual Basic. Developers can also write OLE servers that can provide functionality to other applications.

Developers can create and distribute OLE objects and share them with other applications within the network. Through these distributed OLE objects, Visual Basic supports multitiers.

OLE custom controls (OCXs, now called ActiveX controls) replace Visual Basic controls (VBXs) as the building blocks for applications. The 32-bit OCXs are subsets of OLE technology.

The OLE technology allows developers to encapsulate processes such as legacy code and business rules into OLE Automation Servers which are reusable across the enterprise. Automation Servers can be single- or multiuser and can provide services requested by other objects, either locally or over a network. Automation Server should not be confused with distributed OLE, which is an OS-level feature that performs many of the same functions.

An automation server can be an in-process server or an out-of-process server. In-process servers, also known as OLE DLLs, share the same address space as the applications they support. An out-of-process server exists in its own address space. That is why in-process servers cannot be distributed without their applications and out-of-process servers can.

Out-of-process servers are executables that have predefined OLE interfaces. Developers use these interfaces to browse methods and properties of OLE applications using the Visual Basic Properties browser.

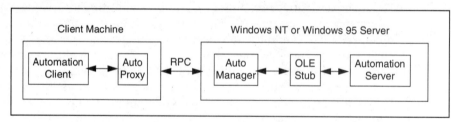

Figure 15.1 OLE Automation Servers

The real benefit of out-of-process servers is that they can execute on remote machines and are accessible over a network which supports application partitioning. Remote Automation takes OLE Automation requests from the client, sends them across the network using RPCs, and receives them on the server, as illustrated in Fig. 15.1. The distributed Automation Server objects communicate with one another using asynchronous notification or through OLE callbacks. Protocol support for TCP/IP, NetBEUI, IPX/SPX, and Named Pipes is provided.

Visual Basic data handling capabilities are centered around Data Access Objects (DAOs) and the JET Database Engine (version 3.0). JET supports the creation, modification, and deletion of tables, indexes, and queries. However, the SQL supported by JET is not fully ANSI-compliant. Visual Basic and JET coordinate database activities using DAOs. These objects enable developers to manipulate information in the database by letting them set properties and access methods encapsulated inside of objects. Security and referential integrity are provided through DAOs. JET also has data replication support with synchronization. JET can also use the multithreading capabilities of Windows 95 and NT.

Visual Basic 4.0 Enterprise Edition can coordinate small teams of developers. It includes a built-in version of Visual SourceSafe, a Microsoft product that manages group activities during source code development. The Enterprise Edition has a remote automation feature that allows developers to segment an application across a network and has mechanisms to speed up data access from back-end servers.

Visual Basic 5.0, expected in early 1997, will replace the remote automation feature of Visual Basic 4.0 with Network OLE, which is a component of Windows NT 4.0. Visual Basic 5.0 will allow users to create OLE controls (ActiveX components) using Basic rather than Java or some other C++ derivative. This version will also support OLE Document Objects that enables Web browsers to launch applications.

Visual Basic 5.0 is expected to add the capability to compile applications.

5

What to Expect in the Year 2000

Hardware and software continues to evolve. New uses of the technology show up all the time. It's hard to stay current, let alone at the cutting edge.

Hardware continues to become more powerful. Chip capabilities continue to double every eighteen months or so. Parallel processing is gaining more and more ground as software and applications that can take full advantage of the technology become available.

The use of ATM for networking continues to grow within organizations. It continues to be considered an enabling technology for enterprise networks. The holdup has been cost. By 2000, it should be affordable.

Object orientation is becoming more and more prevalent in software development tools and is becoming the technology of choice for many applications. The learning curve continues to be a steep one, but organizations that take the risk are reaping the benefits. However, object orientation is not necessarily the right structure for all applications.

Intranets will change the way organizations look at the delivery of information and services. The Internet will offer organizations new ways to market and sell their products. This additional connection into the organization needs to be monitored and security built in.

Client/server technology has changed a lot in the last three years. It's guaranteed to change a lot in the next three years as well.

16

Future Trends in Hardware

With the rate at which hardware is improving, it's impossible to predict what level of capability we can expect on our desktops, in our servers, in the network configurations, or even in our laps!

16.1 New Bus

In early 1995, Compaq, Digital, IBM, Intel, Microsoft, NEC, and Northern Telecom announced a new serial bus called Universal Serial Bus (USB). The bus, which could also be called a special-purpose LAN, operates at 12 Mbps (roughly the speed of Ethernet), supports up to 127 devices, and combines a 12 Mbps data-transfer rate with a 5-volt power line. USB can also set priorities for data streams—for example, giving voice and video priority.

The Open HCI Specification, developed by Microsoft, Compaq, and National Semiconductor in late 1995 and backed by more than 25 companies, defines an industry-standard common hardware interface for operating systems, device drivers, and BIOS to manage the USB.

The idea behind USB is to replace the PC cable clutter. USB's proponents show a diagram of a future PC with only three ports out the back: a USB, a graphics port (for the monitor), and a LAN port—no parallel, serial, graphics, modem, sound/game, and mouse ports. USB is designed to handle all those devices.

USB is designed to be completely plug and play. Devices will be correctly detected and configured automatically as soon they are attached. USB can also add and remove devices at any time, without powering down or rebooting.

Universal Serial Bus has three basic types of data transfer:

- Isochronous or **streaming real-time data**, which occupies a prenegotiated amount of USB bandwidth with a prenegotiated latency. This would be used for voice and video.
- **Asynchronous interactive data**, such as characters or coordinates with few human-perceptible echo or feedback responsible characteristics. This would be used for games.
- **Asynchronous block transfer data**, which is generated or consumed in relatively large and bursty amounts and has wide dynamic latitude in transmission constraints.

However, the USB is still not available, although it is expected sometime in 1997. Its delay has caused some vendors to lean toward an alternative serial bus, the IEEE 1394 standard known by the Apple trademark FireWire. FireWire supports only half as many devices as USB, but offers superior speed (100 to 400 Mbps) for multimedia peripherals.

16.2   More Powerful Chips

The Pentiumn Pro uses the Intel P5 chip, called Triton. Intel has already delivered Triton successors, the 430HX and 430VX. The VX supports superfast synchronous DRAM (SDRAM) as main memory, and both of the chips add the necessary core logic support for USB and are supposed to improve PCI performance yet again. PCI (Peripheral Component Interconnect) is a local bus that provides a high-speed data path between the CPU and peripheral devices. There are typically three or four PCI slots on the motherboard. There may also be one or two built-in PCI controllers (IDE, SCSI, network, etc.) on the motherboard. PCI provides plug-and-play capability, automatically configuring the PCI cards at startup.

The 430HX PCIset (formerly dubbed Triton II) is aimed at data reliability–conscious corporate sites, and the 430VX PCIset (formerly Triton VX) is aimed at consumer PCs, officials said.

These chip sets will primarily improve I/O performance by employing a technology called Concurrent PCI and will link PCs to the USB, paving the way for a host of new plug-and-play peripherals as well as real-time data feeds for voice, audio, and compressed video.

Concurrent PCI increases performance by making more efficient use of the PCI bus, resulting in better video and audio performance and better performance for applications that run directly on Intel processors. Audio applications that run on the Pentium, instead of on a coprocessor, would gain the most.

The 430HX, for corporate PCs, will be the first chip set in the Triton line to support parity checking and error correction code (ECC) for robust data integrity. Current Intel Triton chip sets do not support parity checking and ECC, an issue of grave concern for some users.

Intel has already announced the 440FX PCI set, its second Pentium Pro chip set, intended for high-performance desktop micros and entry-level servers. It brings the key features of Intel's 430HX Pentium chip set, including EDO support, concurrent PCI, and USB, to Pentium Pro systems while offering lower cost and a smaller footprint than Intel's original Pentium Pro chip set.

If history repeats itself (and with Intel it usually does), as Pentium Pro prices decrease and demand increases, these chip sets will eventually become Intel's mainstream micro chip, at least until Intel rolls out the P7.

Intel's 64-bit processor, known as P7, was renamed in 1996 as the Merced chip and is expected to ship in 1997, but most likely in 1998. Merced will be based on a dramatically modified superscalar architecture that employs advanced instruction precoding technology and instruction-level parallelism. Merced, based on RISC technology, is expected to be the first general-purpose microprocessor to implement the concepts behind the very long instruction word (VLIW) architecture. In addition, Merced will feature the multimedia instruction-set extensions—called MMX—jointly developed by Intel and HP. MMX includes extensions to the basic architecture with MPEG, audio, graphics, telephony, and videoconferencing capabilities.

An interesting side note: The 8086 in 1979 had 60,000 transistors. The Pentium Pro has 5.5 million. In 1996, the first Pentium Pros ran internally at 150 MHz; 1997 versions will be running at 250 MHz.

16.3   Improved Memory Chips

Today, the most common type of computer memory is dynamic RAM (DRAM). It usually uses one transistor and a capacitor to represent a bit. The capacitors must be energized (with electronic refresh cycles) every few milliseconds or hundreds of times per second, in order to maintain the charges and prevent memory loss. Data in memory must be refreshed after each transfer, and so the CPU inserts a wait state between each memory access while the data is being refreshed. When speeds are given for memory implementations, they refer to the speed of memory transactions: data from memory to processor.

16.3.1   EDO RAM

Extended data out RAM (EDO RAM) uses a wider effective bandwidth by off-loading memory precharging to separate circuits. As a result, it offers a 10 percent speed boost over DRAM. Burst EDO RAM offers another 10 to 20 percent increase.

Relatively inexpensive, EDO RAM was the predominant RAM architecture by the end of 1995. EDO is a SIMM (single in-line memory module) implementation with 32-bit architecture and 5-volt power consumption. EDO DRAM is not compatible with pre-Pentium machines or even with some of the older Pentiums. For machines running at 120 to 133 MHz, EDO plus cache is typical.

16.3.2 SDRAM

SDRAM (synchronous DRAM) is high-speed DRAM that can transfer bursts of noncontiguous data at 100 Mbps. (A burst is a sequence of signals, noise, or interface counted as a unit in accordance with some specific criterion or measure.) The Joint Electronic Device Engineering Council, an international body that sets integrated circuit standards, is working on the specification for a SDRAM standard.

SDRAM uses a DIMM (dual in-line memory module) implementation, has a 3.3 volt power consumption, and is a 64-bit architecture. A DIMM uses less power and has faster performance than SIMM. A DIMM looks like a wide SIMM and has a 64-bit data path compared with the SIMM's 32bit path, plus the possibility of fewer system compatibility problems. SDRAM is expected to be the predominant technology (over EDO RAM) by the end of 1996 as higher speeds (150 MHz and up) are offered.

16.3.3 RDRAM

RDRAM, or Rambus DRAM, is a new RAM architecture that uses bus mastering (the Rambus Channel Master) and a new pathway (the Rambus Channel) between memory devices (the Rambus Channel Slaves). A single Rambus Channel has the potential to reach speeds of 500 Mbps in burst mode, which is a 20-fold increase over DRAM. The price of RDRAM is expected to stabilize at about 10 percent more expensive than DRAM.

16.3.4 Flash memory

Flash memory is also fairly new. Flash memory is nonvolatile (it doesn't "erase" when the machine is turned off), unlike the other memories discussed above. It also has low power consumption. It's aimed at the digital cellular, digital camera, and digital voice recording markets for use in PCMCIA and small-form-factor PC Cards.

16.4 PowerPC Platform

Apple, IBM, and Motorola jointly developed a common hardware reference platform for PowerPC-based computers. The architecture connects the Macintosh ROM-based operating system with the micro's operating system, which usually resides on the hard drive. A boot ROM is specified that uses open firmware to launch a computer based on various operating systems, including AIX, the MacOS, NetWare, OS/2, Windows NT, and Solaris.

Both IBM and Motorola offer the chips for sale, but IBM owns the architecture. The PowerPC is designed to span a range of computing devices from hand-held machines to supercomputers. For example, it is used in Apple's Pippin multimedia CD-ROM player.

To date, PowerPC chips have been mostly used in PowerMacs, which run a version of System 7 that supports older Mac applications as well. IBM is using the PowerPC chips in certain RS/6000 models and is offering PowerPC systems that run AIX and Windows NT. IBM has announced NetWare and Solaris versions for the PowerPC, but OS/2 on the PowerPC has been dropped.

The PowerPC is a refined version of IBM's RS/6000 single-chip CPU. It is a RISC-based 32-bit multitasking microprocessor that has an internal 64-bit data path to memory similar to the Pentium.

The first PowerPC chip, the 601 (MPC601), runs at 50 and 66MHz and is as fast or faster than a Pentium, but is half the size and uses half the electricity. A low-power 603 is designed for notebooks and runs at 75MHz. The 603e raises the speed to 100MHz and doubles the internal cache to 32KB. An ultra-low power 602 has been designed for consumer products.

The PowerPC Platform (PPCP) is a specification that defines a common PowerPC platform by defining the minimum hardware such as ports, sockets, bootstrap ROM, and cache. Compliant systems must be able to run Mac OS, Windows NT, OS/2, Solaris, AIX, and NetWare. The PPCP was formerly known as the Common Hardware Reference Platform, or CHRP.

16.5 Other Hardware Advances to Watch

Telephony systems that combine data and fax modems with voice-mail and answering-machine functionality will begin to take a more dominant place in the personal as well as corporate arsenal of tools.

Motherboards will be smaller, which will improve component accessibility, reduce clutter, and permit lower power consumption and quieter cooling fans.

16.6 Robust Wireless LANs

Wireless LANs allow users to stay connected to the network as they wander through the halls and into meeting after meeting—just as long as they have their trusty portable computing device. Pen-based portables and hand-held devices are being used to enter inventory, call data up from a central data warehouse, and enter sales data "on the spot." Wireless portables are being used in hospitals and on trading floors.

There are two parts to a wireless LAN implementation: the wireless client adapter and the access point. The client adapter is usually a PC Card (formerly known as PCMCIA) adapter, ISA adapter for desktops and servers, or parallel port "plug" for machines without PC Card slots.

Wireless LANs usually do not replace existing LANs, but instead provide a wireless extension to the wired LAN. The access point provides this link into the physical LAN. An access point is a stationary device that attaches to the wired LAN. An antenna links the wireless clients to the wired LAN via the access point.

Wireless LANs have less bandwidth than wired LANs (2 Mbps versus 10 Mbps). Interference from other electrical equipment is also an issue.

Wireless LANs are of two types:

- Spread-spectrum
- Infrared

16.6.1   Spread-spectrum wireless

Also called frequency hopping, spread spectrum takes an input signal, mixes it with FM noise, and "spreads" the signal over a broad frequency range, hopping from frequency to frequency at split-second intervals. The spread signal has greater bandwidth than the original message. Spread-spectrum receivers recognize a spread signal, acquire it, and "de-spread" it, thus returning it to its initial form (the original message). Spread spectrum is highly secure. Would-be eavesdroppers hear only unintelligible blips.

The advantage of spread-spectrum wireless LANs is roaming. Wireless LAN clients can roam from room to room, floor to floor, without losing the connection. If the client software notices a diminishing signal, it searches the domain for the strongest access-point signal and connects to it. All this happens transparently and without losing connection to the server. Radio frequency spread-spectrum is a technology that reduces interference and supplies an elementary degree of security.

There are two types of spread-spectrum implementations:

- Frequency-hopping spread-spectrum (FHSS) uses a technique by which the signal transmits a short burst on one frequency, then hops to another frequency in the available range for the next burst.
- Direct-sequencing spread-spectrum (DSSS) breaks data into small units called chips and uses a radio transmitter to spread the chips across all the available frequency range.

DSSS is expensive to manufacture and uses more power (1 watt versus 100 milliwatts). Compared to DSSS, FHSS devices are smaller, draw less power, and are cheaper to produce.

Security should be another consideration. FHSS products are tough to crack because they are hopping from frequency to frequency with no particular pattern. DSSS may be easier to crack because its signals can be deciphered by determining the spread code. However, most wireless LAN products come with security features such as data encryption, data scrambling, and user IDs.

The IEEE is working on standards for FHSS and DSSS; they are expected to be released by the end of 1996. When this 802.11 standard is released, it should bring the pricing down because proprietary solutions can be replaced with mass-produced standard chip sets.

16.6.2 Infrared wireless

The use of infrared light has its own set of standards, applications, and limitations. Infrared-based products use high-frequency light for data transmission, cannot pass information through boundaries, and offer limited ranges (between 15 and 30 feet) but are therefore more secure.

The applications for infrared fall into two distinct areas: short-distance links to peripherals, and LAN (or even inter-LAN) connections. Both need a line-of-sight path for communication, but each has its own advantages. Line-of-sight limitations turn out not to be such a big issue, given the low dividers used in many offices and the open spaces between buildings.

Infrared has been used to link notebooks to printers, desktop computers, hand-held organizers, and even cellular telephones. These systems generally have a maximum useful range of 4 to 6 feet and an effective throughput from 50 kbps to about 100 kbps.

Any infrared-equipped product should conform to the standard issued by the Infrared Data Association (IrDA). Drivers for IrDA products are not included with Windows 95, but they can be downloaded from Microsoft's WWW home page.

16.7 More Powerful Servers

Vendors are also looking to ccNUMA (cache-coherent nonuniform memory-access architectures) to scale beyond four Pentium Pro processors in one machine while still leveraging installed SMP applications. ccNUMA, using SCI (scalable coherent interface), is a shared-memory, highly scalable SMP architecture that uses a 1-Gbyte high-speed interconnect to maintain a single system image across multiple processors. SCI is an IEEE standard.

Tandem Computers Inc. is positioning its ServerNet technology as a 100-Mbps alternative to SCI for use as a high-speed interconnect for scalable SMP machines. ServerNet is a shared-nothing approach, offering a connection into I/O streams without interrupting the processor.

Sequent Computer Corp., Data General Corp., and others are expected to roll out a 1-Gbyte-per-second SCI interconnect in a ccNUMA architecture by the end of 1996.

16.8 Parallel Technology

IBM has helped to validate the MPP market by aggressively promoting its SP2 (Scalable Powerparallel) System. The purchase of Pyramid Technology

Corp. by Siemens Nixdorf Information Systems gives Pyramid the backing it needs to build on the reputation of its Nile series platforms as robust SMP servers and RM1000 MPP platforms. Compaq Computer Corp. expects to deliver the capability to cluster its Pentium Pro PC systems for increased performance and improved fault tolerance. The Compaq solution has the potential to be the first mass-marketed parallel system.

SMP, cluster, and MPP are architectural design choices made by the hardware vendor regarding how multiple processors will be incorporated into a single computer. In a typical SMP architecture, the machine has up to a few dozen processors, and each processor shares all hardware resources, including memory, disks, and the system bus. Because each processor can see all of the available memory, communicating between processors is straightforward—one processor can easily view the results generated by another processor simply by looking at the appropriate section of memory.

Clusters usually refer to hardware architectures in which a few SMP machines are linked together by an interconnect. This allows you to harness the collective processing power of multiple SMP machines rather than being limited to the processing power of a single SMP machine. However, in a cluster, each node has its own private memory, and so communication between processors is more complex. A processor on one node cannot simply look at the results generated by the processors on another node. Instead, nodes communicate by explicitly sending messages and data across the interconnect.

MPP machines are conceptually similar to clusters in that they support multiple nodes, each of which has its own private memory, that communicate by passing messages over an interconnect. One difference between MPPs and clusters is that the MPPs usually have uniprocessor nodes rather than SMP nodes. However, the major difference between MPPs and clusters is that the interconnect is much more sophisticated—the bandwidth of the interconnect is often designed to increase as more nodes are added and more advanced connection schemes are used. The benefit of the advanced interconnect is that MPP platforms can handle up to hundreds of nodes, whereas coordinating that many nodes using the message-passing communication mechanism can be a challenge.

No single architecture is universally better than all of the others. In general, SMP is easier to manage and MPP is more scalable. Which platform is optimal completely depends on the specific application. SMP systems seem to be best suited for either business-critical or OLTP applications where the application's growth rate is slow and steady at less than 20 percent annually and the amount of raw data is in the range of 10 to 100 Gbytes.

MPP systems are best suited for either complex analytical or very large decision-support applications where the growth rate is unpredictable or more than 50 percent annually and the amount of raw data exceeds 200 Gbytes. Currently, there is not as much information about clustered systems, because clusters are primarily used as a way to add a second SMP system to an existing SMP system (in order to add fault tolerance in case the first SMP fails).

The gray areas between these three categories will continue to get grayer. There are strong rumors about IBM's forthcoming SP3 product, which will be a massively parallel machine that uses small SMP machines as its individual processing nodes. In addition, Pyramid's RM1000 MPP platform was designed to use SMPs as its processing nodes and to include the fault tolerance advantages of clustering.

Sequent Computer Systems Inc.'s new MPP system, code named Sting, is a different type of hybrid architecture. In an MPP architecture each processing node has its own memory, which is physically separate from the memory on every other node. This creates a more complicated programming environment, because, whereas in the case of an SMP machine, all information in memory is shared among all processors, with an MPP machine, programmers must explicitly send messages among processing nodes if they want to share information between these nodes. However, through a technique known as nonuniform memory access (NUMA), Sequent's Sting computer will create the impression that each processing node's memory is actually just a piece of a larger, globally shared memory.

NUMA architectures are not new, but historically the overhead involved in creating the impression was too high. Sequent claims to have designed a NUMA system in which the overhead is low enough that the impression works. Such a system would have the tremendous scalability of MPP systems and the simpler, easy to maintain shared-memory programming model of an SMP system.

As these lines become grayer as new hybrids reach the market, the notion that SMP, clustered, and MPP architectures are distinct may disappear entirely. Once these distinct classifications are no longer useful, all of these machines will be simply termed "parallel platforms."

16.9   On-Line Analytical Processing Servers

Most OLAP applications are currently in the marketing and finance areas of an organization. For these groups, it makes sense to have a dedicated server that handles the multidimensional databases required for OLAP processing. The servers are designed to optimize the storage of these "cubes" and to provide the query and computational performances expected by the users. With a dedicated server, a user can request matrix operations on the entire "cube" and receive acceptable response times. These client/server architectures usually are set up to perform almost all of the business processing on the server, with only presentation logic and services on the client.

One interesting new trend in the OLAP market is the use of agents. OLAP tools emphasize interactive use. Agents automate repetitive tasks and can run in background on demand or at scheduled times. DSS Agent from MicroStrategy Inc. and MetaCube from Stanford Technology Group, a subsidiary of Informix Software, Inc., include agent features. Alerts can also be created that will scan data for exception conditions and automatically create reports for exceptions that fall within a user-specified range. Agents in these products run on the server. Recently released Gentium from Planning Sciences, Inc., supports agents on both the server and the client. These agents can be run at a scheduled time or, as a response to an event, or the agent can decide if it should run when it is initiated.

Agents extend the use of OLAP beyond ad hoc interactive analysis but are still driven by what users think should be analyzed and how it should be analyzed. The next generation of OLAP products will begin to incorporate data mining techniques (see Sec. 17.8) to search for patterns and trends that the users have not foreseen.

The software for the client side of OLAP includes query and analysis tools and languages and tools to build custom applications. These are offered by the multidimensional server software vendor and are usually proprietary. Most vendors are publishing APIs to such tools as Visual Basic, PowerBuilder, and C. The OLAP Council is working on a draft of a common API specification that will address the display and navigation of data and provide ways to obtain metadata information from the server. The OLAP Council's goal is to facilitate third-party support for multidimensional servers.

16.10 ATM

Asynchronous transfer mode (ATM) technology is having a major impact on high-speed networking and as the network vehicle for multimedia business applications. The ATM protocol removes the boundary between the local and wide area network environments, thus eliminating the protocol conversion that currently must occur if LAN equipment is to interface with WAN equipment.

ATM combines simplicity, support for high-bit-rate transmissions, and the flexibility of the X.25 packet-switching systems used by most business systems applications.

In ATM, the basic unit of data transfer is a cell, a packet of a fixed length with a header (which includes routing information) and an information field. Since these two fields are fixed-format, routing can be handled by simple high-speed switching hardware, realizing higher speeds than those realized with variable-length packet-based networks such as X.25 packet switching and frame relay. The only differences between these older technologies and ATM is that their cell or packet sizes vary, while ATM's is fixed.

Frame relay is actually at the lower end of the ATM spectrum (up to 2 Mbps), but it uses variable-length frames and supports only conventional computer data transfer and not multimedia applications. FDDI is widely available despite its high costs, but it will not survive in the longer term as ATM systems become more widely used.

A product of ISDN standardization in the early 1980s, ATM's primary objective was to allow all types of traffic to be carried over one medium. It can handle voice, data, and video across diverse networks. It also provides a dynamic bandwidth management scheme and dramatic increases in performance.

ATM can also handle multimedia communications over a wide range of scalable speeds. At the lower end of the bandwidth spectrum, 25-Mbps ATM hubs are appearing on the market, the upper end will support speeds of up to 2,500 Mbps.

ATM provides a cell relay service that is totally independent of the network services or multimedia applications it is designed to support. A bandwidth management system will support existing network services such as X.25, frame relay, ISDN, leased lines, and legacy services but will transport them over an ATM structure.

For local business requirements, ATM switches will interconnect to hubs and other switches to form a distribution point for existing (and future) LANs. ATM hubs and routers will link LANs and established connections to enterprise networks, and ATM switches will connect departmental hubs and routers to form the basis of the enterprise networks. At this point in time, the distinction between local and wide area networks will be a moot.

It is conceivable that future ATM networks will provide local area network interconnection services, bandwidth on an as-required basis, and services that have access to the raw ATM cell system. Such a network is illustrated in Fig. 16.1.

ATM has the scalability and capacity to function as a backbone. Other technologies, such as frame relay and ISDN, can serve as lower-speed feeder to that backbone. SMDS is a service that can run over ATM.

Upgrades to high-speed networks will likely be evolutionary, and lower-speed networks will still have their place.

It is hoped by the time we reach the year 2000, ATM, SMDS, and frame relay will have made their marks in the high-speed networking field. ATM has been around since the 1980s and finally had its first commercial service in the mid-1990s. Demand at the wide area level remains to be demonstrated. Acceptance at the private level is more evident in universities and research labs.

Pioneers in ATM are Fore Systems Inc., Newbridge Networks Inc., and Net Adaptive. Right behind them are IBM, Digital, and other traditional computer manufacturers. There are different vendors for different segments of the market, such as central office-type hardware and equipment for the private environment. Data services and video applications also have different vendors. At the WAN level, there are vendors like AT&T, Siemens,

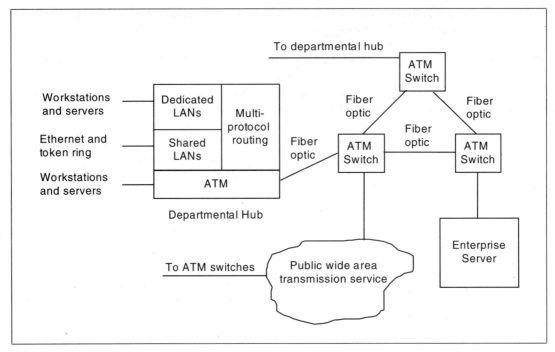

Figure 16.1 ATM network

and Northern Telecom. Switch supplier Fore has a big chunk of the current market.

As organizations look to decentralized system design—client/server—they run into a major stumbling block: Traffic volume can overwhelm transmission capacity. Organizations are forced to upgrade their LAN and WAN facilities to handle the high transaction levels.

Today's LANs range from 4 to 16 Mbps, while WANs often peak at 1.5 Mbps. Optical fiber has increased the capacity of networks two to four orders of magnitude, getting into the 1-Gbps range. ATM and its 53-byte fixed-length cell can provide the high-speed networking capability.

With the push toward faster networks to support multimedia, ATM is also a good fit. The short length of its cell makes it efficient in multimedia environments, and ensures that voice and video can be inserted into the stream often enough for real-time transmission.

The processor power and storage capacity is also opening up new options for network designers. Pentium and PowerPC processors are moving past the 100 Mips mark.

16.10.1 ATM Forum

Lack of standards for ATM remains a problem. To address this problem,

ATM Forum, an ATM advocacy and standards organization, was formed in October 1991 to work on operational issues such as systems management, class of service definitions, and congestion control. It has set the cell structure format and LAN emulation. The LAN emulation specification deploys a LAN emulation server that takes Ethernet and token ring data packets, places them in ATM cells, and then transmits them to devices on ATM LANs. Vendors such as IBM, Fore Systems, and Newbridge Networks are building LAN emulation solutions that adhere to the new standard.

Data standards continue to be a primary focus of the ATM forum.

The ATM Forum's first specification in 1992 defined the User-Network Interface (UNI). The ATM Forum expects to have all the specifications done by the end of 1996.

Desktop ATM25 Alliance is a vendor consortium working on having ATM run at 25 Mbps over regular twisted pair wiring. Led by IBM, Chipcom Corp., and others, the group presented its specifications to the ATM Forum. Since this does not require replacing building wiring, it may propel ATM to the desktop. It is also cost-effective ($1,000 versus $2,000 for the higher-speed ATM with the same hub port and network interface card combination). IBM is offering ATM25 products and is pricing them competitively with token ring products.

16.10.2 ATM APIs

Currently developers must use APIs provided by hardware firms that build workstation adapter cards and switches. There is no standard API set. The services document from the ATM Forum's API Working Group has described what services applications will receive from ATM, but it does not create actual APIs—just the ground rules. Organizations must accommodate existing applications while ensuring that future ones can fully leverage ATM technology.

Work is also under way to adapt applications that use IP or IPX protocols to run over ATM. Applications being earmarked for ATM accommodations include multimedia database routines, desktop publishing, and CAD tools.

Microsoft has proposed an API based on its Windows Socket (WinSock) interface to TCP/IP. The ATM Forum is considering adopting WinSock as part of its standards repertoire.

16.11 Integrating Voice and Data

Lucent Technologies (formerly AT&T's systems and technology business) began testing its Multimedia Communications Exchange (MMCX) server in 1996. This server is a combination of hardware and software that lets users bring these real-time capabilities from the PBX to a LAN. The server can run specialized communications middleware to support real-time voice, video, and data applications over ATM.

MMCX will allow individual micro users to begin and end videoconferences with the ease of a phone call and let them store and manipulate the contents of those sessions as easily as they store and retrieve data now.

General availability is not expected until sometime in 1997.

17

Future Trends in Software

Software changes reflect changes in hardware and provide new ways to support the way organizations do their business.

17.1 Object-Oriented Concepts

It seems as if every product claims to be object-oriented these days. An object is a concept or thing that can be encapsulated (wrapped) to include its own code and properties (attributes, services, data, etc.). Dealing with concepts as objects is a component of most client/server development products, and therefore of the applications built using them. However, if this is as far as the object orientation goes, the product is object-based. Object-oriented products also support object request broker (ORB) technology. As explained below, ORBs provide the mechanisms that "bind" objects across a network.

Because Windows supports encapsulation, OLE can integrate objects within applications, whether they are developed internally or externally. But these OLE objects are considered special "data types" and must adhere to certain protocols if they are to be linked between applications. OLE also has little or no support for inheritance or polymorphism. OLE is, therefore, an object-based technology.

Technology objects are building blocks for application development and for the implementation of business objects. Technology objects include ORB services, databases, and application frameworks. Frameworks are preassembled class libraries that are packaged to provide specific functions.

Business objects

Analysis and design tools that support business modeling are usually purely object-oriented. A business object represents a person, place, thing, or concept in the business domain. That sounds a lot like a database entity. However, in object-oriented terms, the business object is the storage place for the procedures, policy, and control of business data, including such items as the object's business name, definition, attributes, relationships, and constraints. The name is more than just the name of the entity's attributes. It includes what is known about it, what it does, constraint rules, and relationships with other business objects. Once deployed, the objects simulate the ongoing functions of the business.

Business objects provide a way to model and implement into one logical source all that is known and needs to be known about an essential business concept in a way that guarantees consistency throughout the enterprise.

Reuse

Reuse is a holy grail for object technology. The idea behind reusable code is that it can address multiple situations, some of which may not have been thought of yet. The person who creates the object must be able to communicate the problem being solved, the thought process embodied in the software, and how the software should be used to solve the problem.

Reuse sounds a lot like subroutines to veterans of the software industry. Functionally, it is like subroutines. But object code is written to be reused, whereas subroutines hardly ever were. Driven by time-to-market pressures, developers are increasingly measured on how much reused code they incorporate into new applications and how much code they create that can go in the library for reuse by some other application.

Builders and assemblers

To support the notion of reuse, today's object programmers are divided into two groups: builders and assemblers. Builders typically write class libraries, which become reusable components or templates. Templates are reusable software class libraries that include business rules, common design components, and, in some cases, complete applications. Object designers are builders that are the keepers of the object repository. They design common objects (business objects as well as technology objects) and serve as a central resource for both builders and assemblers.

Assemblers construct applications from reusable objects by combining components with application-specific features. Groups of components might be handed back to the builders for transformation into generic components that can be used by other applications.

Although pretested objects can be easily assembled to create an entire application, the key focus is still on how the components are combined. The use of object technology does not guarantee a 100 percent successful application.

Object-oriented development is very appealing to organizations that are under the gun to develop something fast, but still with high quality. However, the variety of approaches can be confusing. Standards for logically integrating objects created by different languages and environments are immature. Forcing reuse within a development organization is complex.

Management must motivate developers to use standard techniques when developing software. Creative developers who want to add bells and whistles must be persuaded to use a possibly less effective technique that is more standard. Good developers can usually write modular code that fosters reuse. Disorganized developers can create unmanageable code regardless of the tool.

The good news is that a well-run development organization can create a library of routines that mirror the business and make them available to developers and end users. Applications can then be "written" by mixing and matching code modules. The bad news is that it takes a lot of discipline and control to create these reusable components so that they are generic enough to be used throughout the organization.

17.1.1   Object request broker

Object request broker (ORB) architecture is a newer technique for enabling objects to extend messages within a single system or across distributed computers. The object orientation provides a higher level of abstraction for connecting objects than an RPC, messaging, or transaction manager approach.

An ORB takes a message from a client program, locates the target object class, finds the object occurrence, performs the necessary translation to allow the invoking and called objects to communicate, and passes back the result. The underlying connections are usually performed by a synchronous RPC or messaging system.

Once a client makes a request, the ORB is responsible for all the tasks required to find the object implementation in the network, prepare it to receive the request, and transmit the request. It is also responsible for communicating the results to the requester.

An object contains both code and data. The functions that an object can perform are defined by its interface. Programs that need the services of an object call those services through the object's interface. Consequently, the internal code and data of an object cannot be accessed by any process except the object's services themselves. If an object is changed but its interface remains the same, the changes will have no effect on the programs that invoke the object.

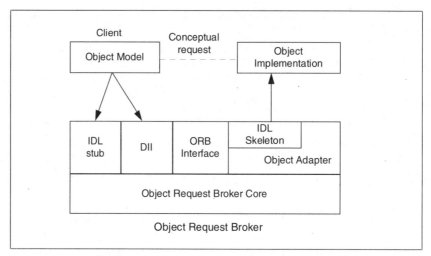

Figure 17.1 Components of ORB architecture

Interfaces are defined using an interface definition language (IDL). The invoking applications make use of the interface information to access local or remote objects, either statically or dynamically. The object interactions are managed by the ORB.

ORB architecture consists of three components: the object model, the object implementation, and the object request broker itself, as illustrated in Fig. 17.1.

The object model is the architecture definition of the objects in a given system. It also contains code and data that are accessible via interfaces defined by an IDL. The interface definition provides information about the operations that are permitted on that object, the arguments each operation expects, what it returns, and what happens when errors (known as exceptions) occur. Programmers never have access to the object itself, only to the interface.

Interfaces are also stored in an Interface Repository, which provides information regarding interfaces and types at runtime. Clients can construct dynamic requests at runtime using the Dynamic Invocation Interface (DII). Clients interface with IDL stubs and the DII via a programming language.

A client process issues a request on an object by using an object reference to the object model. The client process does not need to know where the object is or the current state of the object, such as whether it is currently invoked by another process.

The object implementation actually executes the services defined by the interfaces and requested by the clients.

The ORB provides the intrastructure needed to deliver requests and their parameters to objects and return the results to the clients. In addition to being able to send requests, receive responses, and deliver messages, the

ORB must be able to provide connection management functions and locate objects within the network.

For this to happen, the IDL interface descriptions are compiled to generate a stub and skeleton C++ code that is executed at run time when the object is invoked. Using an object reference, a client can issue requests on the object by making a method invocation, using a stub, or dynamically composing a request using a dynamic invocation interface.

Regardless of how the request is made, the ORB core (the portion of the ORB that is responsible for communication) locates the object, establishes the connection to the object, and delivers the request and all related data from the client to the object implementation. The Basic Object Adapter works with the ORB core to locate the actual object implementation and deliver the request in the form of a method invocation to the skeleton C++ code. The object implementation fulfills the request, and the ORB sends a response back to the client if appropriate. Responses follow the same path as the request.

Some industry watchers predict that distributed objects (objects located on different machines and possibly using different object models) is the way client/server applications will be built in the future. But for now, the technology is still in its infancy, with many technological problems yet to be solved.

One problem is how to ensure that the objects connections work well and do not overload the network.

Another problem is how to make objects that use different models work together. The proposed CORBA 2 (Common Object Request Broker Architecture) addresses interoperability among CORBA-compliant ORBs only, which eliminates non-CORBA-compliant objects such as Microsoft's Component Object Model (COM). Different object models do not understand each other's messages or data types.

Using distributed objects does not address the need for transactional support and integrity. Either the ORB or the transaction manager must provide these functions.

17.1.2 Common Object Request Broker Architecture

Most of the work on object-oriented standards has been spearheaded by the Object Management Group. Its specifications for the Common Object Request Broker Architecture (CORBA) are used within the industry as "the" definition of an ORB, and the two terms are used interchangeably.

The purpose of CORBA is to provide portability and interoperability of objects across heterogeneous systems. It provides the switching mechanism for passing requests and results between objects. This interoperability becomes more critical as organizations want to bring different platforms, databases, legacy applications, and ORB implementations together in an environment that will support the entire enterprise.

CORBA-compliant ORBs also provide

- **Name Services**, which maps requesters to methods through some type of object location service
- **Request Dispatch**, which determines which method should be invoked
- **Parameter Encoding**, which maps the requester's local parameter formats to the recipient's formats
- **Delivery**, which can deliver requests and results using protocols and ISO standards
- **Synchronization**, which provides a means for a recipient to reply to a requester in a timely manner
- **Activation**, which actually invokes the method
- **Exception Handling**, which provides restart/recovery resources
- **Security**, which provides authentication and protection

The CORBA technology and ORB implementations can be used to link legacy applications to client/server applications. An IDL interface for the legacy application turns it into an ORB object. This interface is called a wrapper. The legacy application is then accessible by any ORB client. The wrappers do not modify or disrupt the existing legacy application. If additional functions of the legacy application must be used by client/server applications, the wrapper is modified to reflect the new service.

Given all the choices (RPCs, messaging, ORBs), how does an organization decide? Since RPCs and messaging have the same basic operations, let's compare RPCs to ORBs. An RPC calls a function or a routine but the data remains separate from the routine itself. The routine is executed the same way each time it is invoked. With ORBs, because of the nature of objects (a thing that provides services through methods and typically operates on its own data), the method operates on a set of data that is within that same object. Sets of data do not all have to be handled the same way, even though the method used has the same name.

If your organization is moving toward objects, writing complex applications in C++, and applications are unpredictable in terms of network requests, ORBs are the best bet as long as all objects follow a standard such as CORBA.

If your organization isn't ready to go into objects and legacy applications are still an important link in client/server applications, think RPCs (remote procedure calls). They are an excellent way to partition an application and distribute APIs (application programming interfaces).

Object technology is unarguably the way of the future, but many of us are still trying to incorporate the past with our present. Once we've accomplished that task with RPCs and messaging, we can start to think about our business and its implementation as objects. It's a big leap from host-based to client/server environments, and it's a bigger leap to understanding object technology well enough to retool the organization.

17.1.3   Component Object Model

The Component Object Model (COM) from Microsoft is an object system that prescribes its own model. CORBA is an object model. COM is the underlying object model and implementation for OLE and is used in desktop applications to provide a standard for software-component interoperability. ORBs are used as the infrastructure to construct enterprise-class distributed systems. (Not to be left out, IBM's OpenDoc desktop component model is based on its System Object Model—SOM—which is based on CORBA.)

The COM and CORBA object models differ substantially. The CORBA model is the most familiar to object developers. Its interfaces have methods and properties and may be defined utilizing multiple inheritance. COM, and therefore OLE, uses interfaces and classes differently. The component object can have more than one interface, although a programmer can have a handle to only a single interface. COM interfaces typically have no inheritance and COM itself can support only single inheritance.

COM does not support distributed objects (yet), whereas CORBA does.

However, based on their platform preferences, it is likely that COM will continue to dominate the desktop and CORBA will continue to dominate in the enterprise.

17.1.4   Object-oriented tools

Optima++

Powersoft's Optima++ application development software bundles C++'s impressive performance abilities with a robust design environment to create a product that offers functionality comparable to that of Borland's Delphi 2.0 product. The component-oriented software offers easy Windows application development and a fully compiled language that is effective as a C++ learning tool or as a basis for using reusable code. The product's Reference Card tool displays different user-interface objects via a hierarchical tree that will be familiar to most 32-bit Windows developers. This tool has a Parameter Wizard feature that prompts users for code specifications. Optima++'s effective debugging tools are integrated into the programming environment. Watcom's powerful C++ compiler gives the product its impressive ability to manage and compose programming code.

CommonPoint

IBM's new CommonPoint for AIX product is the first implementation of Taligent Inc.'s object-oriented application development environment. Taligent, jointly founded by IBM and Apple in 1992, was absorbed and became an IBM subsidiary at the end of 1995. CommonPoint is an object-oriented application programming model that runs across 32-bit operating systems. Its compound-document architecture supports embedding of multiple live components, in-place editing, multilevel undo/redo, and OpenDoc and OLE components on supported platforms. Its Centered Computing metaphor allows a user to focus on accomplishing tasks through a user model rather than on the applications and documents.

IBM's implementation of CommonPoint for AIX supplies a set of reusable functions, including text editing, compound documents, graphics editing, database access, real-time collaboration, distributed object computing, heterogeneous communications, multimedia, and localization. Each framework provides a set of prebuilt C++ objects which encapsulate expertise for a particular problem set.

Initial response to CommonPoint for AIX was weak. In an effort to jump-start the product, IBM began integrating CommonPoint with IBM C++ development tools such as Open Class and VisualAge in early 1996. CommonPoint frameworks consist of object-oriented sets of related and integrated application functions. The framework provides developers with reusable functions for creating applications quickly.

17.1.5 Object-oriented databases

Object-oriented analysis and design and object-oriented programming are becoming a desired and preferred way of developing applications rapidly and efficiently through the reuse of application code and entire business objects. It only follows that attention is beginning to be paid to object-oriented database management systems (OODBMS).

The development of OODBMS products has followed two very different paths. One approach is to build a truly object-oriented, nonrelational database structure. OODBMS vendors maintain that the relational data model does not fit with object orientation. These same vendors are working on standards for OODBMS but these standards haven't been released yet. GemStone from Servio Corp. and ObjectStore from Object Design Inc. are examples of OODBMS products that provide access to objects through applications written in C, C++, and Smalltalk.

The other approach is to extend the relational model to accommodate object concepts. This is being attempted in the object-oriented extensions to SQL as included in the draft version called SQL3. Products that support object databases through standard SQL interfaces including ODBC are Objectivity/DB from Objectivity and UniSQL from UniSQL Inc.

17.2 Development Tools

Current versions of client/server development tools are more open, more object-oriented, and more capable of supporting multitier environments. They are offering more hooks into tools such as transaction managers and system management applications that use SNMP or CMIP standards.

17.3   Support for MPP

Massively parallel processors (MPP) are touted as the wave of the future. The hardware is there—and there are more offerings every day.

But the software tools that can take full advantage of MPP platforms are slow in coming. Applications have to be written in such a way that tasks can be done simultaneously rather than in sequence. SMP platforms assign a task to a processor, and then the application waits for the response. MPP expects that multiple tasks for an application will run at the same time. For now, that means that the data must be distributed to take advantage of the parallel processing. For example, a customer service application could be run on a parallel platform by splitting the data among the processors' disk space. Multiple copies of the application software would run on each processor. A request from a customer whose ID began with 1 might be assigned to processor 1, 2 to processor 2, and so on.

17.4   Software for Advanced Microprocessors

Just as corporate America begins to roll in 32-bit operating systems (Windows 95, Windows NT, OS/2 Warp, and Macintosh), vendors are getting their 64-bit operating systems ready. A 64-bit operating system is necessary if a workstation is to realize the potential of a 64-bit CPU architecture because highly complex applications need more data space than the 4.2 Gbytes supported by 32-bit operating systems. IBM's OS/400, Digital's UNIX and OpenVMS, and Silicon Graphics' Irix Unix are all 64-bit operating systems.

Hewlett-Packard and The Santa Cruz Operation (SCO) are cowriting a 64-bit UNIX operating system called Summit 3D that is optimized to run on the Merced CPU, also known as the P7, currently under joint development by Hewlett-Packard and Intel. The operating system will also run on MIPS and PA-RISC architectures and is expected to ship in 1997. It will probably be available before the Merced chip (formerly known as the P7) which is expected in 1998.

Microsoft has announced a 64-bit release of Windows NT by the year 2000 to follow the version of NT that will be released in 1997.

17.5   Trends in Relational DBMSs

Most of the trends in relational DBMSs are centered around distributed data and support for multiprocessors, parallel processors in particular.

17.5.1   Database management on parallel processors

Symmetric multiprocessing and massively parallel processing systems are finding their place in organizations that are looking to

- Utilize large decision-support databases and data warehouses.
- Quickly sift through enormous volumes of collected data.
- Achieve high scalability, operability, and availability.
- Put multiple nodes to work on the same problem.

But the DBMS must be able to use all aspects of parallelism. This means more than parallel queries, which provide the ability to decompose large, complex queries, run the separate components simultaneously, and reassemble them at the end. The DBMS must also be able to do a parallel load, table scan, backup and restore, and database partitioning across processor nodes. It should also have parallel-aware optimizers that can take advantage of the DBMS's parallel capabilities.

In shared-memory SMP systems, the DBMS assumes that the multiple databases executing SQL statements communicate with each other by exchanging messages and data via the shared memory. All processors have access to all data in this case. The data is spread among multiple disks.

In shared-disk systems, the DBMS assumes that all processors have access to the data on the disks, but they may or may not be sharing memory. In this case, the processors have to communicate with each other via messages and data transmitted over the interconnection network.

In a shared-nothing distributed environment, the data is partitioned across all disks, and the DBMS parallelizes the execution of a SQL query across multiple processors. Each processor has its own memory and disk and communicates with other processors by exchanging messages and data over the interconnection network. This architecture is optimized for MPP and cluster systems. This architecture is the hardest to implement because it requires new compilers, parallel support within the operating system, and better programming languages.

The fit between the hardware and software architectures is important. Oracle Parallel Server is based on a shared-disk architecture, and if it is run on an SP2 platform, which is shared-nothing, a software lock manager must be built to cross that architecture.

Data partitioning is key to the effective parallel execution of database operations. With the data from database tables spread across multiple disks, the I/O operations can be performed in parallel. Random partitioning randomly places data across multiple disks on a single server. Intelligent partitioning assumes that the DBMS knows where a specific record is located and does not waste time searching for it.

17.5.2   Parallel queries

A parallel query system breaks a single database query into multiple parallel steps, resulting in improved response times. This approach is highly effective in resource-intense data warehousing and decision-support applications. The query is decomposed into a set of tasks, and each task is assigned to a processor for execution. The more processors there are, the more tasks that can be executed in parallel. The most performance improvement is in complex queries that require data from multiple tables, several join and sorting operations, application of built-in functions, and so on.

One form of parallelism is interquery parallelism, in which different server processors or threads handle multiple requests at the same time. Interquery parallelism has been successfully implemented on SMP systems, increasing throughput, and supporting more concurrent users. But even though multiple queries were processed concurrently, each query was still processed serially by a single process or a thread.

Vendors are now looking at intraquery parallelism, which decomposes the SQL query into lower-level operations which are then executed concurrently, in parallel. Intraquery parallelism can be done horizontally by partitioning the database across multiple disks: A task is performed concurrently on different processors against different sets of data. The other option is vertical parallelism which executes tasks in parallel in sequence; the output from one task is input to another task.

17.5.3 Parallel DBMS vendors

Oracle Corp.

Oracle supports parallel database processing with its add-on Parallel Server Option (PSO) and Parallel Query Option (PQO). PSO was originally designed for loosely coupled clusters of shared-disk systems. It allows multiple instances of Oracle running on multiple computers to share the same data, using a distributed cache manager. PQO is optimized to run on SMPs or in conjunction with PSO.

Oracle's design is based on the concept of virtual shared-disk capability. PQO uses a shared-disk architecture which assumes that each processor node has access to all disks. PSO is required on any distributed memory platform (MPP or clusters) where the shared-disk software is provided by the operating system vendor. Oracle's approach to parallelization of query processing is external and manual. Oracle executes all queries serially unless two conditions are met: The query must include at least one full table scan, and the DBMS must be instructed to parallelize operations. The Oracle PQO query coordinator breaks the query into subqueries and passes these to the corresponding server processes, which work in parallel and return their results to the coordinator for any postprocessing. When executing in parallel, PQO supports both horizontal and vertical parallelism.

Informix Software

Informix Software developed its Dynamic Scalable Architecture (DSA) to support shared-memory, shared-disk, and shared-nothing models.

Informix 7 is a shared-memory implementation that supports parallel query processing and intelligent data partitioning. Informix 8 allows a table to be partitioned across nodes on the network and is designed to support MPP and clusters. The Extended Parallel Server option of Informix 8 supports distributed-memory architectures.

Informix rewrote its database engine for multiprocessing platforms. The original version for Sequent platforms was released in early 1994 as Informix Online Dynamic Server 7.0. It uses shared memory and shared disk, and features database partitioning and parallel query capability. In late 1994, an enhanced version, 7.1, was rolled out for additional platforms, including Sun, Hewlett-Packard, Unisys, Pyramid, and Data General. Informix is in the process of rolling it out for Windows NT. Version 8.0, due out by the end of 1996, will use a high-speed interconnect rather than shared-memory messaging to support loosely coupled, shared-nothing platforms. Initial platforms for Version 8.0 are IBM SP2, HP clusters, AT&T 3600, and ICL Goldrush. Version 8.0 will also add parallel update, insert, and delete to the existing parallel query and load capabilities.

IBM

IBM offers DB2 Parallel Edition (DB2 PE), which is based on DB2/6000 server architecture and is targeted for AIX running on the IBM SP2 platform or clusters of RS/6000. The first release of the product was not optimized to support SMP systems, triggers, and BLOBs. DB2 PE is a shared-nothing architecture in which all data is partitioned across processor nodes. Although DB2 PE can run on a LAN-based cluster of RS/6000, its design is optimized for high-performance SP2 with its very-high-speed internal interconnect. Parallelism is built into the basic architecture. All database functions are fully parallelized.

DB2 Parallel Edition features a modified optimizer that generates a parallel access plan rather than a serial plan that is executed in parallel; intraquery parallelism, in which a single complex query is split up and executed in parallel; and parallel utilities including load, index creation, and backup and restore.

Sybase

Sybase implemented its parallel DBMS functionality in a product called Navigation Server, which is designed to make multiple distributed SQL Servers look to an application like a single server. It is a shared-nothing system which partitions data across multiple SQL Servers and operates on top of existing SQL Servers. All SQL statements and utilities are executed in parallel across SQL Servers, but in the first release of the product, all processing at the SQL Server level remains serial.

In addition to parallel query and load, Navigation Server performs parallel inserts, updates, and deletes. The Navigation Server Manager provides "parallel-aware" administration utilities. Sybase also developed Configurator, a management tool included with Navigation Server that runs on a UNIX workstation and simulates workload to help manage parallel implementations. A new release of the core databases (System 11), purportedly a bottom-up rewrite, was released at the end of 1996.

Computer Associates added parallel capabilities to CA-OpenIngres in 1996. It will handle parallel queries, logical table partitioning, and parallel joins, sorts, load, backup and recovery. CA is targeting lower-end hardware platforms, exploiting SMP on micros.

17.6   On-Line Analytical Processing

On-line analytical processing (OLAP) has become synonymous with multidimensional database technology. Technically, OLAP is the process of analyzing multidimensional databases.

The relational model was developed to address shortcomings in hierarchical and network models. The relational model is good at retrieving records. But business problems such as market analysis or financial forecasting require array-oriented data or multidimensional data. Such solutions need large numbers of records from multiple datasets. The data can be represented in a relational database and accessed via SQL, but the limitations of the two-dimensional tables and SQL pose problems for such complex data access and manipulations. SQL does not handle time series very well either, such as a three-month moving average.

The data model for multidimensional data is a cube. Figure 17.2 compares the two-dimensional table of relational technology with the multi-dimensional (in this case three dimensions) cube of multidimensional technology. A company could create a database of sales figures for each product, but to do the type of analysis the company would want to do, the structure of the database would have to be such that the sales of each product could be determined for each geographic region, for each sales channel, and across time periods. The analyst may also want to slice and

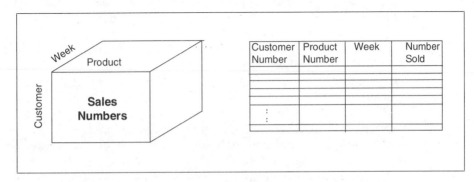

Figure 17.2 Multidimensional data cube compared to a relational table

dice (select portions of the cube to display or use, either slices or portions of a slice—a dice) this cube to look at the data by two dimensions.

Since these are arrays or matrixes, matrix arithmetic can be used to perform a single matrix operation on the cells in the array. This would allow the analyst to quickly aggregate along any of the dimensions of the cube (region, channel, or time).

Excel from Microsoft and Lotus 1-2-3 from Lotus Development Corp., the two major desktop spreadsheet products, have added a similar enhancement to their products. Two dimensions are represented in each worksheet (let's say region and time), and each worksheet within the workbook (using Excel's terminology) represents a different channel. The idea behind slice-and-dice is there, but it is clumsy to use. The same holds true of dimension aggregation. There are third-party products that make the process a little easier.

OLAP systems have been around for nearly twenty years but have been gaining ground as a data model for data warehouses. They were thrust into the limelight in 1993 when Dr. E. F. Codd, the "father" of the relational model, formulated a list of twelve guidelines and requirements for OLAP systems. Suddenly OLAP systems and multidimensional databases were legitimate.

The disadvantages of multidimensional implementations are that they are proprietary and that they support a particular type of application and can show performance benefits for that type of application and performance degradation for other types of applications that need the same data.

The relational database structure is designed for quick update and retrieval of discrete transactions and unambiguous query results. A multidimensional cube is designed for ad hoc query, data analysis, and reporting tasks. The cube concept can be a stumbling block for those schooled in other database technologies.

Most analysis involves interrecord operations, which are difficult for relational systems. The end result is slow performance. Multidimensional databases are very structured and sometimes consist of summarized data. Analysts "twist the cube" to create queries. However, since multidimensional databases have proprietary file structures, they are difficult to integrate with other products and technologies.

To address the integration issue, the OLAP Council was formed in 1995. The original members were Arbor Software Corp., Pilot Software Inc. (now a subsidiary of Dun and Bradstreet), Comshare Inc., and IRI Software, now a subsidiary of Oracle. The council has provided a specification for an API that will provide a standard means of communication between clients and servers. The API for metadata and navigational data access such as drill-down and slice and dice will enable client tools to access any compliant multidimensional database or relational database with the correct interface. The API will begin appearing in the next release of the OLAP products.

Some vendors are building a multidimensional design over their relational implementation. These are called multirelational database systems. The relational schema is organized around a central table that is joined to smaller tables using foreign key references. The central table contains the "facts" or data. The smaller tables are dimensional tables that define the business dimensions. Others, such as Business Objects, give the user an abstract view of the data structure. Using metadata stored in tables within the relational database, the tool reformats data to deliver a multidimensional view of the data. This simulation has some impact on performance, but this is offset by the benefits of providing multidimensional access without moving the data into a proprietary data model.

Use of parallel processors should allow DBMSs to handle multidimensional types of queries. Some DBMS vendors are looking to provide a similar functionality with enhanced indexing. Bit-mapped indexing enhances query speeds, and star indexing is a mechanism for dealing with complex queries like OLAP handles. The center of the star is the business event, and the spokes represent the dimensions, which are displayed through relational tables. And since users should be shielded from table joins anyway, the complexity of a star join should not be a user issue.

As relational databases become more powerful, with parallelization and object-oriented techniques, multidimensional databases may become outmoded.

17.7   New Models for Distributing Applications

Most applications that automate business processes today incorporate many applications with hard-coded interfaces running on the client. Each application depends on the immediate availability of the other applications in order to perform its tasks. In addition, data structures in other applications must be understood by the individual applications.

A new model for distributing applications is attracting attention from organizations with mature three-tier client/server architectures. The model, known as publish and subscribe, is an event-based object-oriented model.

Under this methodology, a business process is modeled as a collection of events that are coded into business objects such as business logic, rules, methods, and data. Each business object generates a type of event and publishes its events through a single interface. A particular type of event may be published by more than one business object.

Each business object can also use the business events produced by other business objects. Also indicating interest (subscribing), the business object is informed when an event is published.

After the event is published, the business object that created it no longer cares about it. In addition, those business objects that receive the published event don't care which business object actually published it.

Any object in the system can be modified at any time. As long as the events it publishes and those it subscribes to do not change, no changes need to be made to the rest of the objects in the system.

New applications are just another publisher of and subscriber to events that are already defined in the system or added to the system specifically for the new application.

This new approach is implemented over a CORBA-based infrastructure, or even with COBOL programs, Visual Basic, or dynamic data exchange.

17.8   Data Mining

Data mining is the process of discovering meaningful correlations, patterns, and trends by digging into (mining) large amounts of data using artificial intelligence and statistical and mathematical techniques. Data mining builds predictive models rather than retrospective models.

Data mining is not industry-specific. Industries that have taken advantage of data mining include retail, insurance, utilities, environmental, financial, medical, manufacturing, and transportation, to name just a few. Data mining has allowed these organizations to see relationships, patterns, trends, exceptions, and anomalies that were not obvious through human analysis.

Most organizations engage in data mining to:

- **Discover knowledge**. They want to determine patterns, trends, and relationships from the data stored in the enterprise. Data mining can also be used to segment, classify, associate, or prioritize data within the enterprise.
- **Visualize data**. If they understand the data, analysts can find ways to display the data to make it easier to understand.
- **Correct data**. Using exception and anomaly identification, an organization can identify erroneous and contradictory information and correct the problems.

Data mining describes a collection of techniques which are aimed at finding useful but undiscovered patterns in collected data. The goal is to create models which predict future behavior based on an analysis of past activity. Some of the barriers to data mining include the highly sophisticated nature of its tools and techniques and the limited number of qualified analysts and statisticians who can interpret the results of the analysis.

Data mining techniques fall into one of two categories:

- **Supervised mining**, currently the most widely used, involves a training phase during which the way the characteristics map to known outcomes is fed into the data mining algorithm. This process trains the algorithm to recognize key variables and conditions that will later become the basis for making predictions with new data.

- **Unsupervised mining** depends on the use of algorithms to detect all patterns. This approach leads to the generation of lots of rules which characterize the discovered associations. The rules are then analyzed for applicability.

Regardless of the techniques used, successful data mining starts with data that has been captured, validated, and corrected. These large amounts of data must be managed easily. Many organizations that are looking to data mining for intelligence about their business are also looking to MPP hardware architectures as the cost-effective platform for handling these very large databases and sophisticated techniques.

There are many examples of data mining use. Organizations like Kmart and American Express use it to target direct mail promotional campaigns, a bank discovered that it could increase credit card revenues by reducing minimum payments, Chase Manhattan Bank uses it to detect fraudulent credit card transactions, the IRS has a system to predict when individuals should be audited, ADP uses data mining to identify likely payroll service customers, and the U.S. Department of Energy has a model to predict the likelihood of oil production for a site.

18

Client/Server and Intranets

There's a new computing paradigm shift beginning to happen that complements and extends the second generation of client/server computing—intranets. Intranets use the hypertext and multimedia technologies used in Web pages on the Internet for internal applications. Some say that intranet technology will replace client/server computing as we know it today. Most disagree, but see it as a welcome addition to the implementation options organizations can choose from. This book takes the latter position.

18.1 Intranets

An intranet uses Web browsers and servers and Internet-based protocols such as TCP/IP and HTTP (Hypertext Transport Protocol) as a platform for internal applications.

Intranets offer the following benefits to organizations:

- Truly open standards
- Ease of use
- Simplicity
- Scalability
- Lower costs

Intranets use the same technology as the Internet, but the applications are limited to internal processes and procedures. Intranets provide a standard browser-based window in which all information is displayed the same way and all processes interface the same way and work the same way.

Organizations are looking at reduced expenses and development time for these applications because programmers and developers need to know only a few basic technologies: hypertext markup language (HTML), common gateway interface (CGI), and a programming language like Java from JavaSoft Division of Sun Microsystems.

18.1.1   The Internet as a platform

The Internet (also referred to as the Net) is a network of connected servers that has been in existence for nearly 30 years. It was originally used to connect universities and government agencies for research, and eventually E-mail and file transfer became its primary uses. The Internet uses a connection-based pricing model, so a user pays a connection fee only to the local node on the network. There are usually no long distance or per byte charges. Organizations started to use the Internet as a way for their geographically dispersed personnel to communicate.

What started the explosion of Internet use was the development of user-friendly graphical interfaces. The first of which was Mosaic, which was created by the University of Illinois National Center for Supercomputing Applications and released on the Internet in early 1993. Mosaic allowed users to navigate the Internet with a point-and-click interface. It also made use of hypertext (links to related information) so the users didn't have to know the file address of the information they wanted to "browse." All a user did was click on "hot" text and the software took over by pulling up the screen of information. Plus the software remembered where the user had been so that the user could get back to previous screens of information within the current session. Users could follow their own thought processes ("I would like to know more about that" and "What does that mean?") rather than a menu of predetermined choices.

The next evolution in Internet software resulted in the World Wide Web (WWW or the Web) and the use of multimedia on what has become known as Web pages. The Web is an Internet service that links documents by providing hypertext links from server to server, allowing a user to jump from document to document no matter where it is stored on the Internet. A home page is created for each server, with links to other documents locally and throughout the Internet.

World Wide Web client programs called Web browsers allow users to browse the Web. Users click on the hyperlinks created on the home page (and subsequent Web pages) to access the information available via that Web site, either locally or located on another Web site.

Web documents are structured with format codes and hypertext links using HTML. These links can include links to text data or multimedia data. For example, by clicking on areas of the screen, a user can see (or hear) a product and in some cases make the product rotate to see it from all angles, read about its features, download sales literature, and leave an address to have a local dealer call.

The initial applications built using Web technology were marketing-oriented. Web sites (accessed by home pages) provided customers—existing and potential—with information about products and services. The Web became a way to communicate with potential customers without having to reach out and find them—they could find you on the Internet.

18.1.2 Reason for the paradigm shift

The remarkable things about the Web are that it expanded so quickly (in less than a year!) and that it is a *truly* open system.

Point-and-click hyperlinking allows users to navigate and locate information easily using standard Web browsers such as Netscape from Netscape Software, Microsoft Explorer from Microsoft, and Mosaic variants from National Center for Supercomputing Applications (NCSA), Internet Division of CompuServe, and IBM. The current de facto standard is Netscape Navigator but Microsoft Explorer is giving Netscape Navigator a run for its money.

Programming languages such as Java from JavaSoft and ActiveX from Microsoft can be used to write dynamic applications (applets) that the users activate as needed (just-in-time). Once activated, the applet is downloaded and run directly from the Web browser without the need to maintain a server connection. For users, the browser becomes the single point of interface for access to all internal and external resources.

Open system

Many organizations have been striving to create a truly open system, and most would have predicted it to be impossible, or at best improbable. By the very nature of its architecture, the Web must be truly open, as every site has a different architecture, but all information must be accessible and readable regardless of what client platform asks for it.

Instead of different software for different client operating systems and back-end data sources being accessed, the Web browser does it all. Web browser software sits on the client. When a Web server responds to a client request from browser software, the server doesn't care whether the client is a Windows 95, Windows 3.11, Windows NT, OS/2, or Macintosh client. The Web browser takes care of any and all translations that must be done. It translates requests to the Web server and takes responses and translates them to the client platform.

In addition, since the protocol for the Internet is of necessity TCP/IP (a nonproprietary protocol), there are not multiple network protocols to be concerned with. TCP/IP is in place in most organizations, and it's a mature protocol for networking. HTTP is the client/server protocol used for information sharing on the Internet.

Java, currently the most widely used programming language for Web pages, doesn't lock organizations into proprietary technologies. Java could be considered open (for now) because it is freely and cheaply licensed to any vendor that wants it.

Single Point of Maintenance

Organizations no longer have to configure machines and then distribute new software releases, or updates and patches, to individual machines. Application releases are maintained in only one place—on a Web server. End users access them on an as-needed basis.

In the traditional client/server model (two or more tiers), different versions of client software had to be maintained to support the various operating systems and GUI drivers. Any attempts at standardization were impeded by a new release of the products or newer platforms—organizations were trying to standardize on a moving target.

With intranet tools like Java, the server application is written once and the client application is written once. The only thing that needs attention to make the application work across all operating systems is the interpreter—the Web browser.

Manageable hardware costs

Client workstations don't need as much horsepower to run just Web-based applications. These very thin clients run just the Web browser and the operating system. The server performs the bulk of data querying and massaging, and of presentation.

By the end of 1996, specialized machines, referred to as network computers, will sell for about $500, rather than the $1,500 for a micro. The devices will connect to a television and access applications and data, via a modem, from a computer network or the Internet. Storage will be on the Web server instead of on a hard drive. However, until productivity tools such as word processors and spreadsheets can run as Web applications, most users will continue to need the power of a micro.

Portable

An intranet application is portable, since the popular Web browsers such as Netscape and Mosaic are multiplatform. Almost all computer platforms offer some sort of Web browser, which can be used as long as the browsers support the same features. The developer writes the application once and lets users install it on their platform of choice.

Viewed as minimal risk

Organizations that have already adopted client/server architectures find that intranets are an extension of that paradigm. TCP/IP is already in place. Adding another front-end tool (the Web browser) is not overwhelming to their users. Learning Java is easy for anyone with C++ background. User

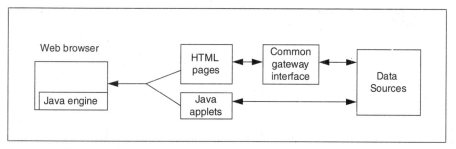

Figure 18.1 Components of an intranet

training costs can be lowered if the Web browser is the consistent user front end and query tool.

When a new corporate application is available, the user links to the appropriate Web browser and runs the new application, either by downloading and executing a Java applet or by receiving an HTML stream from the server or server-based application layer.

Suddenly the idea of "any place, any time" for user access—internal and external users—seems possible and doable, and even better: It uses inexpensive Web technology.

18.2 Underlying Technologies

The components of an intranet and how they interact are illustrated in Fig. 18.1.

18.2.1 Hypertext markup language

HTML is a text-processing markup language that is used primarily for typesetting and hypertext applications. It is used to structure Web page content.

Every hypertext page on the Web is a plain ASCII text document with embedded HTML commands that provide font and graphics information and links to other Web pages and Internet resources. Web browsers interpret these embedded commands to properly display the text and images.

The bulk of an HTML document is plain text. HTML tags, short commands surrounded by angle brackets, are placed around any text that is to be highlighted. For example, <b> and </b> might be the tags around text that is to be displayed in bold. HTML 2.0 is the current standard.

The draft specification for HTML 3.0, issued in March 1995, included support for such features as tables, background images, and mathematical equations. However, the differences between HTML 2.0 and 3.0 were so large that the entire proposal's standardization and deployment proved unmanageable. The draft expired and is no longer being maintained. However, the standards proposed for HTML 3.0 are already in wide use on the Web.

The current proposed version of HTML specifications, 3.2, adds support for tables, applets, text flow around images, and superscripts and subscripts. All new 3.2 tags are backward-compatible with any browser that supports tables, and they all use naming conventions that don't conflict with SGML specifications. The abiding principle of HTML 3.2 is to give Web authors greater control over layout through design elements such as tables and frames.

A significant addition in HTML in 3.2 is cascading style sheets, which let Web designers separate a page's layout and visual structure from its content, enabling more browsers to view at least the basic contents of a page.

HTML tags provide in-line support for standard bitmap graphics formats such as .BMD, .PCX, and TIFF. The progressive .GIF and JPEG formats, where a low-resolution version of the image is rendered almost immediately and then progressively sharpened as the remaining information is received, is becoming more widely used. Adding in-line images requires adding an image tag which is a link to an image file. A reference in a tag is called a uniform resource locator (URL).

Forms can be created using HTML tags. One of the arguments of the Form tag has an action attribute that is used to specify a URL to send the contents of the form to. This URL usually specifies a script or program that can process the incoming data block. These programs use an API called a common gateway interface (CGI), which is discussed below.

The Input tag is used to create text boxes, radio buttons, check boxes, and user-defined command buttons.

However, there are quite a few products on the market that will take care of generating the HTML codes from a form design created by the developer. These are called Web authoring tools. Some of the more popular products are PageMill from Adobe Systems, Inc. and FrontPage from Microsoft. Web authoring capabilities are expected to be included in the next releases of the major micro-based word processing packages as well.

Netscape Navigator Gold 3.0 is a combined Web browser and publishing tool. It offers WYSIWYG editing, and authors can implement proposed extensions to the HTML 3.0 standards such as frames, table creation support, OLE objects, video and audio streaming technologies, and advanced tools such as Java applets and JavaScript scripts. Navigator Gold can be configured to upload files to Internet service providers without a separate file transfer protocol (FTP) program. The current beta version of Navigator Gold can be downloaded for testing. The final version is expected to be released by the end of 1996.

18.2.2 Common gateway interface

A CGI is used by Web server software to communicate with other applications on the server or on the network. It is used to connect to databases and other back-end services, for moving text from one server or platform to another. It is this software, a CGI application, that gives Web servers features, such as forms processing, image mapping, and links to database software and other packages.

For example, if a Web page contains a searchable product catalog, a user can enter a keyword into an HTML form. The CGI application sends the request to a database program and tells the database program to return the results of the search as an HTML page. This CGI application generates a new page each time the database is searched.

CGI applications are also used by Webmasters (the administrator responsible for the management and often the design of a Web site) to count Web-page "hits" (a hit is when a user stops at a site) and send the data to a spreadsheet program for analysis and reporting.

However, there is a downside to CGI applications. Each user's invocation of a server-resident CGI script creates a separate process on the server. Many users translates to many CGI executables being launched. Each process requires its own resources. CGI technology runs out of steam when the number of users increases quickly because CGI applications compete with the Web server software for resources, including CPU time, disk access, and network bandwidth.

CGI applications are potential security risks because they can do things that servers don't normally allow users to do. A well-designed server will provide a way for CGI applications to comply with its internal security measures before it returns a file to a user, but it is easy to code a CGI application to ignore these security measures and access whatever file it wants.

In addition, database management software expects users to stay connected. Web pages do not stay connected to remote applications.

Most developers do not consider CGI a viable solution for high-volume, transaction-oriented systems. Organizations that are attempting to develop intranet implementations for transaction-oriented intranet applications are looking to other software (currently groupware) for the necessary support.

18.3 Intranet Architecture

The use of an intranet shifts the way client/server computing looks. The intranet architecture is definitely segmented into three tiers as illustrated in Fig. 18.2.

The very thin client is on the first tier with browser software and Java applets running as needed as the front-end application; the second tier is a Web server that provides Java code and acts as a gateway to the third tier. The third tier will consist of databases and other Web sites that may be accessed by the Java applet.

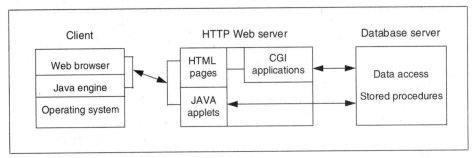

Figure 18.2 Intranet multitiers

United Parcel Service, Inc.'s Web site is a good example of how an Internet application works. At UPS's Web site, users can determine the status of a package they have sent, the transit time between two zip codes, and the price to ship a package given the package's weight, destination, and origin. The system first checks the Web user's credentials against a table of security metrics. Then an HTML form is sent to the user's browser from the company's Web server. The completed form is sent back to the Web server and run through a CGI script or some other program to convert it into SQL and trigger a query to a relational database. The results are formatted back into HTML, passed back to the Web server, and then forwarded to the user's Web browser. The user required no special software and could be running on any platform and there was no "on-hold" waiting. And the entire process takes only a matter of seconds.

The Java language coupled with HTML for layout and graphics allows dynamic applications to be downloaded and run as needed on the client. Rather than just scrolling through static pages, users run Java applets that are linked to the specific Web site they're browsing.

Java and similar object-based development architectures support the movement of executable code, or applets, from server to client, where it is cached before being executed. The client can use applets to do animation, generate a form, perform calculations, do data massaging, or generate local reports.

Web servers send applets to browsers equipped with Hot Java, such as Netscape Navigator 2.0 from Netscape Communications Corp. Hot Java acts as an interpreter to let interactive Java-based programs run on the users' workstations regardless of platform. Applets are interpreted and run within a Web browser regardless of whether the browser is running on a Windows 95 micro, a UNIX workstation, or a Power Macintosh. The developers of Java call this "write once, deploy anywhere."

18.4 Sun's View of Intranets

Java was written as an easy-to-use powerful adjunct to HTML, but not dependent on or limited to the Windows/Intel standard. JavaScript, Sun's

Web-centric answer to Microsoft's Visual Basic, is used to create programs to manipulate data on both the client and the server side.

Java is slated to support a range of client systems. Today's Java applets tend to be either stand-alone applications or simple one-on-one queries that the client downloads, uses, and discards. Java is still missing some components that will be needed before it can be used to support distributed business applications that interact with multiple databases.

One feature that Sun Microsystems is working on is Java Database Connectivity (JDBC), an ODBC-like API for Java and ODBC libraries which would allow applets to link to any SQL-compliant data source. Currently Java programmers have to write these links themselves. Web pages provide similar links via CGIs, but Java is attempting to become independent of Web pages and with them the HTML limitations.

In addition, major database players such as Oracle, Sybase, and Informix have released or are working on Web connections to their databases.

Another feature Sun is working on is support for ORB technology to support the management of interactions across multiple distributed systems and applications. Java applets currently get at such resources through uniform resource locator (URL) links on a Web page. This is inefficient and must be manually maintained and updated by IT.

ORB technology would sit on the Web server and support Java applets and clients by handling the intranet distributed computing components. ORBs would automatically track logical resources across the network as well as the relationships between applications and back-end resources. Java applets would interact with the ORB to find out where they needed to go and how to perform their job.

18.5 Microsoft's Strategy for Internets/Intranets

Microsoft has announced specifications for its ActiveX Internet development platform. ActiveX is an enhancement to Microsoft's OCX (OLE custom controls) technology. OCX controls have been renamed ActiveX controls. Microsoft's strategy includes the following alliances and key strategies:

- Java will be included with Visual Basic (code name Jakarta) by the end of 1996.
- America Online will bundle Internet Explorer as the default browser for AOL subscribers.
- SAP will use Microsoft's Internet server products and ActiveX in SAP's client/server business applications.
- Internet Explorer will be bundled with the next version of Windows 95 (code named Nashville) due to be released in 1997.
- ActiveX technology provides controls that will link existing Windows application standards (OLE) to the Internet.

SQL Server 6.5, which was released mid-1996, has a new wizard that uses stored procedures to format query output as HTML. Developers can indicate the network directory and filename for the generated file. While this creates static output, pages can be refreshed automatically by running queries on a scheduled basis or as a result of a trigger firing. Microsoft also expects to provide wizards that let Web browsers query FoxPro and Access databases.

The Internet Information Server (IIS) is Microsoft's Web server for Windows NT; it can be downloaded free from Microsoft's Web site and is now bundled with Windows NT. It includes the Internet Server API (ISAPI), which developers can use to build Web applications. ISAPI supports ODBC access to data sources, OLE automation, and the ability to call DLL functions. Windows NT 4.0 will include Network OLE, which will integrate with IIS to support distributed applications that can run over TCP/IP networks.

Visual Basic Script (VBS) is Microsoft's programming language for the Internet. VBS is a derivative of Visual Basic and Visual Basic for Applications. VBS is expected to be released by fall of 1996. Microsoft's Sweeper SDK (software developers' kit) is a collection of Win-32 and OLE-based client services and APIs that developers can use to Internet-enable applications. Sweeper is expected by the end of 1996.

18.6   Evaluating Intranet Products

There are three types of products used to create intranet applications.

18.6.1   Languages

The two languages used for intranet applications today are Java and Visual Basic.

Java from JavaSoft is a general-purpose, object-oriented, portable development language that can be interpreted and compiled. Developers use the language to create applets that are displayed by a browser or procedural code that runs on a Web server to implement application logic. JavaScript is from Netscape and is designed to be included directly in HTML documents.

Visual Basic Script (VBS) from Microsoft is used to perform scripting on the client workstation within the browser environment.

Both JavaScript and VBS applets are stored as ASCII text within HTML pages and then downloaded and compiled by the browser at run time.

ActiveX technology provides controls that can be used in applications. However, ActiveX isn't a language in the strict sense of the word. ActiveX components can be used to build intranets and Internet-based applications.

18.6.2   Browsers

Clearly the most widely used browsers are Netscape Navigator from

Netscape Communication Corp. and Internet Explorer from Microsoft. New versions of both are to be released by the end of 1996. And they are both versions 3.0!

The major differences between the two products are the platforms they support and their support for Java and ActiveX extensions. Internet Explorer 3.0 is currently limited to Windows 95 and Windows NT platforms. Internet Explorer is due to be shipped in the summer 1996 but users can download beta versions from Microsoft's Web site.

Netscape Navigator 3.0 supports Windows 95, Windows NT, Windows 3.x, Apple Macintosh, and UNIX. Netscape Navigator 3.0 is also available as a download from Netscape's Web site.

Internet Explorer 3.0 includes complete support for ActiveX capabilities, including applets, the ability to embed ActiveX documents in Web pages, and scripting. Internet Explorer 3.0 is expected to support Java through an ActiveX applet.

Internet Explorer also offers free HTML converters and document viewers so that applications can access Word, Excel, and PowerPoint documents from Web pages. Such capabilities are provided in Netscape Navigator by means of helper applications, which are the calls necessary to view files.

Netscape Navigator does not natively support ActiveX, but third-party support is expected. Netscape Navigator does fully support Java and JavaScript.

Netscape Navigator supports Virtual Reality Modeling Language (VRML), which makes it possible to interact with a three-dimensional world. Internet Explorer 3.0 is also expected to support VRML.

In making the decision, an organization should weigh how firmly entrenched in the Microsoft camp it is against the advantages of open standards and cross-platform deployment.

18.6.3 Development tools

The hooks for intranets (HTML and CGI) are not rocket science. Client/server software companies can easily add support for these protocols to their products—most have already—and call the results intranet tools or products that support the Internet platform. Organizations should be very careful about the development product they choose. It is important to understand exactly how robust the intranet support really is. What follows are just a few tools that show promise for intranet development.

Borland C++

Borland C++ 5.0 includes new Java development tools with a just-in-time compiler, a graphical Java applet debugger, and an integrated version of JAvaSoft's Java Development Kit (JDK). Borland's new AppAccelerator is a just-in-time compiler with significant performance advantages for Java developers.

Latte, the code name for Borland's visual development environment for building Java applications, is expected to be released in phases and to be complete in 1997. Latte has a Delphi-like visual development environment and includes a compiler and debugger.

PowerBuilder

Powersoft's PowerBuilder 5.0, released mid-1996, allows developers to create OLE servers and browser plug-ins for Internet/intranet applications. The PowerBuilder DataWindow will be available as an OCX plug-in, thus allowing developers to add data access capabilities to Internet/intranet applications that run through Web browsers.

PowerBuilder 5.0 allows developers to build distributed objects that are accessible from Web browsers. PowerBuilder 6.0, due in 1997, will allow developers to create OCXs for the Internet/intranet and traditional applications. Browsers will then be able to use all of PowerBuilder's existing capabilities including access to its repository.

PowerBrowser

Oracle's PowerBrowser is a cross between a Web browser, E-mail software, and Oracle Power Objects. It uses a Visual Basic-like language, a WYSIWYG HTML authoring environment, an integrated news reader, an integrated E-mail client, and Web server capabilities. The authoring tool's interface is as simple to use as Visual Basic and Delphi. A PowerBrowser component called Personal Publisher generates the HTML code automatically.

The Basic language is used to write scripts to be executed inside HTML documents. The capabilities of a PowerBrowser application can be extended using Oracle's Network Loadable Objects (NLOs) for executing third-party network-resident applications such as Java applets and VRML scripts.

PowerBrowser includes the native Windows Blaze database for local data storage and can connect to SQL*Net or Oracle's Web Server Option, thus providing HTML and CGI capabilities for Oracle database servers.

18.7   Intranet Applications

The very first Internet-based applications were marketing-oriented and were intended to provide information but did not provide two-way communication. The earliest Internet-based user-interactive applications were customer service–oriented, like the UPS example mentioned above.

Most of today's intranet applications grew from these same ideas and are document-oriented. For many organizations, the savings generated by not printing documents and providing Web-searchable applications instead can more than cost-justify the intranet. Users with Web browsers search pages of information, such as a organization handbook that resides on a Web server inside the corporate firewall. User interaction is limited to fill-in-the-blank queries and data entry.

Intelligent forms and interactive documents are not far behind. Microsoft's Web publisher, code named Internet Studio (originally code named BlackBird), incorporates Java-like extensions to HTML that will support interactive multimedia home pages.

JetForm Corp. offers Web Forms, which allows an organization to take intelligent forms generated by the vendor's back-end software and publish them on a Web server. Clients can download the forms and fill them out using a combination of a Web browser and JetForm Filler for Windows. Symantec's Delrina Group is also working on Web-capable forms.

Legacy applications could be wrapped by intranet infrastructures for access by users running Web browsers. The application's interface is translated into HTML and sent to the browsers. The users' response is converted back into a format that the application can understand.

Some organizations are looking to proprietary groupware platforms such as Lotus Notes, Microsoft's Exchange, and Novell's Groupwise as intranet applications. Other organizations are building their own collaborative environments using Internet-based tools such as its Network News Transfer Protocol (NNTP) and Multi-User Domain (MUD) to create and support discussion groups and chat environments.

The Web can also be used to disseminate static documents rather than printing them or replicating them in a Notes database. Lotus's InterNotes Web Publisher, bundled into Notes 4.0 servers, allows companies to publish Notes-generated documents on Web servers and allows users to access documents on Notes servers via a Web browser.

18.8 What's on the Horizon

JavaSoft announced Java ORB Environment, or JOE, to support Java interaction with Common Object Request Broker Architecture–compliant distributed computing services. Third-party vendors such as Iona Technologies Ltd. are also releasing comparable products. JavaSoft has also announced Java Database Connectivity, a Java-based API analogous to the ODBC protocol.

Novell has licensed Java and will implement it on NetWare so that developers can write Java applications that make use of NetWare services such as NetWare Directory Services.

Symantec Corp. recently introduced Cafe, an integrated environment for Java development with a native compiler and visual Java controls, a project management system, and a graphical debugger. Cafe is for Windows 95 and Windows NT. Caffeine for the Macintosh is expected by the end of 1996.

18.9   What's Still Missing

There are still some holes in this fast-moving paradigm shift.

18.9.1   Security

Security is an issue for Internet applications, but it should not be an issue for intranets because all the interaction of intranet applications takes place behind the safety of a corporate network firewall. And there should (read as must) be a firewall between corporate servers and the Internet. A firewall is a dedicated gateway in the network that provides security from outside network connections and dial-in lines. Routers and other internetworking devices are used to build firewalls because of their access control capabilities.

Firewalls allow an organization to connect its system to the Internet and regulate which information is allowed outside the firewall as well as protect its internal network from intruders.

If internal users must use the Internet for connections, they can have a secured link through the use of a virtual private network (VPN), which is a safe connection of two or more remote PCs or private networks over the Internet. The VPN runs independently of firewalls, avoiding the associated interoperability and limited communications problems that arise between various firewalls. The VPN creates public and private encryption keys that establish tunnels through an Internet firewall into a company's LAN. VPNs are useful for securing Internet communications between remote users, branch offices, suppliers, and companies. They are more cost-efficient than leased lines and provide equal security.

Some organizations are using the secure socket layer (SSL) protocol created by Netscape Communications and built into Netscape Navigator. The SSL protocol secures communication channels between clients and servers and encrypts transmissions. It replaces networking subroutine calls used by the Web software with modified, secure versions of these subroutine calls. These modified calls make use of encryption and digital signatures transparent to both the user and the Web software. The SSL routines handle collecting a public key from a server, creating a unique session key, and encrypt communications using a strong encryption algorithm.

The other security protocol being used is S-HTTP (Secure Hypertext Transfer Protocol). It requires that the Web browser or server software understand and negotiate the details of choosing a method of encryption, exchanging encryption keys, and handling digital signatures. SSL can coexist with S-HTTP because S-HTTP is quite flexible.

There is little, if any, support for directory and authentication services.

18.9.2   Information overload

Organizations must think about what happens once the information is broadcast across the company. Everyone is supposed to have the right information and only the right information. To get what they need, users shouldn't have to wade through mountains of excess information, which they received by mistake or because their information needs were never specified and refined.

18.9.3 Stability of Java

Java is an extremely new language. It just came out of beta in the summer of 1996. There are many concerns about its stability as a new language and how well it can support (or will be able to support) high-availability transaction processing systems. Database connectivity is still limited. There are few standards for multimedia access. Java applets can't run in Windows 3.x. The object management tools necessary to build and maintain libraries of Java applets are slow in arriving.

18.9.4 Speed

Java programs run about 10 times slower than comparable C++ programs because Java is an interpreted language. Java compilers and specialized Java machines will be required to speed things up. Third parties are working on just-in-time compilers.

18.9.5 Bandwidth

Not only do the Java programs run slowly, but all of this downloading of applets and related data and images can bring a network to its knees. As organizations begin to roll out intranets, they must consider the effect on the network traffic and whether the existing bandwidth can handle the increased traffic.

18.9.6 Lack of standards

There are no standard security mechanisms, support for a global directory, or related management tools for tracking, administering, and coordinating users' interactions. IETF has been working on an X.500 global directory for the Internet, but the sheer volume and volatility of the Internet makes a centrally managed global directory impractical.

IT managers have many of the same problems they had when they started down the client/server path. Some of these involve what development rules should be in place. Once again the rules for how applications are designed, deployed, and supported are changing. Now, instead of dealing with full applications, organizations are faced with the management of many applets. In addition, organizations have to predict the behavior of the Web-based applications, which can be even more dynamic than the Windows-based client/server applications ever thought of being.

Management tools that help with capacity planning, performance analysis, and troubleshooting for intranets are arriving on the market. Many of the vendors' names are familiar ones, such as Computer Associates, IBM, and Cabletron Systems, which are extending their existing products to handing intranet- and Internet-based systems. Others are newcomers such as NetCarta Corp., which offers a series of tools for mapping, navigating, and managing Web servers.

18.9.7   Hidden costs

Initial efforts are relatively inexpensive. Most projects use existing staff and TCP/IP networks. However, if the pilot expands, an organization is faced with the need to support multiple browsers, hardware upgrades, process redesign, firewalls, and complex system management.

Organizations that lack a solid TCP/IP network will have high implementation costs. Those with TCP/IP networks in place may have to install T1 lines to provide high enough throughput.

Organizations may not be ready for the content development and maintenance of the Web pages or the management of applet libraries. Content monitoring is a task that IT has not yet been faced with.

A very big unanswered question is, how long will use of the Internet remain free?

18.10   Should You Wait?

This is an exciting technology. If client/server technology seemed like an answer to operational issues of scalability and improved user responsiveness, than intranet technology is going to be your answer to improved user productivity and easier application maintainance.

Finding people within your organization who want to work on this technology should be easy. However, just because it's easy, relatively inexpensive, and fun doesn't mean that an organization should jump on the intranet bandwagon without some planning. This is an enterprise-wide solution in most cases. Functional and divisional differences should be transparent, as the intranet is support for the enterprise itself—the whole, not the parts. There needs to be a clear sense of direction of the enterprise identity that generates a purpose and goal for the use of intranet technology.

Intranets are employee tools. If employees are going to use an intranet, it must deliver content that users deem valuable. Deciding what that content is, who will keep it updated, and what its purpose is demands high-level support. The culture has to be open—employees have to be willing to share "their" data, which in most organizations is often perceived as a loss of power. The IT organization can't make that sharing happen, the push has to come from above. If the information available within the intranet is not useful, employees won't use it.

Make sure you find an pilot application that will shine using this technology. But don't forget to manage expectations and make sure they are realistic. As with any other new technology, be sure you are using the technology for the right reasons, not just for technology's sake.

Look for business needs and opportunities that are looking for a solution—unless, of course, you find a champion who wants you to try this new technology to see what it might do for the organization. In that case, just make sure the application picked is going to be a strategic winner! There might not be a second chance.

Glossary

100Base-T Proposed standard for 100 Mbps LAN transmissions, becoming the Fast Ethernet standard

100VG-Anylan Competing standard from AT&T for 100Base-T transmission

10Base-T 10 Mbps transmissions for LANs, usually Ethernets

430HX Intel Pentium chip that supports error-correction code and is aimed at business machines with 512K of memory

430VX Intel Pentium chip that supports error-correction code and is aimed at home and small business machines

440FX Chip set for Pentium Pro with a high level of data integrity and support for two processors

Active data dictionary A data dictionary used by applications as the code for the application is written

ActiveX Controls that can be used to program applications for the Web (Microsoft)

Advance Peer-to-Peer Network *(See* APPN)

Advanced Program-to-Program Communication *(See* APPC)

API (application programming interface) Set of programming routines that are sued to provide services and link different types of software

APPC (Advanced Program-to-Program Communication) Permits communications between distributed processing programs on different machines; a component of SNA

Application layer of OSI model Contains utilities that support application programs

Application logic Collection of actions, calculations, and decisions that the application must carry out

Application logic component Consists of the tasks and rules that an application uses to complete its task as well as any services required to execute the tasks and rules

Application program interface *(See* API)

Application servers Optimized for one or more applications, containing all necessary code and most, if not all, business rules

Application wrapper Surrounds the complete legacy system, both the code and the data, tricking the legacy application into thinking it is interfacing with an end user sitting at a dumb terminal

APPN (Advanced Program-To-Program Network) Distributed networking feature of SNA, which supports direct communication between users anywhere on a network (IBM)

Asynchronous transfer mode *(See* ATM)

ATM (asynchronous transfer mode) Creates a virtual circuit among two or more points at high speeds; uses fixed-length packets with header and information fields

Atomicity In distributed transaction processing, the entire transaction must be either completed or aborted

Backbone networks Networks that connect other networks

Bandwidth The capacity of a communications channel

Baseband transmission Uses discrete (digital) signals to carry information

BISDN *(See* Broadband ISDN)

BLOBs (binary large objects) Images, video, and graphics are examples

Bootstrap Protocol (BOOTP) Used to configure networked micros; uses the User Datagram Protocol of IP; relatively old

Bottom-up design Designed for homogeneous LAN environments and quick development over formal data modeling

BPR *(See* Business process reengineering)

Bridges Used to connect LANs with different physical and transmission characteristics and protocols

Broadband ISDN (BISDN) Uses fiber-optic cables to obtain speeds of 155 Mbps and higher

Broadband transmission Uses nondiscrete (analog) signals

Bus mastering Special form of multiprocessing; add-in boards called bus masters process independently of the CPU

Business intelligence applications Another term for DSS applications

Business objects Storage place for the procedures, policies, and control of business data, as well as its name, definition, attributes, relationships, and constraints

Business process reengineering (BPR) Use of information technology to improve the performance of a business and cut costs by redesigning work and business processes from the ground up

Business rules Rules that are global to the organization

C1 and C2 Security levels specified by the government

Call level interface (CLI) An interface that passes SQL statements directly to the server without recompiling them

Capture and transmit changes Changes are either captured in a log and transmitted at a later time, or changes are propagated as they occur

CDE (Common Desktop Environment) A graphical front-end for UNIX; a component of UNIX95

Cell switching Used by ATM, combines the efficiency of packet switching with the guaranteed bandwidth of circuit switching

Centralized database One copy at a central location; does not perform well as a query and analysis database; does not scale well

CGI (common gateway interface) Used by Web server software to communicate with other applications on the server or on the network

CHRP (Common Hardware Reference Platform) Now known as PPCP (PowerPC Platform)

CICS (Customer Information Control System) Supports transactional applications in a distributed environment (IBM)

Circuit switching Sets up a temporary connection of two or more communication channels. Users have full use of the circuit until the connection is broken.

CISC (complex instruction set computing) Instructions are decoded by the microcode which is placed in the microprocessor hardware (Contrast with RISC)

CLI *(See* Call level interface)

Clusters Link machines into a single system using an interconnect

CMIP (Common Management Information Protocol) Supports communication among different networks and network management applications; based on OSI standards; competes with SNMP

COM (Component Object Model) Infrastructure upon which OLE layers other software services (Microsoft)

Commit and rollback Facilities aimed at recovering from data errors or software malfunctions; a transaction is either committed or it is rolled back

Common gateway interface *(See* CGI)

Common Hardware Reference Platform *(See* CHRP)

Common Management Information Protocol *(See* CMIP)

Common Object Request Broker Architecture *(See* CORBA)

Common User Access *(See* CUA)

Communication servers A central outing point that provides security and load balancing

Complex instruction set computing *(See* CISC)

Component Object Model *(See* COM)

Compute servers Optimized to do number crunching

Concurrency Keeping all copies of a database in synch (current)

Connection-oriented Provides a reliable two-way connection service during a session

Connectless Frames are transmitted between nodes but a logical link does not need to be established

Consistency In distributed transaction processing, the system and its resources go from one steady state to another

CORBA (Common Object Request Broker Architecture) Provide portability and interoperability of objects across heterogeneous systems (OMG)

CUA (Common User Access) Set of guidelines from IBM that address GUI standards

Customer Information Control System *(See* CICS)

Data dictionaries Contain data about data; impose naming conventions

Data handling component The data required for the application as well as the services needed to access, manage, and retrieve the data

Data Link address Known as the local address; used to send and receive identification

Data Link layer of OSI model Concerned with error-free transmissions and shields upper layers from details about the physical transmission

Data logic The actual formation of the data request

Data marts Data warehouses that are specialized for a particular functional area in the organization

Data mining Discovering meaningful correlations, patterns, and trends by digging into large amounts of data using artificial intelligence and statistical and mathematical techniques

Data services Accepts the data logic output and handles all the front-end and back-end work of the request

Data warehouses Repository of data from production systems that is summarized or aggregated and possibly translated; it has an enterprise-wide focus

Database gateway A software link to data sources

Database servers Provide a single point for storing and updating files

Database wrapper Surrounds legacy data only

Datagrams One-shot, one-way messages

DCE (Distributed Computing Environment) A framework of services for distributing applications in heterogeneous hardware and software environments (Open Group, formerly OSF)

DCOM *(See* Distributed COM)

DDE (Dynamic Data Exchange) Provides automatic information exchange between applications (Microsoft)

Decision-support applications *(See* DSS)

Desktop Management Interface (DMI) A common format for presenting and retrieving management information for desktop machines

DFS (distributed file system) A file system that manages and locates data from remote files and distributes files across multiple networks; converts file names into physical locations

DHCP (Dynamic Host Configuration Protocol) Dynamically configure client addresses as they are required

DII *(See* Dynamic Invocation Interface)

Distributed applications Applications that have their data distributed, their processing distributed, or both

Distributed Component Object Model *(See* Distributed COM)

Distributed COM Used to design software as a set of components that reside on different machines in a network (Microsoft)

Distributed data management Keeps data current among all sites; facilitates the distribution of data to multiple network nodes and the access to that data

Distributed database Pieces of the database are on separate nodes (and each node has copies of the DBMS software); can be fragmented or replicated

Distributed file system *(See* DFS)

Distributed Relational Database Architecture (DRDA) Provides access to distributed relational databases in IBM operating environments and in non-IBM environments that conform to DRDA

Distributed request Contains multiple requests that can be processed on multiple sites, each request can reference data residing on multiple sites

Distributed transaction Contains multiple data requests that refers to data residing on multiple nodes

Distributed transaction processing A business transaction is executed across a network of systems as local transactions; the results of the transaction depend on all local transactions successfully completing

Distributed unit of work In IBM's Distributed Relational Database Architecture, the equivalent to the distributed transaction type of processing

DMI *(See* Desktop Management Interface)

DRAM (Dynamic RAM) Most common type of computer memory; one transistor and a capacitor to represent a bit

DRDA *(See* Distributed Relational Database Architecture)

DSS (decision-support systems) Applications that are used to support decision making

DSSS (Direct-sequencing spread-spectrum) In spread-spectrum wireless transmissions, data is broken into small units called chips and a radio transmitter is used to spread the chips across all available frequency ranges

Durability In distributed transaction processing, the effects of a transaction are permanent and should not be affected by system failures

Dynamic assignment In partitioned applications, resource assignments are made each time an application is run

Dynamic data dictionary A data dictionary that is accessed at program execution

Dynamic Data Exchange *(See* DDE)

Dynamic Host Configuration Protocol *(See* DHCP)

Dynamic Invocation Interface (DII) Component of CORBA that allows CORBA objects to find out at run time which objects they may use (OMG)

Dynamic link library (DLL) Executable code module for Microsoft Windows that can be loaded on demand and linked at runtime, then unloaded when the code is no longer needed

Dynamic RAM *(See* DRAM)

Dynamic Scalable Architecture (DSA) A parallel database architecture for uniprocessors and multiprocessors (Informix)

ECC *(See* Error-correction code)

EDI (electronic data interchange) Transmission of data for standard business transactions from one firm's computer to another firm's computer

EDO RAM (extended data out RAM) Has a wider effective bandwidth by off-loading memory precharging to separate circuits

EIS (executive information system) Interactive informational application written to support one executive's (or a very small group of executives) work style

Electronic data interchange *(See* EDI)

Electronic forms Image of a form that can be routed electronically

Error-correction code (ECC) A memory subsystem design that automatically corrects single-bit errors and detects multiple bit errors

Executive information systems *(See* EIS)

Extended data out RAM *(See* EDO RAM)

Extraction Replication technique where users make their own copies of a dataset from a central location

Fast Ethernet A shared-media LAN where all nodes can share its 100-Mbps bandwidth

FDDI (Fiber Distributed Data Interface) Uses two counterrotating optical fiber rings; tokens can travel on either of the two rings and use either of two station connections

FHSS (frequency-hopping spread-spectrum) In spread-spectrum wireless transmissions the signal transmits a short burst on one frequency, then hops to another frequency in the available range for the next burst

Fiber Distributed Data Interface *(See* FDDI)

File services Actually go to the disk and retrieve the data as stated in the request from the data services

Firewalls A gateway to the Internet that can be designed to prohibit particular services from entering or leaving; network security measure

First-generation client/server architectures Client machines do all the processing and the server handles data services

Flash memory Nonvolatile memory; aimed at PCMCIA and small-form-factor PC Cards

Fragmentation Distributed parts of the database; tables can be fragmented horizontally, vertically, or both

Frame relay High-speed packet switching protocol which provides a connection-oriented frame transport service

Graphical user interface *(See* GUI)

GUI (graphical user interface) User interface that makes use of graphics; event-driven; user-controlled

Hallway clusters   Series of stand-alone systems connected by the network so they can share processing cycles; shared-nothing

Host-based environments   Processing is done on one machine and users are connected via "dumb" terminals; the application on the host is in control

HTML (hypertext markup language)   Text-processing markup language used to build hypertext applications and structure Web page content

HTTP (Hypertext Transport Protocol)   Protocol used to move documents around the Internet

Hyperlinking   Using point-and-click to activate hypertext

Hypertext   A link to another process that is activated by a user clicking on a "hot" area on the screen; cursor usually changes shape when placed over a "hot" area

Hypertext markup language   *(See* HTML)

Hypertext Transport Protocol   *(See* HTTP)

IIS   *(See* Internet Information Server)

Informational application   Based on transaction applications and used to provide information to management

Integrated Services Digital Network   *(See* ISDN)

Intelligent hubs   *(See* Smart hubs)

International Organization of Standards   *(See* ISO)

Internet Information Server (IIS)   A Windows NT-based Web server (Microsoft)

Interoperability   The ability to operate software and exchange information in a heterogeneous network

Interprocess communication   *(See* IPC)

Intranet   An internal application that uses Internet technology (Web pages, HTML, CGI, etc.)

IPC (Interprocess communication)   Used by independent processes to exchange and share data

IPng (IP next generation)   A new version of TCP/IP that will include enhancements and greater addressing capabilities

IPX/SPX   NetWare's native stack; IPX is the network layer, SPX is the transport layer

ISDN (Integrated Services Digital Network)   Designed to carry both voice and data messages on the same line

ISO (International Organization of Standards)   A voluntary organization that defines international standards

Isolation In distributed transaction processing, the effect of a transaction is not evident to other transactions until the transaction is committed

JAD *(See* Joint application development)

Java Database Connectivity (JDBC) An API that allows applets to connect to database servers; based on X/Open SQL call-level interface (JavaSoft)

JDBC *(See* Java Database Connectivity)

Joint application development (JAD) Uses a top-down approach to application development with heavy involvement by the users

LAN switching The ability to replace shared LAN capacity with bigger, dedicated pipes to each desktop

LAN switching hub Has router software; can do remote access, LAN-to-host links, and Token Ring switching; stand-alone for small networks or stackable for daisy chaining hubs

Legacy applications Usually refers to applications that are host-based, could be any application that isn't easily accessible to current technology methods

Legacy screen scrapers Convert host-generated screens into GUI front ends; no changes in the host code are required

Logical Link Control A sublayer of the Data Link layer of the OSI model; creates the logical data link between the sender and the receiver

LSAPI (License Service API) A license system that isolates an application from the licensing policy (Microsoft)

Mail API *(See* MAPI)

Management information base *(See* MIB)

MAPI (Mail API) Provides mail and scheduling (Microsoft)

Massively Parallel Processor *(See* MPP)

MAU (multistation access unit) Device computers are wired into for token ring LANs

Media Access Control A sublayer of the Data Link layer of the OSI model; interfaces with the Physical layer protocols

Merced chip Combined RISC/CISC microprocessor successor to the Pentium Plus (Intel)

Message switching Sends a message to a holding area where it is picked up by a receiving station

Message-oriented middleware (MOM) Provides a single, standard API across hardware and operating system platforms and networks; message-oriented middleware guarantees that messages reach their destination

MIB (management information base) A database of information used by network management software

Middleware Provides the integration between the application programs and other software components in the environment which allows resources to be shared, processing to be distributed and interaction between heterogeneous systems, nodes, and networks to take place

MIME (Multipurpose Internet Mail Extensions) Protocol designed for transmitting mixed-media files across TCP/IP networks such as the Internet; handles binary, audio, and video files

MMCX (Multimedia Communications Exchange) Combination of hardware and software to bring PBX capabilities to a LAN (Lucent Technologies)

MOM *(See* Message-oriented middleware)

MPP (massively parallel processors) Multiple tasks of an application are run at the same time on multiple processors

Multidimensional Representing data in a cube structure to facilitate analysis

Multithreading Process is broken into independent executable tasks (threads); the threads complete their tasks in background

Multitier Client/server architecture with three or more tiers for processing

Named pipes A local interprocess communication mechanism which uses a conversational communication technique

Natural languages Allow users to develop queries free of syntax

Network computers Devices that connect to a television and access applications and data from a computer network or the Internet; storage would be within the network;   the machine has no storage devices

Network layer of OSI model Establishes, maintains, and terminates the network connection between two users and transfers messages and data over that connection

Network-centric A client connects to the network, not to a particular server

Nonpersistent queuing In message-oriented middleware, queuing information is stored in volatile memory which increases performance but leaves it vulnerable to equipment failure

Object Linking and Embedding *(See* OLE)

Object request broker Takes a message from a client program, locates the target object class, finds the object occurrence, performs the necessary translation, and passes back the result

Object-oriented database Database that is based on object concepts

OCX An OLE custom control, now referred to as ActiveX controls (Microsoft)

ODBC (Open Database Connectivity) An API that provides access to relational databases (Microsoft)

ODSI (Open Data Services Interface) Directory service for Microsoft BackOffice

OLAP (on-line analytical processing) Structuring data in multidimensional cubes to facilitate analysis

OLE (Object Linking and Embedding) Set of APIs for implementing object-oriented features in business applications

OLE DB Used to link to nonrelational data and application data linking; ODBC is used for relational databases

OLTP *(See* On-line transaction processing)

OMA (Object Management Architecture) Combines distributed processing with object-oriented computing (OMG)

On-line analytical processing *(See* OLAP)

On-line transaction processing Transaction processing that happens in real time; usually has many users and large shareable databases

OODBMS *(See* Object-oriented databases)

OpenDoc Similar to OLE, designed as a cross-platform technology, platform independent, and to interoperate with other similar architectures such as OLE (Apple, IBM, Borland, and others)

Operational applications Process data in a procedural, predetermined manner

Optimizing queries Determine the fastest and most efficient steps to handle a query

ORB *(See* Object request broker)

OSI model A seven-layer model for network transmissions

Packet switching Breaks a message into small packets and sends them individually over the fast path at that time; the packets are reassembled at their destination

Parallel query A single database query is broken into multiple steps and executed at the same time

Partitioning Breaking an application into components and assigning those components to resources in the network for their execution

PCI (Peripheral Component Interconnect) A local bus that provides a high-speed data path between the CPU and peripheral devices

Persistent queuing In message-oriented middleware, queuing information is disk-based at the expense of speed

Physical layer of OSI model Handles the physical transmission of signals

Point-to-Point Protocol *(See* PPP)

Portability An application should be able to be moved (ported) to another platform as easily as performing a new compile of the code

Portable Operating System Interface *(See* POSIX)

POSIX (Portable Operating System Interface) A UNIX-based specification from IEEE that is viewed as a standard for server operating systems

PowerPC Platform *(See* PPCP)

PPCP (PowerPC Platform) Standard hardware design that uses the PowerPC microprocessor (IBM)

PPP (Point-to-Point Protocol) Protocol that allows a computer to connect to a network with a standard dial-up line and a high-speed modem and have most of the features of a direct connection

Preemptive Multitasking Designated tasks can take priority over tasks that are waiting in queue or currently executing; if executing, they will stop execution to make way for the task with the higher priority

Presentation component The part of the application that controls what the user sees and captures what the user does

Presentation layer of OSI model Handles network security and format translations

Presentation logic Controls the interaction between the user and the application

Presentation services Accepts the input from the user and displays output from presentation logic

Protocol Rules and formats for communications within the same OSI layer across different devices

Prototype A working model of an application

Publish and subscribe A replication technique that uses a primary database (publisher) for making copies to other sites (subscribers)

RAD *(See* Rapid application development)

RAID (redundant arrays of inexpensive disks) Set of physical devices viewed by the system and the user as a single local device; data is usually striped over disk surfaces to recover data if a drive must be reconfigured

Rambus DRAM *(See* RDRAM)

Rapid application development (RAD) A development methodology that delivers working pieces of an application incrementally

RARP *(See* Reverse Address Resolution Protocol)

RDA *(See* Remote Data Access)

RDRAM (**Ramus DRAM**) Uses bus mastering and a new pathway between memory devices; has 20-fold increase in speed over DRAM

Reduced instruction set computing *(See* RISC)

Reengineering *(See* Business process reengineering)

Remote control connection A telephone line connects a micro to a host; the micro acts as a dumb terminal

Remote Data Access (**RDA**) The ISO protocol for multisite transaction processing

Remote data management Data must be managed from a central console, perform unattended, support full replication, and provide administration functions

Remote database computing The presentation services, application logic, and data requests are on the client; data services and file services are on the server; fat client

Remote node connection Needs a dedicated modem and serial port, multiple users can share the port

Remote presentation The presentation services and logic are on the client, everything else is handled by the server; thin client

Remote procedure calls *(See* RPC)

Remote request An application issues a single data request that can be processed from a single remote site

Remote transaction Contains multiple data requests, but all the requested data resides on the same node

Remote unit of work In IBM's Distributed Relational Database Architecture, the remote request and remote transaction types of distributed processing

Repeaters Used to restore a signal's strength to its original strength

Replication Making copies of a database or dataset and distributing it to multiple nodes; copies must be keep in synch

Repository Integrates analysis and design components of development with the back-end code, database, and document generation

Repository technology Extends the concept of a data dictionary to include the management of data and process models, addresses, rules, and definitions

Reserve Address Resolution Protocol Operates at the bottom of the network stack (the hardware link)

Rightsizing The IT architecture fits the business environment

RISC (**reduced instruction set computing**) Instructions are decoded directly by the hardware (Contrast with CISC)

RMOM (remote monitoring) Lets active network monitors feed information about the network to an SNMP-based console without waiting for a request

Routers A hardware device that manages the route selection for data packets

RPC (remote procedure call) Client process calls a function on a remote server and waits for the results before continuing with its processing

Run-time version A translator that sits on the client machine and interprets the high-level code generated by the development tool

S-HTTP (Secure Hypertext Transfer Protocol) The Web browser negotiates the details of choosing a method of encryption, exchanges encryption keys, and handles digital signatures

SAG CLI Call level interface from SQL Access Group (now part of Open Group)

Scalability Architecture is modular; can scale up or down as resource demands change

SDLC *(See* System development life cycle)

SDRAM (Synchronous DRAM) High-speed DRAM that can transfer bursts of noncontiguous data at 100 Mbps

Second-generation client/server Clients connect to the network for application services as well as data services; they are not necessarily provided by the server the client is actually connecting to

Secure socket layer (SSL) Protocol that secures communication channels between clients and servers and encrypts transmissions (Netscape Communications)

Semaphores Govern the allocation of computing resources between individual threads

Service level agreement *(See* SLA)

Service protocol Defines the format and meaning of messages before they are readied for transport

Service wrapper Surrounds systems services such as transaction managers

Session layer of OSI Model Creates, manages, and terminates the dialogues between the users

Shared disk Each processor has its own memory but share disk

Shared memory Memory is accessible and shared by multiple processors

Shared nothing Each processor uses its own memory and disk but CPU cycles are "shared"

Simple Mail Transfer Protocol *(See* SMTP)

Simple Network Management Protocol *(See* SNMP)

SLA (service level agreement) User's expectations of a service provider (internal or external)

Smart hubs, also called intelligent hubs Designed to integrate heterogeneous networks and workstations from multiple vendors

SMDS (Switched Multimegabit Data Services) Provides high-speed cell switching but emphasizes the transmission of bursty traffic over a short period of time

SMTP (Simple Mail Transfer Protocol) A protocol that operates at Layers 5 through 7 of the OSI model; TCP/IP protocol that defines the format of an E-mail message; de facto standard message format on the Internet

SNA (Systems Network Architecture) Uses a seven-layer architecture similar to OSI model but there is not a one-to-one correspondence; provides network facilities for IBM platforms only (IBM)

Snapshots A replication technique where a distributed DBMS generates snapshots of the data and distributes the snapshots; timing is specified by the user

SNMP (Simple Network Management Protocol) A common format for network devices to exchange management information with the network management console(s)

Software distribution Software should be distributed electronically, including configuration of the target machine and installation on the target machine

Spread-spectrum wireless *(See* FHSS and DSSS)

SQL (Structured Query Language) Standard language for data access in relational structures

SQL3 SQL standards that are currently in draft and expected for release in mid-1997

SQL92 SQL standards ratified in 1992

SSL *(See* Secure socket layer)

Stackable hubs *(See* LAN switching hub)

Stored procedures SQL statements that are compiled and stored on the server database; can be invoked directly from applications

Switched Multimegabit Data Services *(See* SMDS)

Symmetric multiprocessor More than one processor can execute at a time; processors within the same system share all processes and resources including disk, memory, and network I/O

Synchronizing distributed databases Maintaining data integrity across distributed databases

Synchronous DRAM *(See* SDRAM)

System development life cycle (SDLC) A system development methodology that has discrete steps

System recovery A system can recover from a media failure such as a disk crash

Systems Network Architecture *(See* SNA)

T1 Channel that can handle 24 voice or data channels at 64 Kbps giving a capacity of 1.544 Mbps speed

T3 Combines 28 T1 lines giving a capacity of 44 Mbps; requires fiber optic cabling

TAPI (Telephony API) Defines and establishes a telephony interface standard to support visual call control

TCP/IP (Transmission Control Protocol/Internet Protocol) A de facto standard for interconnecting otherwise incompatible computers; the connection method used by the Internet

TCP/IP Addresses Addressing is handled by the IP protocol; address uniquely identifies the system on the TCP/IP network and contains the system's network ID and host ID

Telephony API *(See* TAPI)

TI RPC (Transport Independent Remote Procedure Call) A set of RPCs for executing procedures on remote computers; operating system and network independent (Sun Microsystems)

Token ring Local area network which passes a token around the network; workstation grabs the token when it needs to transmit, transmits using the entire bandwidth of the network, and releases the token when transmission is complete

Top-down design A user design or conceptual system design; translates the user requirements into design specifications; designed for larger systems and multiple hardware environments

TP monitors Manage transactions across multiple servers

TP-Lite Transaction management is handled by the DBMS itself

Transaction managers Divide complex applications into transactions, control transactions from their starting point, to remote resource managers, and back again to their starting point

Transaction processing applications Processing the links between an organization and its customers and suppliers

Transaction processing monitors *(See* TP monitors)

Transaction recovery A transaction can recover from a system or application failure

Transactional queuing In message-oriented middleware, adds to disk-based queuing a means of verifying that messages are received and responded to

Transmission Control Protocol/Internet Protocol *(See* TCP/IP)

Transport Independent Remote Procedure Call *(See* TI RPC)

Transport layer of OSI model Corrects all failures that occur at the Network layer

Transport protocol Prepares the message for transport and forwards it to another network node

Triggers Special stored procedures that are automatically invoked by server database software

Two-phased commits In the first phase, each server involved performs its portion of the transaction and signifies it is ready to commit (save) its work; in the second phase, all servers commit their work; if any server fails during the second phase, the entire transaction is canceled and servers are instructed to roll back their work

Two-tier architectures The processing for the client/server application is done by the client and the server it is connected to

Uniform resource locator *(See* URL)

Universal Serial Bus *(See* USB)

URL The name given to a site in the Internet

USB (Universal Serial Bus) A new bus, also called a special-purpose LAN, that can support up to 127 devices and can handle a 12 Mbps data-transfer rate with a 5-volt power line

Virtual LAN Uses software to create logical networks out of the physical infrastructure

Virtual reality modeling language (VRML) A mechanism for delivering interactive 3-D over the Web

VLAN *(See* Virtual LAN)

VRML *(See* Virtual reality modeling language)

WABI (Windows Application Binary Interface) Windows APIs that are used to run Windows applications natively under UNIX (Microsoft)

Web Another name for the World Wide Web

Web browser Software that is used to interface to Web servers and return Web pages

Web publisher Software that is used to create the content of Web pages

Workflow automation   Used to assist in designing new processes in a business processing reengineering project

World Wide Web   The use of multimedia on the Internet

WOSA (Windows Open Services Architecture)   An open architecture and a consistent standard set of APIs to provide interoperability between Windows workstations and services available in heterogeneous environments

WWW   *(See* World Wide Web)

X Client   The client in an X Window System

X Server   The server in an X Window System

X Window Manager   Manages the appearance of an X Window client

X Window System   The client acts as a presentation server and the server runs as a client for that presentation server

XMP (X/Open Management API)   A standards-based process-to-process communication between a managing system and a managed system; supports SNMP and CMIP

XNS (Xerox Network Services)   Foundation for NetWare's IPX/SPX

XOM (X/Open Object Manager)   Used to manipulate data structures associated with managed objects

XPG4   X/Open Portability Guide version 4

Suggested Readings

Anderson, George, *Client/Server Database Design Using Sybase*, McGraw-Hill, 1997.

Bambra, Joe, et al, *Client/Server Application Development Using Informix*, McGraw-Hill, 1997.

Berson, Alex, *Client/Server Architecture*, McGraw-Hill, 1996.

Berson, Alex, et.al, *Sybase System 11*, McGraw-Hill, 1997.

Boume, Kelly, *Client/Server System Testing Guide*, McGraw-Hill, 1997.

Dewire, Dawna Travis, *Client/Server Computing*, McGraw-Hill, 1993.

Gopaul, Mitra, *Client/Server Application Development Using DB2/6000*, McGraw-Hill, 1997.

Green, Bill, et al, *Powersoft's PFC Library Guide*, McGraw-Hill, 1997.

Green, Bill, *PowerBuilder 5 Client/Server Application Development*, McGraw-Hill, 1996.

Horwood, Peter, *Client/Server Application Development Using Optima++*, McGraw-Hill, 1997.

Roseen, Jane, *Client/Server Application Development Using Infomaker 5*, McGraw-Hill, 1997.

Wise, Sid, *Client/Server Systems Performance and Fine Tuning*, McGraw-Hill, 1997.

Yarborough, Bill, *Communications Networks for Client/Server and Distributed Objects*, McGraw-Hill, 1997.

Index

About the Author

D. Travis Dewire is a full-time faculty member of the MIS group at Babson College in Wellesley, Massachusetts. She previously taught in the CIS division of Bentley College.

Dewire has more than twenty-five years of experience in information systems, across many different industries. Her previous books include *Client/Server Computing, Application Development for Distributed Environments*, and *Text Management*. She is also a regular columnist for *Client/Server Computing* magazine.